THE

AMERICAN GARDENER'S ASSISTANT

In Three Parts.

CONTAINING

COMPLETE PRACTICAL DIRECTIONS

FOR THE CULTIVATION OF

VEGETABLES, FLOWERS, FRUIT TREES, AND GRAPE-VINES.

By THOMAS BRIDGEMAN,
Gardener, Seedsman, and Florist.

NEW EDITION; REVISED, ENLARGED, AND ILLUSTRATED,

By S. EDWARDS TODD.

PHILADELPHIA:
PORTER & COATES,

PREFACE.

THE primary object in first publishing THE YOUNG GARDENER'S ASSISTANT, was to enable our respectable seedsmen, while furnishing a catalogue of seed for the use of the Kitchen and Flower Garden, to afford instruction, at a trifling expense, to such of their customers as had not a regular gardener, and thereby save themselves the blame, of those who may not have given their seed a fair trial for want of knowing how to dispose of it in the ground.

The Author, having shown his primary object in adopting the catalogue form, presumes that his readers will not be disappointed if they do not find there the names of all the species or varieties of plants they may wish to introduce into their gardens, the mode of culture of such being generally alike. If a catalogue of this kind was essential, it would occupy more space than is allotted to this book; besides, it would be impossible to keep pace with our enterprising horticulturists and florists, who are continually introducing new species into our country. When, also, it is considered that there are a number of indigenous plants at present unknown to us, it will appear evident that the most extensive catalogue would not be perfect in this respect for any length of time; the Author, therefore, thought it unnecessary to attempt anything more than is essential to the attainment of a tolerable share of the products of the garden, by ordinary exertion. How far he has succeeded in this respect, must be left for the reader to decide.

THOMAS BRIDGEMAN.

KITCHEN-GARDENING.

CHAPTER I.

GENERAL REMARKS ON KITCHEN-GARDENING.

Previous to preparing a kitchen-garden, the gardener should provide a blank-book, and prepare a map of his ground, on which he should first lay out a plan of his garden, allotting a place for all the different kinds of vegetables he intends to cultivate. As he proceeds in the business of planting his grounds, if he should keep an account of everything he does relative to his garden, he would soon obtain some knowledge of the art. This the writer has done for more than twenty years, and he flatters himself that a publication of the results of his practice will be interesting and useful to his readers.

If gardeners would accustom themselves to record the dates and particulars of their transactions relative to tillage, planting, etc., they would always know when to expect their seed to come up, and how to regulate their crops for succession; and when it is considered that plants of the *brassica*, or Cabbage tribe, are apt to get infected at the roots, if too frequently planted in the same ground, and that a rotation of crops in general is beneficial, it will appear evident that a complete register of everything relative to culture is as essential to success in the kitchen-garden as in agriculture proper.

Those who have not a garden already formed, and cannot avail themselves of such a slope of ground or quality of soil as they desire, must take up with such as may be within their reach. If practicable, a kitchen-garden should have a warm and south-easterly exposure. But when the ground slopes to the north and west, as is frequently the case, it is important to have the garden located on the sunny side of a grove, forest, or out-buildings. Every person, previous to choosing a location for out-buildings and a dwelling-house, should select the most desirable situation for the kitchen-garden.

LAYING OUT THE GROUND.

If desirable, a border may be formed around the whole garden, from five to ten feet wide, according to the size of the piece of land. Next to this border, a walk may be made from three to six feet wide; and the middle of the garden may be divided into squares, on the sides of which a border may be laid out three or four feet wide, in which the various kinds of herbs may be raised, and also gooseberries, currants, raspberries, strawberries, etc. The centre beds may be planted with various kinds of vegetables. The outside borders will be useful for raising the earliest fruits and vegetables, and serve for raising and pricking out such young plants, herbs, and cuttings, as require to be screened from the intense heat of the sun.

The mode of laying out the ground is a matter of taste, and may be left to the gardener himself, the form being a thing of trifling importance in the production of useful vegetables; and it matters not whether the ground be laid out in beds of four or ten feet wide, provided it be well worked, and the garden kept neat and free from weeds. One should determine what kind of vegetables he designs to raise as well as the quantity of each kind. If the object be simply to supply one family with vegetables, it is better to appropriate only a small plot of ground to this purpose, as a large garden at a distance from a good market is not always a source of profit, while it requires a great deal of labor to keep it in order. It is far better to have a small plot of ground of only a few square rods thoroughly pulverized, well manured, and properly dressed, than one twice as large, and all these things alluded to, only half done. Very many persons in the country, who raise no garden produce for market, err greatly in laying out gardens much larger than they cultivate profitably.

All standard trees should be excluded from a kitchen-garden, as their roots spread so widely, and imbibe so much moisture from the ground, that little is left for the nourishment of any plant within the range of their influence; and when in full leaf, they shade a large space, and obstruct the free circulation of the air, so essential to the well-being of all plants. Moreover, the droppings from some trees are particularly injurious to whatever vegetation they fall upon. When any plants require a shade it is infinitely better to make a temporary protection with wide boards placed on stones, or billets of wood, than to attempt to plant in the shade of trees. In the absence of wide boards for screening plants from the intense heat of the sun, two or more narrow boards may be placed side by side.

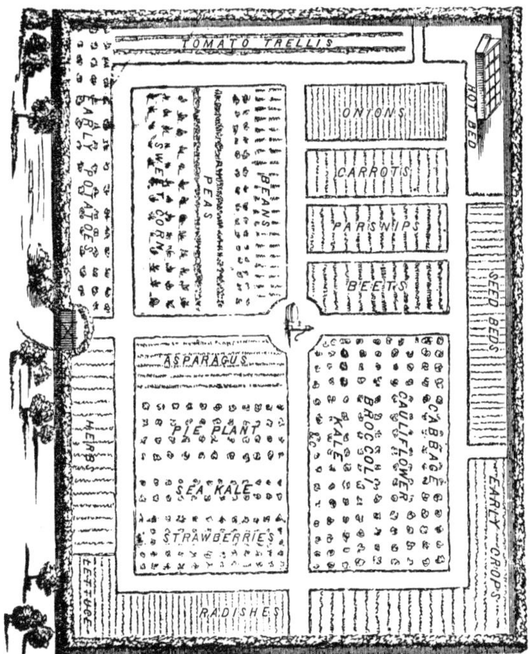

ARRANGEMENT OF THE GARDEN.

The cut herewith given, represents a very satisfactory manner of disposing of different kinds of plants and vegetables in the kitchen-garden. The illustration requires no explanation. The arrangement can be varied to suit the fancy or convenience.

MANURE.—HOW APPLIED.

One important point to be attended to, is to have a supply of good, well-rotted manure ready to incorporate with the soil; and also a portion of ashes, soot, tobacco-dust, and lime, for the purpose of sowing over seed-beds in dry weather, to destroy insects, which sometimes cut off young plants as fast as they come up.

If the ground cannot be all manured every year, as it should be, it is of primary importance that those vegetables be provided for which most need manure. A perusal of the catalogue will enable the young gardener to judge of the kinds of garden products which require it most. Good, rich manure is indispensably necessary for the production of Broccoli, Cauliflower, Cabbage, Lettuce, Spinach, Onions, Radishes, and Salads in general.

In the event of a scanty supply of manure, those kinds of vegetables which are raised in hills or drills, may be manured immediately under the seed or plants by applying a light dressing before the seed is dropped, being careful to cover it with soil, so that the seed may not come in immediate contact with stimulating fertilizers.

As some cultivators, by their method of using manure, show that they have very erroneous ideas as to its real object or utility, I would remind them that manure should be employed with a view to renovate and strengthen the natural soil, and not as a receptacle for seed. In order that manure may have a salutary effect, it should be thoroughly incorporated with the earth by the operation of digging or ploughing. When it is used in hills or on a given spot, it should be well pulverized and mixed with the earth so as to form a compost. These remarks apply especially to strong animal manures, the excrements of fowls, as also to soaper's, tanner's and glue manufac turer's manure, rags, etc. Lime, ashes, bone-dust, poudrette, urate, salt, sulphur, gypsum, nitrate of potash, and other porta ble manures, may be sown broadcast over the land previous to harrowing or raking it, or such manures may be formed into a compost when used in hills or drills. They should in every case be used with caution, as an indiscreet use of them will destroy the seed or plants, and thus defeat the cultivator's object. Many gardeners can corroborate these facts, from having used strong compost as a mould for their hotbeds, thereby poisoning the germs of the seed, and causing the plants to die off prematurely; and it is notorious that a great proportion of failing crops is occasioned by an injudicious mode of using manure.

IMPROVING POOR SOILS.

Much depends on the manures used on particular kinds of soil. The great art of improving sandy and clayey soils consists in giving the former such dressings of clay, cow-dung, and other kinds of manure, as will have a tendency to bind and make them more compact, and consequently more retentive of moisture; and to the latter, coats of horse-dung, ashes, sand, and such other composts as may tend to separate the particles and open the pores of the clay, so as to cause it to approach as nearly as possible to a loam.

SALTPETRE AS A FERTILIZER.

Saltpetre is pernicious to many species of insects; it is also an excellent manure, and may be used to great advantage when dissolved in the proportion of one pound to four gallons of water. This liquid, applied to plants through the rose of a watering-pot, will preserve health and vigor. Soapsuds are equally beneficial, if used occasionally in the same manner—say once a week. These remedies, applied alternately, have been known to preserve melon and cucumber-vines from the ravages of the yellow-fly, bugs, blight, etc., and to keep the plants in a thriving condition.

REPELLING INSECTS.

As liquid, however, cannot be conveniently used on a large piece of land, it may be necessary, if insects are numerous, to sow tobacco-dust, mixed with road-dust, soot, ashes, lime, or the dust of charcoal, in the proportion of half a bushel per acre every morning, until the plants are free or secure from their attacks.

It is necessary that the gardener should have a hogshead set in the ground always at hand in dry weather, containing solutions made of waste tobacco, lime, soot, cow-dung, elder, burdock leaves, etc. A portion of these ingredients, or any other preparation that is pernicious or poisonous to insects, without injuring the plants, thrown into a hogshead kept filled up with water, if used moderately over beds of young plants in dry weather, would, in almost every case, insure a successful crop. Such liquid, however, should never be used when the sun shines; and if applied too abundantly to the leaves, there is danger, sometimes, that the leaves and stems will be destroyed.

Manure should be applied to the most profitable and exhausting crops; and the succession of crops should be so arranged that the ground may be occupied by plants either valuable in themselves, or which may contribute to the increased value of those which are to follow; and the value of the labor required to mature vegetables and prepare them for market, should be always taken into consideration.

VALUE OF PEAT ASHES.

The farmers of Europe consider peat ashes of more value than any others; and I am persuaded that, could they be fairly tested by some of our best cultivators, great good would result to the community. If the farmers in England can afford to keep men under pay, perpetually burning peat for the sake of the ashes, it is natural to suppose that the poor of our community may be placed in easier circumstances, as respects the article of fuel. Thousands of acres of land are to be found in the States of New York and New Jersey, and within a few miles of this city, which abound with peat earth; and the owners of such have already begun to explore their treasures of this description. Good peat burns well in all sorts of stoves and grates, whether made for wood or coal, and also on the hearth; and if the ashes are not used to any better purpose than other ashes have hitherto been, it is the cheapest fuel known. I am persuaded that this subject is worthy of serious consideration; and if the editors of the different papers would arouse the public attention, so as to direct some of our most active citizens to a consideration of this subject, incalculable good would result to the community at large.

PREPARATION OF THE SOIL.

A light, sandy soil will be benefited if worked when moist, as such treatment will have a tendency to make it more compact; on the contrary, if a clayey soil be worked when too wet, it kneads like dough, and never fails to bind when drought follows; and this not only prevents the seed from rising, but injures the plants materially in their subsequent growth, by its becoming impervious to moderate rains, dews, air, and the influence of the sun, all of which are necessary to the promotion of vegetation.

The nearer the ground approaches to a sandy soil, the less retentive will it be of moisture; the more to a clayey, the longer will it retain moisture; and the finer the particles of which the clay is composed, the more retentive will it be of water, and, consequently, the longer in drying, and the harder when dry. But earth of a consistence that will hold water the longest, *without becoming hard when dry*, is, of all others, the best adapted for raising the generality of plants in the greatest perfection. This last described soil is called loam, and is a medium earth, between the extremes of clay and sand.

Many gardens can never be brought into a state of great productiveness on account of an excess of water in the soil. If the soil be heavy, and continues wet and heavy in the spring, let it be drained at once. After this, plough deep, pulverize thoroughly, manure highly, keep the weeds subdued, and in a few years you will have a garden that will produce anything that will grow in your locality. If the soil is heavy, haul on muck, sawdust, chip manure, in great abundance; and when such substances decay, the soil will be light, mellow, and productive.

ROTATION OF CROPS.

Perhaps the next important point to be attended to is the most proper rotation of crops. Virgil, who was a philosopher as well as a poet, very justly observes, that "THE TRUE REPOSE OF THE EARTH IS A CHANGE OF ITS PRODUCTIONS."

It is a curious fact, that a plant may be killed by the poison which it has itself secreted, as a viper may be destroyed by its own venom. Hence it has been very generally noticed, that the soil in which some particular vegetables have grown, and into which they have discharged the excretions of their roots, is rendered noxious to the prosperity of plants of the same or allied species, though it be well adapted to the growth and support of other distinct species of vegetables.

It is proved by experience, that fall Spinach is an excellent preparative for Beets, Carrots, Radishes, Salsify, and all other tap, as well as tuberous-rooted vegetables.

Celery or Potatoes constitute a suitable preparative for Cabbage, Cauliflower, and all other plants of the *Brassica* tribe; as also Artichokes, Asparagus, Lettuce, and Onions, provided such ground be well situated, which is a circumstance always to be duly considered in laying out a garden.

Lands that have long lain in pasture are, for the first three or four years after being tilled, superior for Cabbage, Turnips,

Potatoes, etc., and afterwards for culinary vegetables in general.

The following rules are subjoined for further government:

Fibrous-rooted plants may be alternated with tap or tuberous-rooted, and *vice versa.*

Plants which produce luxuriant tops, so as to shade the land, should be succeeded by such as yield small tops or narrow leaves.

Those which, during their growth, require the operation of stirring the earth, should precede such as do not require cultivation.

Ground which has been occupied by Artichokes, Asparagus, Rhubarb, Sea Kale, or such other crops as remain long on a given spot, should be subjected to a regular rotation of crops for at least as long a period as it remained under such permanent crops. Hence in all gardens judiciously managed, the Strawberry-bed is changed every three or four years, till it has gone the circuit of all the compartments; and Asparagus-beds should be renewed, on the same principle, as often as they fail to produce luxuriantly. Indeed, no two crops should be allowed to ripen their seed in succession in the same soil, if it can be avoided; because, if its fertility be not exhausted by such crops, weeds will accumulate more than on beds frequently cultivated.

SEED AND SEEDING.

I am an advocate for early sowing and planting, even at the risk of losing a little seed, provided the ground be fit to receive it. Some gardeners, as well as some writers, recommend certain fixed days for sowing and planting particular kinds of seed; I think it necessary to guard my readers against being misled. The failure of crops may be often attributed to the observance of certain days for sowing. If some kinds of seed be sown when the ground is wet and cold, they will become chilled in the ground, and seldom vegetate. If they be sown in very dry weather, the germinative parts of the seed may become injured by the burning rays of the sun, or the young plants may get devoured by insects as fast as they come up. To obviate these difficulties, I have generally allowed a week or ten days for sowing the seed, intending the medium as the proper time for the vicinity of New York. With this clearly borne in mind, the reader who observes the difference in the degrees of heat and cold in the different parts of the country, will know how to apply these instructions accordingly.

PLANTING IN DRILLS.

I have, in most cases, recommended drills to be made at certain depths for the different kinds of seed; and when I have stated that the drills should be two inches deep, it is intended that the seed should be covered only one inch, which it will be when planted in these drills and covered; and so in proportion for any other depth required. This may serve as a guide to the young gardener; but circumstances alter cases. If, for instance, some particular crops should fail, this would render it necessary, if the season be far advanced, to risk a further planting of seed, even if the weather be hot and the ground dry. If this be planted a little deeper, it may escape the violent heat of the sun, and in the event of a shower, the ground would become sufficiently moist to bring it up; whereas it sometimes happens that seed sown after a shower does not vegetate until after the season is too far advanced to bring the crop to perfection.

The work of drilling by those who have no machine, may be performed in various ways; in some cases a plough is used, in others a small hoe, or a dibble drawn along the edge of a board or line. It is of little consequence which way the work is done, if it be well done. While I leave the gardener to make his own choice of tools, I would suggest that he be provided with two or three drilling machines; these, every handy man can make for himself; they should be in the form of a garden-rake, with a stout, heavy back, and five teeth, about two inches broad, and tapered so as to enter the ground and leave drills two inches deep. If one be made with the teeth eight inches apart, another twelve, and another fourteen, they will be useful in making drills for the various kinds of seed; and drills thus made serve instead of straining a line when transplanting Cabbage, Lettuce, Leek plants, etc.; the line being stretched at one edge of the bed, and the drilling machine drawn straight by the line, makes five drills at once. If they are straight, they may be kept so, by keeping one drill open for the outside tooth to work in, until the ground be all drilled.

Gardeners practise different methods of covering up seed; some do it with a hoe, others with a rake or harrow; some draw a portion of the earth to the side of the bed, and after sowing the seed, return it regularly over the bed; in some particular cases a sieve is used, in others a roller. Rolling or treading in seed is necessary in dry seasons; but it should never be done when the ground is wet.

Many kinds of seed, such as Asparagus, Capsicum, Celery, Fetticus, Leek, Lettuce, Onion, Parsnip, Parsley, Rhubarb, Salsify, Spinach, etc., will not vegetate freely in dry weather unless the ground be watered or rolled. Where there is no roller on the premises, the following contrivance may answer for small beds as a substitute: after the seed is sown, and the ground well raked, take a board the whole length of the bed, lay it flat on the ground, begin at one edge of the bed, and walk the whole length of it; this will press the soil on the seed; then shift the board till you have gone over the whole bed. In the absence of boards, tread in the seed with your feet, or strike on the bed with the back of your spade or shovel; but this should not be done when the ground is wet.

If it be necessary at any time to sow seed in extremely dry weather, it is recommended to soak the seed in water, and dry it with sulphur. This practice, with attentive watering, will cause the seed to vegetate speedily.

I have, in most cases, recommended seed to be sown in drills drawn from eight to twelve inches apart, in preference to sowing broadcast; because the weeds can be more easily destroyed by means of a small hoe, which, if properly used, greatly promotes the growth of young plants.

If it should be requisite to transplant anything when the ground is dry, the transplanting should always be done as soon as the earth is turned over; and the roots of the plants, before they are set out, should be steeped in mud made of rich compost.

TABLE SHOWING THE NUMBER OF PLANTS ON AN ACRE.

The following table shows the number of plants or trees that may be raised on an acre of ground, when planted at certain distances apart:—

Distance apart.	No. of Plants.	Distance apart.	No. of Plants.
1 foot	43,560	9 feet	537
1½ feet	19,360	12 feet	302
2 feet	10,890	15 feet	193
2½ feet	6,969	18 feet	134
3 feet	4,840	21 feet	98
4 feet	2,722	24 feet	75
5 feet	1,742	27 feet	59
6 feet	1,210	30 feet	48

The preceding table may serve as a guide to such as are not expert in arithmetic, in laying out a garden, as it shows at one view many proportions of an acre of land, in squares of different dimensions. The last line, for instance, shows that, if forty-eight trees be planted on an acre, each thirty feet apart, there may be forty-eight beds of thirty feet square, or thirty beds of forty-eight feet square, formed from the same quantity of land. An allowance of about one-eighth must, however, be made from the above calculation for walks and paths.

DISTRIBUTION OF MANURE.

The table may also serve to show the gardener how to dispose of any given quantity of manure, that may be allotted for an acre of ground. If, for instance it requires three hundred and two trees to plant an acre when placed twelve feet from each other, it will require as many heaps of manure to cover the same quantity of ground, if dropped the same distance apart. It therefore follows, that if one hundred loads be allowed to the acre, each load must be divided into three heaps. If seventy-five loads only be allowed, every load must be divided into four heaps, and so on in proportion to the quantity allowed. But if the gardener should choose to drop his heaps five paces, or fifteen feet apart, he may make such distribution of his loads as to have one hundred and ninety-three heaps on the acre of land; in which case, by dividing each load into four heaps, he will require only forty-eight loads to cover the acre, and he may decrease the quantity still more, by allowing greater distances from heap to heap, or by dividing his loads into smaller proportions, so as to accommodate himself to whatever quantity of manure he may allot to any given quantity of ground.

THE VITALITY OF SEEDS.

As it may not be generally known that some kinds of seed are apt to lose their vegetative qualities much sooner than others, the following hints are subjoined as some rule for the gardener's government, provided the seed is carefully preserved, and not exposed to excess of heat, air, or dampness :—

Parsnip, Rhubarb, and other light, scale-like seeds, cannot be safely trusted after they are a year old. Beans and Peas of different species, Capsicum, Carrot, Cress, Leek, Nasturtium, Okra, Onion, Salsify, Scorzonera, and small herb-seed in general, may be kept two years. Artichoke, Asparagus, Egg-plant, Endive, Fetticus, Lettuce, Mustard, Parsley, Skirret, and Spinach-seed, may with care be preserved three years. Broccoli, Cauliflower, Cabbage, Celery, Kale, Radish, and Turnip-seed will keep four years, if properly attended to. Beet, Cucumber, Gourd, Melon, Pumpkin, and Squash; also Burnet, Chervil, and Sorrel-seed, have been known to grow freely when five, and even seven years old; but it is not prudent to venture seed in the garden, or any other place, when there are any apprehensions that any portion of it has lost its vitality by age, or in any other way.

In order to put such on their guard as may attempt to raise seed either for their own use or for the market, I would observe that great care is necessary; as it is an indubitable fact, that if seed of similar species be raised near each other, degeneracy will be the consequence. It is therefore difficult for any one man to raise all sorts of seed, good and true to their kind, in any one garden.

If roots of any kind become defective, they are unfit for seed, as the annexed fact will show. I once planted for seed some beautiful orange-colored roots of Carrots; but as they had been previously grown with some of a lemon-color, they produced seed of a mixed and spurious variety; and as this is not a solitary instance of degeneracy from the like cause, I have come to the conclusion that, as in the animal frame, so it is in the vegetable system—disorders frequently lie dormant from one generation to another, and at length break out with all their vigor. I would therefore advise seed-growers not to attempt to "bring a clean thing out of an unclean;" but if they find a mixture of varieties among their seed-roots, to reject the whole, or they will infallibly have spurious seed.

SEEDS OF STONE FRUIT.

If the seeds of the Apple, Pear, and Quince, and the pits of the Apricot, Cherry, Peach, and Plum, were not planted in autumn, let it be done as soon as the earth can be brought into tillable condition in the spring, because exposure to frost is usually essential to their vegetating, unless the shells are separated by some means, so that moisture can reach the germs. The chief object of exposing pits to frost is, simply to open the shell.

CAUSES OF FAILURE IN THE GERMINATION OF SEEDS.

As some gardeners attribute all failures of seed to germinate to its defectiveness, I shall offer a few observations to convince such persons of their error.

Seeds denominated hardy and half-hardy, are subject to risk in unpropitious seasons, from unfitness of the soil to promote vegetation, rendered so by cold rains and variable weather. If sprouted seed survive a severe chill, it is the more susceptible of frost, to which it is frequently subjected early in the season. Some species of plants that, in an advanced stage of growth, will stand a hard winter, are often cut off by a slight frost while germinating, especially if exposed to the heat of the sun after a frosty night, or while in a frozen state. Cabbage, Carrot, Celery, Turnip, and many other growing plants, which survive the ordinary winters of England, are here classified as half-hardy, for the reasons above stated.

The most tender species of plants frequently perish from excess of rain. Lima Beans, for instance, have often to be replanted three or four times in the month of May before any will stand. Melons, Cucumbers, Egg-plants, Tomato plants, etc., are sometimes cut off by variableness of the weather. Those who plant tender things in open gardens early in the season, must reconcile themselves to loss in the event of unfavorable weather, instead of throwing blame on the seedsman.

Such species and varieties as, from their nature, are apt to vegetate quickly, are very liable to be devoured by insects before they make any show on the surface. Turnip-seed, for instance, will sprout within forty-eight hours after being sown; and under favorable circumstances, most of the species of this class will come up within a week; but if insects attack the seed-beds in dry weather, a total loss of crops will be the consequence. Every experienced farmer is convinced of this fact, by having frequently to sow his Turnip-ground three or four times before he can get any to stand.

Sometimes a sudden shower of rain will cause plants to grow out of the reach of insects; but every good gardener should have his remedies at hand to apply to seed-beds in general, and especially to those in which plants are raised for the purpose of being transplanted. The seeds of some plants require from two to three or four weeks to vegetate in unfa vorable seasons. Some plants are retarded by cold, others by excess of dry weather; and at such times, seed may fail to vegetate for want of pressure. In the event of drought after heavy rains, seed and young plants often perish through incrustation of the soil, and from other untoward circumstances, which can neither be controlled nor accounted for, even by the most assiduous and precise gardener. It must, however, be conceded, that failures often occur through seed being deposited too deep in the ground, or left too near the surface. Sometimes, for want of sufficiency of seed in a given spot, solitary plants will perish, they not having sufficient strength to open the pores of the earth; and frequently injudicious management in manuring and preparing the soil will cause a failure.

I have been induced to expatiate, and to designate, in the *seventh range of the preceding table*, such plants as are generally cultivated first in seed-beds and afterwards transplanted for the purpose of being accommodated with space to mature in, with a view to answer at once the thousand and one questions asked by inexperienced cultivators.

QUANTITY OF SEED.

Some persons, from ignorance of the nature and object of raising plants for transplanting, ask for pounds of seed, when an ounce is amply sufficient for their purpose. For example, an ounce of Celery-seed will produce ten thousand plants. An ounce of Cabbage-seed will produce from three to four thousand; sufficient, when transplanted, to cover nearly half an acre of land—which land, if sown with spinach, for instance, would require from four to six pounds of seed.

TIME TO COMMENCE GARDENING.

The following directions for the management of a garden are founded on the results of practical experience in the vicinity of New York City, where the soil is generally susceptible of gardening operations towards the end of March. These directions may, however, be applied to all other parts of the UNITED STATES, by a *minute observance* of the difference in temperature. In the extreme northern parts of the State of New York, as well as in all other places similarly situated, the directions for the beginning of April will apply to the latter part of the same month, with very few exceptions. In our SOUTHERN STATES, the directions for APRIL, which may be considered as the first gardening month in the EASTERN, WESTERN, and MIDDLE STATES, will apply to January, February, or to whatever season gardening operations may commence in the respective States. In the *varied climates* of each particular State, if the same rule of application be pursued, success is certain.

FORCING VARIOUS KINDS OF VEGETABLES.

The following simple method of forcing vegetables on a small scale is recommended by a correspondent of a London magazine. The writer says:

"I obtain mushrooms in winter by a very simple process. Provide boxes three feet long, and one foot eight inches deep; a quantity of horse-droppings, perfectly dry, some spawn, and some light dry soil. Fill the boxes by layers of droppings, spawn, and soil, which must be well trodden down. Repeat these triple layers till the boxes are full, and all trodden firmly together. Four such boxes at work are sufficient for a moderate demand; and out of a dozen, four brought in at a time, and placed upon a flue of a greenhouse stove, will produce a fine supply. The surface of these portable beds may be covered with a little hay, and occasionally, though sparingly, watered. It is not absolutely necessary that they be set on the flue of a greenhouse; a warm stable, cellar, or any other similar place, will suit equally well. This plan is also convenient for affording a plentiful stock of superior spawn.

"The same-sized boxes will also do for Asparagus; but for this purpose a sufficient stock of three-year-old plants must be at hand; also eighteen boxes, four of which are the necessary set to be forced at one time for one family. Half fill the boxes with decayed tanner's bark, leaf-mould, or any similar mould; on this pack the roots as thickly as possible, and fill up the boxes with the bark, etc. Any place in a forcing-house will suit them where they can enjoy the necessary degree of heat. Besides Asparagus and Mushrooms, Sea-Kale, Buda-Kale, Angelica, small salad, and various potherbs may be raised in the same manner."

Those who have not the conveniences recommended in a greenhouse, may place the boxes in a hotbed. The glasses being laid on, and the beds covered at night, will soon promote the growth of the plants, and produce vegetable luxuries at a season when garden products in general are comparatively scarce.

It is unnecessary to show of how much value such processes may be in minor establishments, or in a new country. I wish it to be understood, that in order to the successful cultivation of some of the rare vegetables I have treated of, great pains must be taken in every stage of their growth. If the advice I have given be attended to, I flatter myself we shall soon obtain a supply of many of these luxuries of the garden. My directions are founded on the success attending the practice of some of the best gardeners in this country. I have also had sufficient experience to warrant me in this attempt to contribute my mite towards the attainment of this kind of useful knowledge.

HOTBEDS.

For the purpose of raising Mustard, Cress, and other salad herbs, also Egg-plants, Tomato-plants, etc., in small quantities, a hotbed may be made early in the spring, of good heating materials, on the top of which may be laid leaf-mould, old tan, or light compost, to the depth of about nine inches. The various kinds of seed may be sown in boxes or flower-pots, and plunged in the top mould up to their rims, and by being well attended to, a supply of small salads, as well as small seedling-plants, may be raised without much labor or difficulty. This method is also well calculated for raising annual flower-plants at an early season.

ADAPTING PLANTS TO SOILS.

The various species of plants which occupy our greenhouses, gardens, and fields, *require each their peculiar aliment*—they having been collected from all the diversified regions, climates, and soils through earth's remotest bounds; they consequently comprise natives of mountains and rocks, as well as of plains, valleys, and watercourses. The most essential aliment for natives of warm climates and dry soils being HEAT, artificial means are used in cool seasons and unpropitious climates to produce it. Natives of temperate climates require salubrious air, hence they are cultivated to the greatest perfection in our Northern States in spring and autumn; and in our Southern States in the winter; and natives of humid climates, as also amphibious plants in general, require a more than ordinary share of MOISTURE, and grow best in wet soil; but these THREE ELEMENTS collectively constitute the food of plants in general, and should be judiciously imparted to the various species, in due proportions, according to circumstances. I have also shown that the roots of various species of plants require each their peculiar aliment, which is not to be found in all descriptions of land. This is demonstrated by roots of trees being frequently discovered spreading beyond their ordinary bounds in quest of salutary food.

DEEP PLANTING.

Although it has been admitted that excessive deep planting of trees and plants is injurious, and in many cases fatal to their very existence, it does not follow that *all* annuals and biennials are injured by the same means. On the contrary, the earthing up of particular species of plants in a late stage of growth is calculated to promote early maturity, which constitutes the most essential art in gardening for the market; because the earliest crops are always the most profitable. It is moreover a necessary practice in climates where the seasons for gardening are short—as without such practice, many kinds of vegetables could not possibly be matured in due season for gathering before winter.

I would here take the opportunity of proving this last position, by reminding the reader that the effect of deep planting, in the Peach-tree for instance, is discoverable soon after the error is committed, by its fruit ripening prematurely, and this is often the case for a year or two prior to its final decease, and should operate as a salutary lesson against planting *perennial* plants and trees too deep. I would urge gardeners and cultivators to consult the operations of nature in all their rural pursuits; and with a view to aid them, I subjoin the following rules, which are further illustrated under the different heads:

1. In transplanting fruit-trees, let the collar, or that part from which emanate the main roots, be near the surface. A medium-sized tree may be planted an inch deeper than it was in the nursery bed; and the largest should not exceed two or three inches.

2. In the cultivation of such plants as are transplanted, or grown in hills or clusters, as Indian Corn, etc., keep the earth loose but level around them in their early stages of growth, by frequent hoeing, ploughing, or cultivating; and to promote early maturity, throw a moderate portion of earth about the roots and stems at the last or final dressing.

3. In the sowing of seed, remember that IN UNITY THERE IS STRENGTH, and that from the germinative parts of a seed being weak and diminutive, it cannot be expected to perforate through the soil solitary and alone. To insure a fair chance, plant your seed moderately thick, and thin out the surplus plants while young. In planting seed in drills, which is the most eligible plan, the size of the seed and strength of its germ should be considered. Large seed, producing vigorous roots, requires deeper planting than diminutive seed, producing delicate roots and slender stalks.

4. In the choice of compost for exotic or greenhouse plants, imitate the native soil of each peculiar species as nearly as

possible, by a judicious mixture of *maiden earth*, loam, sand, leaf, swamp, and rock mould, decomposed manures, and such other composts as are recommended under the different heads. Remember, that although strong manure is essential to the growth of some plants, it is poisonous to others. PURSUE, THEN, A MEDIUM COURSE. From your soil not being too stiff nor too light, too rich nor too poor, too cool nor too warm, too close nor too porous, if not positively salutary and congenial to all, it must render the situation of each endurable. I again repeat, that temperance in the use of aliment is as essential to the welfare of the vegetable family as it is to the health, happiness, and longevity of mankind.

MEANS FOR REPELLING INSECTS.

There is nothing that protects young crops of Turnips, Cabbage, and other small plants, from the depredations of the fly so well as rolling; for when the surface is rendered completely smooth, these insects are deprived of the harbor they would otherwise have under the clods and small lumps of earth. This method will be found more effectual than soaking the seed in any preparation, or dusting the plants with any composition whatever; but the roller must only be used previous to, or at the time of sowing the seed, and not when the soil is so moist that it will pack and bake, thus forming a crust on the surface of the ground, through which the young plants can never force their way.

Turnip-seed will sometimes sprout in forty-eight hours. Cabbage-seed ought to come up within a week after it is sown; but it sometimes happens that the whole is destroyed before a plant is seen above ground. The seedsman, in this case, is often blamed, but without cause.

A correspondent has communicated the result of an experiment he has tried for preventing the attacks of flies or fleas on Turnips. He says: "Steep your seed in a pint of warm water for two hours, in which is infused one ounce of saltpetre; then dry the seed, and add currier's oil sufficient to wet the whole; after which mix it with plaster of Paris, so as to separate and render it fit for sowing."

As the truth of the old adage, that one ounce of prevention is of more value than a pound of cure, is very generally admitted, I would recommend the following method of preparing a bed for the purpose of raising Cabbage, Cauliflower, Broccoli, and such other plants as are subject to the attacks of insects: After digging or ploughing the ground in the usual way, collect any combustibles that are attainable, as dried weeds, sedge, turf, brushwood, leaves, stubble, corn-stalks, sawdust, or even litter from the dung-heap, which should be placed in heaps on the seed-beds and burned to ashes; then rake the ground over and sow the seed, which will not be attacked by insects while the effects of the fire remain. In the event of extremely dry weather, water the beds every evening until the plants are in full leaf. This is an infallible remedy.

Fish oil is known to be destructive to ants and various other small insects, but it is difficult to apply to plants.

In the summer season, Broccoli, Cabbage, Cauliflower, etc., are particularly subject to the ravages of grubs and caterpillars. To prevent this wholly, is perhaps impossible; still it is not difficult to check these troublesome visitors. It may be done by searching for them on their first appearance, and destroying them. Early in the morning, grubs may be collected from the earth, within two or three inches of such plants as they may have attacked the night previous.

The approach of caterpillars is discoverable on the leaves of Cabbages, many of which are reduced to a thin white skin by the minute insects which emerge from the eggs placed on them. These leaves being gathered and thrown into the fire, a whole host of enemies may be destroyed at once; whereas, if they are suffered to remain, they will increase so rapidly, that in a few days the plantation, however extensive, may become infested; and, when once these arrive at the butterfly, or moth stage of existence, they become capable of perpetuating their destructive race to an almost unlimited extent.

The same remarks apply to all other insects in a torpid state.

Worms, maggots, snails, or slugs, may be driven away by sowing salt or lime in the spring, in the proportion of two to three bushels per acre, or by watering the soil occasionally with salt and water, using about two pounds of salt to four gallons of water; or the slug kind may be easily entrapped on small beds of plants, by strewing slices of turnip on them late in the evening, on which the slug or snail will readily crowd, and may be gathered up early in the morning (before sunrise) and destroyed.

Moles may be annoyed and driven away, by obstructing the passage in their burrows with sticks smeared with tar. First insert a clean stick from the surface through the burrows; then dip others in tar, and pass them through into the floor of the burrows, being careful not to rub off the tar in the operation. Tar is also an effectual remedy against smut in wheat. After being heated in a kettle until it becomes thin, it may be stirred in among the grain until it becomes saturated. The wheat should afterwards be mixed with a sufficient quantity of wood ashes to dry and render it fit for sowing. Before using tar, however, the seed should be steeped in warm water until the germ is about to appear. Otherwise, tar will exclude the necessary moisture to insure germination; and a long time will elapse before the plants come up. And if too much tar be employed, they will *never* come up. A very thin coating of tar is sufficient. Coal-tar is better than pine tar.

To prevent depredations from crows, steep corn in strong saltpetre brine, sow it over the land, or steep your seed-corn; and if the crows once get a taste, they will forsake the field.

CHAPTER II.

ARTICHOKE.

ARTICHAUT. *Cynara.*

VARIETIES.

Cynara Scolymus, or French. | Cynara Hortensis, or Globe.

THE garden Artichoke is a native of the South of Europe, and much cultivated for the London and Paris markets. It is a perennial plant, producing from the root annually its large, squamose heads, in full growth, from June or July, until October or November. The Globe Artichoke, which produces large globular heads, is best for general culture, the heads being considerably larger, and the eatable parts more thick and plump.

Both sorts may be raised from seed, or young suckers taken from old plants in the spring. A plantation of Artichokes will produce good heads six or seven years, and sometimes longer; but if a supply of this delicious vegetable be required throughout the season, a small plantation should be made from suckers every spring, for a successive crop, as the young plants will continue to produce their heads in perfection after the crops of the old standing ones are over.

The best way to obtain a supply of Artichokes from seed is to sow it in the latter part of March, or at any time in April, in a bed of good, rich earth; or it may be planted in drills one inch deep and about twelve inches apart. The ground should be light and moist, not such as is apt to become bound up by heat, or that, in consequence of containing too large a proportion of sand, is liable to become extremely hot in summer, for this is injurious to these plants. After the plants are up, they should be kept free from weeds, and the earth often loosened around them.

The business of transplanting may be done in cloudy or wet weather, at any time after the plants are from nine to twelve inches high. Having fixed upon a proper soil and situation, lay on it a good quantity of rotten dung, and trench the ground one good spade or eighteen inches deep, incorporating the manure therewith. When this is done, take up the plants; and after shortening their tap-roots a little, and dressing their leaves, plant them with a dibble, in rows five feet asunder, and two feet from plant to plant, leaving part of their green tops above ground, and the hearts of the plants free from any earth over them, and give each plant a little water to settle the roots.

WINTER MANAGEMENT.

The winter dressing of Artichokes is an important operation; on it depends much of their future success. This should not be given them as long as the season continues mild, that they may have all possible advantage of growth, and be gradually inured to the increasing cold weather; but it should not be deferred too late, lest by the sudden setting in of hard frost, to which we are subject in the Northern States, the work be neglected, and the plants consequently exposed to devastation and loss.

In the first place, cut all the large leaves close to the ground, leaving the small ones which rise from the hearts of the plants. After this, line and mark out a trench in the middle, between each row, from fourteen to sixteen inches wide, presuming that the rows are five feet apart, as directed. Then dig the surface of the beds lightly from trench to trench, burying the weeds; and as you proceed, gather the earth around the crowns of the plants to the height of about six inches, placing it in gently between the young rising leaves, without burying them entirely under it. This done, dig the trenches one spade deep, and distribute the earth equally between and on each side of the plants, so as to level the ridges, giving them at the same time a neat, rounding form.

The beds may remain in this condition until there is an appearance of hard frost, when they should be covered with light dung, litter, or leaves of trees, to preserve the crowns and roots from intense cold. In this manner the roots will remain in perfect safety all the winter. As soon as the severe frosts are over, the beds must be uncovered, and when the young shoots begin to appear above ground, then, and not till then, level down the beds, throwing the earth into the alleys or trenches, and round them in a neat manner. Then dig in the short manure, and loosen all the earth around the plants. At the same time, examine the number of shoots arising on each stool, and select three of the strongest and *healthiest* on every stool, which are to remain; all above that number are to be broken off close to the roots with the hand, unless you want some for making new plantations, in which case an extra number for that purpose is to remain on the parent plants, until they are about eight or ten inches high, when they are to be slipped off, and planted in a bed prepared in the same manner as directed for the young plants, taking care at the same time to close the earth about the crowns of the roots, and draw it up a little to the remaining suckers.

The spring dressing should be given when the plants are in the above-described state, whether that occurs in February, March, or April, occasioned by the difference of climate in the respective States, or by the earliness or lateness of the spring.

The gardeners near London generally take off the side suckers, or small Artichokes, when they are about the size of a hen's egg. These meet with a ready sale in the markets, and the principal heads that are left are always larger and more handsome. The maturity of a full-grown Artichoke is apparent by the opening of the scales; and it should always be cut off before the flower appears in the centre; the stem should be cut close to the ground at the same time.

Artichokes are esteemed a luxury by epicures. To have them in perfection, they should be thrown into cold water as soon as gathered, and after having been soaked and well washed, put into the boiler, when the water is hot, with a little salt, and kept boiling until tender, which generally requires, for full-grown Artichokes, from an hour and a half to two hours. When taken up drain and trim them; then serve them up with melted butter, pepper, salt, and such other condiment as may best suit the palate.

ASPARAGUS.

ASPERGE. *Asparagus officinalis.*

VARIETIES.

Gravesend.	Large Battersea.
Large White Reading.	Large Green, or Giant.

This plant is a native of cold climates, and is found growing wild in Russia and Poland, where it is eaten by the cattle the same as grass. It will endure the severity of our winters, and produce buds when the weather becomes mild; but as garden products are generally scarce after a hard winter, the gardener who studies his interest will make the most of the spring season, and raise all he can before the market becomes glutted. To this end he is recommended to prepare for forcing this vegetable as soon as the coldest of the winter is past. (*See article on Forcing Vegetables.*)

Asparagus may be raised by sowing the seed in the fall as soon as ripe, or in March and the early part of April. One ounce of seed will produce about a thousand plants. It requires some of the best ground in the garden. The seed may be sown in drills, ten or twelve inches asunder, and covered about an inch with light earth. When the plants are up they will need a careful hoeing, and if well cultivated and kept free from weeds, they will be large enough to transplant when a year old. Some keep them in the nursery-bed until they are two years old.

If the beds are properly dressed every year, they will produce well for twenty years or more. New beds may be made in autumn, or before the buds get far advanced in spring—say in February, March, or April, according to situation and circumstances. The ground for the bed must not be wet, nor too strong or stubborn, but such as is moderately light and pliable, so that it will readily fall to pieces in digging or raking, and in a situation that enjoys the full rays of the sun. It should have a large supply of well-rotted dung, three or four inches thick, and then be regularly trenched two spades deep, and the dung buried equally in each trench twelve or fifteen inches below the surface. When this trenching is done, lay two or three inches of thoroughly-rotted manure over the whole surface, and dig the ground over again, eight or ten inches deep, mixing this top dressing, and incorporating it well with the earth.

ARRANGING THE YOUNG PLANTS.

In family gardens, it is customary to divide the ground thus prepared into beds, allowing four feet for every four rows of plants, with alleys two feet and a half wide between each bed. Strain your line along the bed six inches from the edge; then with a spade cut out a small trench or drill close to the line, about six inches deep, making that side next the line nearly upright; when one trench is opened, plant that before you open another, placing the plants upright ten or twelve inches distant in the row, and let every row be twelve inches apart.

The plants must not be placed flat in the bottom of the trench, but nearly upright against the back of it, and so that the crown of the plants may also stand upright, and two or three inches below the surface of the ground, spreading their roots somewhat regularly against the back of the trench, and at the same time drawing a little earth up against them with the hand as you place them, just to fix the plants in their due position until the row is planted. When one row is thus placed, draw the earth into the trench over the plants with a rake or hoe, and then proceed to open another drill or trench, as before directed; and fill and cover it in the same manner and so on till the whole is planted. Then let the surface of the beds be raked smooth, and the stones removed.

Some gardeners, with a view to have extra large heads, place their plants sixteen inches apart in the rows, instead of twelve; and by planting them in the *quincunx* manner—that is, by commencing the second row eight inches from the end of the first, and the fourth even with the second—the plants will form *rhomboidal* squares, instead of *rectangular* ones, and every plant will thus have room to expand its roots and leaves, growing very luxuriantly.

The above directions are intended for family gardens. Those who may wish to raise Asparagus in large quantities for market, should prepare the ground with a plough, and plant two rows in each bed, which may be carried to any length required. If several beds are wanted, they may be planted in single rows, four or five feet apart, in order that the plough may be worked freely between them. Frequent ploughing will cause the roots to spread, so as to widen the beds; and the winter dressing may be performed in a great measure with the plough. After the Asparagus is cut, the ground between the beds may be ploughed, and planted with Cabbage, Potatoes, or any other vegetable usually cultivated in rows.

WINTER DRESSING OF ASPARAGUS-BEDS.

About the beginning of November, if the stalks of Asparagus turn yellow, which is a sign of their having finished their growth for the season, cut them down close to the earth, carry them off the ground, and clear the beds carefully from weeds.

Asparagus-beds must have an annual dressing of good manure; let it be laid equally over the beds, two or three inches thick, after which, with a fork made for the purpose (which should have three flat tines), dig in the dung quite down to the crowns of the plants, by which means the roots will be greatly benefited; as the winter rains will wash the manure down among them. It is the practice with some gardeners to dig the alleys at every autumn dressing, and cover the beds with the soil taken out; this may be done for the first two years after the beds are made, but not afterwards. When the plants are in full growth, their roots and crowns extend int, the alleys, and digging them up frequently will destroy plants, or render them too weak to produce buds in perfection. The beds will be greatly benefited if covered to the depth of several inches with leaves, sea-weed, or long litter from the livery-stables.

The seedling Asparagus should also have a slight dressing. Remove the weeds, and then spread light dung over it, to the depth of one or two inches, to defend the crown of the plants from intense cold.

SPRING DRESSING OF THE BEDS.

This work should be done from about the latter end of March to the middle of April, or just before the buds begin to rise. After clearing away all long litter, spread the short dung over the whole surface, and dig it in. If the alleys be dug at the same time, it will be beneficial to the plants. Care must be taken at this season not to wound the crowns with the tines of the fork; but forking the beds should not be neglected, as admitting the sun and rain into the ground induces the plants to throw up buds of superior size. To promote such a desirable object, the ground should be kept clear of weeds at all seasons, as these greatly impoverish the soil, and frequently smother the plants.

Every bed of Asparagus should be allowed to grow undisturbed, after the buds or stalks have been removed for a few weeks; otherwise the beds will not produce abundantly next season. There is great danger of injuring the productiveness of Asparagus by cutting off every shoot as soon as it is a few inches high. One stalk at least should be allowed to grow unmolested in every crown after the third or fourth cutting. If the young shoots be cut off for several successive weeks, the top formed in the latter part of the season will be small and the growth feeble.

No fertilizing material should be applied to Asparagus in the spring but lime or salt. During the winter it is an excellent practice to throw all the soapsuds from the kitchen on the asparagus-beds; but as soon as the growing season commences, let salt be spread over the entire surface, until the ground appears as if covered with snow. Such a liberal dressing of salt will destroy all weeds and grass, and promote the growth of Asparagus.

Asparagus-plants will not produce buds large enough to cut for general use in less than three years from the time of planting; but in the fourth year, when the shoots are three or four inches high, they will bear extensive cutting, which should, however, be discontinued when no large buds are thrown up. The best way of cutting is to slip the knife down perpendicularly close to each shoot, and cut it off slantingly about three or four inches beneath the ground, taking care not to wound any young buds proceeding from the same root, for there are always several shoots advancing in different stages of growth.

Asparagus is considered a wholesome vegetable, and should not be kept long after it is gathered. After being well washed, it may be tied in bundles of about a dozen buds each, and boiled in water, slightly seasoned with salt, until tender, which will be in about twenty minutes. Take it up before it loses its true color and flavor, and serve it up on toasted bread with melted butter. Asparagus will never grow luxuriantly when there is an excess of moisture in the soil. Bone-dust is excellent as a dressing for asparagus-beds, if applied in late autumn. Guano and hen manure are also the best kinds of manure for asparagus. If the soil is heavy, apply a thin dressing of sand every season with the manure.

BEANS. (English Dwarfs.)

FEVE DE MARAIS. *Vicia faba.*

The principal cause of these garden Beans not succeeding well in this country, is the summer heat overtaking them before they are podded, which causes the blossom to drop off prematurely. To obviate this difficulty, they should be planted as early in the spring as possible. They are generally planted in England from October to April, for early crops, and from that time to July, for late crops. It sometimes happens that autumn plantings are injured by the coldness of their winters; but an average crop is generally obtained.

In the Eastern, Western, and Middle States, if a few of the best varieties of these Beans be planted in the open ground, as soon in the season as it can be brought into good condition, they will come into bearing in regular succession, according to their different degrees of earliness; and plantings may be repeated every ten days of the first spring month; but it is only from those which are planted early that any tolerable produce can be expected, as they become deficient in quality as well as in quantity on the approach of extreme warm weather. In the Southern States they may be replanted in succession throughout the autumn and winter months, which will cause them to bear early in the ensuing season.

The best mode of planting is in drills, drawn two inches deep, in which the seed Beans may be dropped two or three inches apart, according to their size, and the drills may be from two to three feet asunder. A strong clayey soil, if well drained, is the most suitable; bnt they often do well in moderately light ground, provided it be well trodden, or rolled, after the Beans are planted.

As soon as the Beans are three or four inches high, they will need a careful hoeing; and if some earth be drawn up to their stems three or four times in the course of their growth, it will greatly refresh and strengthen them. When they arrive at full bloom, and the lower pods begin to set, the tops may be broken off. If this be done at the proper time, it will promote the swelling of the pods, as well as their early maturity; for having no advancing tops to nourish, the whole effort of the root will go to the support of the fruit.

DESTROYING GREEN BUGS.

Broad Beans are particularly subject to green bugs. Tobacco-water, or salt-water, will sometimes destroy them, but the most certain way is to watch their first appearance, and pick off that part on which they first settle, and burn it; or if such plants be cut down close to the ground, they will produce fresh shoots, which may bear a good crop. One quart of seed Beans will be required for every sixty feet of row, allowing the smallest sorts to be planted about two inches apart, and the largest four inches. The beans should be gathered young, and shelled while fresh. After having been washed, let them be boiled in plenty of water with a little salt and a bunch of green parsley. They take from thirty to forty minutes to boil, according to age, and may be served up with melted butter gravy. But they are very good when cooked and eaten with fat pork, or good old-fashioned Hampshire bacon.

BEANS. (Kidney Dwarfs.)

Haricot. *Phaseolus vulgaris, etc.*

These varieties of Beans, being natives of India, South America, and other warm climates, will not endure the least cold, and it is therefore always hazardous to plant them in the open ground until settled warm weather. The earliest varieties, if planted towards the end of April or the first week in May, will come to perfection in from six to eight weeks after planting. Some of the later varieties will keep longer in bearing, and are esteemed by some on that account. These, with some of the early varieties, may be planted in the months of May and June; and if a regular succession of young beans be

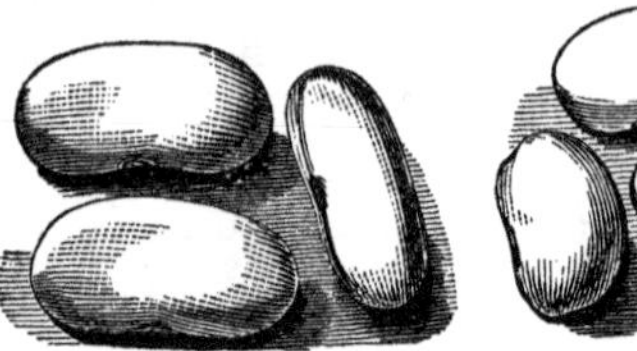

Kidney Beans. Dumpling Beans.

required throughout the summer, some of the varieties should be planted every two weeks, from the last week in April until the beginning of August.

These Beans require a light, rich soil, in which they should be planted in hills, three or four in a hill, or drills about two inches deep, and the Beans two or three inches from each other; the drills may be from two to three feet apart. The Refugees do best when planted in hills.

Some gardeners, anxious to have Beans early, are apt to begin planting too soon in the season, and very frequently lose their first crops. It should be recollected that these Beans are next to Cucumbers and Melons as regards tenderness, and will always grow quicker and yield better, if the planting be delayed until settled warm weather. The early Mohawk is the hardest, and may sometimes succeed well if planted about the middle of April; but it is much safer to delay the planting of any quantity until towards the end of the month.

One quart of Kidney Beans will plant from three hundred and fifty to four hundred hills, according to the size of the Beans, allowing four Beans to each hill, or from two hundred and thirty to two hundred and sixty feet of row, allowing six Beans to every foot.

These Beans should not be suffered to get old and tough before they are gathered. Be careful, in trimming them, to strip off the strings. To effect this desirable object, break them across; and in order to preserve their greenness, soak them in salted water for a short time, then put them into the water while boiling, which should be previously seasoned with salt. When they are tender, which will be in from fifteen to twenty minutes, take them up and drain them through a colander, in order to render them capable of absorbing a due share of gravy, melted butter, etc.

BEANS. (Pole or Running.)

Haricots a rames.

These species and varieties of Beans may be planted early in the month of May and in June, either in hills three feet apart or in drills about two inches deep, and the Beans two or three inches apart in the drills. The poles should be eight or ten feet long, and should be fixed in the ground before the Beans are planted, so as not to injure the roots in making the holes.

The varieties of Lima Beans should not be planted in the open ground until the second week in May, unless the season be very favorable and the ground warm. As these Beans are apt to get rotten by cold and damp weather, let six or eight be planted half an inch deep round each pole, and afterward thinned, leaving three or four good plants in a hill, which should be full four feet distant from each other every way.

Lima Beans require richer ground than any of the other sorts. A shovelful of rich, light compost, mixed with the earth in each hill, would be beneficial. If any varieties are wanted before the ordinary seasons, they may be planted in flower-pots in April, and placed in a greenhouse or garden-frame; and being transplanted with the balls of earth entire, will come into bearing ten or fourteen days earlier than those planted in the open ground. It will require about a quart of Lima Beans to plant one hundred hills. A quart of the smallest-sized Pole Beans will plant three hundred hills and upwards, or about two hundred and fifty feet of row. Lima Beans should be shelled while fresh, and boiled in plenty of water until tender, which generally takes from fifteen to twenty minutes. The mode of cooking and preparing the other sorts is the same as for Kidney Dwarfs.

BEET.

BETTERAVE. *Beta vulgaris.*

Beets, in their several varieties, are biennial; and the best blood-colored are much cultivated for the sake of their roots, which are excellent when cooked, and very suitable for pickling after being boiled tender. When sliced, they make an beautiful garnish for the dish, and the young plants are an excellent substitute for Spinach.

The Mangel-Wurzel and Sugar Beets are cultivated for cattle. Domestic animals eat the leaves and roots with great avidity. They are excellent food for swine and milch cows, and possess the quality of making them give a large quantity of the best-flavored milk. The roots are equally fit for oxen and horses, after being cut up into small pieces and mixed with cut straw, hay, or other dry feed. A small bed of the earliest Turnip-rooted and other esteemed kinds of Beets may be planted in rich, early ground the first week in April, which, being well attended to, will produce good roots in June.

Make drills a foot apart and from one to two inches deep; drop the seed in the drills one or two inches from each other, and cover them with mellow earth. When the plants are up strong, thin them to the distance of six or eight inches from each other in the rows. The ground should be afterwards hoed deep around the plants, and kept free from weeds.

If the planting of Beet-seed for general crops be delayed until May or June, the roots will be much larger and better than those from earlier planting, which, from being frequently stunted in growth by the various changes of weather, become tough, stringy, and of unhandsome shape. In case of the failure of crops, or of unfavorable weather in June, Beet-seed planted the first week in July will sometimes produce large, handsome roots, which may be preserved for winter use.

The most suitable ground for Beets is that which has been well manured for previous crops, and requires no fresh manure provided it be well pulverized. It is always best to thin Beets while young. If the tops are used as a vegetable, they should not be left too long for this purpose, or they will greatly injure the roots of those that are to stand. Beds that are to stand through the summer, should be kept clean by repeated hoeings; and the roots intended for winter use should be taken up in October, or early in November. Allowing Beet-seed to be planted on the gardening plan, it will require at the rate of ten pounds for an acre of land. If cultivated on the field system—that is, by planting them a sufficient distance apart to admit of ploughing between each row—one half the quantity of seed will be sufficient. Thinning out the surplus plants is indispensable to the production of good roots.

An acre of rich, loamy soil has been known to yield two thousand bushels of roots, some of which weighed from fifteen to twenty pounds each. To produce such large roots, they should be cultivated in drills from two to three feet apart, and the plants thinned to ten or twelve inches in the rows. It is generally conceded, however, that moderate-sized roots contain more saccharine matter, in proportion to their bulk, than extra large roots; and that twenty tons, or about seven hundred bushels, are a very profitable crop for an acre of land, and would be amply sufficient to feed ten cows for three or four months of the year. A gentleman in Connecticut computes the products of one-fourth of an acre of good land at eight tons, which, he says, will support a cow the whole year.

Beets will usually produce more milk than turnips; and milk-dealers will always pay more for a bushel of good beets than for an equal quantity of turnips.

BORECOLE, OR KALE.

CHOU FRISE VERT. *Brassica oleracea, etc.*

There are several sub-varieties of this genus of plants besides those above specified, most of which have large open heads, with curled wrinkled leaves. The Dwarf Curled, or Finely Fringed sorts, are much cultivated in Europe for the table; and the coarse and tall-growing are considered profitable for cattle. The Thousand-headed Cabbage, and Cesarean Kale, grow from three to five feet high, and branch out from the stem, yielding an abundant supply of leaves and sprouts in winter and spring.

For the garden, these several varieties may be treated in every respect as Winter Cabbage. The seed may be sown from about the middle of May to the first week in June, and the plants set out in the month of July, in rich ground. They are never so delicious as when rendered tender by smart frosts. They are valuable plants to cultivate, particularly in more Southern States, as they will be there in the greatest perfection during the winter months. If planted in a gravelly soil, and in a sheltered warm situation, they will bear the winter of the Western States; and may be kept in great perfection in the Eastern States, if taken up before the frost sets in with much severity, and placed in trenches, up to their lower leaves, and then covered with straw or other light covering. The heads may be cut off as they are required for use; and in the spring, the stems being raised up, will produce an abundance of delicious greens.

One ounce of good Borecole seed will produce about four thousand plants, and may be sown in a border four feet by ten.

BRUSSELS SPROUTS.

CHOU DE BRUXELLES AGETS. *Brassica oleracea.*

This plant frequently grows from three to five feet high, and produces from the stem small heads resembling cabbages in miniature, each being from one to two inches in diameter The top of the plant resembles the Savoy, when planted late. The sprouts are used as winter greens, becoming very tender when touched by the frost. The seed may be sown about the middle of May, in the same manner as Borecole, and the plants set out with a dibble early in July. The subsequent treatment must be in every respect as for Borecole.

Some gardeners, with a view to furnish the New York markets with greens early in the spring season, when vegetables in general are scarce, cultivate the common Rape (*Brassica Rapus*), it being a good substitute for Brussels Sprouts, which are not always attainable after a hard winter. If Rape-seed be sown early in September, the plants will survive an ordinary winter, and produce top-shoots or sprouts early; but it is best sown as soon as the ground is susceptible of cultivation in the spring. The sprouts should be cut while young, as such greens command the best prices, and are more palatable than when far advanced in growth.

In cooking these sprouts and Kale, Colewort, and greens in general, they should be put into hot water, seasoned with salt, and kept boiling briskly until tender. If it be an object to preserve their natural color, put a small lump of pearlash into the water.

BROCCOLI.

CHOU BROCCOLI. *Brassica oleracea Italiana.*

The several varieties of Broccoli and Cauliflower may be justly ranked among the greatest luxuries of the garden. They need only be known in order to be esteemed. The Broccoli produces heads, consisting of a lump of rich seedy pulp like the Cauliflower, only that some are of a green color, others purple, some brown, and the white kinds so exactly resemble the true Cauliflower, as to be scarcely distinguishable, either in color or taste.

Broccoli is abundant throughout England the greater part of the year; and is raised with as little trouble as Cabbages are here. The mode of raising the purple Cape Broccoli is now generally understood in this part of America; but the cultivation of the other kinds has been nearly abandoned, on account of the ill-success attending former attempts to bring them to perfection.

In some of the Southern States, where the winters are not more severe than in England, they will stand in the open ground, and continue to produce their fine heads from November to April. In the Eastern, Western, and Middle States, if the seed of the late kinds be sown in April, and the earlier kinds in May, in open ground, and treated in the same manner as Cauliflower, it would be the most certain method of obtaining large and early flowers; but as only a part of these crops can be expected to come to perfection before the approach of winter, the remainder will have to be taken up, laid in by the roots, and covered up with earth to the lower leaves in some sheltered situation, where they will come to more perfect maturity.

Those who are desirous of obtaining Broccoli and Cauliflower in a large quantity, so as to have all the different varieties in succession throughout the winter months, should have places erected similar to some of our greenhouses. The back and roof of such a house may be made of refuse lumber, which being afterwards covered with fresh stable-dung, will keep out the frost. The place allotted for Cape Broccoli and Cauliflower should have a glazed roof to face the south; the sashes must be made to take off in mild weather, but they should be always kept shut in cold weather, covered with mats, boards, or litter, to keep out the frost.

The hardy kinds of Broccoli may be preserved without glass, by having shutters provided to slide over the front in extremely cold weather, which may be covered over with fresh stable-dung or other litter. If these plants get frozen, it will be necessary to shade them from the full rays of the sun until they are thawed, which may be done by spreading straw over them while they are in the bed. The sudden transition from cold to heat is more destructive to vegetables than the cold itself.

The proper time for sowing the seed of Purple Cape Broccoli is from the tenth to the twenty-fourth of May. Those who intend to provide a place for the winter-keeping of the other kinds, may sow seed of the most esteemed varieties at the same time, or in two or three separate sowings, a week apart.

In order to insure plants of a luxuriant growth, let the seed be sown in a moderately shaded border. It is best to sow it in shallow drills, drawn three or four inches apart, in which case, one ounce of seed will occupy a border of about four feet in width by twelve in length, and produce about four thousand strong plants. (*See article Cabbage, page* 53.)

When the plants are of sufficient size they should be transplanted into rich ground, which should be previously brought into good condition. This being done, plant them in rows two feet and a half apart, and two feet distant in the rows. As soon as they have taken root give the ground a deep hoeing, and repeat this two or three times in the course of their growth, drawing some earth around the stems.

Some of the Cape Broccoli, if attended to as directed, will come to perfection early in September and in October. The other kinds will produce heads in regular succession throughout the winter and spring months, according to their different degrees of earliness, if an artificial climate be provided for them. These, of course, with whatever may remain of the Cape Broccoli, will have to be taken up early in October, and laid in carefully, with the roots and stems covered with earth as far as their lower leaves. Those who have not a place provided may keep a few in frames, or in a light cellar; but every gardener and country gentleman should have suitable places erected for a vegetable that yields such a delicious repast, at a time when other luxuries of the garden cannot be obtained.

It has been proved by repeated experiments, that the Purple Cape Broccoli succeeds better in our climate than any other variety; and also, that if Broccoli or Cauliflower plants be retarded in growth by extreme heat, they seldom arrive at full perfection. It is therefore important that the time of sowing the seed of Cape Broccoli be so regulated as to allow six weeks of the summer for the plants to grow in, previous to their being transplanted, and about seven or eight weeks between that and the commencement of cool autumn weather, which is essential to mature them.

If seed be sown much before the middle of May, or so early that the plants arrive at full growth in the heat of summer, and thereby become stunted, they generally button, instead of forming perfect heads of flowers, and are consequently of no use but for cattle.

In some of the Southern States late planting of Broccoli and Cauliflower succeeds better than early, because the winters are calculated to mature these vegetables, from their not being subject to injury from *slight* frost in a late stage of their growth.

CAULIFLOWER.

CHOUFLEUR. *Brassica oleracea botrytis.*

This is an excellent vegetable, and great pains must be taken in every stage of its growth to avoid the extremes of heat and cold, which accounts for good Cauliflowers being scarcely attainable in unpropitious seasons, and which the novice falsely attributes to defectiveness of the seed.

To produce early Cauliflower, the seed should be sown between the sixteenth and twenty-fourth of September, in a bed of clean, rich earth. In about four or five weeks afterwards, the plants should be pricked out into another bed, at the distance of four inches from each other every way; and this bed should be encompassed with garden frames, covered with glazed sashes, and boards or shutters. The plants should be watered and shaded a few days till they have taken root; and afterwards they will require light and air every mild day throughout the winter. But the outsides of the frames must be so lined and secured, and the tops of the beds so covered, as to keep out all frost.

The plants should be well attended to until the time of transplanting in the spring; and those who have not hand or bell glasses, so as to enable them to set some out by the latter end of March, should have a frame ready about the last week in February, in order that they may be transplanted to the distance of eight or nine inches apart. This would prevent them from buttoning. If this be not done, some of the strongest plants should be taken out of the beds and planted in flower-pots, which may afterwards be placed in a frame or greenhouse, until the weather be warm and settled, which may be expected soon after the middle of April. They should then be turned out with the balls of earth entire, and transplanted into a bed of the richest earth in the garden, at the distance of two feet and a half from each other every way; the residue may be taken up from the frame the last week in April, or earlier, if the season proves mild, by means of a garden trowel, and transplanted as above.

The plants should afterwards be well cultivated, by hoeing the ground deep around them, and bringing some earth gradually up to the stems, so as to push them forward before the approach of warm weather. When the soil has been drawn up to the plants some little time, fork the ground between the rows lightly over, which will promote their growth. Those out of flower should be liberally supplied with water in dry weather, twice a week, and those in, every other day, which will contribute to their producing very large heads. As the flower-heads appear, the larger leaves should be broken down over them, to defend them from the sun and rain, in order that the heads or pulps may be close, and of their natural color.

Plants from the autumn sowing will generally succeed best, but good Cauliflowers are sometimes produced from seed sown in a hotbed towards the end of January, or early in February. Great pains must be taken to have the bed in good condition to receive the seed. When the plants are up, they must have air every mild day, and as they progress in growth, they should have as much air as possible, consistent with their preservation; but the beds must be kept covered up every night, as long as there is any danger of frost. When the plants are three or four inches high, they must be pricked out three or four inches apart into another bed; and by the latter end of April they may be transplanted into the ground, and treated in every respect the same as the other.

In the early part of May, Cauliflower-seed may be sown in the open border, in drills, as recommended for Broccoli. One ounce of seed will produce about four thousand plants. These plants should be pricked out in June, and transplanted into good ground early in July, to flower in autumn. Those that are not likely to flower by the last of October, should be taken up and provided for in the manner recommended for Broccoli.

Cauliflower as well as Broccoli, should be gathered while the pulp is close and perfect. After having trimmed off some of the outside leaves, let them be boiled in plenty of water seasoned with salt, taking care to skim it, and also to ease the cover of the pot, so as not to confine the steam. Take them up as soon as the fork will enter the stems easily, which will be in from ten to twenty minutes, according to their size and age. Drain them, so as to make them susceptible of absorbing a due proportion of gravy or melted butter. This renders them a palatable and dainty dish.

Many persons are apt to forget, that the successful cultivation of Cauliflower depends on the particular seasons in which the plants are raised and set out. Consequently, instead of raising their own plants in the right seasons, apply for them at the seed-stores and gardens, in May and June. If early Cau liflower do not arrive at or near perfection, by the end of June, the plants get stunted by the heat, and seldom yield anything but leaves, unless the summer should prove mild, in which case some of the early plants may flower in autumn. But it is needless to risk the setting out of early Cauliflower plants later than April for the sake of such chance, because plants raised from seed sown about the middle of May, and transplanted in July, are by far the most likely to produce good fall Cauliflower.

CABBAGE.

CHOU. *Brassica oleracea.*

The early sorts of spring Cabbage may be raised in various ways. Some sow the seed between the tenth and twenty-fourth of September, pricked out and managed the same as Cauliflower plants, only that they are more hardy, and may sometimes be kept through the winter without sashes.

Some prefer sowing the seed in a cold-bed, covered by a garden frame with sashes. If this frame be placed on a warm border, and kept free from frost, and the seed of the early kinds sown the latter end of January, or early in February, these plants will be better than those raised in the fall; as they will not be so liable to run to seed, will be more hardy, and as early as those raised in hotbeds in the spring.

Or, if a heap of fresh horse-manure be deposited on the ground intended for the raising of early plants before the frost sets in, the same may be removed some mild day in January or February, and temporary frames made by driving stakes in the ground, and nailing planks or slabs thereto. The ground being then dug, the seed sown, and covered up with sashes, plants will soon be produced in perfection. The frames should be well protected, by placing the manure around them, and covering the tops with mats and boards, as directed for hotbeds in the Calendar for February and March.

It is customary with gardeners about New York to raise their plants in hotbeds. In order to do this, the beds should be prepared in time to receive the seed by the latter end of February, or early in March. Plants thus produced, as well as those raised as before directed, will be fit to transplant about the middle of April, and should be carefully planted, with a suitable dibble, in good ground, from sixteen inches to two feet apart, according to size and kind. By being hoed often, good Cabbages will be produced in our latitude in June. If seed of the large and early kinds be sown in a warm border early in April, they will produce plants fit to transplant in May, which will make good Cabbages for summer use.

The seed of Red Cabbage may be sown towards the last of April, or early in May; and that of Savoys and late Cabbage in general, may be sown at two or three different times, between the middle and the end of May, in fresh rich ground.

The most certain way of raising good strong plants in the summer season, is to sow the seed in a moderately shaded border, in shallow drills drawn three or four inches apart. One ounce of seed sown in this manner, will occupy a border of about four feet in width by twelve in length, and produce about four thousand strong plants; whereas, if seed be sown broadcast, as is the usual custom, two ounces of seed may not produce so many good plants as the one ounce on the plan recommended.

The Bergen, and other large kinds, should be transplanted the second and third week in July, in rows thirty inches asunder, and the plants about two feet apart in the rows. The Savoys and smaller sorts may be planted about the same time, but from four to six inches nearer every way. Cabbage succeeds best in a fresh, rich soil; and the ground should be deeply hoed or ploughed at least three times during their growth.

As I have been more familiar with the cultivation of vege

tables than fruits, I would state further my views relative to the Cabbage tribe. On New York Island, in the vicinity of the city, it is customary with gardeners to cut their Cabbages gradually as they are required for market, and often to leave their roots standing. These by some are ploughed under, where they not only feed, but generate their peculiar species of insects. Some gardeners take their roots and leaves to the cattle yard or dung-heap, and return them back to the garden the ensuing season in the shape of manure. As a consequence of such practice, good Cabbages are very seldom obtained, even after a routine of other crops, for two or three years.

EVIL OF DEEP PLANTING.

With a view to illustrate the evil of deep planting, I would observe further, that when Cabbage plants are transplanted in proper season and on fresh soil, they generally prove uniformly good; whereas, if it should happen, as it sometimes does for want of suitable weather, that the plants cannot be transplanted until they get crooked and overgrown, so as to require deep planting to support them in the soil, such plants, like diseased Peach-trees, decay first in the bark, between earth and air, and then, from being deprived of a natural circulation of the vegetable juices, die and discharge their putrid matter in the earth, to the destruction of such other plants as may be inserted in their stead. I have frequently known a land of Cabbage plants filled up half-a-dozen times, and the crop at last scarcely worth gathering; whereas could the plants have been set out while dwarfish, and inserted their proper depth in the ground, the cultivator would have been rewarded a hundredfold.

The *Brassica Rapa*, or Turnip-Cabbage, produces its bulb or protuberance on the stems above ground, immediately under the leaves. It is eatable when young, or about the size of a garden Turnip. The seed may be sown in April or May, and the plants afterwards treated the same as Cabbage, only that in earthing up the plants you must be careful not to cover the globular part. They are much more hardy than Turnips. In England the bulbs often grow to upwards of twenty inches in circumference, and weigh from ten to twelve pounds. They are cultivated for the feeding of cows and sheep, as well as for table use. In either case, they are treated like Cabbage, or sowed like Turnips, and afterwards thinned to proper distances.

The *Brassica Napus*, or Turnip-rooted Cabbage, has an oblong thick root in the form of a winter Radish. It is extremely hardy, and will survive very hard frosts. The seed should be sown in rich ground, and treated in every respect as Turnips, observing to thin the plants with a hoe to the distance of sixteen inches apart. Their roots will be much larger and better when treated in this way than if transplanted.

The *Brassica Napus*, variety *esculenta*, is sometimes cultivated as a salad herb. It is held in great esteem by the French as a culinary vegetable, and is called the Navet, or French Turnip. In France, as well as in Germany, few great dinners are served up without it in some shape or other.

HOW TO KEEP CABBAGES.

As numerous species of insects attack plants of the *Brassica* or Cabbage tribe in every stage of their growth, great caution is necessary in their cultivation. For a prevention to the attacks of fleas or flies, see page 29 of the General Remarks. Perhaps the most effectual way of saving plants from grub-worms, is not to transplant any during the month of June. Seed-beds are very seldom attacked; but if they should be, they may be protected by digging trenches around them, and throwing in lime, salt, or ashes, sufficient to prevent the ingress of the worms. If seed of the various kinds be sown at the times recommended, the early varieties will be so far advanced in growth before the grub-worms prevail, as to be out of their reach; and by the time the late-sown plants are ready to transplant, the worms will be harmless, because they turn grey towards the end of June, and by the middle of July, the time recommended for general transplanting, the danger from grub-worms is over.

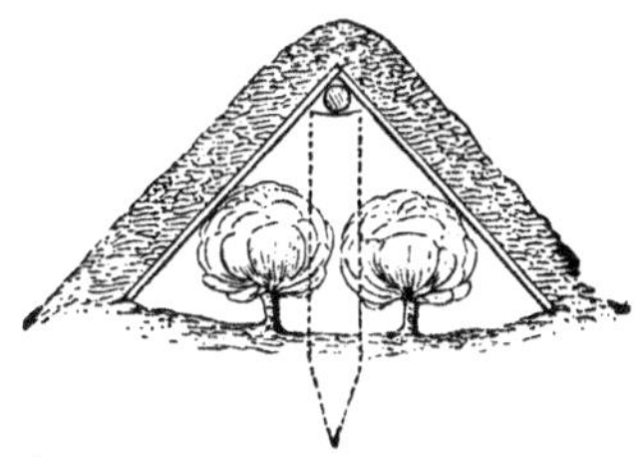

Section of Cabbage Pit.

In the colder portions of the country, those cabbages that have not attained their full growth, if set in rich ground as they grew, in a pit, before cold weather commences, late in autumn, and covered with a roof of boards and earth, as shown by the illustration, will be nicely headed by the opening of spring. The engraving needs no explanation to enable any person to construct a cabbage-pit.

In some parts of New Jersey and Long Island, where we sometimes see forty or fifty acres of cabbage in one field, a deep furrow is ploughed, the heads are cut from the stumps and placed upside down, close together in the furrow, and two furrow-slices turned over the row of heads. The ridge is then smoothed off with a shovel. Some gardeners allow the stumps of the cabbages to extend above ground. But the better way is to remove the stumps.

COLEWORT, OR COLLARDS.

Chou vert. *Brassica oleracea.*

This is a species of Cabbage which is eaten when young; it so nearly resembles the early kinds of Cabbage, that it is seldom cultivated. The English frequently sow the seed of early-head ing kinds of Cabbage as a substitute, which being done at different seasons, enables them to procure a supply of fresh greens from their gardens every day in the year. This is not attainable here, on account of the extremes of heat and cold; but Collards would prove very valuable and acceptable in the event of an unfavorable season for fall cabbage.

If the seed of Early York, Early Dutch, or other early kinds of Cabbage be sown in June, July, and August, and transplanted, as they become fit, into good ground from fifteen to eighteen inches apart, the first planting would make good heads for fall use; and the plants of late sowings, if transplanted in September and October, in a warm border, would produce tender, sweet-eating greens for use in the early part of winter; the latter plantings may be placed ten or twelve inches from plant to plant. These could be easily sheltered on the approach of severe weather, without being taken up. The cultivation of Collards is well adapted to our Southern States, as there they need no protection in winter.

CARDOONS.

CARDON. *Cynara carduneulus.*

The Cardoon Artichoke, a native of Candia, is much cultivated in Europe for culinary purposes, such as for salads, soups, stews. The stems of the leaves being thick and crisp, are the eatable parts, after being blanched. They are in perfection in autumn and winter.

The seed may be sown in a bed of rich earth in the month of April; and one ounce will produce about six hundred plants. When the plants are up strong, they should be thinned so as to leave them four or five inches apart. They may be transplanted in June, at the distance of four feet from each other every way. Observe, before planting, to dress their tops and roots the same as Celery. As they advance in growth, they are to be earthed up for blanching, keeping the leaves close together. This may be done with bass or matting, as practised with Endive. They are afterwards to be earthed up gradually from time to time, until whitened to a sufficient height. As winter approaches, Cardoons must be taken up and laid away like Celery, or they may be preserved with sand in a cellar.

CARROT.

CAROTTE. *Daucus carota.*

The Carrot is a native of Britain, and grows by the roadside in many parts. As a culinary vegetable, it is much used in soups and stews, and forms a dish with boiled beef, etc. The coarse sorts are cultivated as fodder for cows, sheep, oxen, and horses, and are considered profitable, as they frequently yield upwards of four hundred bushels to an acre, when cultivated on the field system.

For the garden, the Early Orange should be cultivated for spring and summer use; but the Long Orange is more suitable for main crops, on account of its bright orange color, as well as for its great size and length. Carrots grow to great perfection in a rich loamy soil; and may be raised in drills drawn about one inch deep, and twelve inches asunder. A small bed may be planted at the latter end of March for an early crop, and from that time to the end of May for successive crops; but the principal crop should not be sown too soon, as the early plantings are apt to produee seed-stalks, and, consequently, stringy and useless roots.

The most suitable ground for late Carrots is that which has been well manured for previous crops, and requires no fresh manure. If the seed be sown in June, and the plants thinned out to the distance of five or six inches from each other when young, and kept hoed, they will yield an abundance of fine roots for winter and spring use, by being taken up in autumn, and preserved either in sand in a cellar, or covered up in pits in a garden, as directed for burying potatoes.

Although Carrot-seed is naturally small and light, it seldom fails to vegetate in favorable seasons. It, therefore, need not be sown too thick in ground not apt to produce weeds. If a root could be insured to grow unmolested in every instance where a seed may be deposited, two pounds would be more than sufficient for an acre of land. But gardeners generally use four or five pounds to the acre, in order that the rows may be more easily traced in the event of a luxuriant growth of weeds. To avoid risking an unequal crop in small gardens, half an ounce of seed should be allotted for every pole, perch or rod, or twenty ounces for a rood of land. On light ground, the use of a roller would be beneficial in dry weather, excess of which is detrimental to the germination of Carrot, as well as of all other light seed.

We herewith give an illustration of a full-grown carrot, before the leaves are removed, for the purpose of stimulating those who have commenced raising a crop of this kind of roots, to persevere in the thorough cultivation of the young plants. Carrots require timely cultivation, while the plants are quite small, before their growth has been checked by weeds.

As soon as the rows can be discovered, if they are sufficiently far apart to admit a horse-hoe, let that implement be run between the rows as shallowly as practicable, to cut up the weeds. This should be done when the sun shines, in order to kill every weed that is disturbed. After cultivating with a horse-hoe, go over all the rows with a hand-hoe, drawing the hoe across the drills every eight inches, cutting up every green thing. After this operation is completed, there will be one or more carrots standing among every little cluster of weeds. Immediately after a good shower of rain, summon all hands, and finish weeding the young carrots, which are tender plants, and will not endure bruising like turnips. When the weeds are pulled up, knock off the earth and spread them carefully around the

An Orange Carrot

young plants. Such weeds will soon decay, and promote the growth of carrots by operating as a mulch, as well as a fertilizer. If no horse-hoe is at hand, all the dressing may be done with a scuffle-hoe, which is far better than an ordinary hand-hoe. With a scuffle-hoe, the operator moves backwards, leaving all the weeds and grass lying up lightly; while, if the hoeing be performed with a hand-hoe, many of the weeds will be pressed by the feet into the mellow soil, where they take root and continue to grow about as well as if they had not been dug up.

The weeds growing in close proximity to carrots should be pulled up when the ground is wet, or at least very moist. For when the sun pours down the scorching heat, a slight disturbance of the ground near the growing carrots will disturb the roots, and the burning sun will wilt them as soon as the weeds that have been pulled up.

CELERY.

CELERI. *Apium graveolens.*

This vegetable, so much esteemed as a salad, is known in its wild state by the name of Smallage; and is found in great abundance by the sides of ditches, and near the sea-coast of Britain. The effects of cultivation are here strikingly exhibited, in producing from a rank, coarse weed, the mild and sweet stalks of the Celery. This circumstance should stimulate the young gardener to aim at improvement in the cultivation of plants in general.

It is customary with some gardeners to raise their early plants in hotbeds; but as plants thus raised are apt to produce seed-stalks, it is much safer to cultivate them in cold beds, prepared as directed for the raising of early Cabbage-plants. The seed for a general crop may be sown the last week in March, or early in April, in rich, mellow ground, and in a situation where the plants can be protected from the parching heat of a summer sun (a border against a north aspect is the most suitable). Some sow the seed broadcast; but the plants will be much stronger if raised in drills. The drills may be half an inch deep, and six inches apart, so that a small hoe can be worked between the rows; and if properly attended to, every ounce of seed sown will produce ten thousand strong plants or more. The early sown plants should be pricked out in a nursery-bed of cool rich earth, as soon as they are two or three inches high, there to remain about a month after which they will be fit to transplant into the trenches.

Choose for this purpose a piece of rich ground, in an open exposure. Mark out the trenches by line, ten or twelve inches wide, and allow the space of three feet between them, which will be sufficient for the early plantations. Dig each trench a spade deep, laying the earth equally on each side between the trenches. Put three inches deep of rotten dung in the bottom of each trench, then pare the sides, and mingle the manure and parings with an inch or two of the loose mould at the bottom, incorporating all well together, and put in the plants.

Previous to planting, trim the plants, by cutting off the long straggling leaves, and also the ends of the roots. Let them be planted with a dibble, in single rows, along the middle of each trench, five or six inches between plant and plant. As soon as they are planted, give them a plentiful watering, and let them be shaded until they strike root and begin to grow. The main crops may be planted in the same way, but in trenches four feet distant from each other, and an inch or two further from plant to plant; or in beds made in the following manner, which, for the ease of preserving the plants in winter, will be found extremely convenient, besides a greater quantity can be raised on a given piece of ground:

Lay out the ground into beds four feet wide, with alleys between, three feet in width. Dig the beds a spade deep, throwing earth on the alleys. When done, lay four or five inches of well rotted dung over the bottom of the beds. Incorporate it with the loose soil, and cover the whole with an inch or two of earth from the alleys plant four rows in each bed at equal distances, and from six to eight inches apart in the rows; after which, give them a plentiful watering, and shade them.

BLANCHING CELERY.

The earthing should never be done when the plants are wet, as this is apt to make the Celery rusty; but should be performed gradually in fine weather as the plants progress in growth, repeating the earthing every two weeks; at which time, care should be taken to gather up all the leaves neatly, and not to bury the hearts of the plants. When they are grown two feet high, and well blanched, they are fit for the table.

As Celery will grow three or four feet high in one season, it will be necessary to delay the planting of that which is intended for winter use until the latter end of July; but the trenches should always be prepared in time, to avoid a serious drought, which often delays the planting till too late in the season. The blanching of Celery for winter use may be delayed until October.

When Celery is raised on a large scale, the trenches may be worked out with a plough, and finished with a spade or hoe. The ground may also be ploughed between the rows previous to earthing it up, which will save much labor.

The *Celeriac*, or Turnip-rooted, may be planted either on level ground or in shallow drills. The root of it swells like a Turnip, and may be preserved in sand through the winter. The French and Germans cut it in slices, and soak it a few hours in vinegar. By such simple preparation it becomes mellow as a pineapple, and affords a delicious and very nourishing repast.

Some gardeners are accustomed to cultivate Celery on the level ground. Others, after making their trenches in the usual way, go to the expense of carting peculiar soil from a distance, with which they replenish their trenches until nearly full. Those who have pursued the latter plan, say that they are rewarded for their trouble by gathering roots of superior size and quality. Those gardeners whose subsoil, or under stratum, is inferior, or ill-adapted for the growth of Celery, should cultivate it in shallow drills or furrows worked out with a plough, by which means they may secure good soil to plant in, and also to earth up with. In such cases the rows must be from four to five feet apart; and frequent ploughing between them would promote the growth of the plants.

Some gardeners prefer to raise celery on level ground, and continue to form a ridge, as the plants grow, by drawing clean earth up against the plants. Others set a four or five-inch drain tile over each plant; and as it grows, fine, rich, clean soil—mostly sand—is worked down in the tiles, keeping the plants in the middle of the orifice in the tile. Others set two planks on the edge, each side of the rows of celery, and fill up between the planks with a clean loamy soil.

THE BEST WAY OF STORING CELERY.

Many people complain of their Celery—one of the most difficult garden crops to raise in perfection—that it does not keep well through the winter; sometimes withers, but oftener rots. It is recommended by some that it should be preserved in the rows where it grows, and that removal more or less injures it. Where the plant is grown in a soil of a dry nature—and Celery never should be grown there—it may be well kept in the row; but we deny most emphatically that removal injures it in the slightest particular.

We pursue two modes, and find both to answer completely. The first is to remove the Celery to high and dry ground. dig a trench spade-deep, stand up a row of plants, then three inches of soil, then another row, and so on until about a half-dozen rows are finished, and then commence another bed, and so on. The soil should be packed firmly, and banked up so that the tops of the Celery are just covered; then spank off roof-fashion, to turn the rain. Over this two wide boards, nailed together, should be placed as a security against moisture. For remember it is water, not frost, as some say, that rots Celery. Frost adds to its tenderness.

Another plan is to sink barrels into the earth, so that the tops are two or three inches below the surface, stand them compactly full of Celery, put close or tight covers upon them, and then a couple of inches of soil. By this mode, somewhat more troublesome than the other, ours kept well for the last two or three years until all was consumed, which was late in spring.

CORN SALAD, OR FETTICUS.

MACHE OU DOUCETTE. *Valeriana locusta.*

VARIETY.—*Olitoria.*

This plant grows spontaneously in the cornfields of England; hence it is called Corn Salad; and from its being sufficiently hardy to stand the winter, and affording an early pasturage, it has acquired the appellation of Lamb's Lettuce. It is cultivated as a salad for winter and early spring use. The seed may be sown in rich, clean ground the latter end of August or early in September.

Some gardeners sow the seed in beds four or five feet wide, with paths between each bed, just sufficient to admit of room for hand-weeding; but it will vegetate more freely if sown in drills half an inch deep, provided it be carefully covered. The drills may be about six inches apart, or just sufficient to admit a small hoe to work between the rows; for if the plants are not cleared of all weeds while young, they will be more plague than profit.

Fetticus must be covered up with straw at the approach of severe weather, to preserve it in good condition for use in the early part of the ensuing spring, as that is the season which most amply remunerates the cultivator. The seed of Fetticus is small and light; but it will admit of being sown thick, say at the rate of from four to six pounds to an acre of land.

CRESS.

CRESSON. *Lepidium sativum.*

Cress is a small salad-herb, and is generally used with Lettuce,

White Mustard, Rape, Chervil, etc. It may be sown very thick in little drills, like salad-seed, and cut before it comes into rough leaf. A small quantity in the salad season, which is spring and autumn, may be sown every week in rich ground, free from weeds.

CRESS (Water).

CRESSON DE FONTAINE. *Sisymbrium nasturtium.*

The Water-Cress is a creeping, amphibious perennial, and is grown very extensively for the London markets. Loudon says, in his Encyclopædia of Gardening, that "The most suitable description of water is a clear stream, not more than an inch and a half deep, running over sand or gravel; the least favorable, deep, still water, or a muddy bottom. It is highly advantageous to make the plantations in newly-risen spring-water, as the plants do not only thrive better in it, but, in consequence of its being rarely frozen, they generally continue in vegetation, and in a good state of gathering, through the whole winter season. The plants are disposed in rows parallel with the course of the stream, about eighteen inches apart. When these plants begin to grow in water one inch and a half deep, they soon check the current so as to raise the water to the height of three inches above the plants, which is considered the most favorable circumstance in which they can be placed. It is absolutely necessary to have a constant current; as where there is any obstruction to the stream, the plants cease to thrive. After they have been cut about three times they begin to stock; and then the oftener they are cut the better."

CUCUMBER.

CONCOMBRE. *Cucumis sativus, etc.*

The *Cucumis sativus*, or common Cucumber, is a native of

the East Indies, and of nearly as great antiquity as the vine. As Cucumbers are much used in New York, it should be an object with gardeners to have them in the market early; directions for raising them out of the ordinary season are therefore given in a future page, under the head Forcing Vegetables, to which the reader is referred. Cucumbers may be raised in the open ground by planting seed the first week of May, in hills four feet apart; or, if the ground be light, basins formed an inch below the level of the surface would be beneficial. Previous to planting, the ground should be prepared by incorporating a shovelful of rotten dung with the earth in each hill, after which four or five seeds may be planted half an inch deep. One ounce of good seed is sufficient for two hundred hills and upwards.

Cucumbers are liable to be attacked by a yellow fly, which sometimes devours young plants. These and other insects may be killed by sowing tobacco-dust, soot, or powdered charcoal round about the vines, when they first come up, or by applying the liquid recommended in page 29 of the General Remarks. After this is done, the plants may be thinned to two or three in a hill, and the ground carefully hoed, drawing a little earth round them at the same time. The vines should be kept free from weeds, and if the weather proves dry, a gentle watering now and then, given in the evening, will be of considerable service.

Picklers may be raised by planting the seed at any time in July. When the vines begin to bear, they should be looked over, and the fruit gathered as soon as it becomes fit, as the plant will cease to bear much if the fruit be permitted to get yellow.

RAISING IN HOTBEDS.

The seed is generally sown in pots or boxes of light, rich mould, and placed in a hotbed; and some sow the seed in the earth of a small bed prepared for the purpose. In either case, as soon as the plants have fully expanded their two seed-leaves, they may be transplanted into pots, putting three plants in each pot; when this is done, apply water warmed to the temperature of the bed, and shut down the glasses, keeping them a little shaded by throwing a mat over the glass, till the plants have taken root. When they are about a month old, they will be fit to transplant into the fruiting-bed.

After the situation of the bed has been ascertained, the heat regulated, and the earth formed into hills, raise one hill in the centre under each sash, so that the earth is brought to within nine inches of the glass; in these hills plant three seedlings, or turn out such as may be in pots, with the balls of earth about their roots, and thus insert one patch of three plants in the middle of each hill. The plants should be immediately watered with water heated to the temperature of the bed, and kept shaded until they have taken root.

The temperature should be kept up to 60°, and may rise to 80° without injury, provided the rank steam be allowed to pass off; therefore, as the heat begins to decline, timely linings of well-prepared dung must be applied all round the frame. Begin by lining the back part first; cut away the old dung perpendicularly by the frame, and form a bank two feet broad, to the height of a foot, against the back of the frames; as it sinks, add more; renew the linings round the remainder of the bed as it becomes necessary, and be careful to let off the steam and give air to the plants at all opportunities.

Give young Cucumber plants necessary waterings, mostly in the evening, in early forcing; and in the afternoon, in the advanced season of hot, sunny weather. Some use water impregnated with sheep or pigeon-dung. As the roots begin to spread, and the vines to run, the hills should be enlarged by gathering up the earth around them, for which purpose a supply of good mould should be kept ready at hand, to be used as required.

When the plants have made one or two joints, stop them by pinching off the tops, after which they generally put forth two shoots, each of which let run till they have made one or two clear joints, and then stop them also; and afterwards continue throughout the season to stop them at every joint; this will strengthen the plants, and promote their perfecting the fruit early.

The following artificial operation is recommended by Abercrombie, Phial, and other writers, as essential to the production of a full crop of Cucumbers under glass. In plants more freely exposed to the open air, the impregnation is effected by nature. Those which some call false blossoms are the male flowers, and are indispensable in this operation.

"The Cucumber," Abercrombie observes, "bears male and female blossoms distinctly on the same plant. The latter only produce the fruit, which appears first in miniature, close under the base, even before the flower expands. There is never any in the males; but these are placed in the vicinity of the females, and are absolutely necessary, by the dispersion of their farina, to impregnate the female blossom, the fruit of which will not otherwise swell to its full size, and the seed will be abortive. The early plants under glass, not having the full current of natural air, nor the assistance of bees and other winged insects to convey the farina, the artificial aid of the cultivator is necessary to effect the impregnation. At the time of fructification watch the plants daily; and as soon as the female flowers and some male blossoms are fully expanded, proceed to set the fruit the same day, or next morning at furthest. Take off a male blossom, detaching it with part of the footstalk. Hold this between the finger and thumb; pull away the flower-leaves or petals close to the stamens or central part, which apply close to the pistil in the bosom of the female flower, twirling it a little about, to discharge thereon some particles of the fertilizing powder. Proceed thus to set every fruit, as the flowers of both sorts open, while of a lively, full expansion; and generally perform it in the early part of the day, using a fresh male, if possible, for every impregnation, as the males are usually more abundant than the female blossoms. By this management, the young fruit will soon be observed to swell freely."

Cucumbers attain the proper size for gathering in from fifteen to twenty days after the time of setting; and often in succession for two or three months or more, in the same beds, by good culture.

If it be desired to have Cucumbers in the open garden at an early season, the plants may be raised and planted in a warm border either in the earth or in hotbed ridges. A hand-glass should be provided for each hill, which must be kept close down every night and in cool days, taking care to admit air when practicable. The plants may be hardened by degrees, by taking off the glass in the heat of the day; and as the weather gets warm, they may be left to nature.

CHIVES, OR CIVES.

CIVETTE. *Allium schœnoprasum.*

This is a small species of Onion, and grows in large turfs. It is propagated by offsets from the roots, and may be planted either in spring or autumn in rows ten or twelve inches apart, and the bulbs three or four inches apart in the rows. They will soon take root, and increase very fast, forming large bunches of bulbs. They make handsome edging for beds or borders.

EGG-PLANT.

MELONGENE AU AUBERGINE. *Solanum melongena.*

The seed of the Purple Egg-plant may be sown in a hotbed about the first of March; and the sashes must be kept down close until the plants come up, after which a little air may be given in the heat of the day. Towards the middle of May, if the weather be warm and settled, the plants should be set out from twenty-four to thirty inches apart, in a rich, warm piece of gronnd; and if kept clean, and a little earth be drawn up to their stems when about a foot high, they will produce plenty of fruit.

Plants of the white variety may be raised in the same manner and transplanted into pots in May; or if some of the seed be sown in a warm situation the first week in May, these may come to perfection in the course of the summer. This variety, though generally cultivated for ornament, is good when cooked.

As Egg-plants will not grow in the open ground until settled warm weather, and are apt to perish from being transplanted too early, the gardener should be provided with small pots, in order that the plants may be transplanted therein early in May, and placed in a frame, there to remain until the first week in June, at which time, if they are turned out and planted with the balls of earth entire, they will soon take root and grow freely.

MANNER OF COOKING.

Select the fruit when at maturity; cut it into slices, and parboil it in a stewpan; when softened drain off the water; it may then be fried in batter made with wheaten flour and an egg, or in fresh butter with bread grated fine and seasoned before it is put in the pan, with pepper, salt, thyme, and such other herbs as may best suit the palate. Some use Marjoram, Summer Savory, Parsley, Onions.

Egg-plant seed will not vegetate freely without substantial heat. If the plants get the least chilled in the earlier stage of growth, they seldom recover. It is therefore important that the frame allotted for them be placed over a well-regulated hot-bed, and partitioned off, so that the sash can be kept down over the plants in cool weather.

Some gardeners raise Egg-plants in the same frame with Cabbage, and such other half-hardy plants as require air every mild day. By such management, one or the other must suffer for want of suitable aliment, *heat* being the principal food of tender plants, and *air* that of the more hardy species.

ENDIVE, OR SUCCORY.

CHICOREE DES JARDINS. *Cichorium endiva, etc.*

The *Chicorium endiva* is a native of China and Japan, and is much used in salads and stews, and as a garnish for the table. The proper kind of seed for early sowing is the Green Curled. A small quantity of this may be sown at different times in April and May, by those who would have it early. This plant is apt to run to seed. For this reason, it will be best to delay the sowing of seed for general crops until June or July. If a small quantity of each esteemed variety be sown two or three times in these months, they will produce a plentiful supply for use in autumn and the early part of winter. One ounce of good Endive-seed will produce about five thousand plants.

When the plants are three or four inches high, they should be transplanted into good ground, at the distance of a foot from each other, and immediately watered. If they are set out in cloudy or wet weather, it will save this trouble. The plants will require to be hoed and attended to in the same manner as lettuce, until grown to a moderate size, when they must be blanched. Select the large and full-hearted plants, and with bass or other strings tie them a little above the middle, not too tight, previously gathering up the leaves regularly in the hand. This must be done when the leaves are very dry, otherwise the plants will rot. *Cichorium intybus* grows spontaneously in many parts of Europe and America. In France it is much cultivated; the tops of the plants are considered profitable for cattle, and the roots are taken up in autumn and dried.

The aromatic and volatile qualities of coffee are, by the combination of this root, rendered more mellow and full upon the palate, and its fragrance greatly increased, producing an agreeable tonic and most exhilarating beverage.

Sow the seed in April in drills half an inch deep and about eighteen inches apart; thin out the plants to six or eight inches in the row. The plant produces beautiful blue flowers, and is worthy of a place in the flower-garden. The roots when dried, roasted as coffee, and ground, may be mixed in the proportion of two ounces of the powder to a pound of coffee.

HORSERADISH.

RAIFORT. *Cochearia armoracia.*

This plant is propagated by cuttings from the root, either cut from the top about two inches long, or by offsets, or otherwise useless parts, from the sides of the main root, retaining the crowns or top-shoots in as many parts as possible. These should be planted as early in the spring as practicable, in rows two feet apart and six or eight inches from each other in the rows.

Select for the bed a good depth of soil, and such as will retain moisture; manure it with well-rotted dung, plough or dig it deep, and the draw-drills a foot apart; then plant with a dibble, cuttings as above described, in every alternate drill, from two to three inches deep. The intermediate drills may be planted with Beet or Carrot-seed, or that of any other root; but Turnip-Beets are the most suitable to cultivate between the rows, as they will grow quick and can be pulled out without disturbing the Horseradish.

The beets must of course be thinned out while young, and kept cultivated by hoeing between the rows, which will also benefit the Horseradish. After the Beets are pulled, hoe the ground again, and keep it clear of weeds, by which method the bed may be cleared every year. Some cultivate Horseradish in a permanent bed; in which case, if, in taking up the roots, some offsets be left in the ground, they will produce a successive supply for future years.

JERUSALEM ARTICHOKE.

Pomme de terre. *Helianthus tuberosum.*

This plant is a native of America. The tubers of the root, which are generally abundant, were, before Potatoes became improved by cultivation, in great esteem, and are yet considered a fine-flavored and nutritious food, when boiled and mashed with butter. They may be easily propagated by cutting the roots into sets, with two eyes in each, and planting them in the same manner as Potatoes, in March and April. To have them in perfection, they should be hoed frequently, and the ground kept loose around them. In digging them for use, care should be taken to gather them out clean, as the least particle left will grow the year following, and encumber the ground, without producing a crop worth raising.

Indian Corn. Mais. *Zea mayz.*

The different varieties of early Corn intended for boiling when young, or others as curiosities, may be planted in the garden the last week in April, or early in May, in hills four feet apart, or in drills. If some of each esteemed variety be planted in separate beds at the same time, they will come in for the table one after the other in regular succession. After this, if any particular variety be preferred, it may be planted at different times in the month of May and June. If the ground be poor, mix a shovelful of old manure with the earth in each hill before the kernels are planted, and after the plants are up strong, scatter a teacupful of wood-ashes around each hill. This, with attentive hoeing, will cause it to produce ears early. Deep digging or ploughing between the hills is very beneficial when the corn is about eighteen inches high.

There is danger of planting Indian Corn too early, as the kernels will rot before they germinate, when the ground is wet and cold. Then, if the weather be so cold after the corn has come up, that it cannot grow, the young plants receive a stunt from which they never recover. The *locality* must always be the guide respecting the time to plant Indian Corn.

My advice has always been to young gardeners, not to plant Indian Corn too early. Wait till the soil is warm, and the growing season well advanced, before planting any kind of corn. Work at the ground where Indian Corn is to be planted; and get it in an excellent condition, thoroughly pulverized, drained, if necessary, and manured bountifully; then when all the trees are in full-leaf, and apple-trees begin to cast their blossoms, put in the seed, and the young corn will often appear in five days. I have known corn planted dry, in my own garden, to come up in four days, when the soil was warm; and I have often waited over two weeks for good seed to vegetate; and even after so long a time, the blades did not appear. Indian Corn must have dry and rich ground, and warm weather, or it will not produce large ears.

In order to have a succession of "roasting ears," or green corn, my practice is to prepare the ground for several rows, side by side. Then two weeks after the first row was planted, put in the seed for another row, and so to the middle of summer. In this way, one may have green corn for a long time.

Indian Corn will mix when different varieties are planted in such close proximity that the pollen from the tassels will be carried to the silken cords, one of which proceeds from the root of every kernel to the end of the growing ear. If varieties are permitted to mix, they soon lose their identity. The product *may* be quite as good, and perhaps better, than the variety planted; and it may *not* be so excellent.

To prevent any and all varieties from hybridizing, cut off

every tassel as soon as it appears. This will not injure the growing corn in the least; and it will always be found a complete security against mixing of the seed, even when varieties widely different are grown in rows side by side. But the tassels must be clipped off before they have pushed entirely out of the sheath, or a portion of the pollen may be blown to the ears, and thus impregnate the young grain. A piece of paper tied over each ear, will shield it from the pollen. I allude to this subject, as it is desirable to know how to keep a good variety pure for several years.

MAIZE FOR SOILING, OR FOR DRY FODDER.

One acre well prepared by thorough pulverization and manuring and seeded with maize, will almost always yield three times as much feed for soiling stock of any kind, as can be produced from any other kind of grain or grass. Growing Maize or Indian-corn feeds largely on coarse manure, which other plants do not appropriate to their growth and development. For this reason, the ground can be, and always should be, highly manured. If a farmer apprehends a scarcity of pasture, he should make preparations at once for putting in one or more acres, for feeding-green, next August, or in September, when pasture fields are often as dry and parched as a barren desert. Should such feed not be required while green, the stalks and leaves, if properly cured, will make excellent dry fodder. Moreover if a crop of Maize is not wanted for green or dry feed, it may be ploughed under, to ameliorate the stubborn condition of a heavy and lumpy soil. Four bushels of Indian-corn per acre will furnish more than three times the amount of vegetable matter for fertilizing a poor soil, than a crop of red clover, peas, or any other material that farmers are accustomed to raise for such purposes. When heavy soils are destitute, in a great degree, of fine mould, which is always eminently essential to the production of bountiful crops of grain and roots, the ground will be extremely lumpy and difficult to till; and should there be an excess of moisture in the soil, in warm weather, the ground will bake, and thus prevent crops of any kind attaining that great development which is obtained when the soil is dry, and well supplied with vegetable mould. When red clover or peas are plowed under for the purpose of renovating the soil, if Indian-corn be put in as soon as practicable after the ground is ploughed, a heavy burden of stalks will grow before frosts occur to injure their growth, which also may be ploughed in, and thus furnish the barren land with two dressings of green manure in a single season.

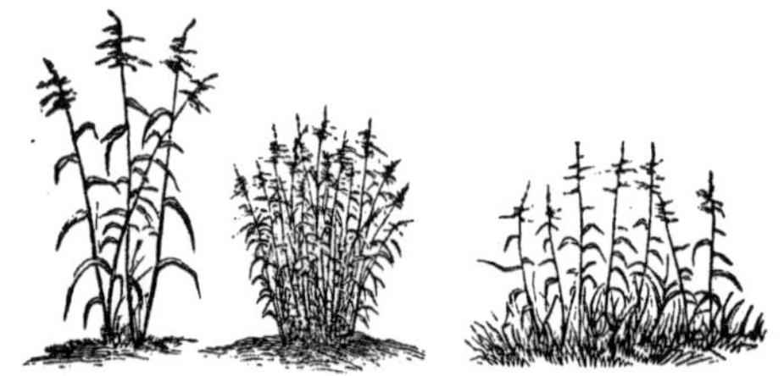

Planted in hills. Sowed thick broadcast. Sowed thin broadcast.

PREPARATION OF SOIL AND SEEDING.

The accompanying illustration will furnish the beginner in this branch of agriculture with some correct notions concerning the growth of Maize. The plants at the left hand represent a hill of Indian-corn, where the stalks grow tall, large, and heavy, having large butts and joints, which cattle will not eat, unless they are well cured and cut into short pieces. The middle figure represents Maize as it appears when the grain is sowed thick. The stalks are small and much more tender than when the seed is sowed thin. The figure at the right hand represents the appearance of Maize that was sowed moderately thick.

In order to produce a bountiful crop of Maize, plow under a liberal dressing of barn-yard manure, always remembering to break up the ground when it is just moist enough to crumble easily. Heavy ground should not be broken up when the furrow slices will turn over in clods. Let the ground be harrowed; and if a grain drill is at hand, drill in the seed, about three inches deep, at the rate of four bushels per acre. A drill is better for putting in such grain than to sow it broadcast, and harrow it in, as a drill will bury all the kernels at a uniform depth, whereas much of the seed will not be covered at all if harrowed in; and a large portion will often be covered sc slightly that the young plants cannot flourish luxuriantly.

Some farmers prefer to put in the seed with a corn planter, in drills about thirty inches apart, which will allow a horse-hoe to work between the drills. Others mark out the ground with a small plough, making channels three inches deep, about thirty inches apart, into which the grain is dropped, or scattered by hand. The seed is then covered by hitching a horse to a small log, five or six feet long, and drawing it sideways over two rows at once. This is a rapid and efficient way to cover the seed when a person has no drill.

The tall white flint, or eight-rowed yellow corn, in our latitude, is the best variety for producing green fodder, whether the crop is to be fed green, or cured, or ploughed under. On many farms there are several acres covered with nothing but noxious weeds, which may every season be made to yield an abundant crop of excellent feed, if properly managed.

HOW TO CURE THE STALKS.

As soon as the Maize is in full bloom, let it be cut, bound in small sheaves, and set up in long shocks in dry weather. During protracted storms, the sheaves should be put in round shocks, and the tops bound tightly to turn as much of the rain as possible. If a person have hay-caps, one may be put on every shock, and thus keep the stalks dry. In pleasant weather, the caps should be removed. When a person has an abundance of barn-room, the sheaves may be set up on open floors, or poles placed on the beams of the building, so that the air may circulate through the stalks. A ton of Maize, well cured, will produce more rich milk than a ton of good hay.

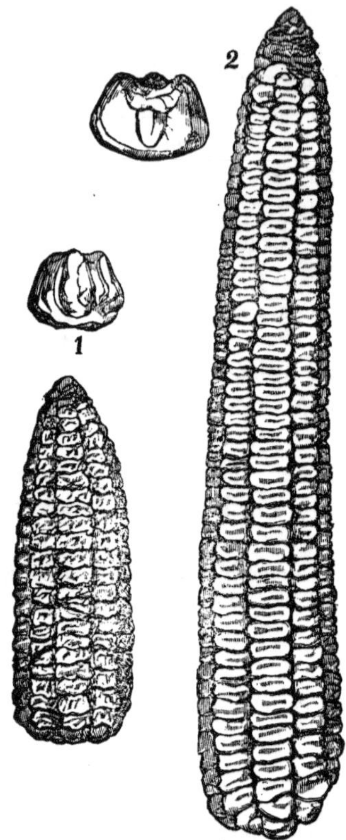

Narragansett Corn. New Jersey White, ½ Dent.

DESCRIPTION OF ILLUSTRATIONS.

Figure 1 represents an ear of Narragansett Corn, which was originated near the Narragansett Bay, Rhode Island, and is highly esteemed by many gardeners.

Figure 2 is the New Jersey White, ½ dent, which is an excellent variety, yielding bountifully in most localities. All the varieties illustrated in this book, and many other kinds, can be obtained at most seed stores in our large cities.

Figure 3 represents the Rhode Island Asylum Corn.

Figure 4 is the Tuscarora Corn, which was originated by the tribe of Tuscarora Indians, in Niagara county, N. Y. It needs improving by selecting the earliest ripened ears for a few years.

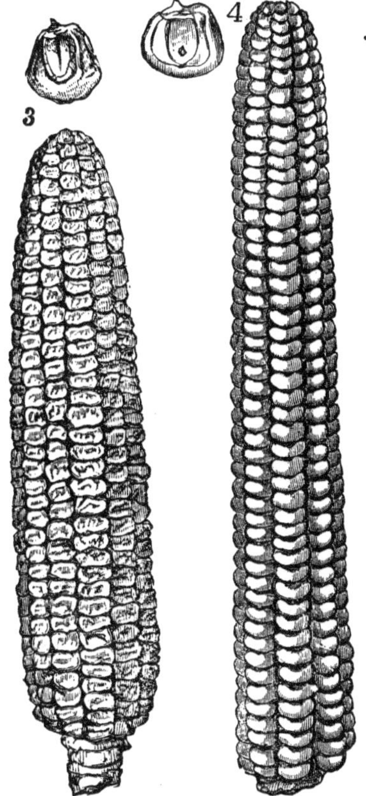

Rhode Island Asylum Corn. Tuscarora Corn.

Figure 5 is the Ohio Dent Corn, which will yield more bushels per acre, in certain States, than can be produced by planting any other variety.

Figure 6 represents the King Philip Corn, which is an 8-rowed variety, having large kernels, long ears, and small cobs. It is an excellent kind of corn for most localities, although in some States it does not succeed satisfactorily. The Improved King Philip is considered a superior variety, not only for market but for meal for home consumption

Figure 7 represents a variety highly esteemed, known as the Rhode Island Premium Corn. The varieties of Indian-corn are almost without number. Some are not worthy of cultiva-

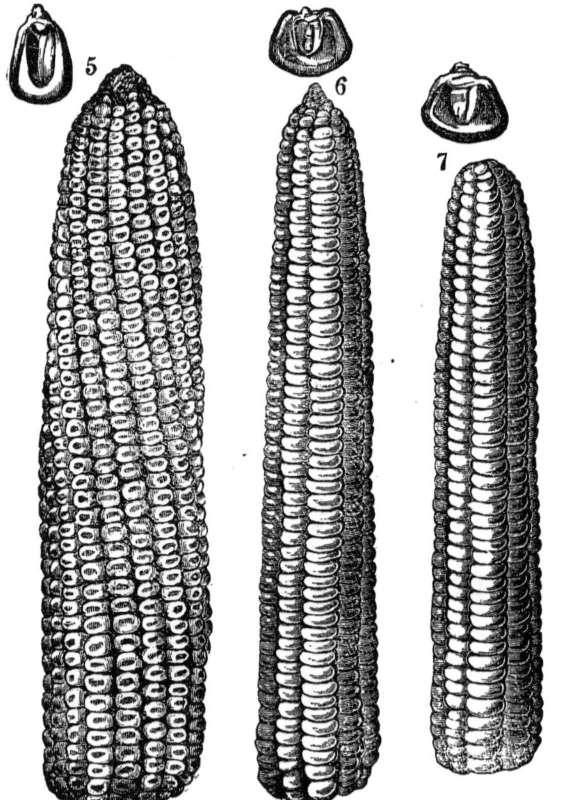

Ohio Dent Corn. King Philip Corn. . hode Island Premium Corn

tion, while others succeed most satisfactorily wherever the soil will produce a large crop of any kind of corn.

METHOD OF CULTIVATING THE HOP.

HOUBLON. *Humulus lupulus.*

Although the Hop is not a culinary vegetable, yet, as it is more or less used in every part of our country, it may not be amiss to treat of its culture. As a great deal depends on the manner in which Hops are cured, I propose giving directions for their management throughout, so as to enable those who choose, to prepare their own. My information is collected chiefly from Loudon's Encyclopædia of Plants.

"The Hop has been cultivated in Europe an unknown length of time for its flowers, which are used for preserving beer. Its culture was introduced from Flanders in the reign of Henry the Eighth; though indigenous both in Scotland and Ireland, it is little cultivated in those countries, owing to the humidity of their autumnal season. Like other plants of this sort, the Hop bears its flowers on different individuals; therefore, the female plants alone are cultivated."

NAMES OF DIFFERENT VARIETIES.

"There are several varieties grown in Kent and Surrey, under the name of Flemish, Canterbury, Goldings, etc.; the first is the most hardy, differing little from the Wild or Hedge Hop; the Golding is an improved and highly productive variety, but more subject to blight than the other. Besides these are the Farnham, or Golden Grape, which is cultivated for an early crop; and for late picking, the Mayfield Grape, or Ruffler, is esteemed, which is a dwarfish variety. Great caution is necessary lest the varieties get mixed, as they will not ripen nor dry equally, and consequently cannot be of one uniform color and quality. In the Hop-growing districts of the State of New

York, where Hops constitute the principal crop of the farm, the Pompey Hop, Grape Hop, and English Cluster are most productive. Still, the Pompey Hop, it is said, is more liable to be injured by rust and insects than the other varieties.

PREPARATION OF SOIL AND PLANTING.

"The Hop prefers a deep loamy soil on a dry bottom; a sheltered situation, but at the same time not so confined as to prevent a free circulation of air. The soil requires to be well pulverized and manured previous to planting. In Hop districts, the ground is generally trenched either with a spade or subsoil plough; and if the ground is at all wet it must be thoroughly under-drained, as Hops will not grow luxuriantly and produce abundantly when there is an excess of water in the soil. The ground requires as thorough preparation for Hops as for a crop of wheat or roots.

"The ground is marked out with a plough, making drills three or four inches deep, and six to nine feet apart. Some experienced Hop-growers say the rows should never be nearer than nine feet in rows both ways. By some, five, six, or seven plants, are placed in a circular form, which circles are distant five or six feet from each other.

"The sets or cuttings are procured from the most healthy of the old stools; each should have two joints or buds. From the one which is placed in the ground the root springs; and from the other, the stalk. Some plant the cuttings at once, covering them with mellow soil about two inches deep, where they are to remain; and by others they are nursed a year in a garden. An interval crop of Beans or Cabbage is generally taken the first year. Sometimes no poles are placed at the plants till the second year, and then only short ones of six or seven feet. The third year the Hop generally comes into full bearing, and then from four to six poles, from fourteen to sixteen feet in length, are placed to each circle: or one pole to each plant, if cultivated in straight rows. The plan adopted for the most part at the present time, is to set stakes about eight feet high at every hill, and attach tarred twine to the tops all over the field. This is called horizontal cultivation. The stakes should be about one and a half inches square, of durable timber, and the whole stake dipped in a trough of coal-tar, to prevent decay and repel insects.

CULTIVATION AND TRAINING.

"The after-culture of the Hop consists in stirring the soil, and keeping it free from weeds; in guiding the shoots to the poles, and sometimes tying them for that purpose with bass or withered rushes; in eradicating superfluous shoots which may rise from the root, and in raising a small heap of earth over the root to nourish the plant; although, if the ground be not excessively wet, it is better to hill but little. Rows of Beans may be planted between the rows of Hops, without injury to the crop of Hops. Grass and weeds must be kept subdued by the repeated use of the horse-hoe and hand-hoes, through the entire growing season.

"Some persons cultivate only a few hills of Hops for the use of their own families; and the hills are planted near the dwelling, and the vines trained on cords over the window. Sometimes the vines are allowed to run thirty feet high. This is objectionable, as such a great length of vine is produced at the expense of the crop of Hops. After the vines have attained a certain height, if there is no support they will soon cease to run; and the energies of the plants will be employed in producing Hops.

"As the Hop is a staminate or male, and pistillate or female plant, if the vines be unproductive, some of the barren hills should be dug up, and others that will bear well set in their places. In field cultivation, the most successful growers of Hops plant about every ninth hill with sets from a staminate or male stalk. By this means all the vines will be fertilized and rendered productive.

"A person should pass through the field every few days, and aid the vines in twining to their supports. It is a striking characteristic of the Hop, as well as of beans, that the climbers always ascend in one direction. Hops run from right to left, and beans in the opposite direction. And if the runners be put around the pole in an opposite direction, and secured there, the ends will turn about as soon as they are free, and go up the pole, or twine the other way. Hop-vines turn around a pole in the same direction that the sun appears to revolve around the earth.

WHEN AND HOW TO PICK.

"Hops are known to be ready for gathering when the chaffy capsules acquire a brown color, and a firm consistence. Each chaffy capsule, or leaf calyx, contains one seed. Before these are picked, the stalks are detached, and the poles pulled up, and placed horizontally on frames of wood, two or three poles at a time. The hops are then picked off by women and children. After being carefully separated from the leaves and stalks, they are dropped into a large cloth hung all around within the frame on tenter-hooks. When the cloth is full, the Hops are emptied into a large sack, which is carried home, and the Hops laid on a kiln to be dried. This is always to be done as soon as possible after they are picked, or they are apt to sustain considerable damage, both in color and flavor, if allowed to remain long in the green state in which they are picked. In very warm weather, and when they are picked in a moist state, they will often heat in five or six hours. For this reason, the kilns are kept constantly at work, both night and day, from the commencement to the conclusion of the Hop-picking season.

"Some Hop-growers, however, prefer large boxes made of thin boards for receiving the Hops as they are picked. These boxes have handles screwed to their sides, so that two persons may handle a boxful conveniently."

MANNER OF DRYING HOPS.

"The operation of drying Hops is not materially different

from that of drying malt; and the kilns are of the same construction. The hops are spread on a hair cloth, from eight to twelve inches deep, according as the season is dry or wet, or the Hops ripe or immature. When the ends of the Hop-stalks become quite shrivelled and dry, they are taken off the kiln, and laid on a board floor till they become quite cool, when they are put into bags. When only a small quantity is raised, they can be spread on a clean floor a few inches deep, and stirred every day till they are quite dry, after which they should be stored in sacks made of coarse cloth."

MANNER OF BAGGING.

"The bagging of Hops is thus performed. In the floor of the room where Hops are laid to cool, there is a round hole or trap, equal in size to the mouth of a Hop-bag. After tying a handful of Hops in each of the lower corners of a large bag, which serve for handles, the mouth of the bag is fixed securely to a strong hoop, which is made to rest on the edge of the hole or trap; and the bag itself being then dropped through the hole, a packer goes into it, when a person who attends for the purpose, puts in the Hops in small quantities, in order to give the packer an opportunity of packing and trampling them as hard as possible. When the bag is filled, and the Hops trampled in so hard that it will hold no more, it is drawn up, loosened from the hoop, and the end sewed up, two other handles having been previously formed in the corners in the manner mentioned above. The brightest and finest-colored Hops are put into fine bagging, and the brown into coarse or heavy bagging. The former are chiefly used for brewing fine ale, and the latter by the porter brewers. But when Hops are intended to be kept two or three years, they are put into bags of strong cloth, and firmly pressed with a screw so as to exclude the air." Hops are also pressed into small packages, in paper bags, weighing half a pound and upwards, to suit the wants of small families.

YIELD PER ACRE.

"The produce of no crop is so liable to variation as that of the Hop. In good seasons an acre will produce 20 cwt., but from 10 to 12 cwt. is considered a tolerable average crop. The quality of Hops is estimated by the abundance or scarcity of an unctuous clammy powder which adheres to them, and by their bright-yellow color. The expenses of forming a Hop plantation are considerable; but once in bearing, it will continue so for ten or fifteen years before it requires to be renewed. The Hop is peculiarly liable to diseases; when young it is devoured by fleas of different kinds; at a more advanced stage, it is attacked by the green fly, red spider, and ottermoth, the larvæ of which prey even upon their roots. The honey-dew often materially injures the Hop crop; and the mould, the fire-blast, and other blights, injure it at different times towards the latter period of the growth of the plant."

The Hop is considered somewhat precarious; but when the season is good, the profit is very great. The average product may be stated at 700 lbs., though it has reached 1600 lbs. to the acre; and in the latter case the expenses amounted to sixty dollars. The ordinary, or average price, may be stated at eighteen cents per pound. The profits on an ordinary crop, according to these assumed data, would be about seventy dollars to the acre. It often falls materially short of this, however, from the want of knowledge and care in gathering and drying the crop.

MEDICINAL PROPERTIES.

The young shoots of both wild and cultivated Hops are considered by some as very wholesome, and are frequently gathered in the spring, boiled, and eaten as Asparagus. The stalks and leaves will dye wool yellow. From the stalk a strong cloth is made in Sweden; and the mode of preparing it is described by Linnæus in his Flora Suecica. A decoction of the roots is said to be as good a sudorific as Sarsaparilla; and the smell of the flowers is soporific. A pillow filled with Hop flowers will induce sleep, unattended with the bad effects of soporifics which require to be taken internally.

STACKING THE POLES.

"The stripping and stacking of the poles succeed to the operation of picking. The shoot or bind being stripped off, such poles as are not decayed, are set up together in a conical pile of three or four hundred, the centre of which is formed by three stout poles bound together a few feet from their tops, and their lower ends spread out. A flat stone, or piece of board, should be placed under every pole to keep the moisture from rising in the wood, which, if not prevented, will hasten the decay of the poles about as fast as if they were in the ground. Those who propose to raise Hops on a large scale, should visit some of the Hop-growing districts in the northern counties of New York, or other States, and examine the modes of culture and kilns for drying.

Leek. Poirreau. *Allium porrum.*

VARIETIES.

Scotch, or Flag.	Large London.

This is a wholesome and useful herb, and is so hardy as to endure the extremes of heat and cold without injury. The seed may be sown in March, or early in April, in a bed of rich earth, in drills about an inch deep, and a sufficient distance apart to admit of a small hoe being worked between the rows, allowing one ounce of seed for every three thousand plants that may be required.

If the ground be kept loose and clean around the plants, they will be fit to transplant in June, or early in July, and should be set out in good ground, in rows twelve inches asunder, and the plants five or six inches apart in the rows. They will grow well in a warm border, which at this season is useless for many kinds of vegetables. After the plants have taken root, they should be frequently hoed, and kept free from weeds.

Those who wish to have Leeks blanched, may plant them in trenches three or four inches deep, and as the plants increase in growth, the earth should be drawn by a hoe into the trenches.

LETTUCE.

LAITUE. *Lactuca sativa crispa.*

It would be easy to furnish a more extensive catalogue of Lettuce, as the varieties are numerous; but as this is one of those kinds of vegetables that can only be raised in perfection during mild and temperate weather, it is needless for the gardener to plant any in the open ground but such as have been tested, and found to stand a tolerable degree of warm weather, which generally prevails in May and June, and consequently cuts short the salad season. Those who have been accustomed to raise head Lettuce in any quantity, know the trouble of preparing the ground and planting, and the loss they would sustain if several thousand plants should run to seed just as they appeared to be perfecting for market. As this is often the case, even with the very best attention, I would caution gardeners to test such plants as they are not acquainted with, before they set out any quantity with a view to their heading.

Lettuce seed of most varieties may be sown from the first to the middle of September, in rich ground free from weeds; they answer very well when sown with Spinach, and should be covered with straw at the approach of severe weather. These plants, if transplanted into warm borders, or in the open ground, as early in March as the weather will permit, will produce fine heads early in the month of May.

The best of the tender kinds of Lettuce should be sown in moderate hotbeds early in March, and if transplanted into good ground by the middle of April, will produce their heads before the approach of warm weather. Such kinds as are known to produce heads in hot weather, also such as are intended to be cut as a small salad while young, may be sown in warm borders in March and April; but those designed for heading should be transplanted as soon as they are an inch or two in height, and kept in a growing state by frequent hoeing, or they may run up to seed as the season advances.

If it be an object with the gardener to have good strong Lettuce plants for transplanting, the seed should be sown very thin. One ounce of good seed is sufficient for a border of six feet in width by eighteen feet in length, and will produce from ten to twelve thousand plants. All kinds of Lettuce intended for heading should be planted in good ground, twelve inches distant from each other every way; the plants should be carefully hoed every other week during their growth. The first hoeing should be done in about two weeks after they are transplanted.

The Coss Lettuce requires to be blanched. This is done by gathering up the leaves of the plants and tying bass around them, when grown to perfection. If Head Lettuce be required at other seasons than the spring, it may be obtained in autumn by sowing seed in August, or in the winter by means of garden frames and glazed sashes. (*See article on Forcing Vegetables.*)

Moisture is the most essential nutriment of Lettuce; and the best varieties may run to seed without forming heads, in the event of extreme dry weather. Those who put off the sowing of seed until May and June, instead of sowing it in March and April, as directed, may procure head Lettuce from some of their strongest plants by transplanting them into rich ground as soon as they are an inch or two in height, and the remainder, if left thin in the beds, may produce small heads by stirring the earth around them with a small hoe or weeding-hook. These are as good for family use as larger heads, and those persons who are fond of Lettuce may raise such throughout the summer. But market gardeners seldom attempt it, unless they have a tract of moist, loamy soil, peculiarly adapted to the growth of head Lettuce, in anything like a propitious season.

Where the soil in a garden is heavy, by mingling a load of sand with a small plot of ground for a bed of Lettuce, heads may be obtained much sooner than they will grow in a heavy soil.

MELON.

MELON. *Cucumis melo.*

The Melon is an exotic plant, growing wild in Asa. It is cultivated in all the warm countries of Europe, and also in Africa and America, where its salubrious and cooling fruit is generally esteemed.

For the varieties of the Musk or Canteleupe Melons, prepare a piece of rich ground early in May; manure, and give it a good digging; then mark it out into squares of six feet every way. At the angle of each square, dig a hole twelve inches deep and eighteen broad, into which put about six inches of old, rotten dung. Throw thereon about four inches of earth, and mix the dung and earth well with the spade; after which draw more earth over the mixture, so as to form a circular hill about a foot broad at top. When your hills are all prepared, plant in each, towards the centre, six or eight grains of seed, distant two inches from each other, and cover them half an inch deep. One ounce of good Melon-seed will plant about one hundred and twenty hills.

When the plants are in a state of forwardness, producing their rough leaves, they must be thinned to two or three in each hill. Draw earth from time to time around the hills and about the roots of the plants. As soon as the plants have spread into branches, stop them by pinching off the top of the first runner-bud. This will strengthen the plants and promote their perfecting the fruit early. After this keep the ground free from weeds by frequent hoeing.

There are many varieties of the melon, highly esteemed in Europe, which do not succeed in this country; the gardener should, therefore, plant only such as have been tested and found to produce good fruit here, or our superior old sorts may become degenerated. After a judicious selection is made, if caution be not used to plant the different sorts remote from each other, and from Cucumbers, Squashes, and Gourds, degeneracy will infallibly be the consequence. To prevent the ravages of flies, etc., see General Remarks, Chap. I.

WATER MELON.

MELON D'EAU. *Cucurbita citrullus.*

The Water Melon, though by some considered a species of the former, is a distinct genus of exotic plants. They afford a very refreshing article of luxury in our warm summers. In order to have Water Melons in perfection, you must fix upon a piece of very rich, light soil; prepare, plant, and manage it in every respect as is directed for Musk Melon, only let the hills be seven or eight feet distant every way. One ounce of seed will plant from forty to fifty hills.

Some persons, who have a soil as rich as manure can make it, can never succeed in raising Water Melons, because there is too large a proportion of clay in the soil. In order to raise large Melons, a rich, sandy soil, or a sandy loam, is essential. I have known Water-Melon seed planted where the ground was so productive as to yield forty bushels of Wheat, or eighty of Indian Corn per acre, when a Melon of fair size and quality could not be obtained with the best of cultivation.

FORWARDING MELONS UNDER HAND-GLASSES.

The directions already given for maturing Cucumbers under glass will apply to Melons, with very few exceptions. Care, however, must be taken that they be kept away from each other at the time of fruiting, as instances often occur of whole crops being entirely ruined by plants of the same genus being raised too near each other. Those who wish to forward Melons may prepare a hotbed, early in the season, for plants. If the ridging system be adopted, and a hand-glass applied to each hill, Melons may be obtained one month earlier than the usual time.

Gardeners raising Melons for the supply of city markets, may gratify the public taste early in the season by pursuing the forwarding, if not the forcing system. Ridges may be prepared in the following manner: In April or May a trench may be dug in a warm border, about two feet deep and three wide, and of sufficient length for as many hand-glasses as are intended to be employed, allowing three feet for every hill. Some good heating-manure should be laid in the pits, managed the same as a common hotbed. To this must be added rich mould to the depth of eight or ten inches. As soon as the mould is warm, the seedlings may be planted, three in each hill, after which the hand-glasses should be set on, and shaded. After the plants have taken root and begin to grow, one side of the glasses should be raised in fine days to admit fresh air; and as the warm weather progresses, the glasses may be taken off in the middle of fine days, so as to harden the plants gradually to the weather; and by the latter part of May they may be removed entirely.

Those persons who live at a great distance from a glass-works may make a protection for Melon-hills by making wooden boxes, without bottom or top, about ten inches wide and fourteen inches long. Then, one pane of glass, ten by fourteen, simply laid on a box, will subserve the purpose of an excellent bell-glass. Such boxes should be at least eight inches high, else the young plants will not have sufficient room to push upwards.

MUSTARD.

MOUTARDE. *Sinapis.*

The *Alba*, or White Mustard, grows spontaneously in the fields of England; it is also cultivated as a small salad, as well as for seed. The seed yields from every hundred pounds, from thirty-three to thirty-six pounds of sweet, mild oil.

White Mustard Seed is much used as a medicine, and persons subject to disordered stomachs often derive great benefit by taking a spoonful of the dry seed two or three times a day. Some use it in pickles, to which it imparts an agreeable flavor, and renders Cucumbers, in particular, more salutary.

The *Nigra*, or Common Mustard, is also a native of England. The condiment called Mustard, and in daily use at our table, is prepared from the seed of this species. The seed of each variety may be sown in clean, rich ground in April and May; and for a fall salad in September, in shallow drills.

MUSHROOMS.

HOW TO DISTINGUISH THE GOOD FROM THE POISONOUS.

The *Agaricus* is said to be the most extensive genus in the vegetable kingdom. The species are determined upon various principles. As some of the kinds are poisonous, it is necessary to describe the eatable Mushroom. Loudon says, it is most readily distinguished when of a middle size, by its fine pink or flesh-colored gills, and pleasant smell. In a more advanced age, the gills become of a chocolate color, and it is then more apt to be confounded with other kinds of doubtful quality;

but that species which most nearly resembles it is slimy to the touch, destitute of fine odor, and has a disagreeable smell.

Again; the noxious kinds grow in woods, while the true Mushroom springs up chiefly in open pastures, and should be gathered only in such places. Unwholesome *fungi* will sometimes spring up on artificial beds in gardens. Sometimes, when the spawn begins to run, a spurious breed is often found to precede a crop of genuine Mushrooms. The poisonous toad-stool, *Agaricus cirocus*, may generally be detected by the presence of a sickly, nauseous smell, though some hurtful kinds are so free from anything disagreeable in the smell as to make any criterion, drawn from that alone, very unsafe. The wholesome kinds, however, invariably emit a grateful, rich odor.

In order to ascertain whether what appear to be Mushrooms are of the true edible kinds, sprinkle a little salt over the inner or spongy part; if, in a short time after, they turn yellow, they are unwholesome; but if black, they may be considered as genuine Mushrooms.

FORCING MUSHROOMS AT ALL SEASONS.

Mushrooms may be obtained at any season of the year, by a proper regulation of the time and manner of forming the beds. A good crop is sometimes collected without making a bed on purpose, by introducing lumps of spawn into the top mould of old hotbeds. The *Agaricus campestris* is most generally cultivated. Dr. Withering mentions other eatable varieties, which grow considerably larger, but are inferior in flavor; he says "that a plant of the variety Georgia was gathered in an old hotbed at Birmingham, which weighed fourteen pounds; and Mr. Stackhouse found one fifty-four inches in circumference, having a stem as thick as a man's wrist."

The methods of procuring and propagating spawn, and of forming Mushroom beds, are numerous. Indigenous spawn may be collected in pasture lands in September and October, or it may be found in its strength and purity in the paths of mills worked by horses, or in any other horse-walks under shelter; it is frequently found in old hotbeds and dunghills in the summer season, and Mushrooms of good quality may often be seen beginning to form on the surface, like large peas. When these are absorbed it is time to take out the spawn, which is generally in hard, dry lumps of dung, the spawn having the appearance of whitish coarse pieces of thread. The true sort has exactly the smell of a Mushroom. If spawn thus collected be required for immediate use, it may be planted in the beds at once, or it will keep three or four years, if laid to dry with the earth adhering to it, and afterwards placed in a warm, dry shed, where there is a current of air; but if it be not completely dried the spawn will exhaust itself or perish, as it will not bear the extremes of heat, cold, or moisture.

HOW TO MAKE MUSHROOM-BEDS.

Mushroom-beds are simply heaps of animal dung and earth, so tempered as to be capable of producing and preserving spawn; but in order to have fruitful spawn at all times, it should be so formed as to be always at command. To this end, a quantity of fresh horse-droppings mixed with short litter should be collected. Add to this one-third of cow-dung and a small portion of good earth, to cement it together; mash the whole into a thin compost, like grafting-clay; then form it in the shape of bricks; which being done, set them on edge, and frequently turn them until half dry; then with a dibble make one or two holes in each brick, and insert in each hole a piece of spawn the size of an egg; the bricks should then be laid where they can dry gradually. When dry, lay dry horse-dung on a level floor, six or eight inches thick; on this pile the bricks, the spawn side uppermost. When the pile is snugly formed, cover it with a small portion of fresh warm horse-dung, sufficient in quantity to produce a gentle glow through the whole. When the spawn has spread itself through every part of the bricks, the process is ended, and they may be laid up in any dry place for use. Mushroom spawn, made according to this receipt, will preserve its vegetating powers for many years, if well dried before it is laid up if moist, it will grow, and soon exhaust itself.

Mushroom-beds are often formed in ridges in the open air, covered with litter and mats, so as to prevent heavy rains exciting a fermentation; and sometimes in ridges of the same sort, under cover, as in the open sheds of hot-houses. They are also made in close sheds, behind hot-houses, or in houses built on purpose, called Mushroom-houses. A moderately warm, light cellar is peculiarly suited for the purpose, in the winter season, as no fire is necessary, and but little water—the application of which frequently proves injurious when not judiciously managed. Mushrooms may also be raised in pots, boxes, hampers, etc., placed in warm situations; also in old beds, in pits with glazed frames, and in dark frames or pits.

The general way of making Mushroom-beds is to prepare a body of stable-dung, moderately fermented, about a yard in thickness, more or less, according to the size and situation in which the bed is to be formed. When the strong heat has subsided, an inch of good mould may be laid over it, and the spawn planted therein in rows five or six inches apart. After this is done, another layer of mould, an inch thick, may be added, and then a coat of straw. Beds well constructed will produce Mushrooms in five or six weeks, and will continue to produce for several months, if care be taken in gathering not to destroy the young ones. As Mushrooms are gathered from time to time, the straw should be spread carefully over the bed.

Beds made in a convenient place, where there is space all around, may be formed so as to make four sloping surfaces, similar to the roof of a house, which, by being spawned on the four sides, will yield abundantly. The celebrated Mr. Nichol makes his beds without spawn. The following are his directions, taken from Loudon's Encyclopædia of Gardening:

"After having laid a floor of ashes, stones, chips, gravel, or brick-bats, so as to keep the bed quite dry and free from under-damp, lay a course of horse-droppings six inches thick. These should be new from the stables, and must not be broken, and the dryer the better. They may be collected every day until the whole floor or sole be covered to the above thickness; but they must not be allowed to ferment nor to heat. In the whole process of making up, the bed should be as much exposed to the air as possible; and it should be carefully defended from wet, if out of doors. When this course is quite dry, and judged to be past a state of fermentation, cover it to the thickness of two inches with light, dry earth; if sandy, so much the better. It is immaterial whether it be rich or not; the only use of earth here being for spawn to run and mass in. Now lay another course of droppings, and earth them over as above, when past a state of fermentation: then a third course, which, in like manner, earth all over. This finishes the bed, which will be a very strong and productive one, if properly managed afterwards.

"Observe, that in forming the bed, it should be a little rounded, in order that the centre may not be more wet or moist than the sides. This may be done in forming the sole or floor at first, and the bed would then be of equal strength in all parts. If it be made up against a wall in a cellar, stable, or shed, it may have a slope of a few inches from the back to the front, less or more, according to its breadth. I have sometimes been contented with two courses as above, instead of three; and often, when materials were scarce, have made them up slighter, thus: three four-inch courses of droppings, with one inch of earth between each, and a two-inch covering at top. Such a bed as this I have had produce for ten or twelve successive months; yet very much depends on the state of the materials, on the care taken in making up the beds, and on the after-management.

"The droppings of hard-fed horses only are useful. Those of horses kept on green food will, of themselves, produce few or no Mushrooms. I have made up beds from farm-horses, fed partly on hard and partly on green food, and from carriage or saddle-horses, fed entirely on corn or hay, treated them in the same way in every respect, and have found, not once, but always, those made from the latter most productive. Droppings from hard-fed horses may be procured at the public stables in towns, or at inns in the country, any time of the year; and if the supply be plentiful, a bed of considerable dimensions may be made and finished within five or six weeks. In as many more weeks, if in a stable or dry cellar, or shed, it will begin to produce, and often sooner; but if the situation of the bed be cold, it will sometimes be two or three months in producing Mushrooms."

EXTREMES OF TEMPERATURE SHOULD BE AVOIDED.

It may be necessary to state further, that extremes of heat, cold, drought, and moisture should be avoided in the cultivation of Mushrooms. If the temperature keeps up to 50° in the winter, the beds will be safe, and the heat in the beds may rise to 60° or even 70° without injury. Air also must be admitted in proportion to the heat, and 60° should be aimed at as a medium temperature. Water, when given a little at a time, is better than too much at once, after the spawn has begun to spread; and the water for this purpose should always be made blood-warm. A light covering of straw may be used to preserve moisture on the surface; and if the beds are made in open frames, or otherwise subject to exposure, the straw may be laid thicker than on beds made in a cellar.

Should beds fail in producing Mushrooms after having been kept too hot or too wet, it may be inferred that the spawn is injured or destroyed; but if, on the contrary, a bed that has been kept moderately warm and dry should happen to be unproductive, such bed may be well replenished with warm water, and a coat of warm dung may be laid over the whole. If this does not enliven the bed, after having lain a month, take the earth off; and if, on examination, there is no appearance of spawn, the whole may be destroyed. On the contrary, should the bed contain spawn, it may be renovated by covering it again, especially if any small tubercles be discernible.

If the heat should have declined, the spawn may be taken out and used in a fresh bed. If beds be formed in hotbed frames under glass, some mats or straw must be laid over the glass to break off the intense heat of the sun.

Although only one species of *edible fungi* has yet been introduced into the garden, there are several eatable kinds. In Poland and Russia there are above thirty kinds in common use among the peasantry. They are gathered at different stages of their growth, and used in various ways—raw, boiled, stewed, roasted; and being hung up, and dried in their stoves and chimneys, form a part of their winter stock of provisions. Great caution is necessary in collecting Mushrooms for food; and none but the botanist should gather any but the kinds we have described. Physicians say, "that all the edible species should be thoroughly masticated before they are taken into the stomach, as this greatly lessens the effect of poisons. When accidents of the sort happen, vomiting should be immediately excited, and then the vegetable acids should be given, either vinegar, lemon-juice, or that of apples; after which give ether and antispasmodic remedies, to stop the excessive vomiting. Infusions of gall-nut, oak bark, and Peruvian bark are recommended as capable of neutralizing the poisonous principle of Mushrooms." It is, however, the safest way not to eat any but the well known kinds.

NASTURTIUM, OR STURTION.

Capucine. *Tropæolum.*

This is an annual plant, a native of Peru, and is highly deserving of cultivation for the sake of its brilliant orange and crimson-colored flower, as well as for the berries, which, if gathered while green and pickled in vinegar, make a good substitute for capers, and are used in melted butter, with boiled mutton, etc.

The seed should be sown in April, or early in May, in drills about an inch deep, near fences or pales; or trellises should be constructed, on which they can climb and have support; for they will always be more productive in this way than when suffered to trail on the ground.

OKRA. GOMBO. *Hibiscus esculentus.*

The green capsules of this plant are used in soups, stews, etc., to which they impart a rich flavor, and are considered nutritious. Its ripe seed, if burned and ground like coffee, can scarcely be distinguished therefrom.

The seed should be planted in good rich ground, the first or second week in May, if settled warm weather, but not otherwise, as it is a very tender vegetable. Draw drills about an inch deep, and three or four feet asunder, into which drop the seed at the distance of six or eight inches from each other, or rather drop two or three in each place, lest the one should not grow, and cover them nearly an inch deep. As the plants advance in growth, thin them out, earth them up two or three times, and they will produce abundantly.

ONION. OIGNON. *Allium cepa.*

Of the several varieties of Onions, the Yellow or Silver Skinned, and Large Red, are the best for a general crop. The bulbs are handsome, of firm growth, and keep well through the winter. The New England White are handsome for the table, and very suitable for pickling, as well as to pull while young, and generally prove a very profitable crop.

Previous to sowing Onion-seed for a general crop, the ground should be well prepared by digging-in some of the oldest and strongest manure that can be got. The earlier this is done in the spring, the better; and the planting should not be delayed longer than the middle of April. The seed may be sown moderately thick, in drills one inch deep and twelve inches apart. Those who cultivate Onions for the sake of their bulbs, may use at the rate of four or five pounds of seed per acre.

As market gardeners, in the vicinity of large cities, find it most profitable to pull a great proportion of their Onions while young, they generally require at the rate of from eight to ten pounds of seed to an acre of land.

When the plants are up strong, they should be hoed. Those beds that are to stand for ripening, should be thinned out while young, to the distance of two or three inches from each other. If a few should be required for use after this, those can be taken which incline more to tops than roots; and if the beds be frequently looked over, and the small and stalky plants taken away where they stand thickest, the remaining bulbs will grow to a larger size. The plants should be hoed at least three times in the early part of their growth; but if the season prove damp, and weeds vegetate luxuriantly, they must be removed by the hand, because after the Onions have begun to bulb, it would injure them to stir them with a hoe.

WHEN TO HARVEST ONIONS.

When the greenness is gone out of the tops of Onions, it is time to take them up; for from this time the fibrous roots decay. After they are pulled, they should be laid out to dry, and when dry, removed to a place of shelter.

The small Onions may be planted in the following spring. Even an Onion which is partly rotten will produce good bulbs, if the seed-stems be taken off as soon as they appear.

The *Allium fistulosum*, or Welsh Onion, is cultivated for spring salad; it forms no bulbs, but is very hardy. If the seed be sown early in September in rich ground, although the tops may die down in the winter, yet the roots in mild climates will continue sound, and put up new leaves early in the spring.

The *Allium cepa*, or common White and Red Onions, are most generally cultivated by market gardeners as a substitute for the *Allium fistulosum*. They sow the seed in the spring and autumn months, the product of which is pulled and sent to the market while young.

The *Allium proliferum*, or Tree Onion, is propagated by

planting the bulbs in spring or autumn, either the root bulbs, or those produced on the top of the stalks; the latter, if planted in the spring, will produce fine Onions. These may be planted in rows with a dibble, the same as Shallots.

The Potato Onion, *Allium tuberosum*, does not produce seed as other Onions, but it increases by the root. One single Onion, slightly covered, will produce six or seven in a clump, partly under ground. The bulbs are generally planted in the spring from twelve to eighteen inches apart; but they will yield better when planted in autumn, as they will survive the winter if slightly covered with dung, litter, or leaves of trees, etc.

WHEN TO SOW THE SEED.

Onion-seed may be sown at any time from March to September; but those only can be depended upon for ripening which are sown in the first and second spring months. It is a singular fact that Onions will not ripen later than August, or the early part of September, however warm the weather may be. They can, however, be preserved in the place where they grow, by spreading some short dung over them in autumn, just sufficient to prevent their being lifted out of the ground in winter. Onions thus preserved, often prove more profitable to market gardeners in the spring than crops which ripen; because ripe Onions are then scarce, and green ones prove a good substitute for Shallots, Welsh Onions, Leeks, etc.

Parsley. Persil. *Apium petroselinum.*

Parsley is a hardy biennial plant, and grows wild in moist climates, but has been greatly improved by cultivation. The leaves of the Common Parsley are used as a potherb, and those of the Extra Curled kinds make a fine garnish. The Large-Rooted are generally cooked for the table in autumn and winter, like Parsnips.

As Parsley-seed, sown late in the season, is apt to lie in the ground some time before it vegetates, and often fails in dry weather, the general crop should be sown in a cool situation by the early part of April, in drills an inch deep, and one foot asunder, allowing at the rate of about six or seven pounds of seed to the acre, or two ounces for every three perches of land. After the plants are up, let them be kept clean by frequent hoeing. The Large-Rooted Parsley should be thinned out while young, and managed the same as Carrots and Parsnips.

In order to have Parsley green through the winter, the old leaves should be picked off in September. If some of the roots be taken up early in November, and laid in a frame, or light cellar, the leaves will keep green a long time. The remainder may be covered up with straw in the place where it grows. If Parsley-seed be sown in frames in spring or summer, it may be preserved for winter use without the trouble of removing it. It frequently happens that Parsley seed will remain in the ground three or four weeks without showing any signs of vegetation, and in the event of extreme dry weather, is apt to decay for want of its most essential aliment —MOISTURE. A few grains of Long Radish-seed, sown about an inch apart in each drill, are well adapted to promote the growth of Parsley; because Radish-seed being quick in germinating, will open the pores of the earth; and the plants, as they progress in growth, will create a shade sufficient to protect the Parsley from the full rays of the sun.

PARSNIP. PANAIS. *Pastinaca sativa.*

This is a hardy biennial plant, common in calcareous soils. It has long been an inmate of the garden, and forms a vegetable dish in the winter, with salt meat, salted fish, etc. Parsnip-seed may be planted from the middle of March till the middle of May, in drills one inch deep and fourteen inches apart; and as this vegetable requires a long season to grow in, the sooner the seed is planted the better. Parsnips grow best in a deep soil, which has been well manured the preceding fall. Sow the seed thick along the drills, at the rate of five or six pounds per acre, and rake them in evenly.

The Parsnip, although when in full growth it will endure the extremes of heat and cold, requires peculiar management to promote and preserve germination in an early stage of culture In order to give the seed a fair chance, it should be planted in ground susceptible of moisture, and not apt to encrust when dry. If cultivated in light ground, it should be rolled or pressed immediately after depositing the seed therein. But this should not be done while the earth is wet. A few grains of Long Radish-seed, sown in each drill as directed for Parsley, will also prove beneficial to Parsnips.

When the plants are two or three inches high, thin them to the distance of six or eight inches in the rows. They should be kept free from weeds, by regular hoeing through the summer; and in autumn they will be fit for use. They improve in flavor after having been frozen, and will endure the severity of a hard winter.

Parsnips require from thirty to forty minutes' boiling, according to their size and age. Some boil them in water seasoned with salt, until tender; but they are better when boiled with salt pork, and afterwards mashed and fried in butter.

PEPPER.

POIVRE OU PIMENT. *Capsicum.*

This family of plants is a native of the East and West Indies; some of their capsules, or pods, are yellow, and others red, when at maturity. They are much used for pickling, and should be gathered for that purpose before they are fully ripe.

The seed of the different kinds of *Capsicum* may be sown in a hotbed in March, or on a warm border, early in May. One ounce of seed will produce about three thousand plants. When the plants arrive at the height of from one to two inches, they should be transplanted into good rich ground, from eighteen inches to two feet distant from each other.

Those who do not want Peppers early in the season, may

sow seed in the open ground in May, in drills two feet asunder, and half an inch deep. When the plants are grown an inch or two high, thin them to the distance of fifteen or eighteen inches in the rows. The ground should be afterwards hoed deep around the plants, and kept free from weeds by repeated hoeings.

The *Capsicum Grossum*, or Bell Pepper, is perennial, and will keep in perpetual bearing in warm climates. In England this species is considered superior to all others, on account of its skin being thick, and also pulpy and tender. The plants are therefore frequently preserved in hot-houses during the winter and spring, and kept in the open air in settled warm weather.

PEAS.

Pois. *Pisum sativum.*

Peas will grow to different heights, according to soil and season. The Dwarf Pea require less distance between the rows and shorter sticks than the tall kinds; and sometimes no supports at all.

Planting the early kinds of Pea should commence as soon in the spring as the ground can be brought into good condition. All the other sorts, as well as the early, will answer for successive crops. A few of the most esteemed varieties should be planted at the same time every two weeks, from March until the end of May. Persons desirous of having Peas throughout the summer and autumn, may plant a few in June, July, and August. In dry weather the Peas should be soaked in soft water five or six hours before planting, and if the ground be very dry, it should be watered in the drills.

Gardeners practise different modes of planting Peas. Some plant them in ridges, others in drills; some in single rows, others in double; some use sticks for the dwarf kinds, and others not.

All the different sorts of Peas may be planted in double or single rows, from four to six feet apart, according to the different heights they may be expected to grow. If two drills be made three inches deep, and about nine inches apart, and the seed dropped along each drill moderately thick, they will yield better than single rows, and will save sticks. When the plants are two or three inches high, let them be hoed, drawing, at the same time, a little earth up to their stems. When they get to double that height, let them be hoed again. At the same time place a row of sticks or brush in the middle of your double rows, and a few shorter and smaller ones on the outside of each row, to assist the Peas in climbing to their main support. You must be governed as to the length of your sticks by the description of your Peas. There is great advantage in having sticks of a suitable height to the various kinds of Peas. The sticks should not only be sufficiently tall, but also branchy, that the plants may readily take hold; and they should be prepared fan-fashion, so that the side branches may extend only along the rows. As the plants progress in growth, let them be repeatedly hoed and earthed up; this will promote a plentiful bearing.

One quart of Peas will plant from one hundred and fifty to two hundred feet of row, allowing the largest kinds to average one inch apart, and the smallest two Peas to the inch.

To have green Peas in perfection, they should be gathered while young, and cooked immediately after they are shelled, or they will soon lose their color and sweetness. Let the water be slightly seasoned with salt, and boiled; then put in the Peas with a small bunch of Spearmint, and ease the cover so as to let off the steam. They require about fifteen minutes boiling, or five minutes more or less, according to the age and care bestowed.

FORCING PEAS IN HOTBEDS.

The best kinds of Peas to force, are those that are the most dwarfish, as they will bear earlier, and make less straw. Peas run less to vine by being transplanted, than when they are sown where they are to remain; and the plants may be raised in a hotbed, or in pots or boxes. They do not require excessive heat, the temperature must be progressive, beginning at about 50° for the nursery-bed, and from that to 60° or 65° for fruiting. When the leaves of the plants are fairly expanded, they may be transplanted into rows from twelve to eighteen inches apart; and the earth in the fruiting-bed should be from twelve to eighteen inches in depth.

As the Peas progress in growth, the earth should be stirred; and when six inches high small sticks may be applied, so that the tendrils of the Peas may easily take hold; and they should be moulded at the bottom. to enable them to support themselves. When they are in blossom pinch off the top. This will greatly promote the forming and filling of the pods. In dry weather Peas will require to be regularly watered; and as the spring advances, they may be exposed to the weather. Should cold storms occur, the tender vines must be protected with wide boards placed edgewise on both sides of the rows, and a board over the top until the weather has become warm. Such shields should be placed around other tender plants, when the weather is cloudy and cold, as they will grow more rapidly in a place where there is but little light, than when exposed to the light of day, chilling winds, and cold storms, with no sunshine. Cold winds and storms frequently chill plants so that they never recover.

POTATO.

POMME DE TERRE. *Solanum Tuberosum.*

The Potato is known to be a native of the southern parts of America, but has been greatly improved by cultivation. The varieties being very numerous, it is unnecessary to point out any particular kinds; some of the earliest should, however, be planted first in the spring, to produce young Potatoes in due season; but they are not so suitable for a full crop as the late varieties.

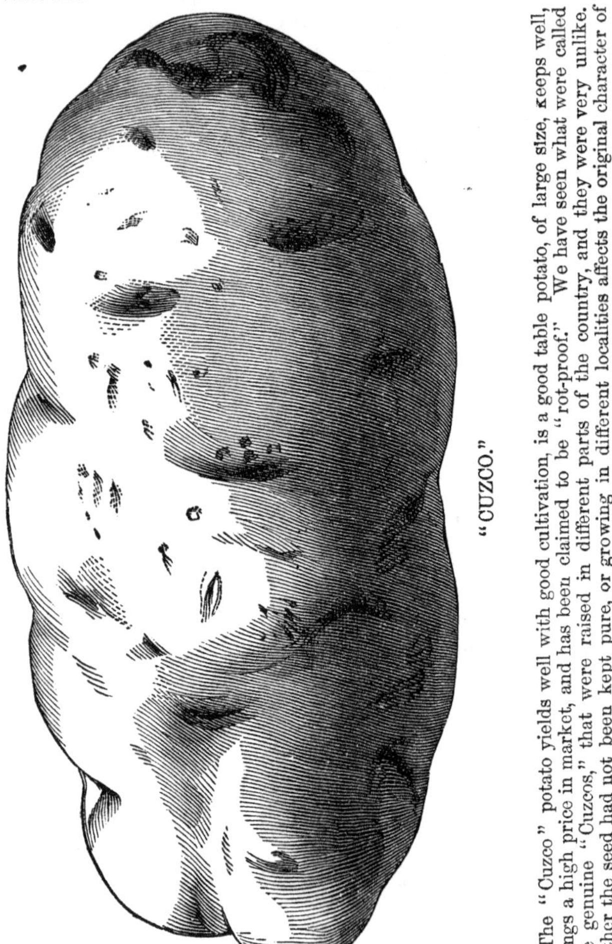

"CUZCO."

The "Cuzco" potato yields well with good cultivation, is a good table potato, of large size, keeps well, brings a high price in market, and has been claimed to be "rot-proof." We have seen what were called the genuine "Cuzcos," that were raised in different parts of the country, and they were very unlike. Either the seed had not been kept pure, or growing in different localities affects the original character of the potato.

Potatoes being of such extensive utility, various expedients have been contrived with a view to find out the best method of preparing the seed. In many parts of England (where Potatoes equal to any in the world are raised), the farmers seldom plant them whole; they take the Potatoes as they come to hand, and in cutting them, take care to have two good eyes in each set; the small Potatoes are deprived of the sprout or nose-end, as it is generally considered that a redundancy of eyes exhausts the set, and produces weak plants, which are not calculated to yield a full crop. I have frequently known from five to six hundred bushels raised from an acre with small Potatoes alone cut in this way. Some prefer planting the sets immediately after they are cut. The better way is to get them cut a week before the time of planting, and to lay them out on a barn or garret-floor to dry.

It will require from twelve to sixteen bushels of Potatoes to plant an acre of ground, according to the size and nature of the seed-roots, the manner of preparing, and mode of planting the same.

Potatoes may be planted from the first week in April until July, either in hills or drills; the best way for a gardener is to plant them in drills four or five inches deep, and about thirty inches asunder. The sets may be dropped six or eight inches apart; and if a small quantity of comb-maker's horn shavings, bone-dust, or sea-weed, be used as a manure for the early kinds, it will expedite their growth. The ground should be hoed as soon as the plants come up, and a few times after this. Level cultivation is better than hilling.

"HOW TO RAISE LARGE CROPS OF POTATOES.

"It is desirable, not only to get the best varieties for seed, but to know how to plant them and to raise the largest and best crop.

"The method I pursue, and which pays better, *far better*, than any of the old systems generally practised, is as follows:

"1. In the fall plough *deeply* and subsoil plough, in all eighteen to twenty inches in depth.

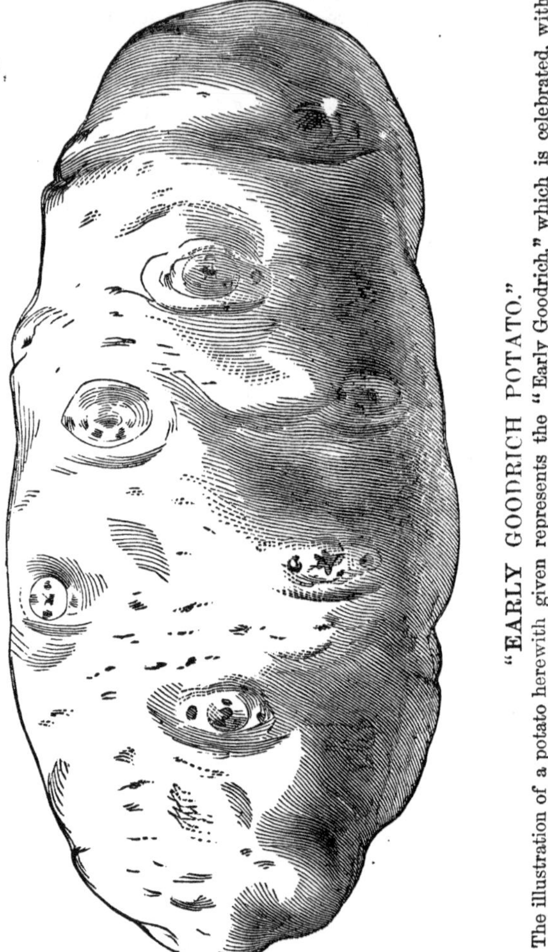

"EARLY GOODRICH POTATO."

The illustration of a potato herewith given represents the "Early Goodrich," which is celebrated, with superior cultivation, for being very early, large, white skin, smooth eyes, white flesh, of first quality, perfectly sound, solid to the core, keeps well, and is highly productive. Average yield on good rich soil, 300 bushels per acre. This and the following illustrations of potatoes were prepared by Mr. A. W. Harrison, of Philadelphia, a distinguished potato amateur. We furnish a fair idea of his mode of raising potatoes.

"2. In early spring, plough and subsoil across the winter furrows; harrow and roll.

"3. Mark out, as for corn, three feet apart each way, opening the furrows eight inches deep.

"4. At the intersection drop a *whole* potato, *the largest you have*, and spread upon it a handful (about forty bushels per acre) of a compost made of eight parts of wood-ashes, four of bone phosphate of lime, four of fine-ground plaster, two of finely slaked lime, and one of salt; or, if preferred, three ounces of artificial fertilizer per hill. Then cover, roll, and spread 1,000 lbs. per acre of good artificial fertilizer.

"5. As soon as the young plants appear, run the cultivator close to and between, but *not over* them, in each direction. Afterwards, and *before* the weeds come up, cultivate, both ways, with Knox's horse-hoe—so arranged as to cut as shallow as possible, and keep the surface *entirely flat.* Repeat this, at short intervals, three times. Then hand-hoe three times, still keeping a flat surface. Allow no hilling at any time, nor any weeds to grow.

"6. As soon as the tops are dead, dig in clear dry weather with heavy five-tined digging forks; spread, under cover, to dry, and store in a cool, dark, dry, airy cellar, spreading half a pint of freshly-slaked lime in powder on each bushel of potatoes.

"7. Gather and compost the dry tops, for application next autumn; then plough and subsoil-plough as before, for next year's crop.

"The following are the advantages of this system of cultivation:

"1. No possible entire failure of the crop.

"2. No rot in healthy varieties.

"3. The largest yield the soil and variety are capable of.

"4. The largest proportion of large potatoes.

"5. No degeneracy of varieties, but continued improvement.

"6. No necessity for rotation of crops: the potato can be thus grown almost indefinitely on the same land, with, perhaps, at long intervals, a seeding to clover to maintain the supply of vegetable fibre in the soil.

"7. No loss by late spring frosts. If the early growth is cut off, the dormant eyes will grow and the crop be saved.

"8. The greatest economy of culture and harvesting.

"9. The highest table quality of potato.

"If the materials for the compost cannot be obtained, top-dress heavily in the fall, after ploughing, with barn-manure, but never use it in the season of planting. It may increase the crop, but tends to engender disease, especially in wet seasons.

"Any further information on the subject will be cheerfully furnished on application.

"*If you wish liberal crops you must give liberal culture.*"

FORCING POTATOES IN HOTBEDS.

Potatoes may be forced in a great variety of ways. Those who attempt to mature Potatoes in frames, will of course provide such of the earliest kinds as are not inclined to produce large tops. Potatoes may be forwarded in growth previous to being planted in the beds, by placing them in a warm, damp cellar. Some forward them in pots and boxes, and afterwards mature them in a hotbed; others plant them in the bed at once, in which case the bed should be moulded from fifteen to twenty inches deep, and the heating materials should be sufficient to keep up a moderate heat for several weeks.

Perhaps the most convenient way to force Potatoes in this climate, is to provide pots for the purpose, and plant one set in each pot, and place them in a warm cellar till a bed can be prepared. While the tuberous roots are forming, and before they fill the pots, prepare the beds for maturing them, and then bury them in the mould with the balls of earth attached to them.

The beds should be kept free from frost, and air should be given at every opportunity. The common round Potatoes may be forwarded, by laying them thick together in a slight hotbed in March, and when they are planted in the borders, a quantity of comb-maker's shavings may be deposited in each hill; this will greatly promote their growth.

POTATO-GROUND MARKER.

The accompanying illustration represents a gauge-marker, for marking out either potato ground or corn ground. It is drawn bv two horses, and makes three marks at one through. The

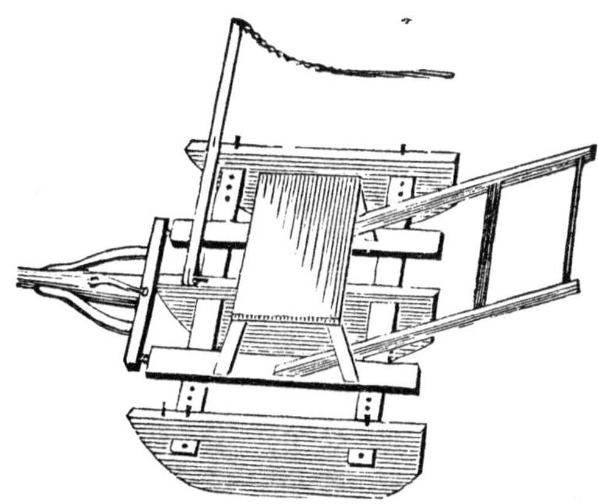

three runners are each about four feet long, eight inches wide, and two inches thick. The two outside runners can be moved towards or away from the middle runner, and secured to the slats that extend through all the runners. The slats are four inches wide, of hard wood, and one inch thick. A wooden pin secures them rigidly in the middle runner, and iron pins in the outside runners. A tongue belonging to some light carriage can be used with such a marker. The braces of the tongue are secured to raves bolted to the slats, as shown by the figure. It can be constructed with a seat, or not. On sod ground a seat will be necessary, as the weight should be increased in order to make a plain mark. The illustration will show how the handles are to be attached. The gauge-marker has a small chain attached to the outer end, which should run in the last mark made by the runner. When the marker is turned around, the gauge is laid over on the other side of the marker.

TRUE'S POTATO PLANTER.

The illustration herewith given represents a machine for making the furrow, cutting the potatoes, dropping the pieces,

covering the seed, and rolling the ground, all at one operation, in a workmanlike manner. It was invented only a few years since, by J. L. True, Garland, Maine. We have seen it operated with one horse, where it planted potatoes with great dispatch and accuracy. Where a farmer plants several acres of potatoes, such a planter will relieve workmen of much hard labor.

A STEEL CULTIVATOR TOOTH.

The following illustration represents one of the best kinds of cultivator teeth that we have ever met with for cultivating potatoes. They are bolted to the wood-work of cultivators, with strong bolts passing through the iron flanges or palms on the upper end of the standard. The steel plates are bolted to the cast-iron standards. When the earth is to be turned towards the growing plants, the teeth are attached with the steel plates or mould-boards outwards. If it is desirable to turn the earth inwards, or away from the plants, the teeth are taken off the cultivator and bolted to the opposite side. Such

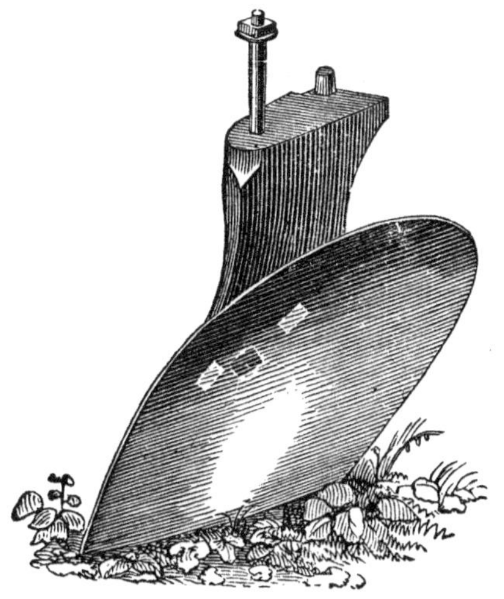

teeth can be obtained of the inventor, M. Alden & Son, Auburn, N. Y., or of Paschall Morris's Agricultural Works, 1120 Market street, Philadelphia, Pa.

HILL'S POTATO-DIGGER.

The illustration on the next page represents a two-horse potato-digger, recently invented by Rev. J. J. Hill, Xenia, Ohio. We saw the first one that was ever made, in operation on Long Island, in the fall of 1865. It works well, and has been thoroughly perfected by the proprietor, R. H. Allen, 189 Water street, New York City. Those farmers who raise large quantities of potatoes will find this a great labor-saving implement.

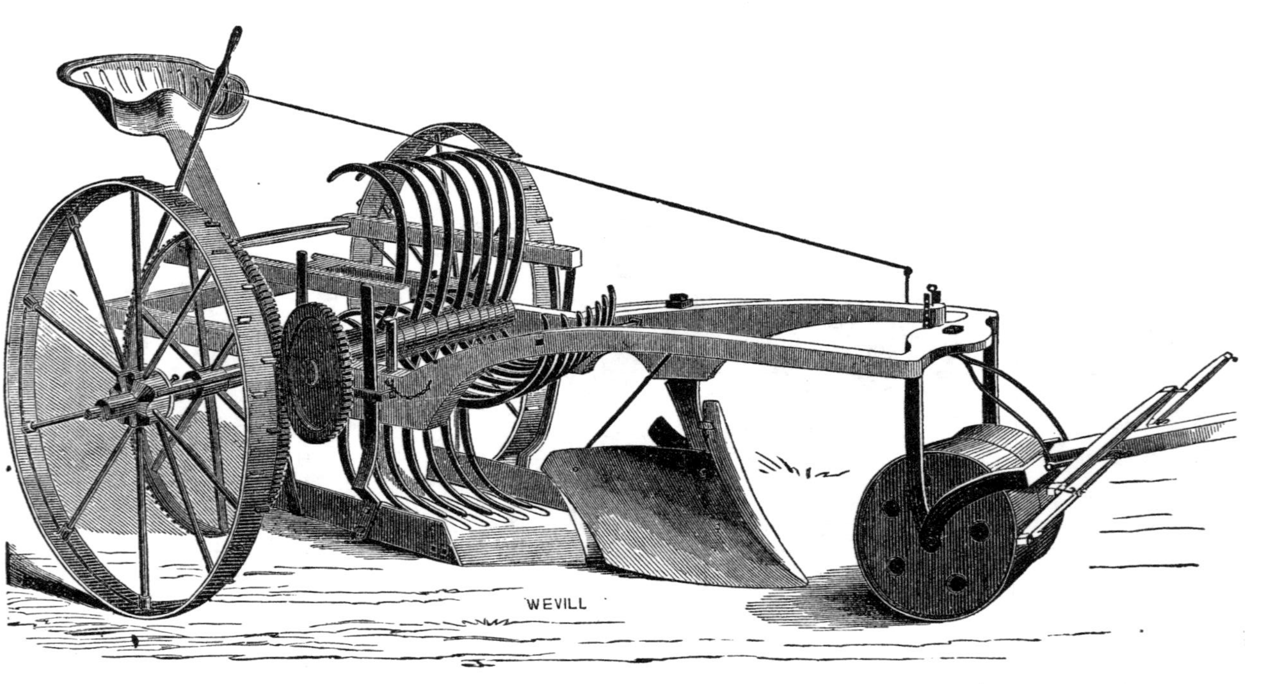
WEVILL

SWEET POTATOES.

POMME DU TERRE DOUCE. *Convolvulus batatas.*

Sweet Potatoes are grown to great perfection in the Southern States, and may be raised in the vicinity of New York, by means of a moderate hotbed, in which they should be planted whole early in April, three or four inches deep, and about the

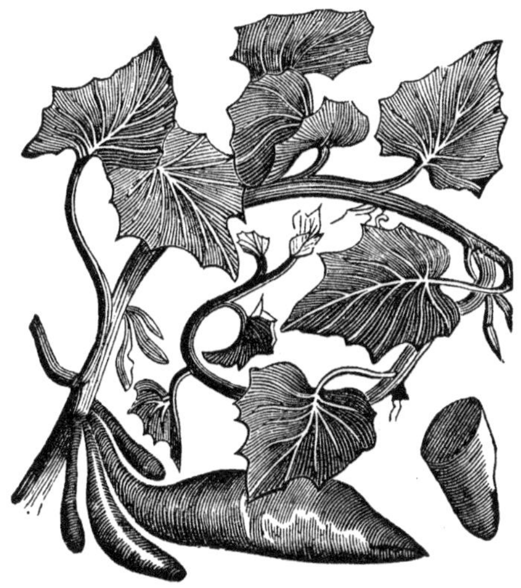

same distance apart. In about a month they will throw up sprouts. When these are three inches above ground, part them off from the Potato, which, if suffered to remain, will produce more sprouts for a successive planting. Transplant the sprouts into rich light soil, in rows four feet apart, and the plants about a foot apart in the rows, or in hills four feet apart. Keep them clear of weeds until the vines begin to cover the ground, after which they will grow freely. In sandy ground it is well to put a shovelful of rotten manure to each plant. A moderate hotbed five feet square, put down early in the month of April, with half a peck of good sound Sweet Potatoes placed therein, will produce a succession of sprouts in May and June, which, if planted and managed as directed, will yield about fifteen bushels of good roots.

PUMPKIN.

Citrouille ou Potiron. *Cucurbita pepo.*

This plant is highly deserving of cultivation, particularly in new settlements. The large sorts are profitable for cattle, as some of the mammoth tribe have been known to weigh upwards of two hundred pounds each. The other kinds are very productive, and may be raised on any waste land. They are generally raised on cultivated farms, between hills of Indian-corn, and may be planted in the garden or open field in May and June, in hills eight or ten feet apart, with three or four seeds in each hill.

One quart of Field Pumpkin-seed will plant from five to six hundred hills. An ounce of the finer kinds will plant from fifty to eighty hills. The finest quality of Pumpkins are known to make good pies, and may also, after being boiled, be worked up with wheaten flour into bread, for which purpose they are fully equal to Indian-meal. The knowledge of this fact may prove advantageous to farmers living at a distance from cities, as they may find a market for their grain or meal readier than for their Pumpkins.

There is a vast difference in the quality of Pumpkins. Some are very coarse-grained, spongy, very watery when cooked, and make exceedingly poor pies; while others are rich, fine-grained, cook dry and mealy, and require but little or no sweetening. Pumpkins of a mammoth size are seldom as good as small ones.

The way to raise good Pumpkins is, to procure and plant none but the best seed. Never plant seed that has been taken from Pumpkins of poor kind. Pumpkins will hybridize, even when they grow several rods apart. Hybrids are always poor. The seed is unfit to plant, as they will not produce excellent Pumpkins. Those seeds sold in markets are seldom reliable. When an excellent Pumpkin is found, dry the seeds with care, and plant a few hills in one corner of a large field, far away from other vines, and continue to save the seeds of the best specimens which the vines produce for several years. After a few seasons, an excellent variety will be obtained; and if the seeds be planted on rich ground, not among growing crops, very large crops may be grown with little labor. When Pumpkins are raised among Indian-corn, it is impossible for them to grow as large and fair as if the vines were not shaded. Moreover, the crop of corn will not be as large, when the soil produces a heavy crop of Pumpkins.

One of the best ways of raising a crop of Pumpkins is, to stick the seed one in a place, eight feet apart in every fourth row of Potatoes, soon after the rows appear. The crop of Potatoes will come to maturity before the Pumpkin-vines have become so large as to shade a large proportion of the ground.

Radish. Radis ou Rave. *Raphanus sativus.*

The different varieties of Radish are extensively cultivated near large cities, chiefly for their roots, which are considered a luxury after a hard winter, and prove acceptable as warm weather approaches, provided they can be obtained in perfection. The plant is also cultivated for the sake of the seed-leaves, which are used as a small salad; and even the seed-pods, if pickled while young and green, are considered by some a good substitute for Capers.

Those who may be desirous of having good Radishes early in the spring, should have a warm border prepared in the very best manner, so as to be ready to sow some of the seed as early in the spring as the seed will vegetate. If the ground should not be in good condition to receive the seed at this time, let it be delayed a few days; and by the first of April have another bed prepared in the open ground, by working in some strong well rotted manure. The seed may be sown broadcast, and raked in evenly, or in drills drawn about one inch deep, and a foot apart.

If you wish to have Radishes in regular succession, sow seed of the most esteemed varieties every two weeks, until the middle of June. If any be sown after this, it should be the seed of those that will endure the heat better than the others, and may be sown in drills, in small quantities, throughout the summer until the latter part of August, when all the varieties may be sown in regular succession till the first of October.

Radishes must have a sandy or loamy soil. It is folly to attempt to raise them on heavy soils, even when such ground is extremely rich. For family use, a load or two of sand may be mingled with a small area of ground in a warm corner of the garden, and made fertile with rich liquid manure a few weeks or more before the seed is planted. A shield on the north side of the bed, made of boards nailed to stakes four or more feet high driven in the ground temporarily, will break off the cold wind, reflect the warm sunshine on the bed, and make the Radishes grow long before other plants appear. In order to have excellent Radishes, save and plant only the largest, earliest, and fairest seed.

It may be necessary here to remind the gardener of the necessity of sowing tobacco-dust, soot, ashes, etc., over his seed-beds, in hot, dry weather, or he will find it difficult to raise Radishes in unpropitious seasons.

FORWARDING RADISHES.

Radishes may be obtained early in the spring by means of a moderate hotbed. The earth in the frames should be a foot in depth, and air should be admitted every day after they are up, or they will incline more to tops than roots. If they come up too thick, they should be thinned to one or two inches apart. Give gentle waterings as occasion requires, with tepid water, and keep them well covered in cold nights. For raising early Radishes without frames, hotbeds may be made in ridges, and arched over with hoop-bends, or pliant rods, which should be covered with mats or canvas cloth at night, and during the day in cold weather. In moderate days turn up the covering; and on fine mild days, take it wholly off, and harden the plants gradually to the weather.

In order to have tender Radishes, it is essential that they be made to grow rapidly. When they grow slowly, and the weather is cold, Radishes are tough and stringy.

ROCAMBOLE.

AIL D'ESPAGNE. *Allium scorodoprassum.*

This and the *Allium sativum*, or common Garlic, are raised in some gardens. Many people consider the Rocambole to be of a milder and better flavor than Garlic, but the bulbs are not so large. The plants are hardy, and will grow in almost any rich soil or situation. They may be propagated either by the roots or seed. The former ought to be separated and planted at the same time, and in the same manner as Shallots. If raised from seed, they may be sown in drills, either shortly after the seed is ripe, or in the succeeding spring. The plants require to be kept clear of weeds; and in the following autumn may be taken up, the bulbs parted, and planted as before.

RHUBARB.

RHUBARBE. *Rheum.*

Rhubarb is a genus of exotic plants, comprising seven species, of which the following are the principal:

1. *Rhaponticum*, or Common Rhubarb, a native of Thrace and Syria, has long been cultivated in British gardens for the footstalks of the leaves, which are frequently used in pies and tarts.

2. *Rheum undulatum* is also cultivated for the same use.

3. The *Palmatum*, or true Officinal Rhubarb, is a native of China and the East Indies, whence its culture has been introduced into Europe. It produces a thick, fleshy root, externally yellowish brown, but internally of a bright color, streaked with red veins. The several kinds of Rhubarb may be propagated by offsets taken from the roots early in the spring, or from seed sown early in autumn, or in March and April, in drills one inch deep and a foot apart. The indispensable points to the production of good roots of the *Palmatum*, are depth and richness of soil, which should be well pulverized before the plants are set out. Prepare beds of fine mould eighteen inches deep, in which set the plants from the seed-bed, ten or twelve inches apart. This must be done when they have attained the height of four or five inches, and have thrown out as many leaves.

The first season is the most critical, and more care is necessary. If the weather be hot, the nursery must be shaded, and at all events frequently watered; for water, though hurtful to old plants, is now of the first importance. Wet weather is the most proper time in which to plant. The beds must be kept free from weeds during the summer, and on the approach of severe weather, covered up with light litter. In the early part of spring, this must be taken off; and in the beginning of April the plants must be transplanted into rich ground.

Those who cultivate the *Palmatum* for the sake of the roots, should dig the ground two or three spades deep, and place the plants three feet apart every way. As to the other varieties, it is not so particular, only the plants must have room in which to grow. In the early part of November, the leaves being then decayed, the beds should be covered with dry litter. Before this is done, a little earth should be drawn round the crowns of the plants. If there be any danger of water lodging make trenches to carry it off. The beds should be stripped of their covering, and the ground well hoed and cleared of weeds. The roots of the *Palmatum* must not be taken up until six or seven years old. The stalks of the other kind may be cut every spring, as soon as the leaves are expanded.

If Rhubarb stalks be required for use early in spring, they may be obtained by placing flour barrels or deep tubs over some of the plants, and covering them up with fresh stable dung, or by any of the methods pointed out in the article under the head of Forcing Vegetables. The stalks of this plant are used for pies and tarts. After being stripped of the skin, or outer covering, and divested of the small fibres, or stringiness to which the plant is liable in an advanced stage of growth, the stalk should be cut transversely into very small pieces, and then parboiled with sugar, and such spices as best suit the palate. Rhubarb may be kept in this way as well as other preserves, and may be used not only in pies and tarts, but will make an excellent pudding, which is done by flattening a suety crust with a rolling-pin, then spreading on the fruit, rolling it up in an oval shape, and boiling it in a cloth. Prepared in this way, the fruit retains its virtues, and the pudding may be served up hot, in slices from half an inch to an inch thick, with butter and sugar spread between the layers. Some boil the stalks to a juice, which being strained through a colander, will keep for years if well spiced and seasoned with sugar.

After the roots have been well washed, and the small fibres cut off, they are to be cut transversely into pieces about two inches thick, and dried on boards, turning them several times a day, in order to prevent the escape of the yellow juice, on which its medicinal qualities depend. In four or five days the pieces may be strung upon strings, and suspended in a shady but airy and dry situation, and in two months afterwards will be fit to dry.

FORWARDING RHUBARB.

Those who may desire to have this excellent substitute for fruit at an early season, may procure it without much trouble. It is customary with some persons in the southern parts of England to keep this plant growing in their kitchens, so that they may have it for use at any time. They have strong neat boxes, made for the purpose, about three feet deep and two wide, and in length, according to the demand, from four to eight feet; these being kept clean, have the appearance of flour-bins, and they sometimes are so contrived as to have shelves over them in imitation of a kitchen dresser. The plants being taken up out of the garden towards winter, are placed as close to the bottom of the box as they can be, with their crowns level; and some sand being thrown over, sufficient to fill up the interstices, and to cover the crowns about half an inch, finishes the operation. No further trouble is necessary, except to give a little water, just to keep the roots moist, as they need no light at all; and if the roots be planted in the garden when the spring opens, they will, after having taken root, vegetate as strongly as before they were removed.

Roots of Rhubarb, taken up in autumn and packed in sand, and deposited in a warm cellar, will produce stalks earlier than if kept in the garden; and if placed in hotbeds they will yield abundantly early in the season.

This plant contains an acid as fine as the Gooseberry, for pies and tarts. A square rod of ground will supply a family; and it may be used till midsummer or later.

SALSIFY.

Salsifis ou Cercifis. *Tragopogon porrifolius.*

This plant grows spontaneously in the open fields of England, and is by some highly valued for its white edible root, and for the young shoots rising in the spring from plants a year old. These, when gathered while green and tender, are good to boil and eat in the same manner as Asparagus. Some have carried their fondness for this plant so far as to call it Vegetable Oyster. It requires the same kind of soil and management as Carrots and Parsnips.

The seed should be sown early in the spring, an inch deep, in drills twelve inches apart. When the plants are two or three inches high, they should be thinned to the distance of six inches from each other, and afterwards hoed. The ground should be kept clean and loose around the plants by repeated hoeing. In the autumn they will be fit for use. The roots may be taken up late in autumn, and secured in moist sand from the air; or suffered to remain out, and dug up when wanted. As the seeds of Salsify do not all ripen uniformly, it should be sown moderately thick, and none but the earliest sowed.

The mode of cooking recommended by an American author is, "To cut the roots transversely into thin pieces; boil them in water, or milk and water; when boiled soft, mash them, and thicken the whole with flour to some degree of stiffness; then fry them in the fat of salt pork or butter." To some they are a luxury. In England the tops are considered excellent food when boiled tender, and served up with poached eggs and melted butter. They are by some considered salutary for persons inclined to consumption.

SCORZONERA.

SCORSONERE. *Scorzonera Hispanica.*

This plant has long been raised in British gardens, for culinary purposes, and especially as an ingredient in soups, on account of its palatable and nourishing roots. Some boil and eat them like Carrots, in which case they should be deprived of their rind, and immersed in cold water for half an hour, or they will be bitter. They are raised precisely in the same manner as Salsify. If the seed be sown early in the spring in a good deep soil, the roots will attain perfection in autumn, and continue good all the winter. They last from three to four years, according to the quality of the earth and the care bestowed upon them; but it is better to raise a few from seed every year.

SEA-KALE.

CHOU MARIN. *Crambe maritima.*

This plant is found on the sea-shore, in the southern parts of England, where it grows spontaneously. As soon as it appears above ground, the inhabitants remove the pebbles or sand with which it is usually covered, to the depth of several inches, and cut off the young and tender leaves and stalks, as yet unexpanded and in a blanched state, close to the crown of the root. It is then in its greatest perfection. When the leaves are full-grown, they become hard and bitter, and the plant is not eatable. Cultivators have differed widely respecting the mode of treating this plant; many, conceiving that stones, gravel, and sea-sand are essential to its growth, have gone to the expense of providing them; but it has been discovered that it will grow much more luxuriantly in a rich sandy loam, where the roots can penetrate to a great depth.

The seed of Sea-Kale may be sown in October, or as early in the spring as the ground can be brought into good condition, in drills an inch and a half deep, and fourteen or sixteen inches asunder. The plants should afterwards be thinned out to the distance of six or eight inches from each other in the rows, and kept clear of weeds by frequent hoeing through the summer. When the plants are a year old, every third row may be taken up, and also every other plant in each row, leaving them fourteen or sixteen inches apart; these may be transplanted into good ground prepared as directed for Asparagus. Plant two rows in each bed, about eighteen inches apart. The best way is to make two drills three inches deep, and with a dibble set in the plants fifteen or sixteen inches from each other; when these drills are filled, the crowns of the plants will be covered nearly two inches, but they will soon push through the earth. The plants left in the seed-bed may form a permanent bed, which should be forked or dug between the rows. Previous to this being done, lay on an inch or two of good rotten manure, and incorporate it with the earth around the plants. Some make new plantations of the old roots, which should be cut up into pieces of about two inches in length, and planted three or four inches deep, at the distance before directed for the plants. At the approach of winter, the leaves will die away and disappear. The beds should then be thickly covered with dung, leaves, or sea-weed. This will not only protect the plants from frost, but will cause them to shoot up early in the spring. As soon as the frost is out of the ground, this may be taken off; or, if well rooted, it may be mixed up with the earth. The crowns of the plants should then be covered to the depth of ten or twelve inches for blanching.

Some blanch it by heaping on it sea-sand; some common sand and gravel; and others with large garden-pots, inverted and placed immediately over the plants. If these pots be covered up with fresh horse-dung, it will forward the shoots in growth, and make them sweeter and more tender. When the plants have been covered in either method three or four weeks, examine them, and if you find that the stalks have shot up three or four inches you may begin cutting. Should you wait till all the shoots are of considerable length, your crop will come in too much at once, for in this plant there is not that successive growth which there is in Asparagus. You may continue cutting until you see the heads of flowers begin to form; and if at this time you uncover it entirely, and let it grow to that state in which Broccoli is usually cut, and use it as such, you will find it an excellent substitute; and this greatly enhances the value of the plant. Sea-Kale is sufficiently hardy to bear our winter frosts without much injury. Care should be exercised not to weaken the roots too much by over-cutting for in that case it would injure their next year's bearing. Some of the shoots should be allowed to grow, to carry on a proper vegetation, and strengthen and enlarge the roots. Great care should be taken in cutting, not to injure the crowns of the roots by cutting the shoots too close to them. Sea-Kale should be dressed soon after it is cut, as the goodness of the article greatly depends on its not being long exposed to the air.

If you choose to force Sea-Kale, dig a trench all around a small bed, about three feet wide, and thirty inches deep; fill it with hot dung, and as it sinks, fill the depression with good soil. This will make the plants grow luxuriantly. To have this rare vegetable in perfection, it should be cooked as soon as gathered. Let it be first soaked in water, seasoned with salt, for half an hour; then wash it in fresh water, and put it into the cooking utensils; keep it boiling briskly, skim clean, and let off steam. When the stalks are tender, which may be expected in from fifteen to twenty-five minutes, according to size and age, take it up, dish it, and serve it up with melted butter, gravy, and such condiments as are most agreeable to the palate.

SKIRRET.

CHERVIS, OU GYROLE. *Sium sisarum.*

This plant is first propagated by seed, and afterwards by offsets taken from the old roots, planted early in the spring, before they begin to shoot. But it is best to raise a small bed from seed every year, as the roots grow longer than those raised from slips, and are less liable to be sticky. The seeds may be sown in drills the latter part of March, or early in April, and managed the same as Salsify or Parsnip. In autumn, when the leaves begin to decay, the roots are fit to use. Skirrets should be planted in a light, moist soil; for in dry land the roots are generally small, unless the season proves wet.

The root of the Skirret is composed of several fleshy tubers as large as a man's finger, and joined together at the top. They are eaten boiled, and stewed with butter, pepper, and salt, or rolled in flour and fried, or else cold, with oil and vinegar, being first boiled. They have much of the taste and flavor of a Parsnip, and are by some considered more palatable.

SHALLOT.

ECHALOT. *Allium ascalonicum.*

The true Shallot is a native of Palestine, and possesses an agreeable flavor; it is propagated by planting bulbs, or offsets, in the fall of the year, which may be set out with a dibble, in rows twelve inches apart, and from four to six inches distant in the rows; or they may be placed in drills, two or three inches deep, and covered up.

Those intended for seed may remain in the ground until June or July; after the tops have decayed the bulbs must be taken up, and the offsets divided; these should be kept in a dry place to plant the ensuing autumn.

SPINACH, OR SPINAGE.

EPINARD. *Spinacia.*

The *Spinacia oleracea*, or common Spinach, is very hardy, and consequently a very important vegetable for cold climates. It merits attention from its being extremely wholesome and palatable, and from its keeping green even after having been cooked. It makes a delicious dish when served up with the gravy of roast meat, melted butter, etc.

As Spinach is the only vegetable which can be raised to advantage near the close of the growing season, the gardener should prepare such grounds as may have been occupied by summer crops; and by having it well manured for this crop, the soil will be in good condition for Beets, Carrots, Parsnips, Turnips, etc., the spring following. If the ground be prepared so as to have several beds sown in succession, from the first to the end of September, the most forward of these, if covered up with straw at the approach of cold weather, will furnish greens for the table when other vegetables are scarce, and the later crops will recover from the effects of a hard winter, and produce a wholesome vegetable early in the spring.

If Spinach-seed be sown in rich ground in March and April, it will grow freely; but it must be cut before the approach of hot weather, or it will run to seed. To raise it in perfection at this season, it should be sown in drills about a foot apart, and be frequently hoed. This will keep it in a growing state, and consequently prevent its running up to seed as quick as it otherwise would.

It is altogether useless to sow Spinach-seed in poor ground. Let the ground be well manured, and the crop will be abundant. Be careful to pick Spinach exceeding clean, and wash it in five or six waters previous to cooking. Some cook Spinach in a steamer over boiling water. Others boil it in water. But the best way is to put it into a saucepan that will just hold it, without water, then strew a little salt upon it, and cover it close. Put the saucepan on a clear quick fire; and when you find the Spinach shrunk and fallen to the bottom, and the juice which comes from it boil up, it is done. In order that it may be rendered capable of absorbing a moderate quantity of gravy, melted butter, etc., which are indispensable with green vegetables, let it be well drained in a sieve, or colander, before it is dished.

SQUASH.

GOURDE GIRAUMON OU POTIRON. *Cucurbita melopepa.*

The several varieties of Squash are very useful in this and other warm climates, as they can be grown in perfection in the summer, and therefore prove a good substitute for Turnips. The seed should be planted in May and June, in hills, prepared in the same manner as for Cucumbers and Melons; and their subsequent management is the same in every respect. The bush kinds should be planted three or four feet apart, and the running kinds from six to nine, according to their nature, as some will run more than others. It is always best to plant five or six seeds in a hill, to guard against accidents; as when the plants are beyond danger they can be thinned to two or three in a hill.

The fruit of the Early Summer Squash is generally gathered for use before the skin becomes hard, and while it is so tender as to yield to the pressure of the thumb-nail. The winter Squashes should be allowed to ripen, and collected together in October, before they are injured by hard frosts.

All kinds of Squashes should, after having been boiled tender, be pressed as close as possible between two wooden trenchers, or by means of a slice or skimmer, made of the same material, until dry, and then prepared for the table in the same manner as Turnips.

In order to raise excellent Squashes, good seed is essential, and rich ground and clean cultivation are indispensably necessary. The seeds should be selected from a ripe and good Squash, and not from a hybrid. Manure may be applied in the hill. If the soil be heavy, let a few shovelfuls of sand be mingled with the soil, where each hill is to grow. When the vines grow rampantly, pinch off the ends of each as soon as they have grown as far from the hill as it is desirable for them to spread. There is nothing gained, but much lost, by allowing the main vines and branches also to attain a great length.

Pull off all the Squashes but two or three on each vine. One good squash is better than three or four of an inferior quality and size.

HOW TO EXTERMINATE THE GRUB.

Many times, when the vines are a few feet long, and young Squashes have appeared, grubs may be found in the middle of the vines, near the root. Sometimes I have found six white grubs, more than an inch long, in a single vine. They bore into the vines an inch or two above the surface of the ground; and the holes may be discovered readily, as foam and fecal matter are constantly being worked out by the worms.

In order to dislodge the grubs, thrust a thin blade of a sharp knife through the vine, and split it open so that the grubs can be discovered and killed. This is the only effectual way to raise Squashes when the grub attacks the vines. Laying the vine open will not injure it.

TOMATO.

TOMATE, OU POMME D'AMOUR. *Solanum lycopersicum.*

The Tomato, or *Love-Apple,* is much cultivated for its fruit, which is used in soups and sauces, to which it imparts an agreeable acid flavor. It is also stewed and dressed in various ways, and is considered very wholesome. The seed should be sown early in the spring, in a hotbed, and the plants set out in the open ground, as soon as the ground has become warm. In private gardens, it will be necessary to plant them near a fence, or to provide trellises. They may be planted four feet distant from each other every way Tomatoes may be brought to perfection late in the summer, by sowing the seed in the open ground the first week in May. These plants will be fit to transplant early in June, and the fruit may ripen in time for preserves or catsup.

MANNER OF PRESERVING TOMATOES.

Tomatoes may be preserved in a stone or glazed earthen pot, for use in the winter, by covering them with water in which a sufficient quantity of salt has been dissolved to make it strong enough to bear an egg. Select perfectly ripe berries, and cover the pot with a plate in such a manner that it will press upon the fruit without bruising it. Previous to cooking these Tomatoes, they should be soaked in fresh water for several hours. Besides the various modes of preparing this delicious vegetable for the table, it may be preserved in sugar, and used either as a dessert or on the tea-table, as a substitute for peaches or other sweetmeats. It also makes good pies and tarts, and excellent catsup.

A celebrated writer observes, that "the common Tomato made into a gravy, by stewing over the fire, and used as a sauce for meat, has been known to quicken the action of the liver and of the bowels better than any medicine he ever made use of; and when afflicted with inaction of the bowels, headache, a bad taste of the mouth, straitness of the chest, and a dull painful heaviness of the region of the liver, the whole of these symptoms are removed by Tomato sauce, and the mind, in the course of some few hours, is put in perfect tune."

HOW TO MAKE CATSUP.

To make catsup, use one pint of salt to one peck of Tomatoes. Bruise, and let them stand two days; then strain them dry, and boil the juice, until the scum ceases to rise, with two ounces of black pepper, the same quantity of pimento or allspice, one ounce of ginger, one of cloves, and half an ounce of mace. Tomatoes are excellent raw, cooked with toasted bread, or eaten in any other way. When I see a dish of luscious peaches and delicious tomatoes side by side, I am in doubt as to which I really like the best, when eaten raw.

TURNIPS. NAVET. *Brassica rapa.*

The turnip is a wholesome and useful plant for both man and beast, and eminently worthy of cultivation.

"Until the beginning of the eighteenth century, this valuable root was cultivated only in gardens, or other small spots, for culinary purposes; but Lord Townsend, who attended King George the First in one of his excursions to Germany, in the quality of Secretary of State, observing this root cultivated in open and extensive fields, as fodder for cattle, and spreading fertility over lands naturally barren, on his return to England brought over some of the seed, and strongly recommended the practice which he had witnessed to the adoption of his own tenants, who occupied a soil similar to that of Hanover. The experiment succeeded; the cultivation of Field Turnips gradually spread over the whole county of Norfolk, and has made its way into every other district of England. Some of the finest grain crops in the world are now growing upon land which, before the introduction of the Turnip husbandry, produced a very scanty supply of grass for a few lean and half-starved rabbits."

Mr. Colquhoun, in his "*Statistical Researches*," estimated the value of the Turnip crop annually growing in the United Kingdom of Great Britain and Ireland, at fourteen million pounds sterling (equal to upwards of SIXTY MILLIONS OF DOLLARS). But when we further recollect, that it enables the agriculturists to reclaim and cultivate land which, without its aid, would remain in a hopeless state of natural barrenness; that it leaves the land clean and in fine condition, and also insures a good crop of Barley, or of Clover; and that this Clover is found a most excellent preparative for Wheat, it will appear that the subsequent advantages derived from a crop of Turnips must infinitely exceed its estimated value as fodder for cattle.

The preceding remarks show the kind of land that may be made capable of producing not only Turnips, but other things of equal value. It must, however, be granted, that some soils naturally suit particular kinds of vegetables better than others; yet, as we have not always a choice, if the soil is light and altogether not suitable for vegetables in general, two crops of Turnips may be grown in one year by sowing seed for the first crop early in the spring, and for the second about the first of August. For general crops, it will be better to have ground manured with short, rotten dung, or compost containing a considerable portion of coal, wood, peat, or soapers' ashes. Most ground that has been well manured for preceding crops, and recently broken up, will do well for Turnips, when there is not an excess of clay and water. If the seed for the first crop be not sown soon enough to mature early in July, the roots are seldom fit for the table, being stringy and wormy; and if the seed intended for a crop for autumn and winter use is sown before August, unless it be a very favorable season, even if they escape the attack of insects and reptiles, the turnips often are defective and unpalatable.

To have turnips in perfection, they must be hoed and thinned out as soon as the leaves are as large as a cent, leaving the best plants from six to nine inches apart. The roots will be better, and the crops greater, if thinned out properly, than if the plants are allowed to grow so closely together that the leaves override and the roots crowd each other.

It is generally admitted that one pound of Turnip-seed is amply sufficient for an acre of ground, yet it is better to use considerably more, because of the difficulty of distributing so small a quantity of seed regularly broadcast. This difficulty is, however, obviated by sowing the seed in drills; and although drilling-in the seed may seem a tedious process to those who have no other means of doing it than by hand, the facilities thus afforded of hoeing between the rows, more than compensate for the extra labor.

I once induced a friend of mine to sow four ounces of Turnip-seed in August, in drills a foot apart, by which means he made it extend over more than half an acre of land; and by hoeing the plants twice, he had the gratification of pulling four hundred bushels of handsome Turnips, which is more than is generally taken from an acre of land cultivated in the ordinary way.

If seed of the Russia or Swedish Turnip be sown in drills, any time in the month of July, or even early in August, they will produce fine roots towards the end of October, provided the land be rich and sandy, or a light loam and the cultivation be thorough. This kind of turnip must be hoed and thinned to the distance of twelve or fifteen inches from each other. If cultivated in the field, frequent cultivation between the rows will be beneficial, and cause the plants to grow luxuriantly.

With many persons the Turnip is a favorite vegetable. In England, a leg of mutton and caper sauce is considered, by epicures, as but half a dish without mashed Turnips. To cook them uniformly, they should be cut in pieces of equal size, after they are pulled, and after being boiled tender, let them be taken up and pressed as dry as possible; at the same time, let a lump of butter and a due proportion of Cayenne-pepper and salt be added, and beaten up with the Turnips until properly mixed. Use the natural gravy from the meat unadulterated, and such condiment as may be most esteemed.

REPELLING THE TURNIP-FLY.

Previous to sowing Turnip-seed, the gardener should procure a suitable quantity of lime, soot, or tobacco-dust, so as to be prepared for the attacks of insects. Turnip-seed will sometimes sprout within forty-eight hours after it is sown; and frequently whole crops are devoured before a plant is seen above ground. A peck of either of these ingredients, mixed with about an equal quantity of ashes, or even dry road-dust, scattered over the ground, morning and evening, for the first week after sowing the seed, will be sufficient for an acre of ground, provided the composition be used in such a way that the wind will carry it over the whole plot. But as the wind often changes, this end may be effected by crossing the land in a different direction each time, according as the wind may serve. If gardeners who raise Radishes, Cabbage, and such other vegetables as are subject to the attacks of insects, were to pursue this course, they would save themselves from considerable loss.

When ashes and other dust is being scattered over Turnips, the work should be done by a careful laborer, who will not walk on the rows of young Turnips, and thus destroy hundreds of plants where they are already standing too far apart. When the seed is put in with a suitable seed-drill, the roller usually marks the place where the young plants may be found.

We have always found that unleached wood-ashes, sifted thinly over the drills soon after the seed was put in, would repel the Turnip-fly most effectually. As the fly is ready for the young plants as soon as the first tender leaves appear, ashes must be sowed before the Turnips have come up, or the crop may be lost. A thin sprinkling is sufficient. If unleached ashes be applied too abundantly, the alkali will destroy the young plants as soon as sufficient moisture comes in contact with the ashes to dissolve it.

AROMATIC, POT, AND SWEET HERBS.

GRAINES D'HERBES AROMATIQUES, ODORIFERANTES, ET À L'USAGE DE LA CUISINE.

Angelica, Garden,	*Angelica atropurpurea.*
Anise,	*Pimpinella anisum.*
Basil, Sweet,	*Ocymum basilicum.*
Borage,	*Borago officinalis.*
Burnet, Garden,	*Poterium sanguisorba.*
Caraway,	*Carum carui.*
Chervil, or Cicely the Sweet,	*Scandix odorata cerefolium.*
Clary,	*Salvia sclarea.*
Coriander,	*Coriandrum sativum.*
Dill,	*Anethum graveolens.*
*Fennel, Common,	*Anethum fœniculum.*

*Fennel, Sweet,	*Anethum dulce.*
Marigold, Pot,	*Calendula officinalis.*
*Marjoram, Sweet,	*Origanum marjorana.*
*Mint, Spear,	*Mentha viridis.*
*Mint, Pepper.	*Mentha piperita.*
*Mint, Pennyroyal,	*Mentha pulegium.*
*Sage, Common,	*Salvia officinalis.*
*Sage, Red,	*Salvia clandestinoides.*
Savory, Summer,	*Satureja hortensis.*
*Savory, Winter,	*Satureja montana.*
*Tarragon,	*Artemisia dracunculus.*
*Thyme, Common,	*Thymus vulgaris.*
*Thyme, Lemon,	*Thymus serpyllum.*

Aromatic Herbs are such as impart a strong spicy odor and savory taste; many of them are used as small potherbs, and for sauces, stuffings, and other uses in cooking. As only a small quantity of these are necessary in private gardens, a by-corner may be allotted for them, and such medicinal herbs as may be wanted in a family.

It may be necessary to explain, as we go along, that there are three principal descriptive names given to plants—namely, Annuals, Biennials, and Perennials. The Annuals being but of one season's duration, are raised every year from seed. The Biennials are raised from seed one year, continue till the second, then perfect their seed, and soon after die; some of these should also be raised every year from seed. The Perennials may be raised from seed; but when once raised, they will continue on the same roots many years. Those marked * are Perennials, and may be propagated by suckers, offsets, cuttings, or parting the roots. The seed of any of the different kinds may be sown early in spring, in drills about half an inch deep, and twelve inches apart, each kind by itself. The plants may afterwards be transplanted into separate beds; or, if a drill for each kind be drawn two feet apart, the seed may be sown in them, and the plants afterwards thinned out to proper distances, according to the natural growth of the different kinds.

Some of the kinds alluded to in the List will spread very

rapidly, and occupy the entire ground, if not kept within proper bounds. To prevent Caraway, Spearmint, Peppermint, or any other plant from spreading, sink boards edgewise eight inches in the ground, entirely around the plot where such plants stand. Then destroy every plant that appears outside of its proper limits. Save a small quantity of the earliest, largest, and fairest of the panicles for seed, and keep the seeds in small papers in open boxes in some out-building where they will be dry and away from mice. When kept in a store-room the vitality of the seed is frequently destroyed by being dried to death.

PLANTS CULTIVATED FOR MEDICINAL AND OTHER PURPOSES.

GRAINES DE PLANTES MEDICINALES.

Bene,	*Sesamum orientale.*
Boneset or Thoroughwort,	*Eupatorium perfoliatum.*
*Balm,	*Melissa officinalis.*
Bean, Castor Oil,	*Ricinus communis.*
Burdock,	*Arctium lappa.*
Catnip,	*Nepeta cataria.*
Celandine,	*Chelidonium majus.*
*Chamomile,	*Anthemis nobilis.*
*Comfrey,	*Symphytum officinale.*
*Elecampane,	*Inula helenium.*
Feverfew,	*Chrysanthemum parthenium.*
*Horehound,	*Marrubium vulgare.*
*Horsemint,	*Monarda punctata.*
*Hyssop,	*Hyssopus officinalis.*
*Lavender,	*Lavandula spica.*
Lovage,	*Ligusticum levisticum.*
*Mallow, Marsh,	*Althea officinalis.*
*Motherwort,	*Leonurus cardiaca.*
*Patience Dock,	*Rumex patientia.*
*Pinkroot, Carolina,	*Spigelia Marylandica.*
Poppy Opium (annual),	*Papaver somniferum.*

*Rosemary,	*Rosmarinus officinalis.*
*Rue, Garden,	*Ruta graveolens.*
Saffron, Bastard,	*Carthamus tinctorius.*
Skullcap, or Mad-Dog Plant,	*Scutellaria lateriflora.*
Snakeroot, Virginian,	*Aristolochia serpentaria.*
*Sorrel,	*Rumex acetosella.*
*Southernwood,	*Artemisia abrotanum.*
*Speedwell, Virginian,	*Veronica Virginica.*
*Spikenard,	*Aralia racemosa.*
*Tansy,	*Tanacetum vulgare.*
*Wormwood,	*Artemisia absinthium.*

Many of the foregoing plants are useful, and may be raised in a small plot of ground appropriated especially to their production. Some of the plants in this list are considered noxious weeds; and all the seed should be gathered and destroyed, except so much as it is desirable to save. It is by no means difficult to keep each kind of these plants on a small plot by itself, as stated on a previous page.

The best time to save plants for medicinal purposes is when they are in full bloom. Spread the stems and leaves on a shelf, or floor, until they are quite dry; then they may be wrapped in papers, or pulverized by rubbing between the hands until thoroughly pulverized, when the powder may be kept in tin or other boxes properly labelled.

FORCING VEGETABLES.

Before I proceed to show the method of forcing vegetables, it may be necessary for me to remind my readers, that in providing an artificial climate, they should consider the nature of the plants they intend to cultivate, and endeavor to supply them with that which is best calculated to nourish and support them. I have, in another part of this work, endeavored to show that heat, light, air, and moisture, are each essential to vegetation, and that these should be supplied in a judicious manner, according to circumstances.

In the midst of our Northern winters, which is the usual time for forcing in England, we are subject to north-west winds, which produce extreme freezing. Now, as we have not yet discovered how to make an artificial air, it will not be safe for the gardener to raise a bottom heat under any kind of vegetable until such time as he can impart a tolerable share of salubrious air, as the heat without air will soon destroy the fruits of his labor.

I shall not attempt to treat of the cultivation of Pineapples, Grapes, Cherries, or other fruits grown in forcing-houses; nor would it be advisable with us to undertake to raise Cucumbers, Melons, etc., in frames throughout the severe winters of our Northern States; but it must be acknowledged that the extreme heat of our summers is as detrimental to the cultivation of some of the most valuable kinds of fruits and vegetables, as the coldness of our winters; and for these reasons, artificial aid is more necessary here in the winter and spring of the year than in England, where a supply of the different varieties of Artichokes, Broad Beans, Borecole, Broccoli, Cauliflower, Kale, Lettuce, Radishes, Rhubarb, Spinach, Turnips, and salads in general, is easily obtained, a great part of the year, from their kitchen-gardens; whereas, if we were to attempt to supply our markets with culinary vegetables at all times, in anything like the abundance that they have them there, we must, out of the ordinary seasons for gardening operations, turn our attention to the protecting and forwarding as well as the forcing system.

The frame being set over the pit, and properly fastened, the fresh dung should be spread regularly in the pit to the depth of twenty or twenty-four inches; if the dung be in a good heating condition, cover it six or eight inches deep with mould, then lay on the ashes, and protect the beds from the inclemency of the weather. In two or three days the rank steam will pass off; it will then be necessary to stir the mould before the seed be sown, to prevent the growth of young weeds that may be germinating; then sow the seed either in shallow drills or broadcast, as equally as possible, reserving a small quantity of the warm mould to be sown lightly over the seed. The beds should afterwards be attended to, as directed for Broccoli and Cauliflower.

The depth of heating materials must be regulated by the season of the year at which the work is commenced, and also to the purposes for which the hotbeds are intended. Beds used for the purpose of raising half-hardy plants, or for procuring seedling-plants late in the spring, may be made in the manner recommended for the common hotbed; but if substantial heat is required to be kept up, the beds must be so contrived as to admit of linings as the heat decreases; and the dung should undergo a regular process of preparation, according to the use it is intended for. Compost heaps should also be provided, in order to furnish suitable mould to the different species of plants; for this purpose, all the old hotbed dung and mould, leaves, tan, turf, sand, and other light manures and decayed animal dung, should be collected together.

In some cases, when a slight hotbed is recommended for forwarding hardy plants, if it should happen that a seedling Cucumber-bed be at liberty, it may answer every purpose for Radishes, Lettuce, or other hardy plants; or such a bed may be spawned for Mushrooms, if required.

If the forcing be commenced before the coldest of the winter is past, great precaution must be used, lest the plants be injured by cold cutting winds, or destroyed by heat for want of air. To prevent the former accident, warm dung should be placed around the frames, and the sashes covered with mats and boards every night. If full air cannot be admitted in the daytime, the sashes must be slidden down to let off the steam; at the same time mats may be laid over the aperture, to prevent cold air entering to the plants.

If the bottom heat in a bed be too violent, which is sometimes the case, means must be used to decrease it. This is generally effected by making holes in the bed with a stake sharpened at the end, or with a crowbar; and filling the holes with water until the heat is sufficiently reduced. In lining hotbeds, if the heat is reduced in the body of the beds, holes may be carefully made to admit heat from the fresh linings, so as to enliven the heat of the bed.

A thermometer should always be at hand at the time of forcing, to be used, when necessary, to regulate the heat in the beds; and the water that is used to plants cultivated in frames, should be warmed to the temperature of the air, or according to the heat required for the various kind of plants.

FORCING ASPARAGUS IN HOTBEDS.

As Asparagus is apt to grow weak and slender by extreme bottom heat, it is forced with greater success, and with less trouble, in flued pits in a hot-house, than in dung hotbeds, because the heat from tan is more regular; yet a suitable bed may be formed in a deep hotbed frame, made in the usual way. If dung alone, or a mixture of dung and leaves be used, it should be in a state past heating immoderately before it is made into a bed.

For the purpose of keeping up a regular heat, a lining of hot dung should be applied around the frame, and changed as occasion requires.

If there be a strong heat in a bed, slide down the sashes till it begins to decline. The temperature at night should never be under 50°, and it may rise to 65° without injury; when the buds begin to appear, as much air must be daily admitted as the weather will permit. In two or three days after the beds are planted, the heat will begin to rise, when the beds should have a moderate supply of water, applied from a watering-pot with the rose attached, and repeated every three or four days.

A frame of ordinary size, calculated for three sashes, will hold from three to five hundred plants, according to their age and size; and will, if properly managed, yield a dish every day for about three weeks. On the above estimate, if a constant succession of Asparagus be required, it will be necessary to plant a bed every eighteen or twenty days.

Rhubarb and Sea-Kale may be, and sometimes are, forced in

the same manner as Asparagus ; but the most general mode is to excite them where they stand in the open garden, by the application of warm dung, and a shield made of boards four feet high to protect the young plants from the cold winds.

INDEX.

A.

B.

C.

H.

I.

J.

K.

L.

M.

N.

O.

P.

R.

S.

T.

V.

Y.

PART II.

FRUIT-GARDENING.

CHAPTER I.

SELECTING FRUIT-TREES IN THE NURSERY.

In the choice of fruit-trees, all possible care and attention are necessary; for, to have trees that do not answer the expectations of the proprietor, is a great disappointment. As the young gardner may need such directions calculated to govern him in his choice, I shall endeavor to furnish them. Whatever species or varieties of fruit-trees are wanted, choose those trees that are vigorous and straight, and of a healthy appearance. Whether they have been grafted or budded, be careful to select such as have been worked on young stocks. Grafts and buds inserted into old, crooked, stunted stocks, seldom succeed well. Trees that are healthy, have always a smooth, clean, shining bark. Such as are mossy, or have a rough, wrinkled bark, or are the least affected by canker, should be rejected. Canker is discoverable in the young wood, and generally two or three inches above the graft or bud. If the tree be an Apricot, Nectarine, Peach, or Plum, and any gum appears on the lower part of it, do not fix upon that. Let the tree you select (if a dwarf) be worked about six inches from the ground, and only one graft or bud should be upon each stock; for when there are more, the tree cannot be brought to so handsome a form.

In some of the following articles, it will be seen that several descriptions of trees may be transplanted with safety, even when far advanced in growth. When trees of four or five years' growth, after having been headed down, that are healthy, and well furnished with fruit-bearing wood close up to the centre of the tree, can be obtained, they will do very well; but great care is requisite in taking up, removing, and planting such. Let the tree be taken up with as great a portion of the roots as possible, taking care not to bruise, split, or damage them; for want of attention to these points, trees often become diseased. Whenever any roots have been accidentally broken, split, or otherwise damaged in taking up the tree, let them be cut off; or if they cannot be well spared, let the damaged or bruised part be pared clean with a sharp knife, and a portion of grafting-wax be spread over the wound, in order to keep the wet from it, which would otherwise injure the tree.

The necessity of pruning-in and dressing mangled roots is particularly required in trees of the stone fruit, such as Apricots, Nectarines, Peaches, and Plums; for without the application of some remedy, they gum at the roots, which defect, if not counteracted, very materially injures the upper part of the trees, which may become so affected as never to recover afterwards; therefore, great care should be taken not to occasion such injury; and when accidents happen, all due caution and application are necessary to promote a healthy and vigorous growth.

A young tree, likely to do well, should have roots nearly corresponding to the branches; at least, it should have one strong root in a similar proportion to the bole of the tree, with a proper distribution of branching fibres. Healthy roots are always smooth and clear; their color varies a little according to the kind of tree; but the older the roots are, the darker the color is.

After the tree is taken up, be careful, in conveying it to the place where it is to be planted, that the roots are not chafed or rubbed. If trees are to be conveyed to a considerable distance, they should be well guarded by straw, or otherwise, in order to prevent injury. All damaged or bruised roots should be pruned, as soon as the tree is taken up; but if it be necessary to prune away any sound, good roots, such pruning should be delayed until the time of planting. In pruning away roots, always let them be finished by a clear cut, and in a sloping direction. When trees are planted at an advanced season in the spring of the year, it will be necessary to prune the tops; and if trees are removed that have been trained three or four years, and are not properly supplied with young wood, they must be cut down either wholly or partially, in order to obtain a sufficiency. In practising this upon Apricot and Nectarine trees, always prune so as to have a leading shoot close below the cut, as it is very rare they will push a shoot below, unless there be a lead. This attention is not so particularly required in the Pear, as such will generally push forth shoots, although no leading ones are left; but in all kinds, the younger the wood is, the more certainly are shoots to be produced. If a tree that has been under training for one or two years, should only have one strong, leading shoot, and two or three weaker ones which do not proceed from it, let the weak shoots be pruned clean away, and shorten the strong one, from which a handsome head may afterwards be formed. For further directions as respects pruning or planting fruit-trees, the reader is referred to the succeeding articles on these subjects.

DESCRIPTIVE LIST OF FRUIT.

In order to assist the reader in making a judicious selection of fruit-trees, I have furnished a short description of such species and varieties as are in great repute for every good quality. Previous to making this selection, I carefully perused Prince's Pomological Manual, Kenrick's American Orchardist, Lindley's Guide to the Orchard and Fruit Garden, and Manning's Descriptive Catalogue of Fruits. Besides these important guides, I had the select catalogues of different nurserymen before me, and have chosen such only as have been most generally recommended. In doing this, I have had difficulties to contend with, of the nature of which none but those who have duly considered the subject can form any idea. The facility with which seedling plants are raised, and the paternal fondness with which people are apt to regard their own seedlings, have occasioned hundreds of names to appear in the various catalogues, which tend not a little to swell the large and increasing list of fruits.

In many instances, the English, French, Spanish, and other names, provisional, local, and barbarous, are given to the same variety; consequently, some fruits appear in the different catalogues under all the varied names; and the patience and labor necessarily requisite for ascertaining which are really distinct varieties, and which are most worthy of cultivation, are correspondingly great.

To exemplify: Suppose from a catalogue of Pears the following names should be selected by a person wishing to plant as many varieties in his orchard—namely, BROWN BEURRE, *Beurre Gris*, *Beurre Rouge*, *Beurre Dore*, *Beurre d'Anjou*, *Beurre d'Or*, *Beurre d'Ambleuse*, *Beurre d'Amboise*, *Poire d'Amboise*, *Isambert*, *Red Beurre*, *Golden Beurre*, *Beurre du Roi*, WHITE DOYENNE, *Doyenne Blanc*, *Doyenne*, *Beurre Blanc*, *Bonne-ante*, *Saint Michael*, *Carlisle*, *Citron de Septembre*, *Kaiserbirne*, *Poire à court queue*, *Poire de Limon*, *Valencia*, *Poire de Neige*, *Poire de Seigneur*, *Poire Monsieur*, *White Beurre*. Here is a list of twenty-nine kinds, as the purchaser supposes, but when the trees produce their fruit, he finds, to his great disappointment and mortification, that he has only two varieties, namely, the Brown Beurre and the White Doyenne.

In making out the descriptive lists, I have generally adopted the names given in the catalogues of the most celebrated nurserymen, as a heading; and have caused the synonymes, or names by which the same variety is known, or has been called, to be printed in *italics;* thus, my lists of about four hundred varieties of the various kinds of fruit, will embrace what has been deemed by some as different varieties, perhaps to the number of nearly two thousand.

In preparing the following articles, the object has been to furnish information which would entertain as well as instruct the reader. Besides the authorities quoted, I have gleaned from those inexhaustible treasures to horticulturists, Loudon's Encyclopædia of Plants, and that of Gardening; but on account of the brevity necessarily observed throughout this work, it has been found impracticable to give many entire extracts. Suffice it to say, that the historical facts are generally collected from these sources.

TRAINING AND PRUNING FRUIT-TREES AND VINES.

In training and pruning fruit-trees and vines, particular attention is required. To supply a tree with a sufficiency of vegetable juices, there must necessarily be living bark and wood in an uninterrupted succession from the root to the extremities of the branches. Pruning, therefore, is useful to remedy any defect, as well as to take off superfluous wood, and prevent unnecessary waste of the sap. Pruning may be performed at different seasons of the year, according to the kinds of fruit, which will be shown under each head as we proceed.

In the spring or summer pruning, be careful not to destroy the germs of future fruits; but merely remove all unserviceable sprigs. In the winter season, make your selection from the wood-shoots of the preceding year; and keep those which appear the most healthy, and cut away those which seem redundant. Beginners had better prefer the spring, as the buds will then be a guide for them to go by. But this business must not be delayed too late in the season, as some kinds of trees and vines are apt to bleed from being pruned untimely. When the sap rises in Grape Vines, before the wound is healed, bleeding ensues, and it is not easily stopped. When this happens, sear the place, and cover it with melted wax, or with warm pitch spread upon a piece of bladder; or peel off the outside bark to some distance from the place, and then press into the pores of the wood a composition of pounded chalk and pitch, mixed to the consistence of putty. Vines will bleed in autumn as well as in spring, though not so copiously. The best preventive is timely or early pruning in the spring, and not pruning until the wood is thoroughly ripe in autumn.

With respect to the manner in which vines, and some particular kinds of trees, should be trained, opinions are at variance. Some advise training the shoots in a straight and direct manner, others in a horizontal manner, and others again in a serpentine form, etc. If vines be trained on low walls or trellises, the horizontal or zigzag manner of training may be adopted. Horizontal training is that in which from a main stem lateral branches are led out horizontally on each side.

It has been remarked, that in order to be a good trainer of vines, a man must have some forethought, and be capable of making his selection as the plants shoot. He must predetermine how he shall prune, and where he shall cut at the end of the season; and so, as it were, fashion the plants to his mind. He has this more effectually in his power, with respect to the vine, than fruit-trees with fruit, on account of its rapid growth

PRUNING THE VINE.

In pruning vines, cut generally two inches above the bud. Some cut nearer, even as near as half an inch, which is apt to weaken the shoot of next season, and sometimes to prevent its vegetating at all; the buds being very susceptible of injury, on account of the soft and spongy nature of the wood. In cutting out old wood, be careful to cut in a sloping direction, and to smoothe the edges of the wood, in order to prevent its being injured by moisture. The pruning being finished, let the loose, shreddy, outward rind on the old wood be carefully peeled off, observing not to injure the sound bark, and clear the trellis of branches, leaves, and tendrils. Let the shoots and branches afterwards be regularly laid in, at the distance above specified, particularly the young shoots that are expected to bear next season. As to others, it is not so material how near the young shoots be placed to the old, even though they sometimes cross them. Choose strands of fresh matting, or packthread, to tie with; and observe to leave sufficient room for the swelling of the shoots and branches next season.

Vines may be pruned too much as well as too little. There is nothing gained by training vines very high. A vine ten

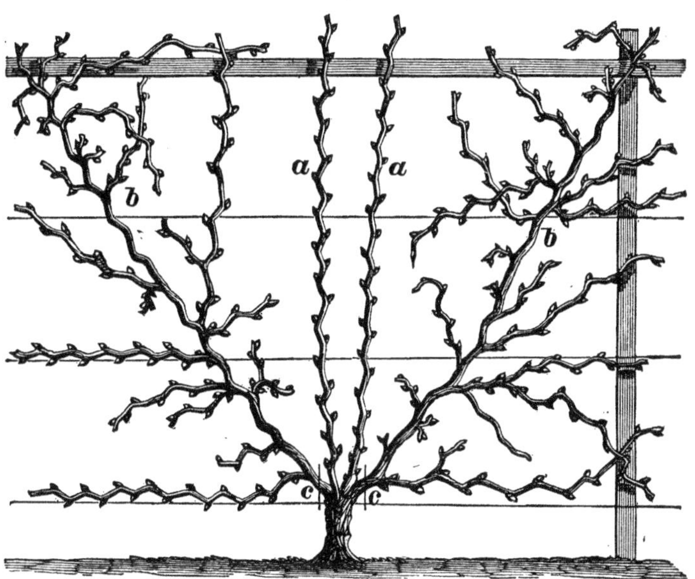

Training a Vine Fan-Shaped.

feet high will be as productive as one forty feet high. The illustration herewith given will furnish an idea of the manner of cutting off the old wood, at *cc*, and throwing all the sap into two vertical canes, *aa*. Or the tops may be cut off at *bb*, and the laterals trained horizontally at pleasure.

PRUNING FRUIT-TREES.

By attending to the proper training of fruit-trees, every advantage is promoted; and by a judicious management in other respects, wood may not only be obtained, but preserved in every part of the tree, so that it will bear fruit to the very bole, which will evidently be greatly to the credit of the gardener, the benefit of the proprietor, and equally conducive to the beauty and welfare of the tree. While trees are young, it is necessary to lay a good foundation for a supply of bearing-wood in future years; for when this is neglected, and they become naked, it is some time before a supply can be recovered. In shortening a branch, always take care to cut in a direction a little sloping; and the middle of all standard trees should be kept as open as possible. It is requisite to have a very sharp knife, that the cut may not be ragged, but clean; and in the operation be careful that the knife does not slip, so that another branch be cut or damaged.

The general pruning of fruit-trees is indifferently performed by many persons, at any time from autumn to spring; and it may be so done without any great injury to them, provided mild weather be chosen for the purpose, and the wood be well ripened. Although it may be advantageous to prune trees early in the winter, when the wood is well ripened, yet, when the wood is green and the buds have not arrived at a mature state, it is requisite in such cases to defer pruning until spring; taking care, however, that it is performed before the moving of the sap. The necessity of this arises from the circumstance that as the wood is not ripened in autumn, the sap is then in an active state, and will continue so until the frost causes it to become stagnant; and if the shoots were shortened while the sap was in motion, the buds would be considerably injured, and the tree weakened. Such unripe shoots are also more liable to suffer by the severity of winter; and wnen the pruning is deferred until spring, all such parts as may have been affected by the weather can be removed to the extent to which the damage has been sustained. As the pruning of such unripe wood in the autumn would be inju rious, so it frequently is when it is done during winter; and the more so according to its severity; because, whenever a cut is made on such green wood, the frost generally affects it, as the sap is not so dense, nor the wood so firm, as to be able to resist the intense cold.

DIFFERENT MODES OF TRAINING.

Whatever method is adopted in training trees, care should be taken to keep the two sides as nearly equal as possible; this may easily be done, whether they are trained in the fan or horizontal method. For espalier trees, the horizontal method has many advantages over any other. The small compass within which the trees are obliged to be kept, requires such a direction for the branches, in order to make them fruitful; and were very high trellises formed, so as to admit of the trees being trained in the fan method, such would be very objectionable, by reason of the shade they would cause, and the trees would also be deprived of the benefit of a warmer temperature, which those less elevated receive.

As some young gardeners may not know what is meant by espaliers, it may be necessary to explain that espaliers are hedges of fruit-trees which are trained up regularly to a frame or trellis of wood-work; they produce large fruit plentifully, without taking up much room, and may be planted in the Kitchen-Garden without much inconvenience to its other products. For espalier fruit-trees in the open ground, a trellis is absolutely necessary, and may either be formed of common stakes or poles, or of regular joinery work, according to taste or fancy.

Standard trees should be pruned low. An excellent mode of pruning is to imitate the cherry-tree, which sends a stem straight upwards, with boughs projecting laterally, on every side, at distances of two or three feet apart. The boughs also should have limbs at suitable distances apart. All the branches should not be cut off the limbs for several feet from the body of the tree, as many of our apple-orchards have been pruned. The entire area occupied by the branches should be well filled up with fruit-producing limbs. In order to do this, one must commence pruning trees when they are young, and prune a little every season, as the branches require. It is decidedly objectionable to allow trees of any kind to grow unpruned for several years, and then give them a severe pruning. Some trees need but little pruning; while others require more or less every year.

BEST TOOLS FOR PRUNING.

The implements employed in pruning, and the manner of using them, are matters of moment. If the operation is commenced when the tree is young, and judiciously followed up, a good knife, a small saw, a mallet, and a chisel fixed on a six-foot handle, to trim the tops and extremities of the branches, are all the tools that are required. A large saw will be occasionally wanted; but an axe or hatchet should never be employed, as they fracture the wood, bruise and tear the bark, and disfigure the tree.

BUDDING AND GRAFTING FRUIT-TREES.

Budding and Grafting, Lindley observes, are operations that equally depend for their success upon the property that buds possess of shooting roots downward, and stems upward; but in these practices, the roots strike between the bark and wood of the stock, instead of into the earth, and form new layers of wood, instead of subterranean fibres. The success of such practices, however, depends upon other causes than those which influence the growth of cuttings. It is necessary that an adhesion should take place between the scion and the stock so that when the descending fibres of the buds shall have fixed themselves upon the wood of the stock, they may not be liable to subsequent separation. No one can have studied the economy of the vegetable kingdom, without having remarked that there is a strong tendency to cohesion in bodies or parts that are placed in contact with each other.

To bud trees, let the following method be adopted: Procure a knife which has a thin blade; the use of the blade is to prepare the buds, and the handle is used to raise the bark of the stocks, so that the buds can be easily inserted. Have some good strong bass in readiness, and then take some good thrifty sprigs from healthy trees of the sorts you intend to propagate. When all is ready, make a cut in the bark of the stock transversely, and from the middle of this cut make another downward, at least two inches in length, so that the two cuts may be in the form of a T; then from one of your sprigs proceed with expedition to take off a bud. This is effected as follows: Insert the knife a little more than half an inch below the bud or eye, force it into the wood, drawing it under the bud, and cut the piece off across the shoot; then immediately let that part of the wood which was cut off with the bud be separated from it, which may be readily done with the knife, by placing the point of it between the bark and wood at one end, and, holding the bark in one hand, pull off the woody part with the other, which will readily come from the bark if the tree from which it was taken be in a vigorous condition. Examine the bark, so as to be satisfied that the bud remains perfect; if there is no hole in it, let it be immediately inserted into the stock, which is done by raising with the handle of your knife the bark of the stock downward on each side from the crosscut, and thrusting the bud in between the bark and the wood, applying it as close as possible. As soon as the bud

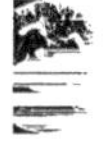

is put into its place, bind it securely with bass, beginning a little below the cut and proceeding upward till you are above the crosscut, taking care to miss the eye of the bud, just so that it may be seen through the bandage of the bass. About a week or ten days after the stocks have been budded, they should be examined, when such as have united will appear fresh and full, and those that have not taken will appear decayed. In the former case the bandage may be left off, and in the latter case, the stock may be budded in another place, provided the first operation was done in the month of July or early in August, as these are the two most preferable months for budding fruit-trees in general. Budding is, however, often attended with success, if done early in September.

SCALLOP-BUDDING

is performed by cutting from a small stock a thin narrow scallop of wood about an inch in length, and taking from a twig a thin scallop of wood of the same length; this is instantly applied, and fitted perfectly at top and bottom, and as nearly as possible on its sides, and firmly bound with wet bass matting. This may be performed in the spring, and if it fails, it may be done again in the month of July. The French practise this mode on Roses.

GRAFTING.

Grafting is the taking a shoot from one tree and inserting it into another in such a manner that both may unite closely and become one tree. These shoots are called scions or grafts, and in the choice of them and the mode of preparing some descriptions of stocks, the following hints will be useful:

Those scions are best which are taken from the lateral or

horizontal, rather than from the strong perpendicular shoots. The shoots of Apples, etc., should be taken from healthy trees late in autumn, or before the buds begin to swell in the spring, and buried half of their length in the ground or in a cool and dry cellar, there to remain until the season of grafting.

For some descriptions of trees the stocks are headed down near to the ground. In nurseries, Apples intended for standards are generally grafted about nine inches high only, allowing them to grow up standard high, and forming their heads upon the second year's shoots. In cider countries, the stock is generally trained up standard high; and when grown sufficiently large for the purpose, it is grafted at the height intended for the head of the tree.

There are various methods of grafting, but the following are those most generally practised.

CLEFT-GRAFTING.

This mode of grafting is generally practised on stocks of from one to two inches in diameter, and may be performed in the following manner: Let the head of the stock be carefully sawed off where the limb is free from knots, and the end pared smooth. Then with a thin knife, split down the stock through the centre to the depth of about two inches, and insert a chisel to keep it open for the reception of the scion, which must be prepared in the form of a wedge, with one or two buds in the upper part, and inserted carefully, so that the inner bark of the scion and of the stock may both exactly meet. Large stocks require two scions, one on each side, and sometimes four are inserted. When done, tie them firmly together with bass, and then cover the grafted part with well-prepared clay, in an oval form, and close it securely.

These directions apply particularly to small limbs or small trees. Those stocks that will pinch the grafts sufficiently tight as soon as the chisel is taken out, do not require any binding. When scions are set in large stocks, it is sometimes necessary to drive in a small wooden wedge to prevent the split stock from crushing the scion. A little caution must be exercised on this subject, to have the stock pinch sufficiently tight to hold the scions securely in the desired position, else they will not live. And if the scion be crushed by too severe pressure, it cannot be expected to live.

SIDE-GRAFTING.

This mode is sometimes practised on those parts of a tree where a limb is wanting. There are two ways in which it may be performed. 1st. The scion may be prepared in the same manner as for splice-grafting, and the bark and wood on the side of the stock cut sloping; the scion being then adjusted as carefully as possible, it must be bound on and covered with clay. 2d. The scion being cut sloping, a crosscut is to be made in the side of the tree on the top of a perpendicular slit; the bark of a tree above the crosscut must be pared down slanting to the wood, and the bark raised as in budding; the scion being then inserted, it must be bound fast, and covered with clay.

SPLICE OR WHIP-GRAFTING.

This mode is often practised on small stocks, and it succeeds best when the scion and stock are of an equal size. The scion, which should consist of young wood of the former year's growth, may be cut to the length of about four inches. This and the stock are each to be cut sloping for an inch or more, and tongued. Tonguing consists in cutting a slit in the middle of the slope of the stock downward, and a corresponding slit in the scion upward; both are now to be joined, so that one of the sides, if not both, shall perfectly coincide, and then securely bound with bass matting and covered with grafting-clay or composition. As soon as the scion and stock are completely united, the bass string may be removed.

SADDLE-GRAFTING.

The celebrated Mr. Knight practised this mode of grafting on very small stocks. The upper part of the stock is prepared in the form of a wedge, by two sloping cuts, one on each side. The scion is prepared by slitting it upward, and paring out the middle part on each side to a point. When the stock and scion are of equal size, the adjustment may be made perfect; but if unequal, one side must exactly meet. The whole is secured by a string of bass matting, and covered with composition or clay; but the string must be removed as soon as a perfect union has taken place.

ROOT-GRAFTING.

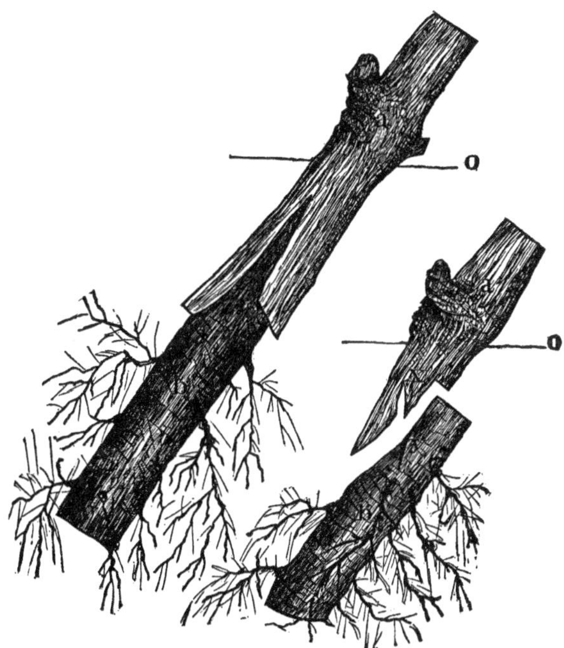

This operation is often performed on Grape-vines, just below the level of the surface, by the usual mode of cleft-grafting. It is also performed on portions or pieces of root where suitable stocks are scarce. The illustration on page twenty-three represents the usual mode of root-grafting. The lines O O represent the surface of the ground. The main thing in all kinds of grafting, is to made a " close fit" between the stock and the scion.

GRAFTING BY APPROACH.

The trees or shrubs to be grafted in this mode must be growing very near to those which are to furnish the grafts. The limbs or branches of each tree, which are thus to be united, must be pared with a long sloping cut of several inches, nearly to the centre; and the parts of each tree thus prepared are to be brought together, and finally secured by a bandage of matting, so that the bark shall meet as nearly as possible. The graft may then be covered with clay or composition; and when a complete union has taken place, the trees or shrubs may be separated with a sharp knife, by cutting off below the junction.

It may be here observed that, as young grafted trees in the nursery progress in growth, the lower side-limbs should be gradually shortened, but not suddenly close-pruned, as they are essential for a time to strengthen the trunks, and to the upright and perfect formation of the tree.

THE BEST TIME TO GRAFT.

The best time to graft Apple and Pear-trees is, when they are in blossom. At that time, sap flows most abundantly, wounds heal more readily, and the stock and scion are far more likely to unite than when the sap is not so abundant. I have always heard it remarked that Cherry-trees should be grafted before the buds begin to swell. But I have always had far better success with scions that were put in when the trees were about to blossom, than with the grafts that were set very early or before the growing season had commenced. The most important consideration is to have good grafts. More scions fail on account of having been injured by being improperly kept than from any other cause.

When beginners prepare the stocks and dress off the ends of the scions with a knife, the cut should be made with a sharp instrument, very true and smooth, and not too sharp-pointed nor too blunt, neither should the end of the scion be too thin nor too thick. If too thin, when the cleft stock closes on it, the scion will be crushed so that it cannot live. If the scion be too thick, the sharpened end will not fit the cleft sufficiently well for the sap to circulate from the stock into the scion. Whatever be the form of the scion, or the shape of the stock, the inside bark of each must be placed together, so that the sap from the stock may pass readily into the scion.

GRAFTING-CLAY AND WAX.

The British Parliament gave Mr. Forsyth a valuable premium for the following important directions for making a composition for curing diseases, defects, and injuries in all kinds of fruit and forest trees, and the method of preparing the trees, and laying on the composition:

Take one bushel of fresh cow-dung, half a bushel of lime rubbish of old buildings (that from the ceilings of rooms is preferable), half a bushel of wood-ashes, and a sixteenth part of a bushel of pit or river sand; the three last articles are to be sifted fine before they are mixed; then work them well together with a spade, and afterwards with a wooden beater, until the stuff is very smooth, like fine plaster used for ceilings of rooms.

The composition being thus made, care must be taken to prepare the tree properly for its application, by cutting away all the dead, decayed, and injured part, till you come at the fresh sound wood, leaving the surface of the wood very smooth, and rounding off the edges of the bark with a draw-knife or other instrument. Then lay on the plaster about an eighth of an inch thick, all over the part where the wood or bark has been so cut away, finishing off the edges as thin as possible. Then take a quantity of dry powder of wood-ashes mixed with a sixth part of the same quantity of the ashes of burnt bones; put it into a tin box with holes in the top, and shake the powder on the surface of the plaster till the whole is covered with it, letting it remain for half an hour to absorb the moisture; then apply more powder, rubbing it on gently with the hand, and repeating the application of the powder till the whole plaster becomes a dry, smooth surface.

If any of the composition be left for a future occasion, it should be kept in a tub or other vessel, and urine poured on it so as to cover the surface; otherwise the atmosphere will greatly injure the efficacy of the application. When lime-rubbish of old buildings cannot be easily got, take pounded chalk or common lime, after having been slaked a month at least. As the growth of the trees will gradually affect the plaster, by raising up its edges next the bark, care should be taken, when that happens, to rub it over with the finger when occasion may require (which is best done when moistened by rain), that the plaster may be kept whole, to prevent the air and wet penetrating into the wound.

As the best way of using the composition is found, by experience, to be in a liquid state, it must therefore be reduced to the consistence of a pretty thick paint, by mixing it up with a sufficient quantity of urine and soapsuds, and laid on with a painter's brush. The powder of wood-ashes and burned bones is to be applied as before directed, patting it down with the hand.

GRAFTING-CEMENT.

Another way of making grafting-wax is to melt equal parts of resin, beeswax, and tallow together. If it be so hard that it cannot be worked with the hands, melt it again and add more tallow. To make it ha der, add more resin. This will be found an excellent coating for wounds made by cutting off limbs of trees. After a tree is pruned, melt the wax in a metallic vessel, but not have it burning hot; then apply it in a liquid state to the wounds with a swab or paint brush. Some persons pour the composition into cold water, and as it hardens take it out and work it up with the hands until it attains a due consistence. It may be spread on brown paper, which being cut into strips of suitable size, is quickly applied, and in cool weather may be warmed by the breath, so as to become adhesive.

Grafting-clay may be made in the following manner: Take equal parts of fresh horse manure, free from litter, cow manure, and good stiff clay; add to this a portion of hair, and work it together in the same manner as masons mix their mortar. It should be well beaten and incorporated several days before it is required to be used.

PROCURING IMPROVED VARIETIES OF FRUIT.

In planting seed for the purpose of procuring improved varieties, care should be taken not only that the seed be selected from the finest existing kinds, but also that the most handsome, the largest, and the most perfectly ripened specimens should be those that supply the seed. A seedling plant will always partake more or less of the character of its parent, the qualities of which are concentrated in the embryo, when it has arrived at full maturity. As this subject is discussed in another part of this work, I shall direct the reader's attention to the operation of *Cross-Fertilization.*

This is effected by the action of the pollen of one plant upon the stigma of another. The nature of this action is highly curious. Pollen consists of extremely minute hollow balls or bodies; their cavity is filled with fluid, in which swim particles of a figure varying from spherical to oblong, and having an apparently spontaneous motion. The stigma is composed of very lax tissue, the intercellular passages of which have a greater diameter than the moving particles of the pollen. When a grain of pollen comes in contact with the stigma, it bursts, and discharges its contents among the lax tissues upon which it has fallen. The moving particles descend through the tissues of the style, until one, or sometimes more, of them find their way, by routes especially destined by nature for this service, into a little opening in the integuments of the ovulum or young seed. Once deposited there, the particle swells, increases gradually in size, separates into radicle and cotyledons, and finally becomes the embryo,—the part which is to give birth, when the seed is sown, to a new individual. Such being the mode in which the pollen influences the stigma, and subsequently the seed, a practical consequence of great importance necessarily follows, viz. that in all cases of cross-fertilization, the new variety will take chiefly after its polliniferous or male parent; and that at the same time it will acquire some of the constitutional peculiarities of its mother. Thus the male parent of the Downton Strawberry was the Old Black, the female a kind of Scarlet. In Coe's Golden Drop Plum, the father was the Yellow Magnum Bonum, the mother the Green Gage; and in the Elton Cherry, the White Heart was the male parent, and the Graffion the female.

The limits within which experiments of this kind must be confined are, however, narrow. It seems that cross fertilization will not take place at all, or very rarely, between different species, unless these species are nearly related to each other: and that the offspring of two distinct species is itself sterile, or if it possesses the power of multiplying itself by seed, its progeny returns back to the state of one or other of its parents. Hence it seldom or never has happened that domesticated fruits have had such an origin. We have no varieties raised between the Apple and the Pear, or the Plum and Cherry, or the Gooseberry and the Currant. On the other hand, new varieties obtained by the intermixture of two preëxisting varieties are not less prolific; but, on the contrary, often more so than either of their parents: witness the numerous sorts of Flemish Pears which have been raised by *cross fertilization* from bad bearers within the last thirty years, and which are the most prolific trees with which gardeners are acquainted. Witness also Mr. Knight's Cherries, raised between the May Duke and the Graffion, and the Coe's Plum already mentioned. It is therefore to the intermixture of the most valuable existing varieties of fruit that gardeners should trust for the *amelioration* of their stock. By this operation the Pears that are in eating in the spring have been rendered as delicious and as fertile as those of the autumn; and there is no apparent reason why those very early, but worthless sorts, such as the Muscat Robert, which usher in the season of Pears, should not be brought to a similar state of perfection.

It is an indubitable fact that all our fruits, without exception, have been so much ameliorated by various circumstances, that they no longer bear any resemblance in respect of quality to their original. Who, for instance, would recognise the wild parent of the Green Gage Plum in the austere Sloe, or that of the delicious Pippin Apples in the worthless acid Crab? Or, what resemblance can be traced between our famous Beurre Pears, whose flesh is so succulent, rich, and melting, and that hard, stony, astringent fruit, which even birds and animals refuse to eat? Yet these are undoubted cases of improvement, resulting from time and skill patiently and constantly in action. But it would be of little service to mankind that the quality of any fruit should be improved, unless we adopt some efficient and certain mode of multiplying the individuals when obtained. Hence there are two great objects which the cultivator should aim at, viz. *Amelioration* and *Propagation.*

LINDLEY'S MODE OF CROSS-FERTILIZATION.

Lindley recommends the operation of cross-fertilization to be performed early in the morning of a dry day; about sunrise is a good time to begin, and before the blossom is entirely expanded. The pollen being at that time humid, is closely attached to the anthers. The blossoms must be carefully opened and the anthers extracted by delicate scissors, care being taken not to wound the filaments, nor any other part of the flower. This being done, the matured pollen from another variety must be carefully placed on the blossom which it is intended to fertilize, and from which the anthers have been extracted; and this operation must be repeated twice or three times in the course of the day. By shaking the blossom over a sheet of white paper, the time when it is perfectly matured will be ascertained. It is necessary to protect the prepared blossom from bees and other insects with thin book-muslin, or gauze, till a swelling is perceived in the germ. When the process has been successful, the pollen which has been placed on the stigma becomes so attached that it cannot be removed with a hair pencil. It changes form and color, and soon disappears, and the blossom will soon wither and fade. But when the process has been imperfect, the pollen is easily detached from the stigma, its appearance is unaltered, and it remains visible with the duration of the flower, which will continue a long time.

GENERAL SUGGESTIONS ABOUT PRUNING.

The Gard'ner at work, ere the birds pipe a tune,
Each fruit-tree inspects, then commences to prune;
The insects destroying, on branches or root,
That injure the blossom, or live in the fruit.

As the season for pruning fruit-trees and vines commences in the various parts of our country at different periods, according to the climate, I would submit a few general remarks on the subject, with a view to prepare the gardener for the performance of the work in a skilful manner, and at the proper season; for be it remembered that untimely or injudicious pruning may produce injury instead of benefit, and in many cases defeat the real object of the operation.

Having given ample directions for the cultivation of the various species of fruit, I would recommend the novice to peruse every article before he enters upon the work of the garden. He will there discover that no single rule will apply to every kind of fruit; *first*, because the mode of bearing is different in almost every distinct species; *secondly*, because the sap rises earlier and continues longer in the branches of some species than in others; and *thirdly*, because some trees, as the Plum for instance, are apt to gum if pruned too soon in the season, and the grape-vine to bleed if delayed too long. For the above, and other reasons that may be given, the gardener should examine all his fruit-trees frequently, with his implements at hand; and if circumstances will not admit of a general pruning, he may cut off dead branches, and clear trees from moss and canker, also search for the nests of insects, and destroy them while in a torpid state. This will assist the natural efforts of the trees in casting off the crude and undigested juices, which, if confined in them, will in a short time destroy them, or some of their branches.

In pruning all descriptions of trees, some general rules may be observed. In cutting out defective branches, prune close to the healthy wood, and also shorten such shoots as have been injured by the winter, to the full extent, or even a few inches beyond, where damage has been sustained.

The limbs of young and thrifty trees should not be too closely pruned, because this would occasion more lateral shoots to put forth than is beneficial to the tree; which, if not rubbed off in the summer while quite young, and as it were herbaceous, will form crowded branches, which may not yield good fruit. In doing this *disbudding*, however, care must be taken to leave shoots in a suitable direction, sufficient for the formation of an open and handsome head to the tree, according to its kind.

It may be observed, further, that in the event of young trees, taken from the nursery, being deficient in fibrous roots, as is sometimes the case, close pruning may be necessary to maintain a proper equilibrium between the roots and the head; but it should be borne in mind that foliage is as essential to the maintenance of the roots as roots are necessary to the promotion of the growth of the head; because the secretion of plants being formed in leaves, it follows that secretions cannot take place if leaf-buds are destroyed.

INSECTS AND DISEASES TO WHICH FRUIT-TREES ARE LIABLE.

Much may be written relative to the various diseases to which fruit-trees are liable, and also to the prevention and destruction of the various kinds of reptiles and insects which frequently deprive us of the first fruits of our garden. The preventive operations are those of the best culture. Autumn ploughing, by exposing worms, grubs, the larvæ of bugs, beetles, etc., to the intense frost of our winters, and the moderate use of salt, lime, ashes, etc., are beneficial. Insects may be annoyed, and sometimes their complete destruction effected, by the use of soapsuds, lye, tar, turpentine, sulphur, pepper, soot, decoction of elder, walnut leaves, tobacco, and other bitter and acrid substances; but perhaps the most effectual way of keeping some of the most pernicious kinds of insects under, is to gather up such fruit as may fall from the trees before the insects have an opportunity of escaping into the earth, or to other places of shelter.

Where trees are planted in a bad soil, or unfavorable situations, they often become diseased. When this happens, the best remedy is good pruning, and keeping the trees clean by a free use of soap and water. If that will not do, they may be headed down, or removed to a better situation. Barrenness and disease are generally produced by the bad qualities of the earth and air, by a want of water, or by the inroads of insects. These incidents generally show themselves in the early part of the year. Leaves and shoots of any color but the natural green; curled and ragged leaves; branches in a decaying state; shoots growing from the roots instead of from the stem or trunk; the stem diseased in its bark; the gum oozing from various parts thereof—are all proofs of the existence of disease. The peach-tree is subject to a disease called the yellows; and the discolored leaves and feeble branches are often ascribed to the worms which so frequently attack the roots. Where these are found, they may be removed by a knife or chisel. But if it should appear that the tree is diseased, it should be removed, to prevent other trees from being infected.

WASH FOR FRUIT-TREES.

The following compositions have been known to protect fruit-trees from the attacks of numerous insects, by being used as a wash to the trees immediately after pruning. The constitution of some trees will bear a much stronger mixture of ingredients than others; but the proportions, as hereafter described, will not be injurious to any, but will be effectual in the destruction of the larvæ of insects.

For Apricot, Nectarine, and Peach-Trees.—To eight gallons of water add one pound of soft soap, two pounds of common sulphur, and half an ounce of black pepper.

For Apple, Cherry, Pear, and Plum-Trees.—To four gallons of water add one pound of soft soap, two pounds of common sulphur, two ounces of tobacco, and one ounce of black pepper.

For Figs and Vines.—To four gallons of water add half a pound of soft soap, one pound of sulphur, and a quarter of an ounce of black pepper. All these ingredients must be boiled together for twenty minutes at least, and when in a lukewarm state, applied to the bark of the trees with a suitable brush.

For the destruction of the Aphis which frequently attacks the Apple, as well as other fruit-trees while young, an application of diluted whale-oil soap to the leaves and branches has been found very efficacious. If whale-oil soap be applied too freely, it may injure young trees or bushes, and sometimes destroy them.

CHECKING THE RAVAGES OF THE CURCULIO.

The most destructive enemy to our fruit is the Curculio, which passes the winter in the earth in a chrysalis state, and if suffered to remain unmolested by the gardener, will be ready to commence its attacks at about the time the blossoms appear on our fruit-trees. The eggs are deposited in the Apple, Pear, and also all stone fruit, at a very early stage of their growth, which soon hatch, and small maggots are produced, which exist in the fruit, causing it to drop off prematurely, with the little enemy within. If this fruit be gathered up, or immediately devoured by hogs, geese, or other animals, a check may be put to their ravages in succeeding years; but if suffered to remain on the ground, they will supply food to myriads of their destructive race, which may not be so easily extirpated.

The most effectual way of preventing the operations of the Curculio is, to spread sheets of cloth beneath the trees and jar them off, by a sharp blow with a mallet against the end of a large iron spike, or pin driven into the body of the tree, when the insects will fall from the trees on the sheets, and may be turned into a vessel of hot water and destroyed.

THE CANKER-WORM.

The canker-worm is another enemy to our fruits, for the destruction of which many experiments have been tried. Some apply bandages around the body of the tree, smeared over with tar or ointment, to annoy or entrap the females in their ascent to the tree; but as these tormentors are frequently on the move from November to the end of June, this must be a very tedious as well as uncertain process. As this insect is supposed to exist within four feet of the trunk of the tree, and not more than three or four inches from the surface of the earth, good culture, and a moderate use of lime, ashes, or any other pernicious ingredient, is the most likely way to destroy them. Every worm should be destroyed, whenever they appear, by crushing, when they are not so numerous as to render it impracticable.

THE BARK-LOUSE.

The bark-louse is another pernicious insect. They resemble blisters, and are so near the color of the bark as to be imperceptible. They often prove fatal to the Apple-tree, by preventing the circulation of the sap. These insects may be conquered by washing the trees with soapsuds, tobacco-water, lime-water, or a wash may be made of soapy water, salt, and lime, thickened to the consistency of cream or paint, with sifted sand or clay, which may be applied with a brush to the trunk and limbs of the trees in May or early in June, and the cracks in the bark should be completely covered.

THE APPLE-TREE BORER.

The Apple-tree borer is said to deposit its eggs beneath the surface of the soil, and the worms are often to be found in the spring of the year by digging round the tree and clearing away the earth to the roots, and may be taken out with a knife or gouge, and destroyed. After the worms are removed the wounds should be covered over with grafting-clay and wood-ashes mixed, and the earth then returned to the roots of the tree. Some use bricklayers' mortar early in the spring around the base of the tree, so as to cover the part where the deposit is made, and prevent their attacks.

There is no effectual way of preventing the borer working in trees, to a certain extent. But, by examining the trees every week, the borers may be cut out before they have entered the wood beyond the reach of a penknife. Young trees that are only a few years old are far more liable to be destroyed by the borer than old trees having a thick, hard, and tough bark. Borers like a tender bark to work in.

VALUE OF WOOD-ASHES FOR FRUIT-TREES.

If all agriculturists and horticulturists were to offer an inducement to the inhabitants of large cities to save their ashes in a dry state, they would be supplied not only with a valuable manure, but an antidote for many kinds of insects; and our citizens would be at less risk from fire, by having a brick vault on their premises for safely keeping them. In England, a private dwelling is not considered complete without an ash-vault; and a good farmer would dispense with his barn rather than be destitute of an ash-house. I have known farmers to supply the cottagers with as much peat as they could burn, on condition of their saving them the ashes; and there are some that will keep men under pay throughout the year burning peat for the same purpose.; and anything that has passed the fire is so valuable, that a chimney-sweep will frequently clean chimneys for the sake of the soot, which is conveyed miles into the country, and sold at a price sufficient to reward the collectors, besides paying all expenses; even the housekeepers' ashes in cities is a marketable article at all times, bringing from ten to twenty-five cents per bushel when kept dry and clean; and a guinea a load was formerly the common price in the villages of Berkshire and Hampshire.

While on this subject, I would urge the importance of a spring dressing of ashes. If cultivators were to prepare turfs from tanners' bark, peat-earth, coal-dust mixed with clay, cow-dung, etc., and get them dried in the summer season, these, by being preserved through the winter, may be burned around fruit-orchards while the trees are in blossom; and if the fires are properly managed, a smoke may be kept up by heaping on damp litter every night; this will prove pernicious to such insects as may reside in the trees, and the ashes being spread on the ground, will serve as a means of destruction to others. An orchard thus managed every year, will need no other manure. The smoking should be effected first on one side of the plantation, and afterwards on the other, or heaps may be prepared in different parts of the orchard, and fire applied according as the wind may serve to carry the smoke where it is most necessary. I know a gardener in the neighborhood of New York who saved his Plums and Nectarines by burning salt hay, after having been used as a covering for his Spinach; and I have no hesitation in recommending it as an excellent remedy for protecting fruit-trees from insects, especially if some coarse tobacco could be procured to add to it. The damper the materials are, in moderation, the more smoke they will create; and if a little tar, pitch, sulphur, or other pernicious combustible be sprinkled among them, it will be beneficial.

Now I would ask—How is it that ashes are not as valuable to the farmers here as they are in Europe? The extreme heat of the summer must certainly engender insects in equal, if not greater proportions; and as respects manure, it must be scarcer in some parts of this extensive country than it is in the densely peopled countries of Europe. Perhaps some may answer, that ashes are already used by our cultivators to a considerable extent; but I would remind such, that from the circumstance of their being mixed up with other manures, and exposed to all sorts of weather (as in our city), they lose their virtue, so that a load may not be worth more than a bushel would be, if kept dry and clean.

THE SITUATION OF AN ORCHARD AND THE SOIL.

The situation of an Orchard or Fruit-Garden should be one that has the advantage of a free circulation of air, and is exposed to the south, with a slight inclination to the east and south-west. When the situation is low and close, the trees are very liable to become mossy, which always injures them, by closing up the pores of the wood; they are also more liable to be affected by blight. Although having an orchard closely pent up by trees, etc., is injurious, nevertheless a screen of forest-trees, at such a distance from the fruit-trees as that the latter will not be shaded by them, is of very great service in protecting the trees in spring from severe cold winds.

A good strong loamy soil, not too retentive of moisture, to the depth of thirty inches, or three feet, is most suitable for an orchard. Great attention must be paid to the sub-stratum, as the ground must be well drained; for if the top soil be ever so good, and the bottom wet, it is very rarely the case that the trees prosper many years; they soon begin to be diseased and go to decay. As it is so indispensably necessary to the success of fruit-trees that the bottom should be dry, if it is not naturally so, it must be made so by judicious draining.

DRAINING ORCHARDS.

When it is necessary to make the bottom dry by draining, it must be done some time before the trees are planted. In performing this work the ground must be trenched, and when the trench is open, stone or brick-bats, etc., must be laid over the bottom to the thickness of six inches, a little coal-ashes or small gravel must be sprinkled over the top of the stones, etc., and then the surface gently rolled. Drains may also be made in different directions, so that any excess of moisture can be taken entirely away from the ground.

If ditches be made between the rows of trees three feet deep, and tiles laid in them, and the hard subsoil returned on the tiles, and trod down well, as it is shovelled in the ditch, the roots of trees will not be very likely to obstruct the water passages. Such drains are better than those filled with stone, or any other material.

IMPROVING SOILS FOR FRUIT-TREES.

It is well known to most cultivators that exposure of soils to the atmosphere greatly improves them, as is experienced by ridging and trenching. Where the soil is stiff and stubborn, small gravel, sand, coal-ashes, lime, light animal and vegetable manure, and other light composts, are very appropriate substances to be applied, and will, if carefully managed and well worked into the ground, soon bring it into a proper condition for most purposes.

Previous to laying out an orchard or fruit-garden, the soil should be manured and pulverized to a great depth. It should be made sweet, that the nutriment which the roots receive may be wholesome; free, that they may be at full liberty to range in quest of it; and rich, that there may be no defect in food.

If orchards are made from meadows or pasture lands, the ground should be improved as much as possible by manuring, trenching, ploughing, etc. If this is not done to its full extent, it should be done in strips of at least six feet in width along where the fruit-trees are to be planted, and at the time of planting let the holes be dug somewhat larger than is sufficient to admit the roots in their natural position, and of sufficient depth to allow of a foot of rich and well-pulverized mould to be thrown in before the trees are planted.

HOW TO TRANSPLANT TREES.

In transplanting trees, they should not be placed more than an inch or two deeper than they were in the nursery-bed, and the earth intended for filling in should be enriched and well pulverized by mixing in some good old manure; and if any leaves, decayed brush, rotten wood, potato tops, or other refuse of a farm are attainable, let such be used around the trees in filling, taking care that the best pulverized mould is admitted among the fine roots. The trees in planting should be kept at ease, and several times shaken, so as to cause an equal distribution of the finer particles of earth to be connected with the small fibres of the roots; and when completely levelled, let the ground be well trodden down and moderately watered, which should be repeated occasionally after spring planting, if the weather should prove dry.

In transplanting trees, care should be taken that the collar or that part from which emanate the main roots, be not inserted too deep in the soil, as this injures the bark, and consequently impedes the natural circulation of the juices. A medium-sized tree may be planted one inch deeper than it was in the nursery-bed, and the largest should not exceed two or three inches.

Newly-planted trees should be watered in dry, hot weather; an occasional hoeing around them will also be beneficial; but care must be taken not to injure the roots.

As some difference of opinion exists among practical men as to the best time for planting fruit-trees, the following extract from Mr. Prince's Treatise on Horticulture is submitted:

TRANSPLANTING IN SPRING vs. AUTUMN.

Spring is the season when we find the most pleasure in making our rural improvements, and from this circumstance probably it has become the general season for planting trees; but experience has proved autumn-planting to be the most successful, especially in those parts of the United States which are subject to droughts, as trees planted in autumn suffer little or none from drought, when those set out in spring often perish in consequence of it. Notwithstanding, with regard to those fruits that have been originally brought from warmer climates, such as the Peach, Apricot, Nectarine, and Almond, which are natives of Persia, Armenia, etc., it is necessary for us to consult the operations of climate also; and, from a consideration of those attendant circumstances, I have come to the following conclusions: In localities south of New York, autumn planting is preferable only for the Apple, Pear, Plum, Cherry, Quince, and all other trees of northern latitude; whereas, the spring is to be preferred for the Peach, Apricot, Nectarine, and Almond, which, for the reasons before stated, might, during severe winters, suffer from the intensity of the frosts. Still I do not mean to assert that trees of those kinds are certain to be injured by the winter, as in very many seasons they are not in the least affected. Many gentlemen, however, of excellent judgment, make their plantations in the autumn, which only serves to prove that even in the most intelligent minds a diversity of opinion exists.

HEELING-IN TREES AND PROTECTING THEIR ROOTS.

As soon as the trees arrive at the place where they are to be planted, let a trench be dug in cultivated ground, the bundles unpacked, the roots well wetted, and immediately covered with earth in the trench, observing to make the earth fine that is spread over them, so as not to leave vacancies for the admission of air to dry the roots, it having been found by experience that the thriftiness of trees the first year after transplanting depends much on the fine fibres of the roots being kept moist, and not suffered to dry from the time they are taken up until they are replanted. Their increase, therefore, must depend principally on the subsequent management on their arrival at the place of destination; for if, when the bundles are unpacked, the trees are carelessly exposed to drying winds, the young fibres of the roots must perish, and the trees, if they live at all, cannot thrive the first season, as they can receive little or no nourishment until these fibres are replaced.

When trees are carried from the nursery to the orchard, if they are out of the ground in the wind and sunshine half an hour, the roots should be protected. Otherwise, all the small ones will lose their vitality. When trees or vines are carried only a few miles, and are out of the ground only one hour, the roots should be dipped in thin mud or clay to protect them from drying winds.

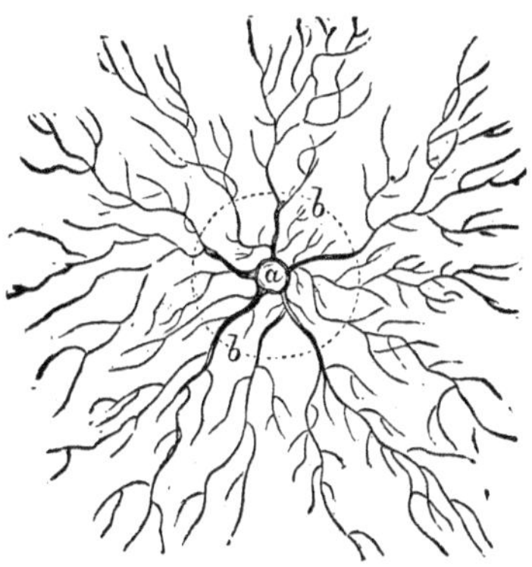

The accompanying illustration is a fair representation of the roots of a fruit-tree before the roots have been disturbed. When trees are dug up in the usual manner, the roots are all cut off, as represented by the dotted lines *b b*, which is sufficient to destroy the vitality of any tree. It is highly important to dig up the entire roots, if possible, when trees are removed.

The accompanying illustrations of trees represent the appearance of trees before and after the tops have been pruned, at the time of transplanting. It is always better to remove a good proportion of the branches, when most of the roots are left in the ground. If all the top be left on, and most of the

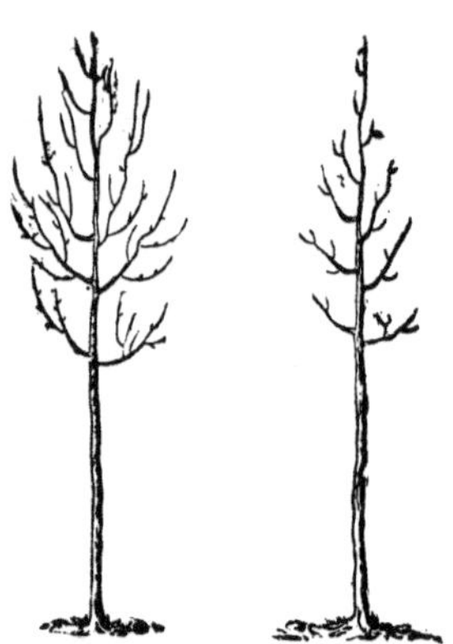

roots cut off, the tree will not thrive so well; and it is far more liable to die.

KEEPING THE SOIL CLEAN.

The ground where trees are planted must be kept cultivated, as young trees will not thrive if the grass be permitted to form a sod around them; and if it should be necessary to plant them in grass grounds, care must be taken to keep the earth mellow and free from grass for three or four feet distant around them; and every autumn some well-rotted manure should be dug in around each tree; and every spring the bodies of the Apple, Pear, Plum, and Cherry-trees, and others that it is particularly desirable to promote the growth of, should be brushed over with common soft soap, undiluted with water. This treatment will give a thriftiness to the trees surpassing the expectation of any one who has not witnessed its effect. Should the first season after transplanting prove dry, regular watering will be necessary, as from neglect of proper attention in this respect many lose a large portion of their trees during a drought.

PLANTING IN PROTECTED SITUATIONS.

Where there is a great extent of close fencing or wall it is advisable to plant trees of the same kind against different aspects. Such as one or two May Duke Cherries against a southern aspect, which will ripen earliest; next, against either an eastern or western; and lastly, against a northern aspect; by observing this method with Dwarf Cherries, Plums, Gooseberries, Currants, etc., the fruit will ripen in succession, and thus a supply is considerably lengthened. The early blooming fruit-trees will sometimes need protection in warm aspects; for which arrangements may be made by keeping awning, matting, netting, etc., at hand, to shelter them in threatening weather, or to screen them from the intense heat of the sun after a frosty night. This, with a sprinkling of water, as the air gets warm, will often prevent any serious consequences from slight frost.

INGREDIENTS FOR A GOOD COMPOST.

As all land possesses inorganic matter, which contains more or less of the elements comprised in the above remedies, and as some land contains more of one element than another, a judicious choice may be made from the above list, with a view to suit all the various kinds of soil; thus, in locations open to sea-breezes, which replenish the earth with salt, that article may be dispensed with, and another substituted; and on land which is not susceptible of being improved by lime, perhaps the salt may be beneficial; but it is presumed that in most cases a compost made of all, or as many of the different articles as are attainable, would produce a lasting benefit to land in general, by sowing, say at the rate of a bushel per acre, once a week, at those seasons of the year when it will avail most in the destruction of reptiles and insects; and as the primary object of using the compost is to prevent our fruits from being destroyed, it would prove most effectual if sown out of a wagon, from which, in passing between the trees, the leaves could be dusted.

The ingredients alluded to consist of ashes, charcoal-dust, plaster-of-Paris, tobacco-dust, lime, salt, soot, pepper, potash, saltpetre, snuff, and sulphur. The proportions may be as follows: Of the first four articles, half a bushel of each; of the next three, a peck of each; and of the last five, say one pound of each; which will make together three bushels of compost.

SCRAPING THE BODIES OF FRUIT-TREES.

To destroy insects on the fruit-trees, and prevent them from creeping up and breeding on them, do as follows:—

Take a strong knife with a sharp point, and a sharp hook-like iron made for the purpose; with these scrape clean off all the moss and outside rough bark, and with the knife pick out or cut away the cankered parts of the bark and wood, in such a slanting manner that water cannot lodge in the sides of the stem of the trees. Having cleared the trees in this way, make up a mixture of lime, soot, and sulphur; put these ingredients into a pot or tub, pour boiling water upon them, and with a stick stir and mix them well together. When this strong mixture becomes cold, and about the thickness of whitewash, dip a brush in the mixture, and apply it to the stems and large branches of the trees, dabbing it well into the hollow parts of the bark.

It will be found eminently more efficacious to apply such liquid as hot as practicable. If it be boiling hot, by the time it is spread out on the cold bark of the tree it will be so cool that the bark will receive no injury in consequence of the liquid being hot. Such hot liquid will destroy the eggs of insects much quicker than when it is cold.—S. E. Todd.

APPLE.

Pommier. *Pyrus malus.*

And now we've arrived near the close of the year,
Winter Apples and *Cranberries* bring up the rear,
All are good of their kind, and we freely declare,
Not one of the *Fruits* we would willingly spare.

The Apple being so closely connected with our wants and enjoyments, is entitled to the first notice in the catalogue of our fruits. The Apple-Orchard is, in truth, the vineyard of our country; and the delicious beverage that can be obtained from some of the varieties of this excellent fruit being calculated to cheer the invalid, as well as to strengthen the healthy, entitles it to high consideration. It is one of our oldest and best fruits, and has become completely naturalized to our soil. None can be brought to so high a degree of perfection with so little trouble; and of no other are there so many excellent varieties in general cultivation, calculated for almost every soil, situation, and climate, which our country affords.

AGE OF APPLE-TREES.

The Apple-tree is supposed by some to attain a great age. Haller mentions some trees in Herefordshire, England, that were a thousand years old, and were still highly prolific; but Knight considers two hundred years as the ordinary duration of a healthy tree, grafted on a crab-stock, and planted in a strong, tenacious soil. Speechly mentions a tree in an orchard at Burtonjoice, near Nottingham, about sixty years old, with branches extending from seven to nine yards round the bole, which in some seasons produced upwards of a hundred bushels of apples.

The Romans had only twenty-two varieties in Pliny's time. There are upwards of fifteen hundred now cultivated in the garden of the Horticultural Society of London, under name. The catalogue of the Linnæan Botanic Garden at Flushing contains about four hundred; and one of our enterprising horticulturists, Mr. William Coxe, of Burlington, New Jersey, enumerated one hundred and thirty-three kinds cultivated in the United States some years ago. They are usually divided into dessert, baking, and cider fruits. The first, highly flavored; the second, such as fall, or become mellow in baking or boiling; and the third, austere, and generally fruit of small size. Besides this division, Apples are classed as pippins or seedlings, pearmains or somewhat pear-shaped fruits, rennets or queen-specked fruits, calviles or white-skinned fruits, russets or brown fruits, and some are denominated burknots.

The Apple may be propagated by layers; and many sorts by cuttings and budding; but the usual mode is by grafting on seedling stocks of two or three years' growth, and for dwarfing, on stocks of the Quince or Paradise Apple. All the principal varieties are cultivated as standards in the orchard, and should be planted from thirty to forty feet from each other, or from any other spreading trees, in order that the sun and air may have their due influence in maturing the fruit.

Many of the dwarf kinds may be introduced into the Kitchen-Garden, and trained as espaliers, or dwarf standards. An Apple-Orchard may be planted at any time after the trees are two years old from the graft; and as trees from young stocks will not come into full bearing until ten or twelve years old, they will bear removing with care at any time within that period.

Old Apple-trees may be grafted with superior varieties by being headed down to standard height. Most commonly, in very old subjects, the branches only are cut within a foot or two of the trunk, and then grafted in the crown or cleft manner. In all the varieties of the common Apple, the mode of bearing is upon small terminal and lateral spurs, or short robust shoots, from half an inch to two inches long, which spring from the younger branches of two or more years' growth, appearing at first at the extremity, and extending gradually to the side. The same bearing-branches and fruit-spurs continue many years fruitful.

PRUNING.

As, from the mode of bearing, Apple-trees do not admit of shortening the general bearers, it should only be practised in extraordinary cases. If trees have not the most desirable form when three or four years old, they should be judiciously pruned to promote regular spreading branches. In annual pruning, the main branches should not be cut, unless in cases of decay; but all superfluous cross branches and dead wood should be taken out, and the suckers removed. Espaliers require a summer and winter pruning.

SELECT DESCRIPTIVE LIST OF APPLES.

SUMMER FRUIT.

American Summer Pearmain, *Early Summer Pearmain.* This apple is of medium size and oblong form; its color bright red on the sunny side, and on the opposite side yellow, streaked or blotched with red; the flesh is very juicy, tender, fine flavored, and excellent. It ripens early in August, and is good either for the dessert or for cooking. Tree a good bearer

Benoni. Fruit of medium size, form round and regular;

the flesh yellow, high-flavored, and excellent; it ripens in July and August. "The tree bears well," says Mr. Manning, "and should be found in every good collection."

Early Bough, *Sweet Bough.* The size of this fruit varies from medium to large; its color pale yellow; its form oblong; its skin smooth; flesh tender, juicy, sweet, and excellent. Ripens early in August in some localities.

Early Crofton, *or Irish Peach Apple.* An Irish apple, of the middle size and flattish shape; of an olive green color, much variegated with red; has a rich saccharine flavor; is much esteemed for the dessert, and is excellent also as a sauce apple. Ripens in August. The tree grows well, and is not apt to canker.

Early Harvest, *Prince's Yellow Harvest, Pomme d'été, July Pippin.* A very early apple, of medium size; bright straw color; flesh white and tender; juice rich, lively, and very fine. The tree bears young, and makes a fine garden espalier; ripening its fruit in July and August.

Early Red Juneating, *Red Margaret, Early Striped Juneating, Strawberry, Eve Apple of the Irish.* Fruit below the middle size; skin greenish yellow, richly and closely streaked with deep red; flesh white, juicy, breaking, sub-acid, very rich and agreeable. Ripens early in August.

Porter. This variety, says Mr. Manning, originated on the farm of the Rev. Samuel Porter, of Sherburne, Massachusetts. The fruit is large, of oblong shape; the skin a bright yellow, with a red blush; the flesh fine, sprightly, and agreeable. Ripens in September and October.

Red Astracan. This beautiful apple is of medium size, and roundish; the skin is dark red, covered with thick bloom like a plum; the flesh is white, tender, and somewhat acid. At perfection early in August.

Red Quarendon. *Devonshire Quarendon.* Sack Apple. A much esteemed Devonshire apple; of medium size; skin of a uniform deep rich crimson, with numerous green dots intermixed; flesh of a brisk, pleasant, and peculiar flavor. A very desirable dessert apple: from August to October; tree very productive.

SUMMER PIPPIN, *Pie Apple.* This fruit, in size and shape, resembles the Fall Pippin; it differs in having a little more red on the sunny side, and in arriving at maturity about a fortnight earlier. It is a very popular apple in New Jersey.

SUMMER QUEEN. A large oblong apple, striped with red on a yellow ground; the flesh is yellow, very high flavored, and excellent. The tree is of vigorous growth, says Mr. Manning, a great bearer, and ripens its fruit in August.

SUMMER ROSE, *Harvest Apple.* A very beautiful and excellent fruit, of moderate size and roundish form; the skin is yellow, striped and mottled with red; the flesh is sweet, juicy, and fine: in July and August; tree a great bearer.

WILLIAMS'S EARLY, *Williams's Favorite Red.* This apple originated in Roxbury, Mass.; it is of medium size; oblong form; the skin a bright and deep red; the flavor pleasant and agreeable. The tree is a great bearer, and its fruit commands a good price in the Boston markets: in August and September.

BEAUTY OF KENT. Fruit very large, roundish, but flat at the base; skin smooth, greenish-yellow, with stripes of purplish-red; flesh juicy, crisp, and tender, with an agreeable sub acid flavor: in October and November.

CANADIAN REINETTE, *Reinette du Canada blanche, Portugal Apple, Grosse Reinette d'Angleterre, Pomme du Caen, Mela Janurea.* Fruit large, broad, and flat; skin greenish-yellow, tinged with brown; flesh yellowish-white, firm, juicy, and of a high sub-acid flavor: from December to March.

CHANDLER. A native winter fruit of Pomfret, Connecticut. Large, roundish, slightly flattened; skin thickly streaked with dull red on a greenish-yellow ground with grey dots; flesh greenish-white, tender, juicy, and rich.

COURT OF WICK PIPPIN, *Fry's Pippin, Golden Drop, Wood's Transparent Pippin, Phillips' Reinette, Knightwick Pippin.* An English winter variety, well adapted for Canada or Maine. Fruit below the middle size, regularly formed, roundish-ovate; skin greenish-yellow, mottled with orange and red at maturity; flesh pale yellow, tender, juicy, and high flavored.

DUTCH MIGNONNE, *Reinette Dorée, Pomme de Laak, Paternoster Apple.* A winter fruit, large, roundish; skin dull orange, streaked and mottled with red, dotted with russet; flesh crisp; juice plentiful, with a delicious aromatic flavor.

EASTER PIPPIN, *Claremont Pippin, Ironstone Pippin, Young's Long Keeping, French Crab.* Fruit middle size, somewhat globular; skin deep green, shaded with a pale livid brown; flesh very firm, and though not juicy, of a good, subacid flavor. This variety will keep sound two years.

HEREFORDSHIRE PEARMAIN, *Winter Pearmain, Royal Pearmain, Royale d'Angleterre.* A fine winter dessert fruit above medium size, form oblong; skin russety-green, mottled with red, and dotted with greyish specks; flesh tender, with pleasant aromatic flavor. Tree an abundant bearer.

LYSCUM, *Osgood's Favorite.* A Massachusetts variety of merit. Fruit large, round; skin greenish-yellow, mottled with red; flesh fine grained, exceedingly mild and agreeable in flavor: in use from September to November.

LYMAN'S PUMPKIN SWEET. A very large apple raised by Mr. S. Lyman, Manchester, Connecticut. Skin smooth, pale yellow; flesh firm, sweet, juicy, and excellent for baking: in the autumn. The tree bears prodigious crops.

NORTHERN SPY. A native variety of the Spitzenberg family. Fruit large, conical, considerably ribbed; skin smooth, yellow ground, nearly covered with rich dark red and purplish streaks! flesh yellowish-white, and of a rich, aromatic, subacid flavor: good from December to May.

PECK'S PLEASANT. This variety resembles the Yellow Newtown Pippin, only it is larger; skin smooth, and when first gathered green, changing to yellow, with bright blush cheek and scattered grey dots; flesh yellowish, fine grained, juicy, and tender, with a delicious high aromatic flavor in winter.

Ross Nonpareil. A delicious Irish variety, approaching in flavor to some kinds of pear; fruit below medium size, roundish; skin covered with a thin mellow russet, faintly stained with red; flesh greenish-white, tender, and of a rich aromatic flavor: in perfection the end of October. Tree a profuse bearer, and worthy of a place in every amateur's garden.

Summer Sweet Paradise. A Pennsylvania fruit of large size; round, a little flattened at both ends; skin rather thick pale green, tinged with yellow, and sprinkled with large grey dots; flesh tender, crisp, juicy, and of a sweet, rich, aromatic flavor: ripe in August and September.

Sops of Wine, *Rode Wyn Appel, Sapson, Sops in Wine.* A handsome little autumn apple for the dessert; skin smooth, crimson, covered with a delicate light bloom; flesh white, with stains of a pinkish hue, firm, crisp, and juicy.

Victuals and Drink, *Big Sweet Pompey.* Fruit large, oblong, rather irregular; skin rough, dull yellow, marbled with russet; flesh yellowish, tender, breaking, and of a rich sprightly flavor: in perfection from October to March. The tree is a moderate bearer.

Winesap, *Wine Sop.* This is a good winter apple for the table, and one of the finest cider fruits; it is of medium size, rather oblong; skin smooth, of a fine dark red and yellow ground; flesh yellow, firm, with a rich high flavor.

AUTUMN FRUIT.

Alexander, *Emperor Alexander, Aporta.* Fruit very large, somewhat cordate, smallest at the crown; of a greenish-yellow colour, striped or marbled with red; pulp tender, sweet, rich, and aromatic; ripens in October, and lasts till Christmas.

American Nonpareil, *Doctor Apple.* A beautiful apple of medium size and roundish form; its color yellow, streaked and stained with red on the sunny side; flesh firm, juicy, and agreeable. A very fine market apple in October and November. Tree a great bearer.

BOXFORD. A very superior variety, says Mr. Manning, which was first cultivated at Boxford, Massachusetts. Fruit roundish, of medium size; skin striped with red and yellow; the flesh yellow, rich, and good. The tree is a great bearer, and ripens its fruit in October.

CUMBERLAND SPICE. A fine dessert fruit, large, rather oblong; of a pale yellow color, clouded near the base; the flesh white, tender, and of a fine flavor. It ripens in autumn, and will keep till February.

DOWNTON PIPPIN, *Elton Golden Pippin, Knight's Golden Pippin.* The Downton Golden Pippin is a most abundant bearer, and the fruit extremely well adapted for market; it is rather larger than the common Golden Pippin; skin nearly smooth; yellow, sprinkled with numerous specks; flesh yellowish, crisp, with a brisk, rich, sub-acid juice; specific gravity 10.79. Ripe in October and November, and will keep good till Christmas.

DRAP D'OR OF FRANCE, *Cloth of Gold.* This apple is very large and handsome; its form globular; its color a fine yellow, with dark specks; its flesh white, firm, and rich-flavored. The tree bears well, and should be found in every good collection. Fruit in perfection from September to November.

FALL HARVEY. This is a large and handsome fruit, the shape flat, the skin light yellow, with a bright red cheek; flesh yellow, firm, rich, and high flavored. Mr. Manning considered it "the finest Fall and Early Winter variety; a good bearer, and deserving extensive cultivation."

FALL PIPPIN, *Cobbett's Fall Pippin, Reinette Blanche d'Espagne, D'Espagne, De Rateau, Concombre Ancien, White Spanish Reinette, Camuesar.* This extremely valuable variety stands in the first class of autumn fruits, and is very large; its form is roundish oblong; skin smooth, yellowish green, tinged with orange; flesh yellowish, crisp, and tender, with a very rich, sugary juice. It ripens in October, and keeps well as a fall apple.

FAMEUSE, *Pomme de Neige.* A Canadian apple of great

beauty; in size medium; skin light green, stained with bright red; flesh white, very tender; juice saccharine, with a musky perfume; ripe in October, and will keep good till Christmas Tree hardy and productive.

Golden Russet, *Aromatic Russet.* A dessert apple, of medium size, and of a pale copper-colored russet; in great repute for its rich saccharine, aromatic, and slightly musky flavor. The tree is hardy and very productive: in October and November.

Gravenstein. Fruit rather large and compressed; of a yellowish green color, striped with red; flesh crisp, and high flavored; ripens in October, and lasts till April. This variety originated in Germany, and is considered the best dessert apple in that country.

Kenrick's Red Autumn. A native apple of largish dimensions, raised by John Kenrick, Esq., of Newton, Massachusetts; color pale green in the shade, but bright red next the sun, and streaked with deeper red; the flesh white, stained more or less with red; tender, juicy, and rich, with an agreeable sub-acid flavor; ripe in October.

Kilham Hill. This apple, one of the most saleable varieties in Salem markets, originated on the farm of Dr. Kilham, in Wenham, Essex county, Massachusetts; the size is above medium; form a little oblong; the skin yellow, striped with red; the flesh is yellow and high flavored; from September to November.

Monmouth Pippin. This variety originated in Monmouth county, New Jersey. It is above medium size, of greenish color, striped with red; flesh firm, and of pleasant flavor. It is considered one of the most saleable and productive varieties of the season; and will keep good till after Christmas.

Orange Sweeting, *Yellow Sweeting, Golden Sweeting.* This variety is much cultivated near Hartford, Connecticut, for the Boston, Providence, and Philadelphia markets; the fruit is rather large, flattened at its base and summit; the color yellow, or orange; flesh very sweet and excellent: from September to December.

Red Ingestrie. A first-rate dessert apple, of medium size, and bright yellow color, deeply tinged with red; raised by Mr. Knight, President of the London Horticultural Society. The tree bears well in America, and ripens its fruit in October, which is very rich, juicy, high flavored, and grateful to the palate.

Red and Green Sweeting, *Prince's Large Red and Green Sweeting.* The fruit is of oblong shape; color green, striped with red; the pulp is very sweet, tender, and of delicious flavor: from September to November.

Seek no Farther, *Rambo, or Romanite.* This apple is much cultivated in Pennsylvania and New Jersey. Its form is flat, resembling the Vandervere in appearance, but is a more juicy fruit; the skin pale yellow, streaked with red; flesh tender and sprightly during the autumn months.

Stroat, *Straat.* A fine autumn apple, introduced by the late Jesse Buel, Esq., of Albany; in size medium; form rather oblong; skin yellowish green; flesh yellow and tender; juice rich and lively; in use from September to December.

Yellow Ingestrie. A beautiful apple, raised by Mr. Knight, President of the London Horticultural Society. The size is small, form round and regular; the color of the skin golden yellow, with some black spots; the flesh yellow, firm, and delicate. The tree is an abundant bearer, and ripens its fruit in October. The late Judge Buel considered this variety as likely to rival the Lady-apple as a fashionable fruit.

York Russeting. A very large russety apple, well known about Boston. Its form is rather oblong; its flesh pleasant and agreeably acid; an excellent apple: from October to December.

WINTER FRUIT.

Æsopus Spitzenberg. A beautiful apple; large and oval; of red color, covered with numerous white specks; the flesh is yellowish; slightly acid, and of the finest flavor; ripens in October and continues good till February.

Baldwin. No apple in the Boston markets is more popu

lar than this; it is rather above medium size; its form round; its color bright red, streaked with yellow; its flesh is juicy, rich, saccharine, with a most agreeable acid flavor. The tree bears fruit abundantly, which ripens in November, and keeps till February or March.

Barcelona Pearmain, *Speckled Golden Reinette, Reinette Rouge, Reinette Rousse, Reinette des Carmes, Glace Rouge, Kleiner Casseler Reinette.* This variety is said to be a very productive and excellent dessert apple; fruit of medium size; oval, not angular; color brownish yellow in the shade, deep red next the sun; flesh firm, yellowish, with a rich aromatic agreeable acid: from November till February.

Beauty of the West. A large, oblate, beautiful fruit, of yellow and red color; its flesh juicy, rich, saccharine, and firm. A good marketable apple from November until March.

Bell Flower. A very large and beautiful Apple; its color bright yellow, with an occasional blush on the sunny side; its form oblong; the flesh tender, juicy, rich, and finely flavored, and is alike excellent for the dessert and for cooking. It ripens early in November, and will keep all the winter. It is a valuable market fruit.

Blenheim Pippin, *Woodstock Pippin, Blenheim Orange.* Fruit large, roundish, of a yellowish color, tinged with red next the sun; pulp sweet and high flavored: ripe in November, and keeps till March: a very superior dessert apple.

Blue Pearmain. This variety is well known about Boston as a large apple, of red color, covered with a dense blue bloom, and of a delicious flavor; good as a dessert or for cooking: from October to January. The tree grows strong, and is very productive.

Court Pendu, *Capendu, Court Pendu Plat, Garnon's Apple.* An estimable dessert apple, of medium size; in shape round, depressed; the color yellow, a good deal covered with full red; it is of a high saccharine flavor and of close consistence; the fruit keeps till February or March. The tree grows upright, and bears well.

DANVERS WINTER SWEET, *Epses Sweet, Danvers Sweeting.* This variety originated at Danvers, near Salem, Massachusetts; fruit of medium size; a little oblong; skin yellow, slightly tinged with red; its flesh sweet and excellent cooked, or as a dessert: from November to April. The tree is a great bearer, and of rapid growth.

DOMINE, *Domini.* A first-rate winter apple, of medium size and greenish yellow color, clouded with brown blotches; the flesh is juicy, tender, and excellent. Tree a great bearer.

GOLDEN BALL, *Golden Apple.* A beautiful and superior fruit from the State of Maine; of large size and golden yellow color; flesh firm; juice very rich, sweet, aromatic, with a good proportion of acid. It will keep good from November to April.

GOLDEN HARVEY, *Brandy Apple.* A dessert apple, not larger than the Golden Pippin; color light yellow, with a flush of red, and embroidered with a roughish russet. It is called Brandy Apple from the superior specific strength of its juice, being 10.85; it is of remarkably close texture, very rich in flavor, and will keep till April or May.

GREEN SWEET, *Green Sweeting, Green Winter Sweet.* This apple is much cultivated in Massachusetts. It is of medium size; the skin dull green, approaching to yellow; the flesh very sweet and delicious. It possesses the valuable property of retaining its soundness till May or June.

HUBBARDSTON NONESUCH. A large Apple of globular form; red and yellow color, streaked and blotched; the flesh is juicy and of excellent flavor; from December to March. The tree is of vigorous growth, a great bearer, and worthy of extensive cultivation.

JONATHAN. *King Philip, New Spitzenberg, Philip Rick.* A winter fruit very generally admired in the State of New York. It is of medium size; the skin of pale yellow and bright red color, occasionally tinged with purple; flesh tender, juice abundant, and highly flavored. This fruit will keep till May.

LADY APPLE, *Pomme d'Api.* Fruit small, flat; of pale yellow color, tinged with a deep red on the side; flesh crisp, sprightly, and pleasant: ripens in November, and continues till April. It is a very saleable fruit on account of its great beauty.

LADIES' SWEETING, *Winter Sweeting.* This apple is above medium size; conical; skin yellow, streaked and mottled with red; flesh juicy, sweet, and high flavored: from November to May.

LEMON PIPPIN. An old and much esteemed dessert apple; of medium size and oval shape, much like a lemon both in form and color, having a firm texture, brisk flavor, and plenty of acid: from October to March. Tree handsome and a great bearer.

MAIDEN'S BLUSH, *Hawthornden.* Fruit large, roundish; skin pale greenish-yellow, tinged with blush; the pulp is white, tender, juicy, and acid; and the fruit is good for the table as well as for all kitchen purposes: in September and October. The tree is hardy and prolific.

MALCARLE, *Charles Apple, Mela Carla, Pomme Finale.* A far-famed fruit. In the climate of Italy, this is supposed to be the best apple in the world. It is cultivated extensively in the territories of Genoa, as an article of export and commerce to Nice, Barcelona, Cadiz, and Marseilles. The fruit is rather large, its form inclining to globular. Its beautiful waxen skin is a little marbled with a very faint green near the eye; its color in the shade is a pale yellow, tinged with flaming crimson next the sun; the flesh is white, tender, delicate, sweet, with the fragrant perfume of roses. It ripens in September, and will keep till spring.

MENAGERE. Mr. Manning pronounced this to be the largest apple he had seen; the form is flat, like a large English turnip; the skin of a light yellow; the flesh pleasant, but more adapted to the kitchen than the dessert: from October to February. It bears well trained as a dwarf.

MINISTER. A native apple of large size, and oblong shape; the skin a light greenish-yellow, striped with bright red; flesh yellow, light, high-flavored, and excellent. Mr. Manning considered this as one of the finest fruits that New England ever produced. It ripens in November, and will keep till after Christmas

Monstrous Pippin, *Baltimore, Gloria Mundi, Ox Apple* Fruit of enormous size, often weighing twenty five ounces or more; of a pale yellowish-green and bluish color, with white spots; and of a sprightly flavor, excellent for cooking: ripens in October, and continues fit for use till January.

Murphy. This apple in appearance resembles the Blue Pearmain; the shape is more oblong, the size not so large; the skin pale red, streaked or blotched with darker red, and covered with blue bloom; flesh white, tender, and good. Raised from seed by Mr. Murphy, and introduced to notice by Mr. Manning.

Newtown Pippin, *American Newtown Pippin, Yellow Newtown Pippin.* This variety, when perfectly matured, is considered by some the finest apple in our country; its skin is green, changing to an olive yellow at maturity, having a thin russet covering the greatest part of the base; flesh pale-yellow and firm; juice saccharine, and possessing a rich and highly aromatic flavor; from December to April.

Newtown Spitzenberg, *Matchless.* A beautiful apple of medium size; skin streaked, and tinged with red and yellow; flesh yellow, rich, and highly flavored: from October to February.

Norfolk Beaufin. Fruit middling size, flattish, of a deep red and pale green color; the flesh is firm and savory; the tree hardy, upright, and a good bearer; fruit excellent for use in the kitchen, and highly esteemed for the dessert. It ripens in November, and is frequently to be obtained in England in July following.

Ortley Pippin, *Ortley Apple, Vandyne, Woodman's Song of Prince.* A fruit very much resembling the Yellow Newtown Pippin, but a little more oval; skin olive yellow at maturity; partially covered with pink and russet; flesh yellow, crisp, and breaking; very juicy, with the same pine-apple flavor which distinguishes the Newtown Pippin: good from November to April.

Pennock's Red Winter, *Pelican.* Fruit very large and compressed; of deep red color, streaked with yellow; flesh tender, juicy, and of a sweet and pleasant flavor: ripens in November, and will keep good till March. It is a very popular apple in the Philadelphia markets.

Pumpkin Sweet, *Ramsdell's Red Pumpkin Sweet.* A beautiful fruit, over medium size, round, inclined to oblong; of a dark red color, covered with dense blue bloom; flesh tender, rich, and sweet. It ripens in November, and keeps till January. The trees bear prodigious crops.

Rhode Island Greening. Fruit large and depressed; skin at maturity greenish yellow; flesh slightly acid, and of the finest flavor: ripens in November, and continues till April. A most estimable apple for cooking as well as for the dessert.

Ribstone Pippin, *Formosa Pippin, Traver's Apple, Glory of York.* Fruit of medium size, roundish, and partially depressed; of a pale yellow color, tinged with red; pulp slightly acid, and of fine flavor: ripens in November, and continues till April. It is one of the most popular dessert apples in England.

Roxbury Russet, *Boston Russet, Pineapple Russet.* This variety is cultivated extensively in Massachusetts for the Boston markets, and for exportation. The fruit is of medium size; of a fine yellow russet color, mixed with dull red; flesh white, juicy, rich, sub-acid, and excellent; for use in winter, and will keep till June.

Swaar Apple. A much celebrated winter table fruit in some parts of New York and New Jersey; it is a large apple of uncommon flavor and richness; skin of a greenish yellow, tinged with blush. The tree is very productive, and highly deserving cultivation in every collection of fine fruit. Good till March.

Vandevere. An apple of medium size, the form flat; skin pale red, with rough yellowish blotches; flesh yellow and tender; juice plentiful, rich, and sprightly: from October till January.

Western Russet, *Putnam's Russet.* This variety is extensively cultivated in Muskingum county, Ohio, where it is esteemed above all others of their fine winter varieties. It is above the middle size, of a greenish-yellow color, covered with russety blotches, and will keep all the winter.

White Winter Calville, *Calville Blanche d'Hiver, Bonnet Carre.* This fruit is large; its color at maturity bright yellow, tinged with red; its form rather flat; flesh white, tender, and pleasant: from November till March. Tree an abundant bearer.

Wine Apple, *Hay's Winter, Large Winter Red, Fine Winter.* A variety highly esteemed in the Philadelphia markets; the fruit is large, of bright red color, striped with yellow, the stalk end russety; its flesh is rich, aromatic, and pleasant: from October to February. The tree bears young and abundantly.

CIDER FRUIT.

Campfield, or Newark Sweeting. This apple is next in reputation, as a cider fruit, to the Harrison, and is often mixed with that apple in equal proportions when ground; it is of the middle size, skin smooth, of red and yellow color; the flesh is white, firm, sweet, and rich.

Granniwinkle. Fruit of moderate size, rather oblong; the skin a dark red, somewhat rough; flesh yellow, sweet, and rich. It is commonly mixed with the Harrison for making cider of a superior quality: ripe in November.

Hewe's Virginia Crab. From this fruit is obtained the celebrated Crab Cider; it is of small size, nearly round; skin of a dull red, streaked with greenish yellow; the flesh is fibrous and astringent; juice acid and austere.

Harrison, *Harrison's Newark.* This fruit is much celebrated in New Jersey as a cider apple; it is somewhat ovate, below the middle size; the skin is yellow, with black spots; flesh yellow, firm, rich, and sprightly. Ten bushels will make a barrel of exquisite cider, from which may be taken fourteen quarts of distilled spirits.

APRICOT.

ABRICOTIER. *Prunus Armeniaca.*

The *Margaret Apple*, the pride of our clime,
With the *Apricot*, *Raspberry*, true to their time,
Are pleasant companions, as summer e'er met,
Though others, as welcome, are coming on yet.

The fruit of the Apricot is next in esteem to the Peach; and as it ripens three or four weeks earlier, should be more generally cultivated. The flowers appear in April, on the shoots of the preceding year, and on spurs of two or more years' growth; and the fruit ripens in July and August. The London Horticultural Society's catalogue describes fifty-four sorts; and Messrs. Prince have eighteen in their catalogue. Besides these, is the Peach Apricot, a large fruit, supposed to be a hybrid between a Peach and an Apricot.

Our enterprising fellow-citizen, Mr. William Shaw, has succeeded for many years in maturing large quantities of this excellent fruit on standards; but they ripen best when trained against close fences. In England, some of the varieties are cultivated as standards and espaliers; but they seldom bear much fruit under ten or twelve years, and then the fruit is abundant and of the finest flavor. They are commonly cultivated as wall trees, in an east or west aspect; for if they are planted to face the south, the great heat causes them to be mealy before they are eatable. New varieties are procured from seed, as in the Peach, and approved sorts are perpetuated by budding on plum-stocks.

The varieties of the Apricot, in general, bear chiefly upon the young shoots of last year, and casually upon small spurs rising on the two or three-years-old fruit branches. The Moorpark bears chiefly on the last year's shoots, and on close spurs formed on the two-year-old wood. The bearing-shoots emit the blossom-buds immediately from the eyes along the sides, and the buds have a round and swelling appearance.

PRUNING APRICOT-TREES.

Apricot-trees may be planted at any time after the head is formed; some head them down in the nursery bed, and remove them to their destined places when five or six years old. Standards will require only occasional pruning, to regulate such branches as may be too numerous, too extended, or cross-formed, and to remove any casually unfruitful parts and dead wood. The regular branches forming the head of the tree should not be shortened unless necessary.

The general culture of the wall Apricots comprehends a summer and winter course of regulation, by pruning and training. The fan method is generally adopted, but some prefer training horizontally. With young trees some contrive to fill the wall by heading down twice a year.

The winter, or early spring management, comprehends a general regulation both of the last year's shoots and the older branches. A general supply of the most regularly situated young shoots must be everywhere retained for successional bearers the ensuing year. Cut out such branches as are not furnished with competent supplies of young wood, or with fruit spurs, to make room for training the most promising branches retained. Generally, observe in this pruning to retain one leading shoot at the end of each branch; either a naturally placed terminal, or one formed by cutting (where a vacancy is to be furnished) into a proper leader. Let the shoots retained for bearers be moderately shortened. Reduce strong shoots in the least proportion—cutting off one-fourth or less of their length. From weak shoots take away a third, and sometimes a half. This shortening will conduce to the production of a good supply of lateral shoots the ensuing summer from the lower and middle placed eyes; whereas without it, the new shoots would proceed mostly from the top and leave the under part of the principal branches naked, and the lower and middle parts of the tree unfurnished with proper supplies of bearing-wood. Never prune below all the blossom buds, except to provide wood, in which case cut nearer to the origin of the branch. As in these trees small fruit-spurs, an inch or two long, often appear on some of the two or three years' branches furnished with blossom-buds, these spurs should generally be retained for bearing. As each tree is pruned, lay in the branches and shoots from three to six inches distance, and nail them straight or close to the fence or wall.

The summer pruning is principally to regulate the young shoots of the same year. In the first place, take off close all the irregular foremost shoots, taking care to retain a competent supply of close side-shoots, with a good leader to each parent branch. Continue these mostly at full length all the summer, regularly trained in, to procure a sufficiency to choose from, in the general winter pruning for new bearers the next year. If the summer regulation commences early, while the shoots are quite young and, as it were, herbaceous, those improper to retain may be detached with the finger and thumb; but when of firmer growth, they must be removed with the knife. If any strong shoots rise in any part where the wood is deficient, they may be topped in June, which will cause them to produce several laterals the same year, eligible for training in, to supply the vacancy.

Sometimes the fruit is much too numerous, if not destroyed by insects often growing in clusters; in which case thin them while in a young, green state, leaving the most prominent fruit singly, at three or four inches distance, or from about two to six on the respective shoots, according to their strength. The Apricots so thinned off, and the first principal green fruit, are very fine for tarts.

SELECT DESCRIPTIVE LIST OF APRICOTS.

BREDA, *Abricot de Hollande, Amande Aveline, Royal Persian.* Fruit medium size, of a round form, and deep yellow color; the pulp is soft and juicy; the tree is a great bearer and the fruit, which ripens early in August, is in great esteem.

BRUSSELS. Highly esteemed for its productiveness; fruit medium size, inclining to an oval form; of a yellow color, and next the sun covered with numerous dark spots; the flesh is of a greenish-yellow color, of a brisk flavor, and not liable to become mealy: ripens in August.

BLOTCHED-LEAVED ROMAN, *Blotch-Leaved Turkey, Variegated Turkey, Abricot Macule of the French.* Fruit middle size, in form slightly compressed, inclining to oval; skin dull straw-color, with orange or red spots; flesh pale straw-color, soft, dry, rather mealy; kernel rather bitter. A very hardy and productive variety; ripe towards the end of July.

EARLY ORANGE, *Royal George, Royal Orange.* The fruit of a medium size; of a deep yellow color, spotted with red or dark purple next the sun; flesh deep orange, succulent, and well flavored; not perfectly a freestone: ripens early in August.

HEMSKIRKE. Fruit middle-sized, roundish, slightly compressed; of a bright yellow color; flesh tender, juicy, with a particularly rich, delicate flavor, resembling that of the Green Gage Plum: ripe in July.

LARGE EARLY APRICOT, *Abricot Gros Precoce, Abricot de St. Jean, Abricot de St. Jean rouge, Abricot gros d'Alexandrie.* Fruit somewhat oblong; skin downy, orange, spotted with red; flesh orange, juicy, and rich, parting from the stone. This is the earliest of all apricots; in France it has ripened by midsummer-day, whence its name of *A. de St. Jean.*

MOORPARK, *Anson's, Temple's, Dunmore's Breda.* The tree is of vigorous growth, and extraordinarily productive; the fruit is very large; of a bright gold color, or orange, with dark spots next the sun; flesh orange color, melting, and excellent: ripens in August.

MUSCH, *Musch.* A fine new variety from Persia; in shape round; of a deep yellow color, and remarkable for the transparency of its pulp, through which the stone is visible; the flesh is very fine and agreeable: ripens in July.

PEACH APRICOT, *Abricot Peche, Abricot de Nancy, Ansen's Imperial.* This is a first-rate fruit; form variable, generally flattened; skin slightly downy; fawn-color next the sun, tinged with reddish spots or points; pulp yellow, melting, juice abundant, high flavored, and excellent: ripens early in August.

PURPLE, *Alexandrian Abricot, Abricot Angoumois, Abricot Violet, Black Apricot.* A small, globular, downy fruit, a little oblong; of a pale red color, becoming deep red or purple next the sun; flesh pale red, but orange next the stone; a little acid, but good: ripens in August.

RED MASCULINE, *Abricot Precoce, Abricot Hatif Musque, Early Masculine.* This is an old and very early variety, the fruit of which is small, of a roundish form, and greenish red color; the pulp is tender; the tree a good bearer, and the fruit esteemed for its earliness and tart taste: ripens in July.

ROYAL, *Abricot Royale.* This fruit is next in size to the Moorpark; rather oval, compressed; of dull yellow color, slightly red; flesh pale orange, firm, juicy, sweet, and high flavored, with a slight acid: ripens early in August.

TURKEY, *Large Turkey.* A superior apricot; fruit of a medium size; deep yellow color, with red blotches next the sun; form globular: flesh firm, juicy, rich, and excellent: ripe in July and August.

WHITE APRICOT, *White Masculine, Abricot Blanc.* Fruit, in size and figure similar to the Red Masculine. Skin nearly white; flesh white, very delicate; juice sweet, with an agreeable peach-like flavor. Ripe in July.

CHERRY.

CERISIER. *Prunus cerasus.*

The accompanying illustrations of choice Cherries will furnish a correct idea of the comparative size of each variety.

The Cherry of the cultivated varieties is said to have been first introduced into Italy in the year 73 from a town in Pontus, in Asia, called Cerasus, whence its specific name; and it was introduced into Britain one hundred and twenty years afterwards.

The Romans had eight species in Pliny's time—red, black, tender-fleshed, hard-fleshed, small bitter-flavored, and heart-

Early Purple Guigne. Black Tartarian. Black Eagle.

shaped. There are now upwards of two hundred in cultivation. The French divide their Cherries into griottes, or tender-fleshed; bigarreaux, or heart-shaped; and guignes, or small fruit. The fruit of many varieties is somewhat heart-shaped, whence they are called ox-heart, white-heart, and black-heart. Why some sorts are called dukes, is not so obvious. The morello cherry is very different from the other varieties, bearing almost exclusively from the preceding year's wood, and the pulp of the fruit having the consistence and flavor of the fungi called morel; whence the name. The Chinese Cherry is valuable on account of its bearing an excellent fruit, and ripening it in forcing-houses.

Cherries are grafted or budded on seedlings from Cherry-stones, and from seedlings of the red and black mazzard. For dwarfing, they are worked on the morello, or perfumed Cherry; the latter is preferred in Holland. In this country, the budding system is more frequently practised on the various species of stone fruit than grafting.

PRUNING CHERRY-TREES.

Cherry-trees, in general, produce the fruit upon small spurs or studs, from half an inch to two inches in length, which proceed from the sides and ends of the two-year, three-year, and older branches; and as new spurs continue shooting from the extreme parts, it is a maxim in pruning both standards and espaliers, not to shorten the bearing branches when there is room for their regular extension.

The Morello is, in some degree, an exception, as it bears principally on the shoots of the preceding year, the fruit proceeding immediately from the eyes of shoots; and bears but casually, and in a small degree, on close spurs formed on the two-year-old wood, and scarcely ever on wood of the third year. Therefore, in pruning, leave a supply of young shoots on all the branches from the origin to the extremity of the tree, for next year's bearers.

All kinds of Cherry-trees, except the Morello, are apt to grow very tall. To remedy this, and to enable them to form handsome heads, the leading shoot should be cut off when of about three years' growth from the bud; after which give only occasional pruning, to reform or remove any casual irregularity from cross-placed or very crowded branches, and take away all cankery and decayed wood.

Dwarf Cherry-trees may be introduced into the Kitchen-Garden, and trained as espaliers. When Morellos are planted in an orchard, they may be placed from fifteen to twenty feet apart. Trees of the duke kind may be planted from twenty-five to thirty feet apart; and the heart-shaped, in general, will require to be from thirty to forty feet from each other, or from any spreading trees.

Cherry-trees may be removed the first year after the bud is established; but they will bear removal at any time before they come into bearing, which is about the fifth year.

The gum which exudes from Cherry-trees is equal to Gum-Arabic; and Hasselquist relates, "that more than one hundred men during a siege, were kept alive for nearly two months, without any other sustenance than a little of this gum taken sometimes into the mouth, and suffered gradually to dissolve." The wood of the wild Cherry-tree is hard and tough, and used by turners and cabinet-makers.

SELECT DESCRIPTIVE LIST OF CHERRIES.

DUKE AND ROUND FRUIT.

Ambree de Choisy, *Belle de Choisy* of Downing. *Cerise. Doucette*, *Cerise de la Palembre* of the French gardens. A middle size roundish fruit, highly deserving of cultivation. Skin transparent, red, mottled with amber; flesh amber-colored, tender, and sweet. It bears well as a standard, and ripens its fruit in June.

Archduke, *Royal Duke*, *Griotte de Portugal*, Portugal Duke. A large globular-formed red cherry; like the May Duke, it grows in clusters, but the tree grows more vigorously than that variety, and yields an abundance of fruit, which hangs a long time on the tree, improving in flavor in July.

Belle et Magnifique. A fine round cherry, much esteemed in Massachusetts. The tree is vigorous and productive; the fruit truly magnificent; its color red, mottled with white spots, and abounding in acid; valuable from its late maturity in July.

CARNATION, *Cerise Nouvelle d'Angleterre*, and *Cerise de Portugal*, of Downing. *Late Spanish*, *Griotte d'Espagne*, and *Griotte de Villenes*, of Prince. Fruit round, of a pale red color; flesh firm, with a very good-flavored juice; makes excellent preserves, and is good for the table in July.

DOWNER'S LATE RED, *Downer's Favorite*. A large round cherry, deserving a place in every garden, raised by S. Downer, Esq., of Dorchester, Massachusetts; color light red; flesh firm and of a fine sprightly flavor; ripening after most other superior varieties are gone, on which account this variety is highly prized in the markets.

CHERRIES.

KENTISH, *Early Kentish*, *Early Richmond*, Virginian May, *Long Stem Montmorency*, *Montmorency à longue queue*. Mr. Prince says that other varieties are sold erroneously under the above names. The fruit of this variety is round; skin red; flesh sprightly acid; juice abundant; excellent for the table and kitchen. It will hang long on the tree, in favorable weather, in June and July.

LATE DUKE, *Cerise Anglaise tardive*, *Unique nouvelle*. Fruit large, above the size of a May Duke; obtuse heart-shaped, rather flat; skin a shining dark red; flesh amber-colored, tender, juicy, and high flavored. Tree a great bearer, and ripens its fruit in July.

MAY DUKE, *Early Duke*, and *Cerise Guigne* of Downing. *Holman's Duke*, *June Duke*, *Griotte de Portugal*, and *Royale hative*, of Prince. Fruit of medium size, roundish, growing in clusters; the skin, when fully ripe, very dark red: the flesh is soft and juicy, with a very pleasant acid. This excellent variety ripens about the middle of June.

MORELLO, *English Morello*, *Milan*, *Cerise du nord*, Griotte du nord. Fruit of medium size, round; of a dark red color, nearly black at maturity; flesh deep red, tender, juicy, and blended with an agreeable acid; ripe in July, and hangs some time on the tree. This variety is excellent for preserves and for brandy.

PLUMSTONE MORELLO. A tree of moderate size, of the Duke or Kentish species; a very large, dark, round cherry, nearly black; of a rich acid flavor. The stone is very large, and resembles that of a plum; a native of Virginia, introduced by William Prince, of the Linnæan Botanic Garden, Flushing.

WATERLOO. A large, roundish, dark cherry, inclining to black at maturity; the flesh is firm and of an excellent flavor; raised by a daughter of Mr. Knight, and so named from perfecting its fruit soon after the battle of Waterloo. The tree is of strong but irregular growth, and ripens its fruit in July.

HEART-SHAPED AND BIGARREAUX.

AMERICAN AMBER, *Early Amber, New Honey.* A beautiful heart-shaped cherry, of medium size, and dark pink or amber color; flesh rich, sweet, and excellent. It ripens early in June.

AMERICAN HEART, *Arden's White Heart.* A medium-sized cherry, of pale yellowish color; obtuse heart-shaped, flesh tender and palatable, but not high flavored. The tree, which ripens its fruit in June, is very productive.

BELLE DE ROCMONT, *Bigarreau de Rocmont, Cœur de pigeon, Flesh Col. Bigarreau.* A beautiful heart-shaped fruit, of pale yellowish and red color, marbled and glossy; flesh firm, white; juice sprightly and of an agreeable flavor: in June and July.

BIGARREAU, Black. *Manning's Black Bigarreau.* This variety is considered highly deserving a place in every good collection; it originated in Mr. Manning's nursery at Salem; the fruit is large, color black; flesh sweet, and of a peculiar rich flavor. The tree grows handsome, is very productive, and ripens its fruit in July.

BIGARREAU, *Graffion, Turkey Bigarreau, Yellow Spanish, White Bigarreau, Imperial Guigne Ambree, White Orleans.*

Very large, obtuse, heart-shaped; yellowish-amber color, but fine red next the sun; flesh firm, white, sweet, and well flavored; a beautiful and excellent fruit: ripe in June and July. This variety commands the highest price in market.

BIGARREAU WHITE, *White Oxheart*, and *Harrison's Heart*, of Downing. *White Bigarreau Tradescant*, and *Bigarreau blanc le gros*, of Prince. Fruit large; obtuse heart-shaped; of pale yellow and white color, mottled with red; flesh white, and well flavored; ripe in June and July.

BLACK EAGLE. A beautiful variety, raised by Miss Knight, of Downton Castle, 1806; fruit of globular form, and middle size; skin dark purple, or nearly black; flesh very tender, rich, and of excellent flavor. The tree grows strong, very upright, and ripens its fruit early.

BLACK HEART, *Guignier à Fruit noir.* Fruit rather large, heart-shaped, dark purple, approaching to black at maturity; flesh dark red, tender, of excellent flavor; ripe early in July. Tree a good bearer.

BLACK TARTARIAN, *Black Circassian, Fraser's Black Tartarian, Black Russian, Ronald's Large Black Heart, Fraser's Black Heart.* A very large heart-shaped fruit, of a most superior quality; color dark-shining purple or black; flesh firm, dark red or purple; sweet, and of most excellent flavor: in June and July. The tree grows rapidly and is very productive.

DAVENPORT'S EARLY BLACK, *New May Duke.* This variety is considered as one of the finest and most productive of early cherries known. The fruit is of medium size, heart-shaped, of a dark glossy black color; flesh firm, and of a pleasant sub-acid flavor. It ripens a week or ten days earlier than the May Duke.

ELKHORN, *Black Oxheart, Tradescant's Black, Bigarreau gros noir, Large Black Bigarreau.* A large black, heart-shaped cherry, well suited to bear carriage to market from the firmness of its flesh. This variety ripens the second and third week in July, when other kinds are scarce.—(*Prince.*)

ELTON. This excellent variety was raised by Mr. Knight in 1806; the tree is very vigorous and productive; the fruit is pretty large, heart-shaped; pale glossy yellow in the shade, but marbled with bright red next the sun; flesh firm, sweet, and rich; ripens soon after the May Duke.

FLORENCE. A very fine heart-shaped cherry; of a yellow amber color, marbled with bright red in the shade, bright red next the sun; flesh tolerably firm, juicy, rich, and sweet: ripe end of June and in July.

GRIDLEY, *Apple Cherry.* A native fruit of medium size, which originated on the farm of Mr. Gridley, of Roxbury, near Boston; the color is black, the flesh firm, and of a fine flavor: in July. The tree grows vigorous, and is very productive.

KNIGHT'S EARLY BLACK. The blossoms of this variety appear very early; its fruit resembles the Waterloo; of a rich dark hue; its flesh is firm, juicy, and abundantly sweet: by the middle of June.

MAZZARD, BLACK. This cherry grows wild, and is cultivated also in abundance in various parts of England. It is the principal fruit employed for the making of cherry brandy, and the stocks of the species are best adapted for nursery-men to bud and graft the better kinds on.

NAPOLEON BIGARREAU, *Bigarreau Napoleon, Lauermann, Gros Bigarreau de Lauermann.* The tree of this variety is remarkable for the vigor and beauty of its growth; it produces a fine large white fruit with red spots; the flesh is remarkably white, solid, and of a sweet, agreeable flavor: early in July.

WHITE BIGARREAU. Mr. Manning represents this as one of the largest and finest cherries known. The form is obtuse, heart-shaped; skin pale yellow, with a bright red cheek; flesh very firm, juicy, sweet, and fine flavored: ripe in July. Mr. Manning observes that this variety has the reputation of being a shy bearer, but that in his orchard it yields an abundance of fruit; and that, owing to the hardness of its flesh, it is not liable to injury from birds. On this account, he says, it is highly deserving of cultivation.

WHITE HEART, *Remington White Heart, Late White Heart.* A moderate-sized cherry, of pleasant flavor; chiefly valuable for its very late maturity, being towards the end of August It is said to have originated in Rhode Island.

WHITE TARTARIAN, *White Transparent Crimea, Fraser's White, Guigne de Russie blanc.* A beautiful cherry, pale yellow, approaching to amber next the sun; a much-admired fruit, of excellent flavor; a good bearer, ripening early in July.

ALLEN'S SWEET MONTMORENCY, *Late Montmorency.* A seedling raised by J. F. Allen, Esq., of Salem, Massachusetts. Fruit of medium size, nearly round; skin pale amber, mottled with red; flesh yellowish, tender, sweet, and excellent. It is a good bearer, and ripens its fruit late in July.

BAUMANN'S MAY, *Wilder's Bigarreau de Mai.* A very early variety imported by Col. Wilder; fruit rather small, oval heart-shaped; skin deep rich red; flesh, when fully ripe, sweet and good; ripe by the end of May.

BIGARREAU CHINA, *Chinese Heart.* A fine variety raised by the late Mr. W. Prince, of Flushing, L. I. Fruit of medium size, oval heart-shaped, with a distinct suture line; skin, when fully ripe, glossy red, mottled with numerous light spots; flesh firm, and of a rich peculiar flavor: late in July.

BIGARREAU HOLLAND, *Spotted Bigarreau, Armstrong's Bigarreau.* Fruit very large, of a regular heart-shape; skin pale yellow, mottled and spotted with bright red; flesh juicy, sweet, and excellent: towards the end of June.

BIGARREAU TARDIF DE HILDESHEIM, *Hildesheim Bigarreau.* Fruit of medium size, heart-shaped; skin yellow, mottled, and marbled with red; flesh pale yellow, firm, with a sweet and agreeable flavor. This variety ripens here in August, and is considered by Thompson the latest sweet cherry known.

DOWNING'S RED CHEEK. An excellent seedling cherry raised at the nursery of A. J. Downing, Newburgh. Fruit rather large, regularly obtuse heart-shaped; skin thin, white, with a rich dark crimson cheek; flesh yellowish, of a sweet and luscious flavor: about the middle of June.

DOWNTON. A beautiful variety raised by T. A. Knight, of Downton Castle, England. Fruit very large, blunt heart-shaped; skin cream-color, stained and marbled with red dots a delicious cherry early in July.

EARLY PURPLE GUIGNE, *Early Purple Griotte.* An early variety ripening towards the end of May, newly introduced from England. Fruit of medium size; skin dark red and purple; flesh purple, tender, juicy, and delicious.

MANNING'S MOTTLED, *Mottled Bigarreau.* A beautiful heart cherry, raised by Mr. Manning from a seed of the Bigarreau; fruit above medium size, roundish heart-shaped; skin glossy amber color, mottled with red; flesh, when fully ripe, yellow and tender, with a delicious juice: ripens late in June.

TRANSPARENT GUIGNE, *Transparent Gean, Transparent.* Fruit small, borne in pairs, and heart-shaped; skin glossy, thin, and nearly transparent; color yellowish white, delicately mottled with fine red; flesh tender, melting, and sweet: ripe early in July.

CHESTNUT.

CHATAIGNER. *Castanea.*

The Chestnut is well known as a large tree, spreading its branches finely where it has room; but planted closely, will shoot up straight to a great height. It is supposed to have been originally from Sardis. It is so common as to be considered a native of France and Italy, and some consider it as naturalized in England. It is also indigenous in America. The London catalogues contain the names of thirty-two sorts under cultivation. The Chestnut is, like the Walnut, both a timber and fruit-tree. Some of the oldest trees in the world are of this species. The American Chestnut differs so little from the European, that no specific distinction can be drawn. It is one of the largest trees of the forest, the wood being extremely durable, and in high esteem for posts and rails to construct fences; and the nuts are very delicious. The *Castanea pumila*, or Chinquapin nut, is a small tree, or rather shrub, growing to the height of thirty feet in the Southern States, but seldom exceeding ten in cold latitudes. The fruit is very sweet and agreeable to eat.

There is a variety with striped leaves, which is very ornamental. The most esteemed of the French kinds are called Marron. Some excellent fruit-bearing varieties are cultivated in England, France, Italy, and Spain, as also in other parts of Europe.

MANNER OF PROPAGATING.

Chestnuts are increased by grafting or budding in the usual methods; but the plants for coppice wood, or timber, are best raised from nuts. Some varieties ripen their fruit a few days earlier than others; but none of these have been fixed on or perpetuated by nursery-men so as to render them available to purchasers. The fruit is a desirable nut for autumn or winter, and is eaten roasted with salt, and sometimes raw; and in some countries it is not only boiled and roasted, but ground into meal; and puddings, cakes, and bread are made from it.

Chestnut-trees will not succeed on wet, nor on heavy soils. The largest and finest trees are found on high ridges of clayey loam, gravelly loam, or sandy loam. By pruning the trees and keeping the soil cultivated around them, as far, or farther than the lateral branches extend, the fruit may be greatly increased both in quantity and quality.

In order to raise trees from the nuts, select the largest and fairest specimens as soon as they fall from the tree, and keep them where they will not become very dry until late autumn, when the nuts must be planted in well prepared soil in drills, and covered two inches deep with mould or fine street dirt. If the nuts are allowed to dry, their vitality will be destroyed. It is essential to their vegetation that the nuts freeze and thaw during winter. The fruit is better to remain on the trees till the frost has opened the burrs.

ALMOND.

AMANDIER. *Amygdalus.*

Although Almonds are not much cultivated in this part of our country, they are entitled to notice. The species are fruit-trees, or ornamental trees and shrubs, both much esteemed for the gay color and early appearance of their flowers. These vary in their color from the fine blush of the apple-blossom to a snowy whiteness. The chief obvious distinction is in the fruit, which is flatter, with a coriaceous covering, instead of the rich pulp of the Peach and Nectarine, opening spontaneously when the kernel is ripe. It is a native of Barbary, China, and most eastern countries. There are twelve sorts described in the catalogue of the Linnæan Botanic Garden at Flushing; some of which are represented as new varieties from France and Italy, where they are cultivated extensively for their fruit.

In France, they have above a dozen species or varieties, besides a hybrid called the Almond Peach. The common and bitter Almond are only to be distinguished by the taste of the kernels of their fruit, which is the only part used. The tender-shelled is in the greatest esteem, and next, the Sweet and Jordan. The bitter cuticle or skin of Almonds is taken off by immersion in boiling water. The sweet Almond and other varieties are used as a dessert in a green or imperfectly ripe, and also in a ripe or dried state. They are much used in cookery, confectionery, perfumery, and medicine.

The Almond is propagated by seed for varieties or for stocks; and by budding on its own or on Plum-stocks for continuing varieties. The Almond-tree bears chiefly on the young wood of the previous year, and in part upon small spurs or minor branches. It is therefore pruned like the Apricot and Peach, and its culture in other respects is the same.

CRANBERRY.

Canneberge. *Oxycoccus.*

This genus of plants is well distinguished from the *Vaccinium*, or Whortleberry, by the narrow revolute segments of corolla; and are pretty little trailing evergreen plants, to which a peat soil or rather moist situations are absolutely necessary. They are very little changed by culture.

The *Oxycoccus macrocarpus* is a red acid fruit, highly valued as a sweetmeat, or for tarts. It is well known that this excellent fruit grows in many parts of our country spontaneously, and that the mere gathering of it is all that bountiful nature requires at our hands; but it is well worth cultivating where there are none. This fruit will keep a whole year, if properly preserved in closely covered stone jars, and is considered by many as superior to the best currant jelly, and may be kept for many months in a raw state without injury.

The *Oxycoccus palustris* bears edible berries, which are gathered wild both in England and Scotland, and made into tarts. Lightfoot says, that twenty or thirty pounds' worth are sold each market-day, for five or six weeks together, in the town of Langtown, on the borders of Cumberland. Nicol says the American species is more easily cultivated than the English, but is inferior to it in flavor. There is reason to believe that the quality of fruit of each of these species is subject to variations, which have not yet been practically distinguished. Their cultivation is now so well understood that both may be considered with propriety as inmates of the fruit-garden. Some raise them from seed sown early in the spring; but it is best to set out plants, and lay the runners as they progress in growth.

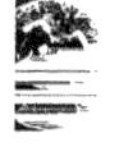

It is customary in England to prepare beds on the edges of ponds, which are banked up so as to admit of the wet getting underneath them; bog or peat-earth is considered essential for the roots to run in; but it has been discovered that they can be cultivated in damp situations in a garden, with a top-dressing of peat or bog-earth; and if they are once suited as to the soil, the plants will multiply so as to cover the bed in the course of a year or two, by means of their long runners, which take root at different points. From a very small space a very large quantity of Cranberries may be gathered; and they prove a remarkably regular crop, scarcely affected by the state of the weather, and not subject to the attacks of insects. Sir Joseph Banks gives an account of his success in cultivating this fruit. "In one year, from 326 square feet, or a bed about eighteen feet square, three and a half Winchester bushels of berries were produced, which, at five bottles to the gallon, gives one hundred and forty bottles, each sufficient for one Cranberry-pie, from two and a half square feet."

Cranberries thrive best in a wet soil, but will grow on almost any land, by giving it a top-dressing of peat, bog, or swamp-earth. As soon as such ground can be brought into tillable condition, get plants that were produced from layers of the last season, and set them out in rows about two feet apart; they will soon cover the ground by their runners, which, on being laid, will produce an abundance of plants well adapted for additional plantations in succeeding years.

CURRANT.

GROSSEILLER A GRAPPES. *Ribes.*

This is a genus of well-known shrubs, much cultivated for the fruit. It is a native of the northern parts of Europe, and found in hedges and woods in England; and there are some species indigenous in America. The fruit, being of an agreeable sub-acid taste, is generally relished both as a dessert and in pies and tarts. It is also much used in making wine, and is grown to a considerable extent for that purpose. There are ten species cultivated in the garden of the Horticultural Society of London, comprising twelve varieties of red, ten of white, five kinds of black, together with a champagne, mountain, rock, upright, and Pennsylvanian. Any number of varieties of the red and white

Red Dutch Currants.

may be procured from sowing the seed; but they are generally propagated by cuttings of the last year's wood, which should be of sufficient length to form handsome plants, with a clear stem ten inches high, which may be planted immediately upon losing their leaves in autumn, or very early the ensuing spring.

The Currant will grow in almost every soil, but succeeds best in one loamy and rich. The best flavored fruit is produced from plants in an open situation; but they will grow under the shades of walls or trees, and either as low bushes, or trained as espaliers. They bear chiefly on spurs, and on young wood of from one to three years' growth; and therefore, in pruning, most of the young wood should be cut to within two or three buds of that where it originated. After the plants are furnished with full heads they produce many superfluous and irregular shoots every summer, crowding the general bearers, so as to require regulating and curtailing, both in the young growth of the year and in older wood.

The principal part of the work may be done in winter, or early in spring; but a preparatory part should be performed in summer, to eradicate suckers, and thin the superfluous shoots of the year, where they are so crowded as to exclude the sun and air from the fruit. In training espaliers, and for standards, two branches are trained in a horizontal direction along the bottom of the trellis, perhaps half a foot from the surface of the earth; and the growth from these, or of all upright shoots,

Cherry Currants.

which will admit of being arranged at the distance of five or six inches from each other, is encouraged. Fan standards are sometimes trained with the branches radiating from the crown of the stem.

The black Currant, or *Ribes nigrum*, is common in moist woods in Russia and Siberia, and in certain localities in America. Its culture is similar to that of the red; but as it is less apt to bear in spurs than on young wood, the shoots should not be so much shortened in this as in the other.

Currant bushes should be planted at different distances, according to the situation and mode of training. When planted in beds, borders, or squares, they should be six feet apart, but if trained as espaliers they may be eight feet apart. Many people dislike the flavor of black Currants. They are therefore not much used in the kitchen as dessert, and seldom in wine-making. They make a jelly or jam, in estimation as a gargle for inflammatory sore throats. In Russia and Siberia wine is made of the berries alone, or fermented with honey, and with or without spirits.

HOW TO START NEW BUSHES FROM CUTTINGS.

Select the sprouts that grew the previous season, and cut off the butt-end, retaining about eight or ten inches of the top-end. Cover the butt-end with grafting-wax, and transplant them with a dibble, at least six inches deep, in soil thoroughly pulverized and enriched. Press the earth gently around the cuttings, and spread straw or some other material around them to keep the ground moist, to promote the growth of roots. All the buds should be pinched off the cuttings below the surface of the ground, if the bush is to be trained to a single stem. If the buds below the surface of the ground be not removed, strong shoots will spring from them, which will overgrow the main stem. If currant bushes be well pruned, the soil around them kept in a good state of fertility, weeds and grass subdued, and the fruit thinned out properly before it has attained much size, currants may be produced twice as large as they usually grow.

SELECT DESCRITIVE LIST OF CURRANTS.

Black English, *Common Black.* This species is most generally cultivated in private gardens for medicinal purposes; the berries are plentiful, of large size, and frequently hang on the bush two months, improving in flavor.

Black Naples. In this variety the fruit is larger, the clusters more numerous, and each cluster produces more berries than the ordinary kinds, on which account it is highly esteemed.

Champagne. The berries of this variety are of a pale red color, which, being transparent, causes it to be generally estimated as a dessert fruit. It is a prolific bearer.

Large Red, *Red Dutch.* This is the most desirable kind of the red-fruited currant cultivated; the bush, when properly trained and pruned, grows strong and upright, and produces an abundance of fine large berries.

WHITE CRYSTAL, *White Grape.* An excellent variety, the berries of which are large, and of a beautiful clear transparent brilliancy; hence its name.

WHITE DUTCH. This variety is held in great esteem for different purposes; the clusters and berries are large, of a yellowish-white color, and delicious flavor. The bushes are often so productive that the branches of the bearing-wood trail beneath the weight of the fruit.

MISSOURI CURRANT. This species is quite distinct from the ordinary kinds; its berries are purple, and although of rather agreeable flavor, they are not to be compared with those under general cultivation.

To these may be added *Knight's Sweet Red, Wilmot's Large Red, Wentworth Red, Victoria,* and *Green Fruited,* and some other kinds.

Some nursery-men's catalogues contain many other names, a great proportion of which are, probably, a repetition of the same fruit. Where the Currant is cultivated for the purpose of making wine, the White and Red Dutch are to be preferred to all others. For the dessert, the White Crystal and Champagne are great favorites, on account of their transparent clearness. Those bushes growing in the shade produce fruit much inferior to what it would be, were the bushes exposed to the sunshine and air during most of the day.

The Currant Worm which destroys the bushes, may be exterminated in the same manner as recommended for the extirpation of the Gooseberry Worm, page 93, which see.

FIG.

FIGUIER. *Ficus carica.*

The Fig-tree may be propagated from seed, cuttings, layers, suckers, roots, and by grafting; the most generally approved method is by layers or cuttings, which come into bearing the second, and sometimes the first year. No tree is more robust or more prolific; even plants in pots or tubs kept in a temperature adapted for the Orange-tree, will fruit freely, and ripen two crops a year, and by being taken care of through the winter, will go on growing and ripening fruit without intermission. Mr. Knight has obtained from his hot-house in England, eight successive crops in a year, by bending the limbs in a position below the horizontal. The trees will produce tolerable crops in the second year if rung or decorticated. Its maturity is also hastened by pricking the fruit with a straw or quill dipped in olive oil, or even by slightly touching the fruit with oil, at the finger's end. In Fig countries the fruit is preserved by dipping it in scalding lye, made of the ashes of the Fig-tree and then dried in the sun.

RINGING OR DECORTICATION.

Girdling, decortication, ringing, or circumcision, as it is sometimes variously called, consists in making two circular incisions quite around the limb, through the bark, at the distance of about a quarter of an inch asunder, more or less, according to the size and thickness of the tree; then by making a perpendicular slit, the ring of the bark is wholly removed. Ringing or decortication is applicable to every kind of fruit-tree, and to the vine. Its operation is twofold. First, in the early production and abundance of blossom-buds which it induces; and second, in increasing the size of the fruit and hastening its maturity, according to the season in which the operation is performed.

When Figs are cultivated in a garden, a good loamy soil should be provided; and they may be trained to close fences or trellises, in sheltered situations. At the approach of winter they must be protected; those trained to close fences may be secured through the winter by a covering of matting; and such as may be in open situations should be liberated from the trellis, and laid down close to the ground, and covered hree or four inches with earth; or trenches may be formed of that depth sufficient to contain the branches, which should be fastened down with hooked pegs, without cramping them: such of the strong central branches as will not bend may be enveloped in litter. They should be pruned before they are laid down in November, and on being raised again in April, they may be trained as before. Figs may be cultivated in private gardens as easily as the vine.

Those persons desirous of learning the names of different kinds of figs, may consult the descriptive lists of nursery-men. The fig-trees at Arundel are planted six or eight feet apart, and from a single stem allowed to continue branching conical heads, pruning chiefly irregular and redundant growths, and cutting out decayed or injured wood.

FILBERT AND HAZEL-NUT.

NOISETIER AVELINIER. *Corylus.*

The Filbert, in many varieties, and also the common Hazel-nut, grow spontaneously in the woods of Britain, and some few varieties are indigenous in this country. The kinds of Filberts generally cultivated are the white, red, cob, clustered, and frizzled. There are many varieties of each. As this shrub is so easily cultivated, it is a matter of astonishment that the nuts from this genus of plants are so scarce in our markets. In different parts of England there are Filbert orchards. In the Filbert grounds about Maidstone, in Kent, it is a prevailing practice to cultivate Hops, standard Apples, and Cherries, among the Filberts. When these come into a bearing state, the Hops are taken up and transplanted elsewhere, and the fruit-trees only suffered to remain. The spare ground is then planted with Gooseberries, Currants, etc. *The Red Filbert* is allowed to have a finer flavor than the White. *The Cob-nut* is large, with a thick shell; but the kernel is sweet and of considerable size. *The Barcelona* is a good large nut, with a thin shell. *The Cosford* is very sweet, kernels well, and the tree is a great bearer. *The Bond Nut* and the *Lambert Nut* are of large size, roundish shape, and very prolific bearers. *The Frizzled Filbert* is highly esteemed. It is beautiful when in the husk, and its flavor is very similar to that of the *White Filbert;* the shell of which is also thin, and its kernel sweet and fine.

All the different kinds may be grown as dwarf standards; or they will bear well if planted in clumps. But as they produce an abundance of suckers, these should be parted off frequently, and planted in a nursery-bed for stocks, as the bearing plants will cease to produce fruit in any quantity, if the suckers are allowed to form a thick bush. They may be propagated by seed, by suckers, by layers, or by grafting in the spring upon seedling or sucker-stocks.

The Filbert bears principally upon the sides of the upper young branches, and upon small shoots which proceed from the bases of side-branches cut off the preceding year. The leading shoot is every year to be shortened, and every shoot that is left to produce fruit should be clipped; which prevents the tree from being exhausted in making wood at the end of the branch. Such branches as may have borne fruit must be cut out every year, in order to promote the growth of a supply of young fruit-bearing branches.

Filberts and hazel nuts cannot be profitably grown in our cold climate, except on a small scale within a good forcing-house. For this reason, it will be folly for any one to attempt to raise an abundant crop of these nuts in a climate like New England and the Northern States. Fruit and flowers of any kind that are not adapted to the climate will not grow profitably, even when the cultivation is of a superior character. What is true of filberts and hazel nuts, is equally true of many other productions of the farm and garden.

GOOSEBERRY.

GROSEILLER. *Ribes grossularia, uva, crispa, etc.*

The *Gooseberry* green, the first fruit of the year,
In pudding or pie, affords exquisite cheer;
But e'en should the season their pleasure forefend,
In such a dilemma, green *Rhubarb's* a friend.

The Gooseberry is a native of several parts of Europe, and is indigenous in America, as far north as 68°. It is cultivated to greater perfection in England than in any other part of the world. In Spain and Italy this fruit is scarcely known. In France it is neglected. In Lancashire, England, and some

A Cluster of Houghton's Seedling.

parts of the adjoining counties, almost every cottager cultivates the Gooseberry, with a view to prizes given at what are called Gooseberry Prize-Meetings.

In Lindley's Guide to the Orchard and Fruit Garden, seven hundred and twenty-two varieties are described, from which the following are selected, as in most repute for size, flavor, and other good qualities:

Red Varieties.

British Crown, *Boardman's*. This variety is noted as being a fine-flavored fruit, especially for tarts; the largest berry weighing 18 pennyweights and 10 grains.

Champagne. The fruit of this variety is held in great esteem for its delicious flavor; the berry is of a medium size, somewhat oblong and hairy.

Capper's Top Sawyer. This is a late fruit, of oblong shape, and hairy near the base; the heaviest weighiug 22 dwts. 17 grains.

Crown Bob, *Melling's*. This variety won eighty-five prizes in two seasons; the largest berry weighing 21 dwts. and 12 grains. It is a late fruit, of oblong shape, bright red color, and hairy.

Early Red, *Wilmot's*. This variety is considered as first-rate of its color. It has a thin skin; is of large size, very early, of excellent flavor, and incredibly productive.

Marquis of Stafford, *Knight's*. This much-esteemed late variety is hairy, of medium size, bright red color, and delicious flavor.

Old Rough Red. This is a favorite fruit for family use; the berries are of medium size, of dark red color; excellent for preserving as gooseberry jam, and for bottling in an unripe state.

Over-all, *Bratherton's*. The average weight of the berries is 20 dwts. It is a highly esteemed fruit.

Triumphant, *Denny's*. This is a medium-sized early berry, weighing about 16 dwts. It is considered equal in quality to any gooseberry of its color.

Warrington. This is a favorite fruit for private gardens; the berries are of medium size, very rich flavored, and ripen gradually without deteriorating.

YELLOW GOOSEBERRIES.

We may mention as good berries, and worthy of cultivation,

the Bunker Hill, Britannia Cottage Girl, Golden Gourd, Golden Yellow, Gunner, Invincible, Regulator, Rockwood, Sovereign, and Viper.

GREEN GOOSEBERRIES.

Of this variety we may enumerate the Angler, Early Green, Favorite, Greenwood, Green Gage, Green Myrtle, Heart of Oak, Independent, Jolly Tar, Laurel, Ocean, and Wistaston.

WHITE GOOSEBERRIES.

Bonny Lass, Governess, Lady of the Manor, Lioness, Nailer, Queen of Sheba, Smiling Girl, White Bear, and White Eagle. There are many other kinds enumerated in the large catalogues of nursery-men.

HOW TO PROPAGATE GOOSEBERRIES.

The Gooseberry may be propagated by all the modes applicable to trees or shrubs; but that by cuttings is usually adopted for continuing varieties; and that by seed for procuring them. The cuttings should be taken from promising shoots just before the leaves begin to fall in the autumn; the greatest part of the buds should be taken off, leaving only two or three buds on the top. Cut them at such a length as the strength and ripeness of the wood will bear; and plant them in good pulverized soil. On the approach of winter, lay some moss or litter around them; and, by being well cultivated, they will be fit to transplant when they are a year old. Gooseberries are propagated by cuttings in the same manner as recommended for the propagation of Currants on a previous page.

PRUNING AND TRAINING.

The Gooseberry produces its fruit not only on the shoots of the preceding year, and on shoots two or three years old, but also on spurs or snags arising from the older branches along the sides; but the former afford the largest fruit. The shoots retained for bearers should therefore be left at full length, or nearly so. The first pruning should be done before the buds swell, so as not to endanger their being rubbed off in the operation. Cut out all the superfluous cross-shoots, and prune long ramblers and low stragglers to some well placed lateral or eye; retain a sufficiency of the young well situated laterals and terminals to form successional bearers. In cutting out superfluous and decayed wood, be careful to retain a leading shoot at the end of a principal branch. The superfluous young laterals on the good main branches, instead of being taken off clean, may be cut into little stubs of one or two eyes, which will send out fruit-buds and spurs.

Some persons not pruning the Gooseberry bush on right principles, cause it to shoot crowdedly full of young wood in summer, the fruit from which is always small, and does not ripen freely with full flavor; on which account it is an important point in pruning, to keep the middle of the head open and clear, and to let the occasional shortening of the shoots be sparing and moderate. Between the bearing branches keep a regulated distance of at least six inches at the extremities, which will render them fertile bearers of good fruit.

The prize cultivators of this fruit in Lancashire are particular in preparing a very rich soil, and they water occasionally with the liquor which drains from dunghills; and there are some who, not content with watering at the root and over the top, place a small saucer of water under each Gooseberry, only six or eight of which are left on a bush. This is technically called suckling. There are others who ring some of the branches; this is done by cutting out small circles of bark around them; and by pinching off most of the young wood, the strength is thrown to the fruit.

When bushes are procured from the public nurseries, let the general supply be in such kinds as will ripen in succession. They may be planted in the kitchen-garden, in single rows, along the side of the walks or paths, or in compartments by themselves, in rows from six to eight feet apart from row to row, and five or six feet apart in the rows; or in small gardens, they may be trained to a single tall stem, and tied to a stake. This, though six or eight feet high, occasions scarcely any shade, and it does not occupy much room, nor exclude air, while, at the same time, the stem becomes closely hung with berries, and makes a pleasant appearance in that state. Persons of taste may train them on arched trellises, and if they are judiciously managed, the ground around them may be more easily cultivated; the fruit may be kept from being splashed with rain, and may be easily gathered when wanted, or preserved by shading with mats. Those who may have a choice of soil and site, should fix on a good, rich, loamy earth, and plant some of the choice kinds in a northern and eastern aspect, near the fence, to come late in succession.

The Gooseberry may be forced in pots or boxes, placed in pits, or in the peach-house or vinery. Unripe Gooseberries may be preserved in bottles against winter; some, after filling the bottles in a dry state, stand them in a slow oven, or in hot water, so as to heat them gradually through without cracking them; they will keep a whole year if closely corked and sealed as soon as cold.

GOOSEBERRY SAW-FLY.

This insect has taken almost entire possession of our Gooseberry and Currant bushes; and of its close resemblance to the *Gooseberry Saw-Fly* of Europe, there can be no doubt. It first attacks the gooseberry; but when these leaves become scarce those of the currant are greedily devoured.

When the flies emerge from their winter quarters in the ground the latter part of April or early in May, the female begins to deposit her eggs on the under side of the newly expanded leaves, choosing the sides of the veins or nervures as a fitting place. With the saw-like appendage for which the family is remarkable, the female commences cutting into the leaves, and in the opening deposits her egg. The larva is hatched in about a week, and commences feeding on the leaf, increasing in size and frequently changing its skin, till it is about three-quarters of an inch in length. It is now of a dull pale-green color, the first thoracic segment being deep yellow, the penultimate being also of the same color. The feet, tail, and head are black, and each segment is dotted black also, some having as many as twenty-four spots arranged in lines down the back, while those on the sides are more irregular, with one large one at the base of each foot. They have six pectoral, sharp, horny feet; the fourth segment appears destitute of feet, but the six following are each furnished with a pair of legs, which assist them in walking. They have also a pair of feet at the extremity of the last segment.

In the fly state it assumes an ochreous color. The body is orange, sometimes bright. The wings are iridescent; and, when expanded, are about two-thirds of an inch in length. The antennæ are almost as long as the body, bristly, brownish above, and nine-jointed; the crown of the head and eyes are black, as are also three large confluent spots in the centre of the trunk, and also a large patch on the breast or sternum.

The broods of caterpillars appear in succession occasionally from March till October, but in greatest numbers in June. Sometimes they severely attack the gooseberry in July and August, and after denuding the bushes of their foliage, they descend into the earth, spinning themselves a yellowish cocoon of an elliptical form, and remain in their pupa state till the following spring. Those of the early summer brood descend in like manner, but in the course of three weeks or less, undergo their transformation, and again appear as perfect flies. See Dr. A. Fitch's Report on Insects for a more complete description of this worm.

INFALLIBLE REMEDY FOR THE GOOSEBERRY AND CURRANT WORM.

The only effectual remedy for the extermination of this worm that is so destructive to Currants and Gooseberries is, powdered White Hellebore (Veratrum Album), sprinkled with a dredging-box over the leaves and branches. The bushes should be turned up, and the powder scattered on the leaves and small twigs in the middle of the bushes. A very light dusting will be sufficient. The worms never eat any more after the powder falls on the surface, even if they have not gnawed holes through the leaves. White Hellebore can be obtained at the drug stores. A few cents will purchase enough to destroy all the worms on a long row of bushes. Great caution must be exercised in using the powder, as it will cause violent sneezing if a very small quantity be snuffed up. This powder will not injure the leaves nor the fruit in the least, notwithstanding it is exceedingly poisonous to the worms.

To protect Gooseberries and other fruits from mildews sprinkle the leaves with soapsuds; and while they are wet, sow sulphur lightly over them. This may be done two or three times a week if necessary, as it is better to use a little of the ingredients frequently than too much at once. A solution made of saltpetre and stone lime is also a good remedy; but it must be used with caution.

GRAPE.

VIGNE. *Vitis vinifera, vulpina.*

Oh, Bacchus! thy *Grapes* now in bunches hang down;
Some *press* them too freely their "sorrows to drown;"
Let "Temperance in all things" be ever our guide—
No evil can flow from the generous tide!

THE Grape-Vine is described by Loudon as a trailing, deciduous, hardy shrub, with a twisted irregular stem, and long, flexible branches, decumbent, like those of the bramble; or supporting themselves, when near other trees, by means of tendrils, like the pea. The leaves are large, lobed, entire, or serrated and downy, or smooth, green in summer; but when mature, those of varieties in which the predominating color is red, constantly change to, or are tinged with some shade of that color; and those of white, green, or yellow Grapes as constantly change to yellow, and are never in the least tinged either with purple, red, or scarlet. The breadth of the leaves varies from five to seven or ten inches, and the length of the foot-stalks from four to eight inches. The flowers are produced

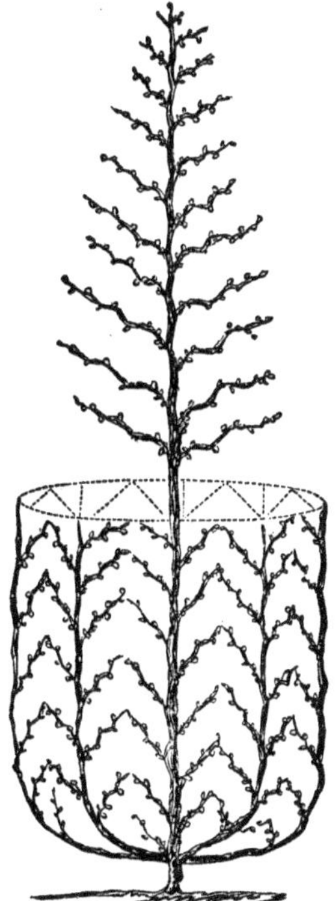

Combined Urn and Fountain.

on the shoots of the same year, which shoots generally proceed from those of the year preceding. They are in the form of a raceme, of a greenish-white color and fragrant odor, appearing in the open air in June; and the fruit, which is of the berry kind, attains such maturity as the season and situation admit, by the middle or end of September. The berry, or Grape, is generally globular, but often ovate, oval, oblong, or finger-shaped; the color green, red, yellow, amber, and black, or a variegation of two or more of these colors. The skin is smooth, the pulp and juice of a dulcet, poignant, elevated, generous flavor.

LIST—SWEET-WATER MUSCADINE, RED HAMBURGH.

The weight of a berry depends not only on its size, but on

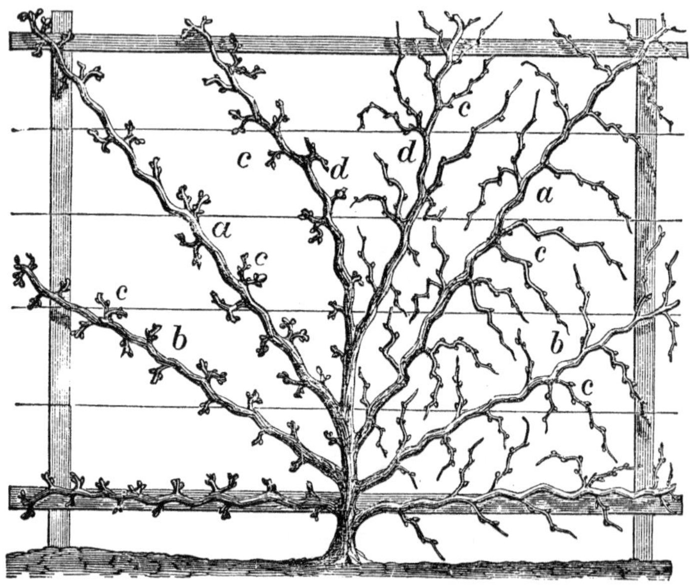

Field-Training on Trellises.

the thickness of its skin and texture of the flesh, the lightest being the thin-skinned and juicy sorts, as the Sweet-Water or Muscadine; and what are considered as large-berried of these varieties, will weigh from five to seven pennyweights, and measure from one to two-thirds of an inch in girth. A good-sized bunch of the same sorts may weigh from two to six pounds; but bunches have been grown of the Syrian Grape, in Syria, weighing forty pounds, and in England weighing from ten to nineteen pounds. A single vine, in a large pot, or grown as a dwarf standard, in the manner practised in the vineyards in the North of France, ordinarily produces from three to nine bunches; but by superior management in gardens in England, the number of bunches is prodigiously increased; and one plant, that of the red Hamburgh sort, in the vinery of the royal gardens at Hampton Court, has produced two thousand two hundred bunches, averaging one pound each, or in all nearly a ton. That at Valentine, in Essex, has produced two thousand bunches of nearly the same average weight.

THE AGE OF GRAPE-VINES.

The age to which the vine will attain in warm climates is so great as not to be known. It is supposed to be equal or even to surpass that of the oak. Pliny speaks of a vine which had existed six hundred years; and Bose says there are vines in Burgundy upwards of four hundred years of age. In Italy there are vineyards which have been in a flourishing state for upwards of three centuries; and Miller tells us that a vineyard a hundred years old is reckoned young. The extent of the branches of the vine, in certain situations and circumstances, is commensurate with its produce and soil. In the hedges of Italy and woods of America they are found overtopping the highest elm and poplar trees; and in England, one plant trained against a row of houses in Northallerton, covered a space, in 1585, of one hundred and thirty-seven square yards. It was then above one hundred years old. That at Hampton Court, nearly of the same age, occupies above one hundred and sixty square yards; and that at Valentine, in Essex, above one hundred and forty-seven square yards. The size to which the trunk, or stem, sometimes attains in warm climates, is so great as to have afforded planks fifteen inches broad, furniture and statues; and the Northallerton vine, above mentioned, in

1785 measured four feet in circumference near the ground; and one branch of the Hampton Court vine measures one hundred and fourteen feet in length. Vine timber is of great durability.

OBSERVATIONS ABOUT VARIETIES.

The varieties of the Grape in countries where it is grown for the wine-press, are as numerous as the vineyards; for as these,

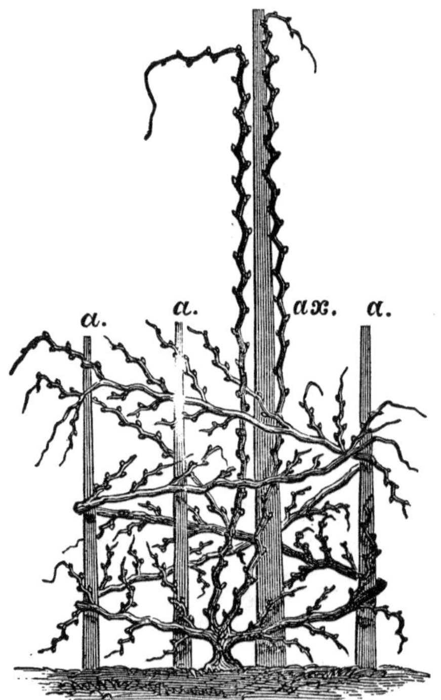

The Spiral System of Training Vines

for the most part, differ in soil, aspect, elevation, or otherwise, and as the vine is greatly the child of local circumstances, its habits soon become adapted to those in which it is placed.

When it is considered that a vineyard once planted will last two or three centuries, it will readily be conceived that the nature of a variety may be totally changed during only a part of that time. The varieties mostly in esteem for wine-making are small berries, and bunches with an austere taste. The Burgundy, as modified by different soils and situations, may be considered the most general vineyard Grape of France, from Champagne or Marne, to Marseilles or Bordeaux.

William Robert Prince, in his Treatise on the Vine, pub-

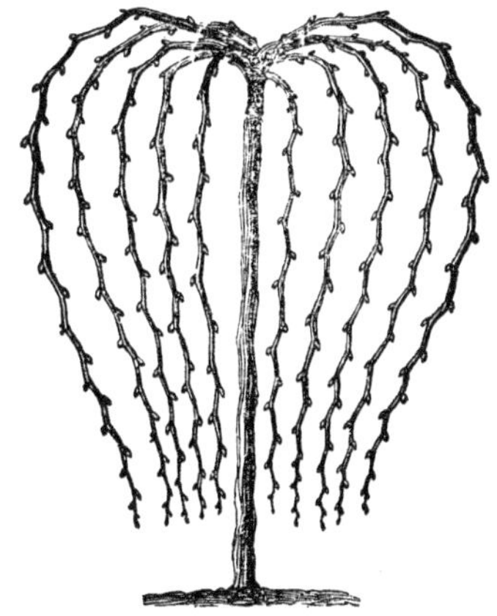

The Weeping Vine.

lished in 1830, enumerated about five hundred and fifty varieties under cultivation in the vineyard attached to the Linnæan Botanic Garden at Flushing, including about ninety American native Grapes; but no sufficient evidence has as yet been exhibited of the foreign varieties flourishing in vineyards here equal to what they do in Europe. Mr. Loubat once attempted to establish a vineyard on Long Island, which he abandoned after six years' arduous exertion. The following have been found to succeed best in private sheltered gardens in the vicinity of New York:—the Sweet-water, the Chasselas, the Muscadine, the White Tokay, the Black Hamburgh, the Blue Cortiga, the Miller Burgundy, the Austrian Muscadel, the Messlier, the Morilon, the Black Prince, Blanc, and some excellent seedling sorts from the imported Lisbon Grapes. To plant a vinery for a full crop of good Grapes of various flavors, take a white and red Muscat, a white and red, or black Muscadel, a white Raisin Grape, a white and red Hamburgh, a Stilwell's,

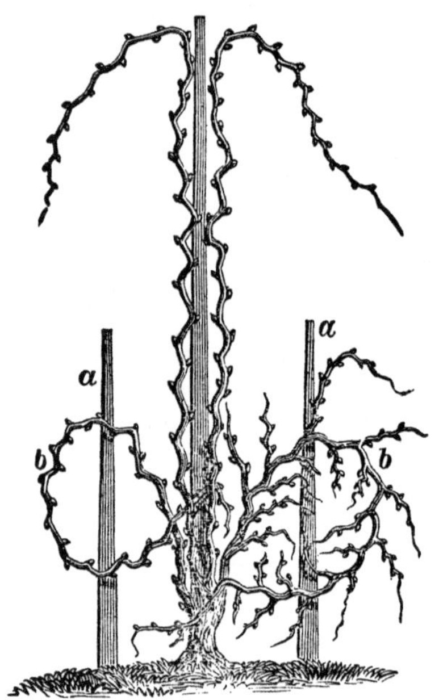

Renewal System on Stakes.

and red Sweet-water, a white and red Nice, a black Damascus, a red Syracuse, and a black Constantia. The above list contains some of the most esteemed table Grapes of all colors and flavors which will ripen in succession.

To the preceding list we may add the following, which are excellent varieties, and succeed well:—Ionia, Isabella, Concord, Hartford Prolific, Catawba, Delaware, and some others,

BEST VARIETIES FOR WINE.

The best wine in Italy and Spain is also made from Grapes of this description; but in both countries many of the larger-berried sorts are grown on account of their producing more liquor. The sweet wines, as the Malmsey, Madeira, Constantia, Tokay, etc., are made from sweet-berried Grapes, allowed to remain on the plants till dead-ripe. That wine is the strongest, and has most flavor, in which both the skins and stones are bruised and fermented. The same thing is true in making cider; but in both processes bruising the stones or kernels is neglected. The vine was formerly extensively cultivated in Britain for the wine-press, but its culture is now confined to the garden as a dessert fruit; and they have in that country not only the best varieties, but they grow the fruit to a larger size, and of a higher flavor, than is done anywhere else in the world. This is owing to the perfection of their artificial climates, and the great attention paid to soil and subsoil, and other points of culture. The fruit is produced in some vineries during every month in the year; and in the London markets (generally) it is to be had in the highest degree of perfection from March to January.

SOIL AND ITS PREPARATION.

The vine will thrive in any soil that has a dry bottom; and in such as are rich and deep it will grow luxuriantly, and produce abundance of large fruit. In shallow, dry, chalky, or gravelly soils, it will produce less fruit, but of better flavor. Speechly recommends dung reduced to a black mould, the dust and dirt of roads, the offal of animals or butchers' manure, horn shavings, old rags, shavings of leather, bone dust, dung of deer and sheep, human excrement, when duly meliorated by time, a winter's frost, and repeatedly turning over. Abercrombie says that dung out of a cow-house, well rotted, is a fine manure for the vine. He recommends drainings from dunghills to be used over the ground once in ten or fourteen days from the time the buds rise till the fruit is set; and that fresh horse-dung be spread over the ground in autumn as a manure, and also to protect the roots from the inclemency of the weather. Some, however, disapprove of manuring high, as being calculated to produce wood rather than fruit.

Whatever the soil may be, whether light or heavy, fertile or barren, grape-vines will not flourish well if there be an excess of moisture in it. Underdraining is the first requisite. The next thing is thorough and deep pulverization, either with a subsoil-plough, or by spading two or three spits deep. If the soil be heavy, the more sand, sawdust, or chip manure one can mingle with it the better it will be for the vines. If there be a large proportion of sand, let clay be mingled with it. Clay will render it more productive for Grapes as well as for grass, or a crop of cereal grain.

It has been proved by repeated experiments that the best manure for vines is the branches pruned from the vines themselves, cut into small pieces, and mixed with the soil by means of a garden-hoe. Dr. Liebig, in his "Organic Chemistry," mentions several instance of vines being kept in a thriving condition for from ten to thirty years by the trimmings of vines alone. The discovery was made by poor peasants, who could not afford to buy the ordinary kinds of manure. Vines cut into small pieces will be found an excellent fertilizer on heavy soils, when there is an excess of clay; and it is a good practice to dispose of all prunings in that manner. If the pieces be covered lightly with earth as soon as they are cut, they will decay in a few months, and make excellent mould.

MODES OF PROPAGATING GRAPES.

The general mode of propagating the vine is by cuttings, either a foot or more long, with a portion of two-year-old wood; or short, with only one bud, or one bud and a half joint. Vines may be obtained at the nurseries, propagated either from layers, cuttings, or eyes. Plants raised from cuttings are generally preferred. Many are of opinion that it is a matter of indifference from which class the choice is made, provided the plants are well rooted and in good health, and the wood ripe. A mode of very general utility is to select the plants in the nursery a year before wanted, and to order them to be potted in very large pots. Varieties without end are raised from seed, and it is thought that by propagating from the seed of successive generations, some sorts may ultimately be procured better adapted for ripening their fruit in the open air than now known. A seedling-vine, carefully treated, will show blossoms in its fourth or fifth year. If it produces a fair specimen of its fruit in the sixth year, then a new generation may be obtained so often. But seed ought never to be sown, except for experiment.

If the ground be mellow, vines may be laid down in a channel and covered with mellow soil and a flat stone or two bricks laid over the place where the roots should start. About every two feet, a bud on the vine should be exposed to the air and light, from which a cane will spring. Vines treated in this manner will form a system of good roots in one season; and when one year old, excellent plants may be taken up and transplanted when they are to produce grapes.

TRAINING GRAPE-VINES.

The illustration on the next page represents the pyramidal mode of training grape-vines, which is practised in large vineyards to a greater extent than any other mode of training. A strong stake, not over seven or eight feet long, is set a few inches from the root of each vine, and in some instances the main vine is wound around the stake and tied with pieces of old rope. The ends of the canes are pinched off as soon as they extend beyond a given limit.

GRAFTING GRAPES.

The following method of grafting the vine is recommended

by Mr. Loudon: Select a scion with one good eye; pare it beneath the eye and on the opposite side in the form of a wedge. Select from the stock to be grafted on, a branch of the preceding year; cut this off a little above the second eye

Pyramidal Training.

from its base; then with a sharp knife split it down the centre nearly to the old wood. Out of each half of the stock, but chiefly out of that half which is opposite the bud, pare off as much as is necessary to make it fit the scion, which must be inserted with its eye opposite to the eye which is left on the top of the stock, and bandaged together carefully with bass matting. Some use grafting-clay, others composition; in either case, a small hole for the eye of the graft, and another hole for the eye left on the stock, must be left open. Tie over a little moss, to be occasionally sprinkled with water. It is essential that the young shoot on the top of the stock should be allowed to grow for ten or fifteen days; then cut it off, leaving only one eye and one leaf to draw the sap and keep alive the circulation, till both scion and stock are perfectly united.

SELECT DESCRIPTIVE LIST OF NATIVE GRAPES.

ALEXANDER, *Constantia of Vevay, Madeira of York, Pa., Winne, Schuylkill Muscadel.* A good wine fruit, of large size, blackish color, and oblong form; very juicy and pungent; a great and sure bearer.

BLAND, *Bland's Madeira, Bland's Virginia, Mazzei, Powel.* A pale-red grape, of large size and round shape, rather musky, but the juice is sweet and lively.

CAROLINA PERFUMED. A medium-sized fruit, of purple color and rather an unpleasant odor; it is, however, considered as well adapted for wine, being rather pungent, very juicy, and pulpless.

CATAWBA, *Red Muncy, To Kalon.* A fine variety, above medium size, of dark red color, in form round, in flavor delicious for the dessert, and highly productive: it ripens soon after the Isabella.

CUNNINGHAM. A native of Prince Edward's county, Virginia; the berries are round, black, of medium size, and not liable to rot; they are said to resemble, in taste, the Nigrillo of Madeira, and are considered good for wine as well as for the table.

ELSINGBURG. Fruit small, round, of purple color, and delicate musky flavor, without pulp; good for wine, and as a dessert fruit; the vine is very hardy and productive.

HIDE'S ELIZA. Berries large, oval, of violet color, and excellent flavor; alike suited for the dessert and for wine.

ISABELLA. A well known and highly estimated variety. Fruit large, oval, of rich purple color, covered with bloom; skin, under good cultivation, thin; flesh juicy, rich and vinous; an excellent dessert fruit.

LUFBOROUGH. A sweet fox grape of large size and round

shape; skin dark purple; pulp dissolving in a saccharine musky juice; good for wine.

MADDOX. A good wine grape, not liable to rot; it is of medium size; roundish; of a brownish red color, and a brisk vinous flavor.

NORTON'S VIRGINIA SEEDLING, *Longworth's Ohio.* An early fruit of medium size and dark purple color; it ripens in September; makes excellent wine; it is also generally approved as a dessert fruit.

POND'S SEEDLING. A large purple grape of roundish form, thin skin, and of rich pungent flavor; adapted for wine as well as for the table.

SCUPPERNONG. This species is very prolific; the berries are large, roundish, and of a color varying from brick red to black; makes peculiar Muscat wine, and is highly esteemed as a dessert fruit.

WARREN, *Madeira.* A round fruit of medium size and dark purple color; it is considered by some as the most luscious of all native grapes; it makes excellent wine.

WOODSON. A small round black Virginian variety, from Prince Edward's county; it is celebrated as a very proper fruit for the manufacture of *sparkling wine;* it ripens later than most other varieties, but yields abundantly.

SELECT DESCRIPTIVE LIST OF FOREIGN GRAPES.

[Those designated thus * will ripen in the open air. Those marked thus † require but little forcing in favorable seasons.]

* BLACK CLUSTER, *Black Morillon, True Burgundy, Early Black, Auverna.* Bunches rather larger than those of the Miller's Burgundy; berries middle size, somewhat oval; skin of a very black color; juice rich and sweet; the fruit ripens in the open air about the middle of September.

BLACK DAMASCUS, *Worksop Manor Grape.* Bunches middle

size; berries large, globular; skin thin, of a fine black color flesh delicate; juice rich, and of exquisite flavor when properly cultivated under glass.

† Black Frontignan, *Black Frontignac, Violet Frontignac, Muscat Noir, Black Constantia* of some. Berries of medium size, round, and grow close on the bunches; skin black; flesh tender; the juice of a rich vinous musky flavor; it ripens in October, in favorable seasons without fire-heat.

† Black Hamburgh, *Warner's Black Hamburgh, Potier Bleu, Victoria* of some collections. Bunches tolerably large, with two short compact shoulders; berries pretty large, of an oval figure; skin rather thick, of a deep purple color, nearly black; flesh tender; juice sugary and rich: a good and regular bearer. *Wilmot's New Black Hamburgh* is said to bear larger berries.

Black Lombardy, *West's St. Peter's.* Bunches long, with large shoulders; berries large, roundish oval; skin thin, very black at maturity; juice plentiful and high flavored; it requires a high temperature, and is then a great bearer.

Black Muscat of Alexandria, *Red Muscat of Alexandria, Red Frontignac of Jerusalem.* Bunches large and shouldered; berries large, oval; skin thick, of a reddish color, becoming black at maturity; flesh quite firm, with a rich vinous flavor: requires a vinery with fire-heat.

† Black Muscadine, *Black Chasselas, Chasselas Noir.* Bunches of medium size, compact; berries globular; skin black, covered with fine bloom; juice rich if well ripened: it requires a vinery.

† Black Prince. Bunches rather long; berries large, oval; skin dark blackish purple, covered with a thick blue bloom; flesh white, abounding with sweet well flavored juice: this variety will ripen here in the open air, and bear profusely in the vinery with the easiest culture.

Black St. Peter's, *Black Palestine, Saint Peter's.* Bunches pretty large and long; berries rather large, almost globular; skin thin, of a black color; flesh delicate, with a very excellent and well-flavored juice: this is one of the best sorts for a vinery without fire-heat, and the fruit may be preserved on the vine for early winter use.

CHASSELAS MOSQUE, *Musk Chasselas.* Bunches of medium size; berries middle-size, round; skin thin, yellowish-white; flesh tender; juice rich and abundant: the highest-flavored chasselas known, having much of the flavor of the Muscat of Alexandria when properly forced.

CHASSELAS ROUGE, *Red Muscadine, Red Chasselas.* The berries of this variety are something larger than those of the Black Muscadine; they are of a dark red color, when highly ripened in the vinery; juice sweet and luscious.

* EARLY BLACK JULY, *July Grape, Madeleine Noire, Maurillon Hatif.* The earliest of grapes. Bunches small and compact; berries small, quite round, of a black color, covered with a blue bloom; flavor moderately sweet, but not rich or perfumed: it ripens here in the open air early in August.

* ESPERIONE, *Hardy Blue Windsor, Turner's Black Cumberland Lodge.* Bunches handsomely shouldered, and differing little in size from the Black Hamburgh; skin of a deep purple color, covered with a thick blue bloom; flesh adheres to the skin, and is of a pleasant flavor: the vine is very prolific.

GRIZZLY FRONTIGNAN, *Grizzly Frontignac, Muscat Gris.* Bunches middle-size, with small narrow shoulders; berries round, of medium size; skin thick, pale brown, blended with red and yellow; flesh very rich, musky, and high flavored: this is one of the best varieties for the vinery.

LOMBARDY, *Flame-Colored Tokay, Red Rhenish, Wantage.* Bunches very large, frequently weighing six or seven pounds, being from twelve to eighteen inches in length; berries large, of somewhat oval figure; skin of a pale red or flame color; flesh firm, with pretty well flavored juice: this variety requires fire-heat to bring it to perfection.

* MILLER'S BURGUNDY, *Miller Grape, Le Mennier, Morillon Taconne.* Bunches short, thick, and compact; berries small, roundish, very closely set together; skin thin, with fine blue

bloom ; flesh tender, abounding with sweet, high-flavored juice ; each berry contains two small seeds.

* PITMASTON'S WHITE CLUSTER. A pretty hardy English variety. Bunches of medium size, compact and shouldered ; berries middle-size, round ; skin thin, light amber color, occasionally shaded with russet when fully ripe ; flesh tender, juicy, sweet, and excellent.

† RED HAMBURGH, *Warner's Red Hamburgh*, *Brown Hamburgh*, *Gibraltar.* The berries of this are of a dark red or purple color, with a thin skin, and juicy, delicate flesh. The size and figure of both the bunch and the berry are very much like the Black Hamburgh, except the latter being less oval, and growing more loosely on the bunches. When the berries are imperfectly ripened, they are of a pale brown color, hence it is called Brown Hamburgh.

* ROYAL MUSCADINE, *Amber Muscadine*, *Early White Teneriffe*, *Golden Chasselas*, *White Chasselas.* Bunches large and shouldered ; berries round, larger than those of the Sweetwater; skin thin, at first greenish-white, but turning to an amber color when fully ripe; flesh tender and of a rich flavor.

SYRIAN. Bunches enormously large, with broad shoulders; berries large, oval; skin thick, white at first, but amber color when fully ripe; flesh firm, juicy, and sweet. A bunch of this variety was gathered in Mr. Speechly's vinery at Welbeck, England, four feet and a half in circumference, weighing nineteen pounds and a half. The Syrian grape is supposed to be the sort mentioned in Numbers xiii. 23.

VERDELHO, *Verdal*, *Verdilhio*, *Madeira Wine Grape.* Bunches rather small, loose, inclined to shoulder; berries oval, small, rather unequal in size; skin thin, almost transparent; juice, when fully matured in the vinery, of a rich saccharine flavor.

WHITE FRONTIGNAN, *White Frontignac*, *Muscat blanc*, *White Constantia.* Bunches rather long, without shoulders; berries middle-size, round, rather closely set; skin thin, of a greenish-yellow, covered with a thin bloom ; flesh tender, very rich, and of a high musky flavor, when cultivated in the vinery.

WHITE HAMBURGH, *White Raisin, White Portugal, White Lisbon, Raisin Muscat.* Bunches large, loosely formed ; berries large, of an oval figure ; skin thick, of a greenish-white color ; flesh hard ; juice sweet, and slightly acid. Bunches of three pounds weight have been gathered in vineries near Boston.

WHITE MUSCAT OF ALEXANDRIA, *Jerusalem Muscat, Passe-longue Musque, Malaga, Tottenham Park Muscat.* The most delicious of all grapes, but requires to be grown under glass in this climate. Bunches large, and well shouldered ; berries large, oval ; skin thick, of pale-amber color when fully ripe ; flesh firm ; juice of a sweet, musky, and most delicious flavor.

* WHITE MELIER, *Melier blanc, Early White Malvasia, Early Chasselas.* Berries middle-size, somewhat of an oval figure ; color yellowish-white ; flesh sweet, juicy, and agreeable in flavor : ripens in August.

WHITE NICE. Bunches very large, with loose shoulders ; berries roundish, of medium size ; skin greenish-white, becoming yellowish when ripe ; flesh crisp, and of good flavor. Mr. McIntosh has gathered from his vinery in England bunches weighing eighteen pounds.

* WHITE SWEET-WATER, *Early White Muscadine, Early Sweetwater.* Bunches middle-size ; berries round, growing close ; skin whitish, sometimes shaded with a light russet ; flesh sweet, watery, saccharine, and luscious : the fruit ripens in the open air towards the end of August.

* WHITE TOKAY, *Gray Tokay, Tokai blanc.* Bunches of medium size, compact ; berries oval, closely set ; skin dull white ; flesh very delicate, sweet and perfumed : good for wine and for the dessert. It will ripen in the open air.

SELECT DESCRIPTIVE LIST OF NATIVE GRAPES.

DIANA. A seedling of the Catawba, raised by Mrs. Diana Crehore, of Boston. Fruit resembling the Catawba, but paler in color; bunches loose; berries round, juicy, and fine flavored; it ripens two weeks earlier than the parent.

GILBERT'S WHITE SHONGA. This variety was found by Garret Gilbert, of the city of New York, on the Shonga Mountains in 1825, and planted in his garden. It is a great bearer, of similar habits with the Isabella, differing from that kind only in color, and coming to maturity a little earlier.

LENOIR, *Sumpter*, *Clarence.* This variety was introduced by Mr. Lenoir, of the Santee river, Carolina. Bunches large, very handsome; berries small, round; skin purple, with a light bloom; flesh tender, sweet, and excellent.

MISSOURI, *Missouri Seedling.* Bunches of medium size; berries small and round; skin black, with a little bloom; flesh tender, sweet, and pleasant.

OHIO, *Segar Box Grape*, *Longworth's Ohio.* The cuttings from which Mr. Longworth's first stock originated, were left at his residence by an unknown friend, in a cigar-box. Bunches from six to ten inches long; berries round and small; skin thin, purple; flesh tender and melting: a good dessert fruit.

SHURTLEFF'S SEEDLING. Raised by Dr. S. A. Shurtleff, of Pemberton Hill, Boston. Bunches large, often weighing a pound; berries oval, of medium size; skin thick, light purple, with a greyish bloom; flesh firm, and of excellent flavor: the fruit is fit for the table in September.

UCHEE GRAPE. A native grape found on the banks of the Uchee creek, Russell county, Alabama. The bunches are long, very compact, and of a jet black color; the berries yield but little juice, which is extremely rich, and makes delicious wine without sugar.

WHITE SCUPPERNONG. Bunches short and close set; berries large, of a roundish figure; skin white, with some dark specks; juice sweet and rich: it is a great bearer, ripening its fruit early.

☞ The Managers of the American Institute having at their nineteenth Annual Fair, held at Castle Garden, in the City of New York, awarded premiums for Native Wine, I here insert a copy of the Judges' Report.

"*Report on Native Wine tested October 21st*, 1846, *by* C. Henry Hall, W. Niblo, *and* Adoniram Chandler, *Committee of Judges on Wine.*"

"The five kinds of wine described below, were sent by Mr. N. Longworth, of Cincinnati, Ohio, to whom a Silver Cup was awarded.

"No. 1.—A fine light wine, called 'Ladies' Wine,' with sugar added before fermentation; delicious in flavor. and will compete with foreign sweet wine.

"No. 2.—A light dry wine, from the Catawba grape; sound, of peculiar flavor, resembling that of Hock, and of the Bouquet.

"No. 3.—A good dry wine, of pure juice, different vintage from the last described, but good sound wine, although not high flavored.

"No. 4.—A dry wine from the pure juice of the Herbemont Grape. It is sound, of the peculiar flavor of the grape, and will without doubt be admired.

"No. 5.—From the Missouri Grape, five per cent. brandy. The wine is thin in body, and wanting flavor, perhaps arising from our not having had a fair chance of tasting it at perfection, it having been recently shaken up."

A Silver Medal was awarded for each of the bottles described below.

A bottle of wine furnished by Mr. T. L. Prevost, Greenville, Greene county, was tested, which was represented to be four years old. "A sort of Hock, of fine flavor, but in a state of fermentation, the sugar not being dissolved and the spirit formed."

A bottle from Mr. Charles Peabody, made by him from a native grape found on the banks of the Uchee creek, in Russell county, Alabama, was pronounced by the judges, "a pleasant wine, sweet, like Malmsey, and if no sugar has been added to the juice, as is represented, it is remarkable in its character."

It is recorded in the *Southern Cultivator*, "that some of the most celebrated wine connoisseurs of Columbus describe the wine made from the Uchee Grape as having the body of Port, with a little of the Muscat flavor, and equal to the best imported."

TRAINING AND PRUNING.

There are various methods adopted in training and pruning the vine; and it appears impossible to lay down rules to suit every cultivator. The vine having, like other trees, a tendency to produce its most vigorous shoots at the extremities of the branches, and particularly so at those which are situated highest, it generally happens, when it is trained high, that the greater portion of the fruit is borne near the top; and it has been observed that the fruit produced on the vigorous shoots, which naturally grow at the extremities of the long branches, is generally more abundant, and of finer quality than that produced on the short lateral ones, from which circumstance some fruit-growers contend that high training is best calculated for private gardens.

In some parts of Italy, vines are cultivated together with Mulberry-trees, and are allowed to mingle and hang in festoons. Thus silk and wine are produced on the same spot; and it is considered that when vines are allowed to grow over trees, on the side of a house, or on bowers, or extended on tall poles, without much trimming, they will produce more fruit, and are not so liable to mildew.

Dr. G. W. Chapman, of New York, having paid some attention to the cultivation of native grapes, observes that the vine, in its natural state, seldom or never throws out bearing-shoots until it reaches the top of the tree on which it ascends, when the branches take a horizontal or descending position. From this fact he considers horizontal training preferable to that in-the fan shape. From the experiments he has made, he has found that the shoots coming from those parts of the branches bent downwards, are more productive than from those ascending. He considers deep digging around the vine, even to the destruc-

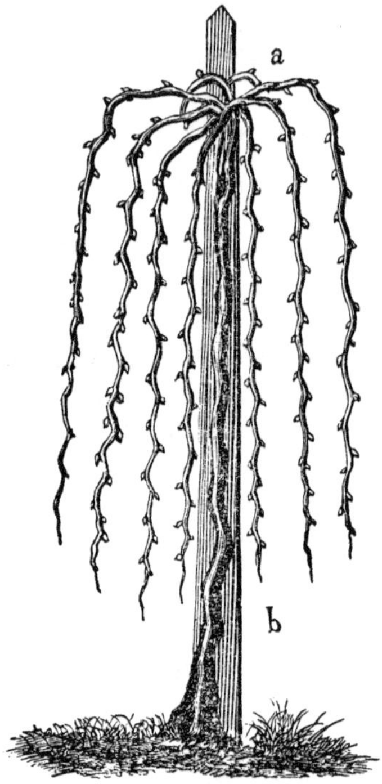

tion of some of the extending roots, as calculated to promote the growth of more fruit and less wood than if allowed to spread near the surface; and he disapproves stopping the shoots before the fruit until early in July.

LAYING DOWN VINES IN WINTER.

Mr. William Wilson, of Clermont, leaves his foreign vines

their whole length at the time of trimming in October. In November, they are laid on the ground at full length, fastened down with pins, and covered lightly with earth. In this state they lie all the winter. In April, as soon as the weather will permit, they are uncovered, and left lying on the ground ten or twelve days. By the first of May the vines are trained to stakes or poles of the length of ten feet and upwards; and by the middle of June the stakes are entirely covered by new shoots of the vine, and with plenty of fruit, which ripens in September. Mr. W. says, that until he pursued his present course, his fruit was frequently blasted and mildewed; but that he has now vines twenty or thirty feet long, which run up the fruit-trees adjoining; others, being carried up eight or ten feet, are stretched horizontally. It is seldom he gathers fruit within three or four feet of the ground, and he has never any blasted or infected with mildew. He keeps the ground cultivated by frequent hoeing; but he says he has used no manure for ten years or more.

PREPARATION OF SOIL AND PLANTING.

Edward H. Bonsall has a vineyard of American Grapes at Germantown, Pa., in a high state of cultivation. In a letter to the author, from which the following is extracted as appropriate to our subject, he says:

" Mr. Bonsall's vineyard is situated between the Schuylkill and Delaware rivers, four miles from the former, and eight from the latter, at an elevation of three hundred feet above their level; has an aspect facing S.S.E., with a substratum of light isinglass soil, and seems well suited to the purpose. He says: ' From my experience, both on my premises and at other places, it is my opinion that we should reject almost all the foreign varieties, especially where our object in cultivating them is to make wine.' He has upwards of thirty varieties of American vines under cultivation; he recommends preparing the ground by ploughing with two ploughs with strong teams, one immediately behind the other, in the same furrow, each of them set deep; and after the ploughing is completed, to be harrowed thoroughly. Then in the direction the rows are intended to be planted, parallel furrows are run across the field, at the distance of eight feet from each other; these are afterwards crossed at right angles, five feet asunder. In the opening, at the intersection of these furrows, cuttings from nine to twelve inches long are planted, and arranged with a view to the vines being, when grown, at distances of four by seven feet from each other. He frequently plants two cuttings in a place, some of which are used to fill up with, in case of failures. He says that in 1829 he planted in nursery-beds from two to three thousand cuttings as late as the middle of April to the middle of May, with better success than at any previous time. In this case the slips should be kept in a cool, damp place, where vegetation may be held in check. To insure their freshness, sprinkle them occasionally with water. Previous to planting, cut them a proper length, and place them with their lower ends three or four inches in water, in a tub above the ground, where they may soak three or four days. At this season the temperature will be likely to be such as to spur vegetation at once into healthy and vigorous action. The autumn, or early in the spring, is preferable for rooted plants. In the autumn of the first year, after the frost has killed the unripened part of the young shoots, they should be pruned down to the mature, firm wood, and then with a hoe hilled over with the surrounding soil, which will completely protect them through the winter. If left without protection the first winter, many of them will perish."

TRAINING ON WIRE TRELLISES.

Mr. Bonsall says his mode of training, as far as he is aware of it, is entirely peculiar to himself, which he describes as follows: "I take chestnut posts, the thickness of large fence-rails, seven feet in length; these I plant along the rows, at distances of ten feet from each other, and at such a depth as to leave five feet above the surface of the earth. Then taking three nails to each post, and driving them to within half an inch of their heads, the first two and a half feet from the ground, a second midway between that and the top, and the third near the top, I attach No. 11 iron annealed wire firmly to one of the nails in the end post, pass on to the next, and stretching it straight and tight, give it one turn round a nail in the same line as the one to which it was first attached. Having in this manner extended it along the three courses, the whole length of the row, my trellis is formed. I have had a portion of my vineyard fitted up in this way for three years, and experience has confirmed the superior fitness of the plan. It is not its least recommendation, that it possesses in a degree the character of labor-saving machinery. A very important and extensive labor-making portion of the operations in the vineyard during the summer is the attention required by the growing shoots to keep them properly trained up. They grow and extend themselves so rapidly, that where the strips of the trellis are lath, or where poles are used to support vines, unless very closely watched, they fall down in every direction, in a very unsightly and injurious manner. Here the wire being small, the tendrils or claspers eagerly and firmly attach themselves to it, and thus work for themselves in probably two-thirds of the instances where the attention of the vigneron would otherwise be required. There is a free access afforded to the sun and air, and no hold for the wind to strain the frame. After the vines have attained a full capacity for production (say five years from the cutting), my view is to prepare them for bearing an average of fifty clusters to each, leaving several shoots of from three to five joints on a vine for this purpose. When fresh pruned, they will not be more than four feet high, at their greatest age."

The modes of training in vineyards and vineries are alike suited to the garden. Low training may be practised in borders or hedge rows in large gardens; and high training in sheltered situations, on high trellises or arbors. By proper management, the vine may be elevated to the middle story of a house by a single stem, and afterwards trained to a great height according to the taste of the proprietor.

INFLUENCE OF CLIMATE.

Dr. R. T. Underhill, of New York, has a vineyard at Croton Point, near Sing Sing, where, after having sunk thousands of dollars in attempting to raise the most celebrated foreign varieties, he abandoned the project as visionary, and commenced planting the Isabella Grape in 1832, and the Catawba in 1835. Mr. Underhill has now upwards of twenty acres of these grapes, chiefly of the former, under the most successful cultivation. He says that the Isabella Grape ripens two or three weeks earlier than the Catawba, and that these two varieties are, in his estimation, the best adapted for general purposes; the former yielding with him a more valuable crop than any other with which he is acquainted. He says that the quality of this fruit has improved very much within a few years, the clusters and berries being much larger and sweeter; and that they are capable of still greater improvement by high cultivation.

"In this latitude (south of the highlands of the Hudson), I find that the Isabella Grape ripens quite as well when planted in a level field, protected from the north and west winds by woods or hedges, as on declivities. Several of my vineyards are thus located, and, as far as I can perceive, the fruit ripens at about the same time, and is of the same quality as those planted on steep side-hills. I think, however, that north of the highlands, side-hills would be preferable. To prepare the ground for a vineyard, the best way is to turn over the whole of the surface soil from fifteen to eighteen inches in depth, early in the spring, by ploughing twice in the same furrow. This will place the richest part of the soil in a position where it will give the greatest supply of nourishment to the vines. Few vineyards in this country have been prepared in this way. But the cost is so small and the advantages so great, that it

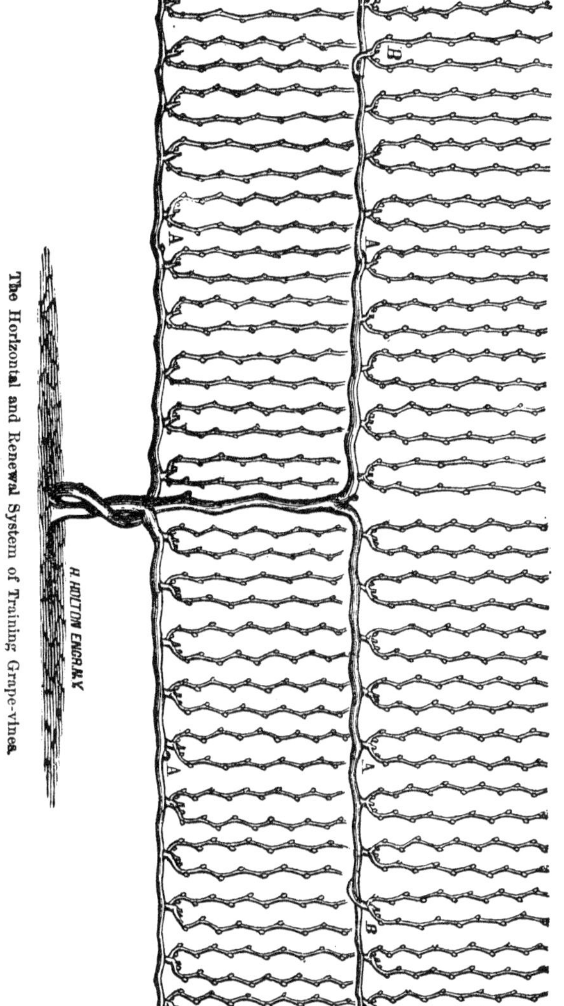

The Horizontal and Renewal System of Training Grape-vines.

should be done wherever there are no rocks or large stones to prevent it."

HORIZONTAL TRAINING.

A vine may be trained horizontally under the coping of a close fence or wall, to a great distance, and the borders in an east, south-east, and southern aspect of large gardens may be furnished with a variety of sorts, which will ripen in great perfection, without encumbering the borders; or the plants may be trained low, like currant-bushes; in which case, three or

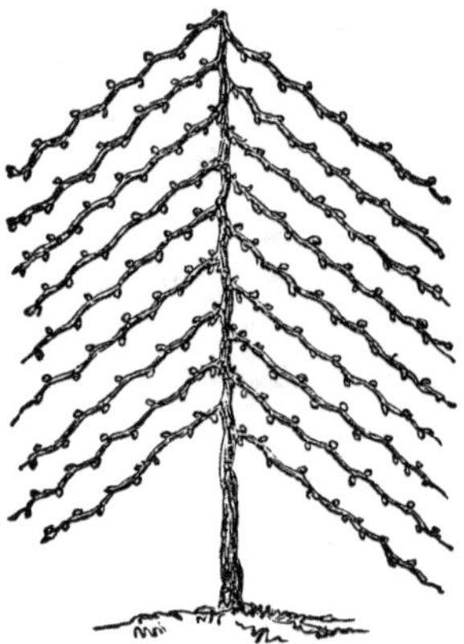

Training in the Form of a Tree.

more shoots, eighteen inches or two feet in length, may diverge from the stem near the ground, to supply young wood annually for bearing. The summer pruning consists in removing shoots which have no fruit, or are not required for the succeeding season; and in topping fruit-bearing shoots, and also those for succeeding years when inconveniently long and straggling. For as, by this mode, the shoots destined to bear are all cut into three or four eyes at the winter pruning, no inconvenience arises from their throwing out laterals near the extremities, which topping will generally cause them to do.

In training vines as standards, the single stem at the bottom is not allowed to exceed six or eight inches in height, and from this two or three shoots are trained or tied to a single stake of three or four feet in length. These shoots bear each two or three bunches, within a foot or eighteen inches of the ground; and they are annually succeeded by others which spring from their base, that is, from the crown or top of the dwarf main stem. This is the mode practised in the north of France and in Germany. In the south of France and Italy, the base or main stem is often higher, and furnished with side shoots, in order to afford a great supply of bearing-wood, which is tied to one or more poles of greater height. The summer pruning, in this case, is nearly the same as in the last. In the winter pruning, the wood that has borne is cut out, and the new wood shortened, in cold situations, to three or four eyes, and in warmer places to six or eight eyes.

PINCHING AND RUBBING OFF BUDS.

Nicoll observes that "most of the summer pruning of vines may be performed with the fingers, without a knife, the shoots to be displaced being easily rubbed off, and those to be shortened, being little, are readily pinched asunder." After selecting the shoots to be trained for the production of a crop next season, and others necessary for filling the trellis from the bottom, which shoots should generally be laid in at the distance of a foot or fifteen inches from each other, rub off all the others that have no clusters, and shorten those that have, at one joint above the uppermost cluster. For this purpose, go over the plants every three or four days till all the shoots in fruit have shown their clusters, at the same time rubbing off any water-shoots that may rise from the wood.

Train in the shoots to be retained as they advance. If there be an under trellis, on which to train the summer shoots, they may, when six or eight feet in length, or when the Grapes are swelling, be let down to it, that the fruit may enjoy the full air and light as it advances towards maturity. Such of these shoots as issue from the bottom, and are to be shortened in the winter pruning to a few eyes, merely for the production of wood to fill the trellis, may be stopped when they have grown to the length of four or five feet. Others that are intended to be cut down to about two yards, and which issue at different heights, may be stopped when they have run three yards, or ten feet, less or more, according to their strength. And those intended to be cut at or near the top of the trellis, should be trained a yard or two down the back, or a trellis may be placed so as to form an arbor; or they may be placed to run right or left a few feet on the uppermost wire.

The stubs or shoots on which the clusters are placed will probably push again after being stopped, if the plants be vigorous. If so, stop them again and again. But after the Grapes are half grown, the shoots will seldom spring. Observe to divest the shoots, in training, of all laterals as they appear, except the uppermost on each, in order to provide against accidents, as hinted before, in training the newly-planted vines. When these shoots are stopped, as directed above, they will push again. Allow the lateral that pushes to run a few joints, and then shorten it back to one, and so on as it pushes, until it stops entirely. When the proper shoots get ripened nearly to the top, the whole may be cut back to the originally shortened part, or to one joint above it, if there be reason to fear that the uppermost bud of the proper shoot will start. Divest the plants of all damp and decayed leaves as they appear, as such will sometimes occur in continued hazy weather, and be particularly cautious not to injure the leaf that accompanies the bunch; for if that is lost, the fruit will be of little value.

THINNING THE GREEN FRUIT.

"Everyone of penetration and discernment," Nicoll observes, "will admit the utility of thinning the berries on bunches of Grapes, in order that they may have room to swell fully; and, further, that of supporting the shoulders of such clusters of the large-growing kinds as hang loosely, and require to be suspended to the trellis or branches, in order to prevent the bad effects of damp or mouldiness in very moist seasons. Of these, the Hamburgh, Lombardy, Royal Muscadine, Raisins, St. Peter's, Syrian, Tokay, and others, should have their shoulders suspended to the trellis, or to the branches, by strands of fresh matting, when the berries are about the size of garden peas. At the same time, the clusters should be regularly thinned out with narrow-pointed scissors, to the extent of from a fourth to a third part of the berries. The other close-growing kinds, as the Frontignacs and Muscats, should likewise be moderately thinned, observing to thin out the small seedless berries only of the Muscadine, Sweet Water, and flame-colored Tokay. In this manner, handsome bunches and full-swelled berries may be obtained; but more so, if the clusters of overburdened plants be also moderately thinned away. Indeed, cutting off the clusters, to a certain extent, of plants overloaded, and pushing weak wood, are the only means by which to cause them to produce shoots fit to bear fruit next year; and this should be duly attended to so long as the future welfare of the plants is a matter of importance."

ROSE-BUGS ON GRAPE-VINES.

"When the rose-bugs first appear on the vines, they are so feeble as to be unable to fly even for a few yards. I directed my men to take each a cup, with a little water in it, and go through the vineyards every morning, removing every bug from the vines; and this was done quite rapidly by passing the cup under the leaf and merely touching it, when the bugs instantly dropped, and were received in the cup containing the water. When the cup was full, they were soon destroyed by crushing them with the foot. This plan was persevered in every morning as long as a bug could be found, and was attended with such success, that they have given me very little trouble since. I also tried ploughing my vineyards just before winter set in, so as to expose to the weather the insect in the larva state, which will certainly destroy the young tribe that have not descended below the reach of the plough. For two years past the number has been so small that I have omitted this process for their destruction."—*R. T. Underhill.*

MULBERRY.

Murier. *Morus.*

There are several species of the Morus or Mulberry. The white kind is commonly cultivated for its leaves to feed silkworms, though in some parts of Spain, and in Persia, they are said to prefer the Black Mulberry. In China, both sorts are grown for this purpose. The most esteemed variety of the white is grown in Italy, and especially in Lombardy, with vigorous shoots, and much larger leaves than the other. The *Morus multicaulis* is cultivated in many parts of France, and is by some preferred to all other varieties. It is said that a less quantity of foliage from this variety will satisfy the silkworms. The late Andrew Parmentier, Esq., was the means of introducing several choice varieties from that country; and our nursery-men, in general, have of late years turned their attention to the cultivation of such as are best adapted to silkworms.

In France, the white Mulberry is grown as pollard Elms are in England. In Lombardy it is grown in low, marshy ground. In China it is also grown in moist loamy soil; and both there and in the East Indies, as low bushes, and the plantations rooted up and renewed every three or four years. In many parts, when the leaves are wanted for the worms, they are stripped off the young shoots, which are left naked on the tree; in other places the shoots are cut off, which is not so injurious to the tree, while the points of the shoots, as well as the leaves, are eaten by the worms.

PROPAGATION BY SEEDS.

The plants are sometimes raised from seed, and one ounce of seed will produce five thousand trees, if sown in rich loamy soil in the latter part of April, or early in May. But the young plants will require protection the first winter. The berries are put in a sack of coarse cloth, crushed with a foot or with the hands, and the pulpy matter all washed out, leaving the seeds quite clean. They are then spread out on boards or cloth, and dried in the shade, and kept in a cool and dry apartment till planting-time. The soil should be very mellow, and in a good state of fertility. The seeds may be planted in drills four feet apart, and not more than one inch deep. Half an inch deep is better. If the soil be heavy, cover the seed with leaf-mould, or some other fine and mellow dirt. Cultivate between the drills with a horse-hoe; and dress out the young plants as if they were carrots.

PROPAGATION BY LAYERS.

The different kinds of Mulberry are more commonly propagated by layers and cuttings put down in the spring. The ground is well prepared and enriched the previous year; and the cuttings are taken from the trees early in the spring, or even in the winter, and kept like scions till the ground is ready to receive them. Transplant the cuttings as recommended for currants (which see on a previous page), and cultivate in drills till the young trees are of a suitable size to transplant. The Italian variety is frequently grafted on seedling stocks of the common sort, in order to preserve it from degenerating. In the East Indies, the plants are raised from cuttings, three or four of which are placed together, where they are finally tc remain.

THE FRUIT.

Mulberry-trees are valuable for their fruit; and in England

the black and red kinds are in great esteem, and much cultivated. The fruit of the white Mulberry is white, and less acid than that of the black species. The black is naturally a stronger tree than the other; the fruit is of a dark, blackish red, and of an agreeable aromatic and acid flavor. The red Mulberry has black shoots, rougher leaves than the black Mulberry, and a dark, reddish fruit, longer than the common sort, and of a very pleasant taste. The fruit of the yellow Mulberry is sweet and wholesome, but not much eaten, excepting by birds. The timber, however, is valuable, from its abounding in a slightly glutinous milk of a sulphurous color, and is known in Europe under the name of fustic wood, for dying a yellow color. In Russia, the fruit of the *Morus tartarica* is eaten fresh, conserved, or dried. A wine and a spirit are also made from them; but the berries are said to be of an insipid taste.

All the species of the Morus are remarkable for putting out their leaves late, so that when they appear, gardeners may safely set out their green-house plants, taking it for granted that all danger from frost is over. From this circumstance, plantations of Mulberry-trees may be made in this country in the spring of the year with greater safety.

The Mulberry produces its fruit chiefly on little shoots of the same year, which arise on last year's wood and on spurs from the two-year-old wood, mostly at the ends of the shoots and the branches. In pruning, thin out irregular crossing branches, but never shorten the young wood on which fruit is produced. If any of the dwarfish kinds are cultivated as espaliers for their fruits, cut so as to bring in a partial succession of new wood every year, and a complete succession once in two years, taking the old barren wood out, as may be necessary. As the blossom-buds cannot be readily distinguished from others in the winter, the best period for pruning is when the blossoms first become visible in the spring.

THE PAPER MULBERRY.

There is another genus of plants, known as the Paper Mulberry, which is very ornamental, called *Broussonetia papyrifera.* Though a low tree, it has vigorous shoots, furnished with twc large leaves. The fruit, which is small, is surrounded with long purple hairs, changing to a black purple color when ripe, and full of juice. "In China and Japan it is cultivated for the sake of the young shoots, from the bark of which the inhabitants of the Eastern countries make paper. The bark being separated from the wood, is steeped in water, the former making the whitest and best paper. The bark is next slowly boiled, then washed, and afterwards put upon a wooden table, and beat into a pulp, which being put in water, separates like grains of meal. An infusion of rice, and the root of manihot, are next added to it. From the liquor so prepared, the sheets of paper are poured out one by one, and when pressed the operation is finished."

"The juice of this tree is sufficiently tenacious to be used in China as a glue, in gilding either leather or paper. The finest and whitest cloth worn by the principal people at Otaheite, and in the Sandwich Islands, is made of the bark of this tree. The cloth of the Bread Fruit tree is inferior in whiteness and softness, and worn chiefly by the common people."

VALUE OF THE WOOD.

The wood of Mulberry is more durable than the best of White Oak, when it is exposed to the influences of the weather. For fence-posts, it will out-last white cedar; and it is nearly equal in durability to red cedar. I know of posts in Connecticut that have been set in the ground for fifty years and are yet sound.

NECTARINE.

PECHERA FRUIT LISSE, OU BRUGNONS. *Amygdalus nectarina.*

The varieties of this fruit resemble the Peach in every respect, except that the skin is smooth, of a waxen appearance, and the flesh generally more firm. Although of the same genus as the Peach, which is so plentiful in this country, the fruit of the Nectarine is quite a rarity, and seldom appears in our markets. There are seventy-two varieties cultivated in the Horticultural Gardens of London under name.

It is generally allowed that their failure here is occasioned by the attacks of insects. The most efficacious method that I have heard of for securing anything like a crop of Nectarines, is to fumigate the trees in the evening, when the air is calm and serene, at the season when the fruit is ready to set. Tobacco is the most effectual antidote for these insects; but a friend of mine collected a quantity of salt hay that had been used for his Spinach the preceding winter; with this he created a smoke, first on one side of his plantation, and afterwards on the other, by which means he obtained a good supply of fruit. Our enterprising horticulturist, Mr. W. Shaw, has succeeded in gathering fine fruit by training his trees against a close fence; and it has been discovered by others that the Nectarine, like the Grape-vine, will yield best in sheltered situations. That eminent horticulturist, Mr. David Thomas, observes that "A vast quantity of fruit is annually destroyed by the Curculio, which causes the Plum, Apricot, and Nectarine prematurely to drop from the tree. To prevent this loss, let the tree, after the blossoms fall, be frequently shaken by a cord connected with a swinging-door, or with a working pump-handle; or let the bugs be jarred from the tree on sheets spread beneath the tree and killed. Or keep geese enough in the fruit-garden to devour all the damaged fruit as it falls. We know that this last method is infallible."

As some may object to shaking or jarring fruit trees, for fear of disturbing the fruit, such are here reminded, that if the blossoms set more fruit than can be supported, it will not come to full perfection, and the trees may be injured in their future bearing; for these reasons, when fruit sets too thick, it should be thinned in an early stage of its growth.

The Nectarine, as also the Peach-tree, is subject to injury

by an insect different from the Curculio species, which feeds on the sap beneath the bark, principally near the surface of the earth, but if not checked, will commit ravages on the trunk and root, so as to eventually destroy the tree. The egg is supposed to be first deposited in the upper part of the tree; and in the months of June and July it becomes a very small maggot, which drops to the ground and approaches the tree near the surface. If the ground be kept clear around the roots, as it ought always to be, the worm can readily be detected by a small speck of gum, which appears on the tree after it has made its entrance, which gumminess will increase in quantity as it progresses. But if the trees are thoroughly examined about once a week, or ten days, and the gum, wherever found, removed by means of a small knife or pointed wire, the worm may be at once defeated from making any havoc on the trees. An orchard of several acres may be kept free from worms by going over it a few times. After a shower of rain is a good time, as the gum can then be more easily discovered; and when it is removed, the wound will soon heal up, and the danger is over, provided the ground be kept cultivated around the trees, and the collar, or that part from which emanate the main roots, be near the surface.

ILL EFFECTS OF PLANTING TOO DEEP.

This is an important precaution, and should be attended to at the time of transplanting all descriptions of trees and smaller plants; because *deep planting* prevents the essential circulation of the juices of plants in their regular and natural courses, and consequently causes disease and premature death; and it must be admitted, that from the circumstance of this fruit being generally raised on standard trees, and in a light soil, our cultivators are apt to plant too deep; and thus act contrary to sound judgment and philosophy, with a view to save the trouble and expense of staking or otherwise supporting their newly-planted trees, which precaution is absolutely necessary to their preservation, even in less tempestuous climates, and in stiff as well as in light soil.

SALTPETRE FOR NECTARINES.

Saltpetre dissolved in the proportion of one pound to five gallons of water, and applied around the stems and roots of trees, as recommended for plants in general, is, in my opinion, one of the best remedies for the destruction of various kinds of insects. It is, moreover, allowed by modern and learned physiologists to contain the most essential nutriment for all descriptions of trees or smaller plants, when judiciously used. Other remedies are recommended to be applied for the destruction of these insects around fruit-trees, besides those previously mentioned; as dissolved potash, coal-tar, sulphur, vinegar, and soapsuds. Culture, upon correct principles, will operate not only as a radical cure, but as a preventive to all defects in trees and plants; which, to be healthy and productive, should be so managed that the sap and nutrimental juices can circulate through every pore which nature has designed for their perpetuity.

PROPAGATION BY BUDDING.

The Nectarine is generally budded on stocks of the same species, or on the Peach or Plum, two or three years old. Knight recommends growing Almond-stocks for the finer kinds of Nectarines and Apricots, as likely to prevent the mildew, and as being allied to the Peach. Dubreuil recommends a Plum-stock for clayey soils, and the Almond for such as are light, chalky, or sandy. The same opinion is held by the Montreal gardeners. The Flemish nursery-men graft both the Peach and Nectarine on the Myrabella Plum, a small cherry-shaped fruit.

The budding may be performed in July or August, in the side of the stock; which will, if properly managed, shoot the following spring, and attain the length of three or four feet the first year. After the budded trees have ripened their first year's shoots, they may either be planted where they are to remain, or retained in the nursery for two, three, or four years, till in a bearing state. Whether the plants be removed into the orchard at a year old, or remain in the nursery, the first shoots from the bud must be headed down in a judicious manner, in order to promote the most desirable form. In annual pruning, thin out superfluous branches and dry wood, and shorten the bearing-shoots. Nectarines may be trained to a close fence or wall, in private gardens; in which case, such plants should be chosen as are budded low. (See article on Apricot.) The Nectarine may be raised from the seed, planted the same as Peach-pits.

SELECT DESCRIPTIVE LIST OF NECTARINES.

FREESTONE NECTARINES.

Aromatic. A middle-sized, rather globular fruit, skin pale straw-color, with deep red or brown next the sun; flesh pale straw, but red at the stone; juice of a rich vinous flavor; ripe early in August.

Boston, *Lewis's Seedling.* A fine native variety, raised by Mr. Lewis, of Boston; fruit of medium size; heart-shaped; color bright yellow, mottled with red; flesh yellow, firm, pleasant, and peculiar in flavor; ripe in September.

Elruge, *Claremont, Temple's, Vermash of some collections.* One of the very best and most highly flavored Nectarines; fruit medium size, of a green or pale yellow color, with violet cheek; pulp whitish, melting, very juicy, rich, and high-flavored; ripens early in August.

Fairchild's Early. Fruit very early, but small; of globular shape, yellow in the shade, deep scarlet next the sun; flesh yellow, not juicy, but well flavored; ripe in July and August.

Perkins's Seedling. A very large beautiful Nectarine, raised by S. G. Perkins, from the Boston, *Lewis's Seedling;* the form is globular; color bright yellow, with dark crimson on one side; flesh tender, juicy, and high flavored; ripe in September

Pitmaston's Orange. A good-sized globular, almost heart shaped fruit, of a rich yellow color, but dark crimson or purple next the sun; flesh golden yellow, but red next the stone, from which it separates; it is melting, juicy, saccharine, and high flavored; ripe in August.

Scarlet. A middle-sized fruit, somewhat ovate, of a beautiful scarlet color next the sun, and pale red on the shaded side; the flesh separates from the stone, and is at maturity in August.

Vermash. *True Vermash.* This fruit is rather of small size and roundish form, tapering towards the eye; the skin is of a very deep red color next the sun, and of a greenish hue on the other side; flesh white, rich, melting, and juicy; at maturity in August.

Violet, *Violette Hative, Petite Violette Hative, Lord Selsey's Elruge, Large Scarlet.* Fruit variable in size, generally medium; pale yellowish-green, but darkish purple and red next the sun; flesh melting, juicy, rich, and excellent; ripe in July and August.

White, or Flanders Nectarine, *New White, Emerson's New White, Neale's White.* A middle-sized, roundish, very pale fruit, slightly tinged with red next the sun; flesh tender and juicy, with a fine vinous flavor; ripe in August.

CLINGSTONES, OR PAVIES.

Brugnon Violet Musqué, *Brugnon Musqué.* Fruit large, of a deep red and yellow color; skin very smooth; flesh yellow, but red at the stone; saccharine, vinous, musky; at maturity in August and September.

Early Newington, *Large Black Newington, Lucombe's Seedling.* Fruit below the medium size, ovate; skin pale green, and on the sunny side of a deep red color; pulp super-excellent; considered by some as the best of all Nectarines; ripe in August and September.

Golden. Fruit medium size, of the finest orange color, delicately and beautifully mottled with red next the sun, which gives to it a clear waxen appearance; flesh firm, yellow, pale red at the stone, and has a poignant rich flavor; ripens in August and September.

Red Roman, *Roman Red.* A very excellent Nectarine, of large size; the skin dark red next the sun, and of a yellowish hue on the other side; flesh yellowish, but red next the stone; it abounds with rich juice when fully ripe, in August and September.

Scarlet Newington, *Late Newington, Sion Hill.* This variety is much esteemed, the fruit is large, of a beautiful red color next the sun, and of a fine yellow or amber on the other side; its quality is excellent, being rich and juicy; early in September.

Tawny Newington. Fruit large, somewhat ovate; tawny-colored, marbled with dull red or orange next the sun; flesh pale yellow, but red at the stone; very juicy, sugary, and of the most delicious flavor; ripens in August and September. This, in England, is considered one of the best of clingstone Nectarines.

ORANGE, LEMON, &c.

Oranger, Citronier. *Citrus.*

Notwithstanding this fruit, and also the Lemon and Lime, are attainable at all seasons of the year, by supplies from our Southern States, the West Indies, and the South of Europe, yet the plants are entitled to our notice on account of their being so easily cultivated, and from their affording an ornament by exhibiting their fruit the whole of the year. The Orange is generally cultivated as a green-house plant; but may be kept in a light room throughout our severe winters, provided the temperature is not suffered to be below the freezing point, 32 degrees. Its recommendations are, handsome evergreen, shining, tree-like form; most odoriferous flowers, and brilliant, fragrant, and delicious fruits, which succeed each other perpetually, and are not unfrequently seen on the tree at the same time, in two or three stages of growth.

All the species of Citrus endure the open air at Nice, Genoa, and Naples; but at Florence and Milan, and often at Rome, they require protection during the winter, and are generally planted in conservatories and sheds. Loudon says that in the south of Devonshire, and particularly at Saltcombe, may be seen in a few gardens, Orange-trees that have withstood the winter in the open air upwards of a hundred years. The fruit is as large and fine as any from Portugal. Trees raised from seed, and inoculated on the spot, are found to bear the cold better than trees imported.

Any of the varieties of the Orange, Lemon, Lime, Shaddock, Citron, etc., may be grafted or budded on stocks of the common Orange or Lemon; but seed of the Shaddocks and Citrons produces the strongest stocks, and on these may be grafted such kinds as may be needed for a conservatory. The most suitable time for budding is July and August; but this operation may be performed at any time when the sap is in motion. The directions for the management of green-house plants apply also to this family of plants.

PEACH.

PECHER. *Amygdalus Persica.*

The *Peach*, plump and ripe, brings us excellent fare,
Let the *Nectarine*, too, in this eulogy share—
Their flavor how grateful—their juices how fine,
Unequall'd in taste by the fruit of the vine.

It is generally considered that the Peach is of Persian origin. In Media, it is deemed unwholesome; but when planted in Egypt, becomes pulpy, delicious, and salubrious. It has been cultivated, time immemorial, in most parts of Asia.

When it was introduced into Greece is uncertain. The best Peaches in Europe are supposed to be grown in Italy, on standards.

Although this fruit will thrive in any sweet, pulverized soi that is properly prepared, a rich sandy loam is the most suitable. Next to the selection and preparation of a suitable soil, a choice of good healthy trees is of the utmost importance. The seed for stocks should be selected from the vigorous growing young, or middle-aged healthy trees; and the buds should be taken from some of the choicest fruit-bearing trees that can be found. Let the stocks be fairly tested before they are budded; and if any infection exist in the stocks, or in the vicinity where the choice buds are found, reject them if you wish to rear a healthy progeny; as more depends upon these particular points than many are aware of.

BUDDING PEACH-TREES.

In this country the Peach is generally budded on stocks of its own kind; but in England it is often budded on damask Plum-stocks, and some of the more delicate sorts on Apricot stocks, or old Apricot-trees cut down; or on seedling Peaches, Almonds, or Nectarines. (See article Nectarine.) Cobbett says: "There are thousands of Peach-trees in England and France that are fifty years old, and that are still in vigorous fruitfulness." He attributes the swift decay of the Peach-trees here to their being grafted on stocks of their kind. Mr. Michael Floy, of the Harlem Nursery, makes the following observations on this subject, which he says are the result of thirty years' experience as a nursery-man in the vicinity of New York:

"In this country Peaches are generally budded on Peach-stocks. Their growth is rapid, and they will form a tree large enough to transplant from the nursery, the first and second year after budding. Notwithstanding the rapid growth of our peaches, and their coming to maturity so early, with but little care and trouble, it must at the same time be admitted that they too often decay with almost the same celerity. A question here will naturally arise on this subject. What can be done to remedy this?

"CAUSE OF PREMATURE DECAY.

"I think the Peach-stock is defective, and is not sufficiently strong and lasting to make a permanent tree. The roots are soft and delicate, very liable to rot in cold heavy ground, particularly if suffered to stand in a sod, or where the ground is not kept clean, dry, and manured every season. *Secondly.* Supposing that the trees are planted in a warm free soil (which is the proper soil for the Peach) they are liable to the attacks of the worm, which eats into their roots, and barks the trees all around, until the trees are completely destroyed. No better method of destroying these worms has been discovered than simply digging round the trees, and examining the infested plants, and where gum is seen oozing out, there the worm may be generally found and destroyed.

"I think an effectual remedy against this intruder may be found, by budding Peaches and Nectarines on the common bitter ALMOND STOCK. The worm does not like this stock. Peach scions will take on it, and grow about as freely as on the common Peach-stock. *Thirdly.* The Peach-stock causes the Peaches and Nectarines to grow too rapidly, making strong shoots, these producing secondary or lateral shoots; and the fruit of the following summer is produced on the top of these lateral shoots, instead of being produced on the principal or first shoots. This causes naked wood at the bottom; and a straggling, unsightly tree, whose branches being heavy at the top with the fruit, are broken down by high winds."

The illustrations of peach-trees represent the right way and the wrong way of pruning peach-trees. If the branches be not shortened in every year, the limbs will become long and bare, except at the ends; and the fruit will be very inferior. On the contrary, if the ends of the limbs be clipped off the inside of the top will be filled with bearing-branches of excellent fruit. Beginners should aim to have the tops of their peach-trees well filled up with bearing branches. By pruning a little

Peach-Tree badly Pruned.

A Peach-Tree well Pruned.

every year, there will be no difficulty in doing it in a most satisfactory manner.

THE YELLOWS.

For several years past Peach-trees have been subject to what has been deemed a disease called the yellows, from the circumstance of the trees having a yellow and sickly appearance. Much curious philosophy has been spent on this subject without arriving at any satisfactory conclusion. As a remedy for the yellows Mr. Floy recommends budding the Peach on Plum-stocks. He writes:—"The Plum-stock is undoubtedly the best for Peaches and Nectarines in the *Northorn* and *Eastern* States; but especially for open dwarfs or espaliers, for which I give the following reasons:—*First.* The Plum-stock prevents the too rapid growth of the shoots, and causes the principals to bear the fruit the following season, instead of producing lateral shoots the same season, and causing the tree to be more dwarf. The branches are strong and fruitful to the bottom of the shoot, thereby having more fruit in a smaller compass. *Secondly.* It makes harder and less pithy wood, and enables it the better to withstand the cold; and this may be easily proved by cutting the branches of each. The shoot on the Plum-stock will be twice as hard and firm as the one on the Peach-stock. But, *Thirdly,* and the most important reason is, that the Plum ceases to send up its sap early in autumn, causing the Peach to perfect its wood before the cold weather sets in."

It is also evident that a tree deprived of its functions or means of growing luxuriantly, is in a similar situation to a diseased animal. If disease be not checked before the juices of the tree become putrid, it will not only die, but will contaminate the earth in which it is planted, to the destruction of its neighboring inmates of the garden or field. All experienced nursery-men admit this to be the case with diseased Peach-trees, and some have actually abandoned their Peach-orchards, and chosen fresh ground for new plantations.

It is precisely the same with smaller vegetable plants. A diseased Cabbage, for instance, by its excremental and corrupt juices being spent in the ground, will render the cultivation of the same or allied species a casualty; and daily observation teacheth, that young and thrifty plants often fall a prey to worms and reptiles which were generated by a previous crop.

Deep planting and injudicious culture are the causes of most of the diseases and failures of fruit-trees; and in this way I account for Peaches being less plentiful than they were when left almost to nature; which was the case, I am informed, in the beginning of the present century. That this malpractice in horticulture is general, the most superficial observer may discover by comparing the thrifty growth of those trees scattered by nature in our highways and byways with many of those aided by the art of man. If any of my readers should require proof of my assertions, I can show them from the window of the room where this article is being written, scores of living, or rather dying evidences of the evil of deep planting.

PRUNING AND TRANSPLANTING.

All the varieties of the Peach produce their fruit upon the young wood of a year old, the blossom-buds rising immediately from the eyes of the shoots. The same shoots seldom bear after the first year, except on some casual small spurs on the two years' wood, which is not to be counted upon. Hence the trees are to be pruned as bearing entirely on the shoots of the preceding year, and a full supply of regular grown shoots must be retained for successional bearers. Cut out the redundant shoots, and all decayed and dead wood, and reduce some of the f rmer bearers, cutting the most naked quite away.

A Peach Orchard may be planted at any time after the bud is established, until the trees are three or four years old, which may be placed from fifteen to twenty feet from each other, or from any other spreading trees. The dwarf kinds may be introduced into the kitchen-garden, and trained against fences, as directed for the Apricot, or as espaliers or dwarf standards.

A judicious pruning of Peach, Nectarine, and other kinds of young trees is necessary to prevent the long, straggling growth of limbs which are frequently bare of shoots for some distance from the body of the tree, which should be shortened, to cause the production of lateral shoots. An annual summer pruning is essential to the well-being of a tree, as by shortening the wood of the preceding year's growth, a symmetrical tree containiug a good supply of bearing-wood may be formed. By this treatment the longevity of a tree will be promoted, provided the work is done with judgment and care, so as not to render the tree impervious to the influence of the sun and air; for, be it remembered, the head of a tree must always be kept moderately open, for the purpose of giving the fruit the best possible chance of ripening perfectly.

Divest young budded and grafted trees of all shoots from the stocks, below the bud or graft, as they appear; also rub off all useless buds in early-shooting wall trees.

DESCRIPTIVE LIST OF PEACHES.

FREESTONE PEACHES.

Astor. An excellent variety, originating in the city of New York; the fruit is above medium size; skin pale yellow, with red cheek; flesh melting and pleasant flavored; juice sweet and plentiful; ripe the latter end of August and early in September.

Beers's Red Rareripe, *Middletown Late Red Rareripe.* Fruit very large, of oblong shape; skin nearly white, with a red cheek; flesh firm, juicy, and high flavored. This variety originated with Joseph Beers of Middletown, New Jersey; it ripens there from the middle to the end of September, and is represented as a good market fruit.

Belle de Vitry, *Admirable Tardive, Bellis, Beauty of Vitry* A large fruit, of fine red color next the sun; on the opposite side a yellowish white; flesh white, stained with red at the stone; firm, juicy, sweet, vinous, aud excellent; ripe early in September.

Bellegarde, *Galande, Violette Hative, Noire de Montreuil. Smooth-Leaved Royal George of some.* The tree is vigorous and productive; fruit above medium size, globular; skin greenish-yellow, and on the sunny side rich deep red, with dark purple streaks; flesh pale yellow, very melting, saccharine, and juicy; a first-rate fruit, early in September.

BUONAPARTE. A fine early variety, introduced by Joseph Buonaparte, and recommended by Caleb R. Smith, of Burlington, New Jersey, as being the best market fruit known at that place; its color is red, mottled with yellow; flesh melting; juice sweet and delicious, in August.

BREVOORT'S SEEDLING MELTER, *Brevoort's Morris.* A superior Peach, raised by Henry Brevoort, Esq., of New York. Skin of a dingy white color, with red cheek; flesh white, firm, rich, and sugary; ripe by the middle of August.

COLUMBIA. Fruit of medium size; skin rough and thin; color dull red; flesh yellow, fibrous, similar to a pineapple; juicy and rich. It is supposed that this Peach originated with Mr. Cox. It is a singular variety.

COOLEDGE'S FAVORITE, *Cooledge's Early Red Rareripe.* A large handsome globular fruit; skin red, tinged with crimson; flesh very melting, juicy, and of delicious flavor, in August. The tree is vigorous and very productive.

CRAWFORD'S EARLY MELOCOTON, *Early Crawford.* Fruit large, oblong; skin yellow and red; flesh yellow, juicy, sweet, with an agreeable acidity. It originated with Mr. Crawford, Middletown, New Jersey. The tree is a great bearer, and the fruit is considered one of the most marketable varieties, in August and September.

CRAWFORD'S LATE MALACATUNE. Fruit very large, round; skin yellow and red; flesh yellow, sweet, juicy, and excellent. It is highly estimated at Middletown for its productiveness and adaptation for market; in September and October.

DOUBLE MONTAGNE, *Sion Early, Double Mountain, Montauban.* A beautiful and excellent Peach of middle size; skin greenish white, but soft red, marbled with a deeper red next the sun; flesh white and melting, juice plentiful and highly flavored; ripe in August.

Early Orange, *Orange Freestone, Yellow Rareripe, Yellow Melocoton, Golden Rareripe, Early Yellow.* Fruit under a medium size, inclining to the oval shape, apex full, with a small tip; skin greenish yellow; flesh fine and yellow; juice rich and sweet, but not plentiful; ripe in August and September. There are several varieties under the same name, some of which are inferior to the true Orange Peach.

Early Royal George. *Red Magdalen of Prince.* A superior variety, of medium size and rather globular form; skin yellow, with red cheek; flesh melting and delicious; in August. There are several varieties cultivated under this name, differently described.

Eastburn's Choice. Fruit large, nearly round; skin pale yellow, with a red blush; flesh yellowish white; juice exceedingly pleasant and sprightly, in September and October. The tree is represented as hardy, luxuriant, and vigorous, by the Editor of Hoffy's Orchard Companion, of Philadelphia, from which this description is taken.

Emperor of Russia, *Serrated Leaf, New Cut-Leaved Unique.* The fruit of this species is deeply cleft, one half of it projecting considerably beyond the other; the skin is downy, of a brownish yellow and red color; flesh melting; juice sweet and delicious; towards the end of August. This sort was found by Mr. Floy in New Jersey, 1809, and all the stones of this fruit are said to produce plants with jagged leaves.

George the Fourth. An excellent Peach, of medium size and globular shape; of pale yellow color in the shade, and dark red next the sun; flesh yellow, but red at the stone, from which it separates; a fruit of very superior flavor when at maturity, which is early in September. It originated in the garden of Mr. Gill, Broad street, New York.

Green Nutmeg, *Early Anne, Avant Blanche.* This early variety is said to have originated in Berkshire, England. The fruit is small; its color yellowish green; its pulp melting, juicy, of very pleasant flavor, and ripens in July and August.

Murray's Early Anne is a variety raised from the seed of this. It is esteemed for its early maturity.

Grosse Mignonne, *Veloutée de Merlet, Grimwood's Royal George, Large French Mignonne, Vineuse,* according to Lindley; and the following synonymes are added by Kendrick: *Belle Beauté, Smooth-leaved Royal George, Royal Souverain, Pourpre de Normandie, Royal Kensington, Early Vineyard, Transparent,* and *Morris's Red Rareripe.* One of the most beautiful and delicious varieties in cultivation. Fruit large, depressed, hollow at the summit, with a deepish suture; skin rather downy, or rich deep red, thickly mottled on a greenish ground; flesh pale yellow, rayed with red at the stone; melting, juicy, and of a rich vinous flavor when in perfection, which is early in September.

Heath Freestone, *Kenrick's Heath.* This variety was first obtained from the late General Heath, of Roxbury, near Boston. The fruit is very large, oblong, and beautiful, frequently weighing half a pound; color pale yellowish green, with crimson or violet next the sun; its flesh is melting, juicy, rich, vinous, and agreeably acid; ripens in September and October.

Hoffman's Pound, *Morrison's Pound, Hoffman's Favorite.* This fruit is by some called the *Morrisania,* from it having been first obtained by Mr. Floy from Governeur Morris; but it originated with Martin Hoffman, Esq., of New York. The fruit is very large, skin brownish white and red; flesh yellow, firm, very juicy and delicious, parting from the stone; greatly esteemed from its ripening late in September and October.

Late Admirable, *Royale, Royal, Bourdine, Téton de Venus of Prince and Downing.* Fruit large, roundish, inclining to oblong; suture deeply impressed along one side, having the flesh swelling boldly and equally on both sides, with a slight impression on the summit; skin downy, of pale green color, streaked with dull tawny red; flesh white, delicate, melting, and highly flavored; a magnificent Peach, ripening in September.

Malta, *Pêche Malte, Belle de Paris, Malte de Normandie, Italian Peach.* Fruit above the medium size; color pale yellowish green, marbled with purplish red; flesh yellow, juicy, rich, vinous, and of superior flavor; ripens at the end of August.

MADELEINE DE COURSON, *Madeleine Rouge, Rouge Paysanne, Red Magdalen. Royal George and New Royal Charlotte of some collections.* An excellent fruit, of large size; color yellow and red; ripens at the end of August; flesh firm, white, but red at the stone; sugary and rich.

MONSTROUS LEMON, *Largest Lemon.* This variety was first discovered in the garden of Mr. Tiebout, now Union Place; the fruit is of the largest size, and in the gardens of two persons in New York has weighed seventeen ounces, as stated by Mr. Prince, who says that the tree requires a sheltered situation, and that the fruit is late in ripening; October.

MORRIS'S RED FREESTONE, *Red Rareripe. Grosse Mignonne and Royal Kensington according to Prince.* Fruit nearly round, of large size, apex a little sunken; skin greenish yellow, with red cheek; flesh delicious and melting; a first-rate variety; ripe towards the end of August.

MORRIS'S WHITE FREESTONE, *White Rareripe, Luscious White Rareripe, Philadelphia Freestone. Lady Ann Stewart of Downing and Prince.* Fruit large, and inclining to the oval form, suture even, but not deep; apex a little sunken; skin white or rather yellowish; flesh white, juicy, rich, and sweet; ripe in September.

NEIL'S EARLY PURPLE, *Early Purple of Miller, Johnson's Purple Avant, Padley's Early Purple, Veritable Pourprée Hative, Pêche du Vin.* One of the most beautiful of Peaches, of medium size; skin yellow, but on the sunny side of a fine deep red and purplish color; it ripens by the middle of August; flesh melting, juicy, with a rich vinous flavor; an excellent fruit.

NEW ROYAL CHARLOTTE, *Queen Charlotte, New Early Purple, Kew Early Purple.* A delicious Peach, rather above medium size; skin pale greenish white, with deep red next the sun; flesh greenish white, rich, and agreeable; ripe in August.

NOBLESSE, *Mellish's Favorite. Vanguard of Prince and*

Winter. The tree is of a vigorous growth, and very productive; fruit large, somewhat oval, of a pale red color, marbled with different shades; pulp juicy, rich, and melting when at maturity, which is in August and September.

PRESIDENT. This variety originated at Bedford, on Long Island. It is a rich, melting, juicy fruit, of large size, roundish, with a shallow suture; skin very downy, dull red next the sun, pale yellowish green in the shade; the surface covered with small red dots; a first-rate Peach; ripe in September.

PRINCE'S LATE YELLOW FREESTONE. A beautiful fruit, of a greenish-yellow color, tinged with red; flesh firm and rich. A partially ripe specimen of this variety was exhibited by Mr. Prince in the Horticultural room of the American Institute, October 24, 1843.

RARERIPE YELLOW, *Yellow and Red Rareripe, Red Velvet, Large Yellow Nutmeg. Marie Antoinette of some.* This variety is large; skin yellow and red; flesh firm, rich, and delicious, in August and September. It is considered one of the most valuable market varieties.

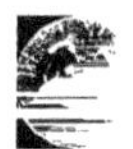

RED CHEEK MALACATUNE, *Hogg's Melacoton, Alberge Incomparable, Lady Gallatin, Probyn Peach.* The fruit of this variety is of large size and oval form; its color is yellow, with a red cheek on the sunny side; the flesh is also yellow, melting, rich, juicy, and luscious. There is another variety of this fruit, which originated with Mr. Polls, of New York, said to be very productive, and of excellent quality; ripens in September.

ROBINSON CRUSOE, *Early Robinson Crusoe.* Fruit large, round, and handsome; skin pale red, marbled with dark red; flesh juicy, sweet, and delicious; ripe in September. The stone from which this variety was raised by Dr. Coxe, of Philadelphia, was brought by Lieutenant Coxe from the far-famed island of Alexander Selkirk or Robinson Crusoe.

SMOCK FREE, *Smock's Freestone.* An esteemed market variety at Middletown, New Jersey, where it originated, in Mr. Smock's orchard. Some specimens of the fruit have measured

twelve inches in circumference. It is of oblong shape, skin pale yellow and dark red; flesh juicy, a little acid, and very palatable; in September and October.

SWEET WATER, *Early Sweet Water. American Nutmeg of Prince.* This variety is said to have originated at Flushing; its form is round, and its color whitish green, with a red blush at maturity, which is early in August. The flesh is very tender, melting, rich, and juicy.

TETON DE VENUS. *Royale of some collections.* There are two or three varieties bearing this name; the fruit of the best variety is large, globular, of a pale yellowish-green color, marbled with red; flesh greenish yellow, but red at the stone; a delicious flavored Peach; ripe in September.

VAN ZANDT'S SUPERB, *Waxen Rareripe.* This variety originated with Mr. Van Zandt, of Flushing; its form is oval; its skin smooth, somewhat mottled, and of a beautiful waxen appearance; flesh melting, and of excellent flavor; in August and September.

WALTER'S EARLY. Fruit large; color white in the shade, and red next the sun; flesh red, very juicy and delicious. It is considered one of the most productive and early Peaches cultivated at Middletown, New Jersey, where it ripens about the middle of August.

WASHINGTON PEACH, *Boyce Peach, Washington Freestone. Early Rose of some.* A first-rate Peach; color a pale yellow in the shade, but pale red next the sun; flesh very juicy and delicious; ripens towards the end of August. A peculiar trait in this Peach is its rapid growth; it will, while ripening, in about ten days nearly double its ordinary size, weighing over half a pound.

WHITE BLOSSOM, *Willow Peach, Snow Peach, White Blossomed Incomparable.* This variety originated on Long Island; the fruit is white, of an oval form and handsome appearance; the flesh is also white, melting, juicy, and pleasant; it is much used for preserves when not over ripe, and is at full maturity in September.

YELLOW ADMIRABLE, *Abricotée, Admirable Jaune, Pêche d'Orange, Grosse Jaune, Pêche de Burai, Sandalie, Hermaphrodite, Apricot Peach.*

MONSTROUS PAVIE OR POMPONNE, *Gros Melocoton, Gros Persique, Rouge Pavie Monstreux, Pavie Camu.* Fruit very large, roundish, with an obtuse nipple; skin downy, of a fine red and greenish-white color; flesh white, deep red at the stone, juicy, and vinous; excellent for preserving; in September and October.

NEW YORK WHITE CLINGSTONE, *Williams's New York. New Newington of some catalogues.* Fruit large, round, with a pointed apex; skin white, tinged with rose; flesh yellow, melting or soft, but adhering closely to the stone; juice very plentiful, sweet, luscious, and high flavored; ripe in September.

OLDMIXON CLINGSTONE. Of all clingstone Peaches this is considered the most delicious; the skin is yellow, with a bright red cheek, marbled; flesh red at the stone, rich, juicy, sweet, and high flavored; the fruit ripens gradually in September. This variety is cultivated in Massachusetts under the above name; but Mr. Manning says that he has cultivated this fruit with the Old Newington and the Catharine, and could never perceive any difference in the fruit or trees.

OLD NEWINGTON, *Newington.* The fruit of this variety is large, rather globular, of a fine bright red and pale-yellow color, marbled with dashes and streaks of a deeper color; the flesh is yellowish white, but red at the stone; also juicy, rich, sweet, and well flavored; the tree is very productive; in September.

ORANGE CLING, *Round Alberge.* A beautiful native Peach, of round shape, and bright yellow or orange color; flesh orange color, aromatic, rich, and juicy. The tree is a great bearer, and from the beauty of its fruit, which ripens in September, is entitled to extensive cultivation for the market.

PAVIE MADELEINE, *Pavie Blanc, Melecoton, Myrecoton, Merlicoton, Persique à Gros-Fruit Blanc.* The fruit of this variety is of medium size, somewhat broadly globular; skin pale yellowish white and marbled red; flesh yellowish white to the stone; juice sugary and of an agreeable flavor; toward the end of August and September.

Prince's Climax. Fruit very large, oval; skin yellow, mottled with crimson; flesh yellow, and of rich pineapple flavor; ripe in September, and good in October.

Selby's Cling. Fruit large, highly esteemed; skin white and red; flesh melting, juicy, and of peculiar rich flavor; ripe in September and October.

Smock's Clingstone. Fruit very large, oblong; skin yellow and red; flesh juicy, rich, a little acid; it ripens in October at Middletown, New Jersey, and is considered one of the most productive and profitable late market fruits.

Tippecanoe Peach, *Hero of Tippecanoe.* This variety originated with George Thomas of Philadelphia, and the fruit has been much admired at the Pennsylvania Horticultural exhibitions; it is of large size, of a beautiful yellow color, with a fine red blush; flesh yellow, firm, and juicy, possessing an agreeable acidity; it ripens late in September.

SELECT DESCRIPTIVE LIST OF PEACHES.

Baltimore Beauty. A native variety. Fruit rather small, roundish oval; skin deep orange, with a rich brilliant red cheek; flesh yellow, but red at the stone, sweet, and very good. Ripens early in August.

Bergen's Yellow. A native of Long Island. Fruit large, often measuring nine inches in circumference; skin deep orange, with dark red cheek; flesh deep yellow, melting, juicy, and delicious. Ripens early in September.

Coles' Early Red. A good early market fruit of medium size; skin pale red, mottled with darker red; flesh melting, juicy, rich, and very sprightly.

Druid Hill. A seedling Peach, raised by Lloyd N. Rogers, of Druid Hill, near Baltimore. Fruit very large, roundish; skin greenish white, clouded with red; flesh juicy, melting, and rich; towards the end of September.

Early York, *Large Early York*. Fruit of medium size, roundish; skin pale red, dotted and mottled with dark red; flesh greenish white, full of rich sprightly juice. Ripens towards the end of August.

Early Newington Freestone, *Newington Peach*. A large and exceedingly high-flavored Peach; skin pale yellowish white, dotted and mottled with a rich red; flesh white, but red at the stone; juicy and melting: end of August.

Haines' Early Red. A popular orchard fruit in New Jersey, of medium size; skin pale white, nearly covered with bright red; flesh greenish white, very juicy, sweet, and melting. Ripe about the middle of August.

La Grange. A late Peach, raised by Mr. John Hulse, Burlington, New Jersey. Fruit large, oblong; skin greenish white, tinged with red; flesh juicy, melting, and delicious. Ripe towards the end of September.

Oldmixon Freestone, *Oldmixon Clearstone*. A large American Peach, slightly oval; skin pale yellowish white, marbled with deep red; flesh white and tender, with a rich vinous flavor: early in September.

Pool's Large Yellow, *Pool's Late Yellow Freestone*. A large and handsome Pennsylvania Peach of the Melocoton family; skin deep yellow, with a dark red cheek; flesh juicy, and of excellent flavor: late in September.

Rareripe, *Late Red*, *Prince's Red Rareripe*. One of the finest of all peaches. Fruit large and heavy, roundish oval; skin downy, pale yellow, thickly marbled with red and fawn-colored specks; flesh white, but deep red at the stone; very juicy, melting, and of an unusually rich flavor. Ripens the second and third week in September.

PEAR. POIRIER. *Pyrus.*

The *Peach* and the *Pear*-tree have still ample store,
And the *Plum*, most inviting, "makes urchins adore."
A bountiful feast is spread over the land,
For great is the Giver, unsparing His hand.

The Pear-tree, in its wild state, is thorny, with upright branches, tending to the pyramidal form, in which it differs

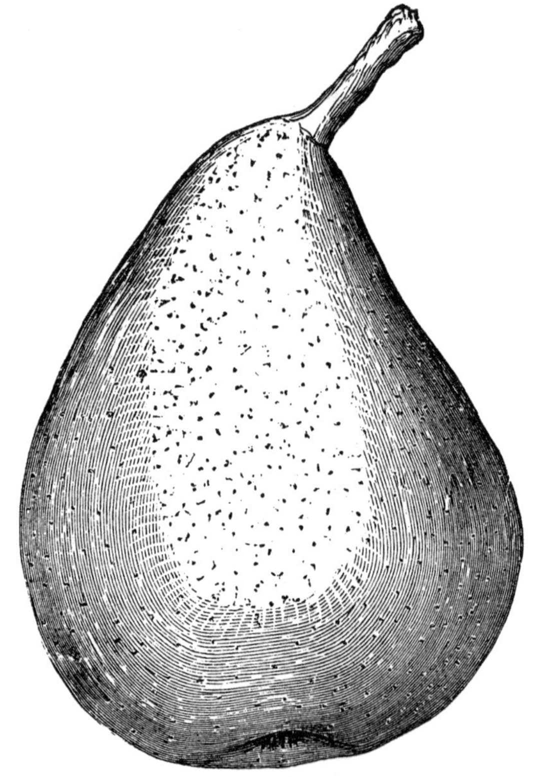

Beurré Clairgean.

materially from the Apple-tree. The twigs, or sprays, hang down. The leaves are elliptical, obtuse, serrate. The flowers in terminating, villose corymbs, produced from wood of the preceding year, or from buds gradually formed on the several years' growth, on the extremities of very short protruding shoots, technically called spurs. The Pear-tree is found in a wild state in England, and abundantly in France and Germany, as well as in other parts of Europe, not excepting Russia, as far north as latitude 51. It grows in almost any soil. The cultivated tree differs from the Apple, not only in having a tendency to the pyramidal form, but also in being more apt to send out tap-roots; in being as a seedling-plant longer in coming into bearing; and when on its own root, or grafted on a wild Pear-stock, much longer lived. In a dry soil, it will exist for centuries, and still retain its health, productiveness, and vigor. The Romans had thirty-six varieties in Pliny's time. There are now several hundreds in the French and British nurseries, and a still larger number in America.

CHARACTERISTICS OF A GOOD PEAR.

Dessert Pears are characterized by a sugary, aromatic juice, with the pulp soft and sub-liquid, or melting, as in the *Beurres*, or Butter Pears, or of a firm and crisp consistence, or breaking, as in the Winter Bergamots. Kitchen-Pears should be of a large size, with the flesh firm, neither breaking nor melting, and rather austere than sweet. Perry Pears may be either large or small; but the more austere the taste, the better will be the liquor. Excellent perry is made from the wild Pear.

PROPAGATION OF PEARS.

Pear-trees are propagated by grafting in the spring, or budding late in the summer, and also by seed taken from the best sorts, for the purpose of obtaining new varieties. In raising Pear-stocks, the wild Pear is preferred in Europe, as being calculated to produce plants more hardy and durable than the cultivated sorts; and for dwarfing and precocity, the Quince is preferred.

The Pear is a much handsomer upright growing tree than the Apple; more durable, and its wood hard and valuable for the turner and millwright; but its blossoms, being white, are less showy than those of the Apple.

A Pear-Orchard may be planted at any time after the trees are two years old from the graft; and as some varieties of trees from young stocks will not come into full bearing until ten or twelve years old, they will bear removing with care at any time within that period. They may be planted at from twenty to thirty-five feet distance from each other, according to the nature of the tree. The dwarf varieties may be planted in the kitchen-garden, and trained either as espaliers or dwarf standards.

Standard Pear-trees will require but little pruning after the heads are once formed; in doing which, the branches should be permitted to extend on all sides freely. Several years may elapse before any cross-placed, irregular, or crowded branches require pruning; yet there are some kinds whose form of growth resembles the Apple, which will need frequent pruning.

IMPROVEMENT OF VARIETIES.

"That some of the fine old varieties of the Pear have deteriorated in some parts of the country, is unquestionable; this is ascribed to various causes; *first*, that the varieties have *run out*, as it is termed; *second*, to the use of diseased stocks, or scions from diseased, or aged, or unthrifty trees, or both; *third*, to the deleterious influence of the salt air, near the sea-board; *fourth*, to the want of proper attention to soil and culture. We cannot subscribe to the soundness of the reason first assigned; there are too many instances of varieties of fruit whose origin is so remote that it cannot be traced, still continuing in full vigor; and the kinds which have deteriorated in some sections of the country still maintain their celebrity in the interior, and more especially in the virgin soil of the West.

Which of the other causes assigned has tended to deteriorate the fine kinds alluded to, we will not undertake to determine; one or more of them may have had their influence, but we think that proper attention to propagation, soil, and culture, may in general, if not in every instance, restore the valuable old varieties to their pristine excellence; and in this vicinity there is decisive evidence of the improvement of that superior old variety, the White Doyenne, Saint Michael, or Virgalieu."

SELECT DESCRIPTIVE LIST OF PEARS.

SUMMER FRUIT.

AH! MON DIEU. A beautiful Pear, introduced by J. B. Mantel, of Bloomingdale, New York. Size medium; form handsome; color rich yellow with bright red cheek; flesh juicy; flavor sweet and perfumed. Tree vigorous and productive, the fruit growing in clusters of four or five together.

AMIRE JOANNET, *Early Sugar*. This fruit is described by Mr. Manning as small, of oblong form; light yellow skin, with a small portion of red; flesh white, and when not overripe juicy and good. It ripens in July, about ten days before the *Petit Muscat*, to which it is superior in flavor.

BELLE DE BRUXELLES, *Beauty of Brussels*, *Cours Complet*. A large early Pear of pyramidal form; skin a beautiful clear yellow, with red cheek; flesh white, fine, and of an agreeable flavor; ripe early in August.

BEURRÉ D'AMANLIS. A fine early Pear, imported from France by J. B. Mantel, of Bloomingdale, New York. Size large; form large-bellied; color green, changing to yellow, with a fine blush when fully ripe, and russet spots; flesh melting, juicy, sweet, and excellent; ripe in August and September. Tree vigorous and productive.

BLOODGOOD PEAR, *Early Beurré*. Fruit large; form nearly oval; skin a dull yellow, covered with dark russet spots; flesh tender, melting, and pleasant. Mr. Manning says: "It comes early into bearing and produces abundant crops every year in August."

CRAWFORD, *Early Crawford.* A fine early Scotch Pear, of medium size, round at the eye, diminishing at the stem; the skin is entirely of a light yellow; the flesh juicy, tender, and good. Ripens its fruit in August.

Theodore Van Mons.

DEARBORN'S SEEDLING. This variety originated in the gar den of the Hon. H. A. S. Dearborn, of Roxbury. The tree is of vigorous growth; fruit of medium size, rounded at the crown, and regularly diminishes in a parabolic manner to the stalk; the skin is smooth, thin, green, with russet spots; at maturity it turns to a delicate yellow; flesh very melting, and of the finest flavor. Ripens in August.

Early Rousselet, *Rousselet Hatif, Early Catharine.* This is a small Pear with a long curved neck; skin yellow, with brownish russet; flesh very fine, rich, and high-flavored; in August and September. The tree yields immense crops.

Honey Pear, *American Honey.* This Pear in size and shape resembles the Seckel; the skin is yellow, with a large portion of dull red; the flesh sweet, juicy, and good.

Jargonelle, English, *Beau Present, Saint Sampson, Grosse Cuisse, Madame Saint Lambert, Poire des Tables des Princes.* Fruit rather large, oblong, of a pale green color, a little marked with red; flesh melting, juicy, with a slightly acid, rich, and agreeable flavor. It ripens early in August, is one of the most productive of all Pears, and the very best in its season.

Julienne of Coxe, *L'Archeduc d'Été, Summer Beurré, Summer Doyenne, Summer St. Michael,* of Boston. *Bloodgood Pear of some collections.* Fruit medium size, smooth, bright yellow at maturity, with a faint blush next the sun; form rather ovate, tapering towards the stalk; flesh perfectly melting, rich, and juicy. The tree bears young, and most profusely, and matures its fruit in August and September.

Madeleine, *Magdalene, Citron des Carmes, Early Chaumontelle.* This Pear is of medium size, pale yellow, with an occasional blush next the sun; flesh white, melting, perfumed. A fine early fruit, ripening in July and August.

Rousselet de Rheims, *Musk or Spice Pear.* Fruit small, pyramidal, greenish yellow at maturity, but brown red next the sun, with russety spots; flesh half beurré, fine, very perfumed. Good to put in brandy, and to dry; in August and September

Sabine d'Été, *Bellissime d'Amour, Epargne of the French. English Red Cheek.* This Pear is of pyramidal form, terminating in a round blunt point at the stalk; color yellow, but fine scarlet next the sun; the whole surface smooth, regular, and polished; flesh white, melting, juicy, and highly perfumed; the tree is an abundant bearer, and ripens its fruit in August.

STEVENS'S GENESEE. Its color is mellow green, with russet blotches; its flesh is represented as white, juicy, and melting; flavor sprightly, rich, and very delicious. Time of ripening, towards the last of August.

SKINLESS PEAR, *Poire sans Peau*, *Fleure de Guignes.* A small oblong Pear; the skin, which is very smooth and thin, is pale green, marbled with red and yellow; flesh crisp, sweet, and of pleasant flavor. The tree is very prolific, ripening its fruit in August.

SUMMER FRANC REAL, *Franc Real d'Été*, *Fondante*, *France Cannel*, *Gros Micet d'Été*, *Milan Blanc*, *Prebles Beurré.* Fruit above medium size; shape oblong, thickest about one-third from the eye; skin yellowish green; flesh melting, rich, and excellent; ripe early in September.

SUMMER MELTING, *Summer Beurré*, *Fondante d'Été.* An excellent summer Pear of pyriform shape; color yellow, tinged with brownish red; flesh soft, melting, and sweet. The tree bears young, and ripens its fruit in August.

SUMMER ROSE, *Thorny Rose*, *Epine Rose*, *Poire de Rose*, *Rosenbirne Kraft.* A Pear of medium size, in form resembling an Apple; the skin is dull yellow, spotted with russet and marbled with red; a very productive variety, ripening its fruit early in August.

WILLIAMS'S BONCHRETIEN, *Bartlett*, *Williams's Early*, *Autumn Superb of Prince.* The fruit is large, oblong; the stalk thick and fleshy, an inch long; the color at maturity yellow, tinged with red; flesh whitish, very melting, and delicate; juice perfumed, sweet, and abundant. Tree very productive, and fruit ripe early in September.

AUTUMN FRUIT.

ANDREWS, *Amory*, *Gibson.* Fruit oblong; skin yellowish green, with a dull red cheek; flesh melting, juicy, and high-flavored. Mr. Manning represents it as "a very valuable pear, producing its fruit early and abundantly." Ripe in September and October.

AUTUMN BERGAMOT, *Common Bergamot, York Bergamot, Bergamotte d'Automne, Andrews.* Fruit globular, depressed; skin rough, yellowish green, and dull brown, with greyish spots; flesh pale, melting, juicy, sugary, and perfumed; ripe in September and October. This variety has been cultivated in

Doyenne Robin.

England from the time of Julius Cæsar, and is still considered by many a first-rate Pear in its season.

AUTUMN SUPERB. This is a large Pear, full and round at the eye, diminishing to a point at the stem; the skin is yellow, mixed with dull red; the flesh melting and good. Mr. Manning says it bears young, and that the fruit ripens in October.

Belle et Bonne, *Belle de Flanders, Schone und Gute, Gracieuse.* Fruit very large, globular, depressed; the stalk long, skin greenish yellow, but next the sun yellow, with spots of russet; flesh white, sweet, exceeding rich, and agreeably perfumed. The tree is very productive, and the fruit ripens in September. This variety has been cultivated under the erroneous names of *Charles d'Autriche, Belle de Bruxelles,* and *Bergamotte Crassane,* which are distinct fruits.

Belle Lucrative, *Fondante d'Automne.* A beautiful Flemish Pear; middle-sized, roundish, tapering at the stalk; skin yellow, slightly russeted, and tinged with pale red; flesh melting, sweet, and juicy, with a slight musky perfume; early in October.

Beurré Bosc, *Calebasse Bosc.* Fruit large and very long; terminated with a crown, near three inches in diameter; somewhat calabash-formed; skin grey fawn-color, but russety-yellow at maturity; flesh white, melting, highly flavored, and delicious. It ripens in October.

Bleecker's Meadow, *Large Seckel of Prince. Meadow Pear of Winter & Co.* A native fruit of medium size, roundish form, and of a yellow color, tinged with dull red; the flesh melting, juicy, sweet, musky, and of delicious flavor. Ripe in October. A prolific bearer.

Brown Beurré, *Beurré Rouge, Beurré d' Or, Beurré Dorée, Beurre du Roi, Beurré d'Amboise, Isambert, Red Beurré, Golden Beurré, Pore d'Amboise.* This was formerly considered the best of all Pears in its season. Fruit rather large, of greenish yellow and dusky red color, covered with thin russet; flesh melting, buttery, rich, and excellent; at perfection in October and November.

Capiumont, *Beurré de Capiumont, Calebasse Vass.* This variety is much esteemed in the vicinity of Boston; fruit of medium size; skin yellow, tinged with fine red or cinnamon; flesh yellowish, melting, very rich, and high-flavored; in September and October.

Capsheaf. A medium-sized Pear, much cultivated near

Providence, Rhode Island ; the shape is rather globular ; skin a light cinnamon russet ; flesh white, melting, and juicy. The tree bears well, and the fruit ripens in October.

CHARLES D'AUTRICHE, *Gracieuse, Charles of Austria.* A fine and beautiful fruit, large, three and a half inches long, and three inches broad; color greenish yellow with brown spots, and partially russeted; flesh white, melting, juicy, and deli cious; ripe in October and good in November.

Beurré Nantais.

CUMBERLAND. A native fruit from Cumberland, Rhode Island, of large size and oblong shape; skin orange color, with bright red cheek; the flesh melting, juicy, and good; ripe in October. The tree is of vigorous growth, and bears abundantly.

CUSHING. A native fruit from Hingham, Massachusetts; of medium size and oblong shape; skin, when ripe, smooth, of a light yellow, mottled with dull red on one side; flesh white, melting, sprightly, and good. It comes early into bearing, and produces plenty of fruit in September and October.

DELICES D'ARDENPONT, *Delices d'Hardenpont de Toulouse. Beurré d'Ardenpont of some.* Fruit above medium size; oblong, pyramidal; skin yellow at maturity, and partially covered with a thin cinnamon-colored russet; flesh yellowish white, nearly melting; juice pleasant, sweet, and abundant; in October and November. The tree is a good bearer.

DIX. A native variety originating in the garden of Mr. Dix, in Boston; fruit large, oblong; skin, when ripe, yellow, with a blush of red; flesh melting, juicy and rich; in October and November.

DOYENNE SANTELETE. A new, fine, handsome Flemish Pear; fruit above the middle size, pyramidally oblong; skin pale green, speckled with grey russet; flesh white, a little gritty, but tender; juice saccharine, with a slight musky perfume. The tree is hardy, and ripens its fruit early in October.

DUCHESS OF ANGOULEME, *Duchesse d'Angoulême.* A Pear of first-rate excellence. Form roundish oblong, tapering towards the stalk; skin dull yellow, with broad russet patches; flesh white, rich, melting, very juicy, and high-flavored, with a most agreeable perfume. Specimens of this fruit have been shown in England, weighing twenty-two ounces; at perfection in October and November.

FLEMISH BEAUTY, *La Belle de Flanders. Imperatrice de la France. Brilliant, Bosch, Bouche Nouvelle.* A fine Flemish Pear in great repute; it is of large size, obovate, obtuse at the stalk; greenish-yellow russet, tinged with crimson; flesh rather firm, yellowish white, sweet, rich, and excellent; it ripens in October.

FREDERICK OF WURTEMBURG, *Roi de Wurtemburg, Capiamont of some collections.* A large and splendid Pear, of pyramidal form and fine yellow color, covered with beautiful crimson on one side; flesh melting and of delicious flavor. The tree bears while young, and very abundantly.

FULTON. A fine Pear of medium size, raised from seed by Mr. Fulton, of Topsham, Maine; shape roundish turbinate; skin dark yellow; russeted; flesh melting, juicy, and of delicious flavor; ripe in September, and lasts a month. The tree is a great and constant bearer, and highly deserving of cultivation.

Comte de Flander.

GANSEL'S BERGAMOT, *Broca's Bergamot, Ives's Bergamot, Bonne Rouge.* Fruit varying from middle size to large; ovate flattened; color dull green, slightly red next the sun; flesh white, melting, sweet, rich and high-flavored. A delicious Pear; ripe in October, and good till Christmas.

Golden Beurré of Bilboa. Fruit of medium size, oblong, color a bright golden yellow, with patches of russet; melting and of fine flavor. A beautiful Pear-tree, a great bearer, and worthy of cultivation; ripe in October.

Gore's Heathcot. A native variety, highly esteemed in Massachusetts. Fruit of medium size; form long; skin of a uniformly light yellow; flesh melting, juicy, and high flavored. The growth of the tree is handsome and vigorous, producing abundant crops in September and October.

Green Sylvange, *Sylvanche Vert*, *Bergamotte Sylvange.* A most superior Pear, of medium size, skin rough and green, speckled with grey or black. The flesh is greenish near the skin, white in the centre, soft, saccharine and juicy; fruit in perfection from October to Christmas. The tree is a great bearer, and specimens of the fruit have been known to weigh thirteen ounces.

Hacon's Incomparable. *Norfolk Seedling*, *Downham Seedling of Winter & Co.* Fruit middle-sized, of pale yellow color, mixed with green, partially covered with orange russet; flesh yellowish white, slightly gritty, but very tender, juicy, sweet and rich; and possessing a high musky and perfumed flavor. The tree is a great bearer, and the fruit excellent. Ripens in November and December.

Harvard, *L'Epergne*, *Boston Eparne* This variety is highly prized in the Boston markets; fruit above medium size; oblong, swollen at the crown; skin russety yellow, tinged with red; flesh white, juicy, and melting. Ripens in September and October.

Henry the Fourth, *Henri Quatre.* Fruit of medium size, oblong, skin a dull yellow, mixed with brown and green; flesh yellow, rather gritty, juicy, and melting, with a peculiar rich flavor; ripe in September and October.

Long Green of Autumn, *Verte Longue*, *Mouthwater.* Mr. Manning says that this is one of the best of the old varieties; its form is very long; skin at maturity a light green; flesh white, melting, and rich-flavored. The tree is of vigorous growth, bears well, and the fruit is ripe in September and October.

MARIE LOUISE, *Marie Chrétienne.* Fruit oblong, tapering towards both ends; size varying from medium to large; skin nearly smooth, yellowish green, and cinnamon-colored russet; flesh white, melting, juicy and rich. It ripens in October and November, and is an excellent fruit in its season.

MOOR FOWL EGG. Fruit rather small, globular, ovate, swollen in the middle; skin orange-brown next the sun, with spots of russet; flesh yellowish white; a little gritty, but tender and mellow; juice saccharine, a little perfumed. This is a hardy Scotch variety; ripe in September, and good in October.

NAPOLEON, *Medaille, Sauvageon Liart. Roi de Rome, and Wurtemburg of Prince.* Fruit large, form of the Colmar; skin smooth; color bright green, but at maturity pale green; flesh very melting, with an unusual abundance of rich agreeable juice. At perfection in October and November.

PRINCESS OF ORANGE, *Princesse d'Orange, Princesse Conquette.* The fruit is roundish; the skin bright reddish-orange russet; flesh yellowish white, sugary and rich, in some seasons perfectly melting, but occasionally a little gritty. A beautiful Pear, and of good quality; in October.

SECKEL, *New York Red Cheek, Red Cheek Seckel, Sycle.* An excellent native fruit, in size rather small; color varying from yellowish to brownish russet, but bright red next the sun; flesh melting, spicy, and of a most extraordinarily rich flavor. This fruit grows in clusters, in great abundance, and is at perfection in September and October.

SWAN'S EGG, *Moor Fowl Egg of Boston.* Fruit small, of an oval turbinate figure; color yellowish green, and dull russety brown; flesh tender and melting, with a rich, saccharine, musky flavor. An excellent fruit; ripe in October. The tree is remarkably tall, upright, vigorous, and productive.

URBANISTE, *Beurré du Roi.* The fruit is of medium size, pyramidally ovate; skin pale green, inclining to yellow, with green streaks; flesh white, but reddish yellow next the core; it is quite melting, juicy, and very sweet, with a little perfume; it ripens from the middle of September to November.

WASHINGTON. A native fruit from New Jersey, of medium size and oval form; the skin is light yellow, covered with small brown spots, with a tinge of red; the flesh melting and of ex-

Des Nonnes.

cellent flavor. The tree bears well, and is worthy of general cultivation; fruit ripens in September.

WHITE DOYENNE, *Doyenne Blanc, Beurré Blanc, Bonne ente, St. Michael, Carlisle, Citron de Septembre, Kaiserbirne, Poire à courte queue, Poire de Limon, Poire de Seigneur, Poire Monsieur, Valencia, White Beurré, Virgalieu of some collections*

Fruit pretty large; roundish oblong; skin pale citron yellow, with cinnamon-russet, speckled; flesh white, juicy, very buttery and delicious; ripe in September and October. An old and once celebrated variety, still admired by many, although excluded from some nurseries or cultivated under new names.

Wilkinson. A native Pear from Cumberland, R. I. The tree bears young, and is very fruitful; size above medium; form oblong; skin yellow, with a brownish blush near the sun; flesh white, juicy, and melting. At perfection in October and November.

WINTER FRUIT.

Beurré d'Aremberg, *Beurré d'Arembert, Duc d'Aremberg, Poire d'Aremberg, Beurre Deschamps, Beurré des Orphelins of Deschamps, Colmar Deschamps.* The English and French writers speak of this Pear as one of the best in cultivation. The tree is a great bearer, comes early into cultivation, and the fruit will keep till March. Fruit large, turbinate; skin of a delicate pale green, dotted with russet, which becomes of a deep yellow at maturity; flesh whitish, fine, very juicy, perfectly melting, and very extraordinarily rich, sweet, high-flavored, and excellent.

Beurré Diel, *Diel's Butterbirne, Dorothée Royale, Beurré de Yelie, Beurré Royale, Poire de Melon. Beurré Incomparable of some.* This ranks amongst the best of Pears. The tree is of vigorous growth; fruit, when in perfection, four inches long and three inches broad; the skin at maturity is bright orange, with reddish russet; flesh clear white, melting, juicy, and of a delicious aromatic flavor; from November to January.

Beurré Rance, *Beurré Epine, Hardenpont de Printemps.* This is said to be a first-rate Pear. The tree is vigorous, and a good bearer; fruit middle-sized, oblong; skin deep green, with russety specks; flesh green, melting, having a rich delicious flavor, with very little acid. It shrivels in ripening, but will keep till April.

Bezy Vaet, *Bezy de Saint Vaast.* A most excellent Pear,

somewhat the shape of the Swan's Egg, but larger; skin dull green, covered with russety spots; flesh yellowish; perfectly melting, sweet, and agreeably perfumed; at perfection in November and December.

CATILLAC. Fruit very large, rather turbinate; pale yellow, stained with red; flesh firm and breaking; its flavor astringent; an excellent baking Pear; from November to April. Specimens of this variety have been known to weigh upwards of two pounds.

CHAUMONTEL, *Bezy de Chaumontelle, Poire de Chaumontelle, Beurré d'Hiver.* This noble old variety is a fruit varying in size from large to very large; its color at maturity yellow, tinged with brownish red next the sun; its form variable; flesh melting, juicy, sweet, musky, excellent; in season from November to February.

COLMAR, *Colmar Souverain, Poire Manne, Bergamotte Tardive, Incomparable.* This fruit is rather large; skin smooth, of a green color, changing to a yellow at maturity; form pyramidal; flesh melting, juicy, saccharine, and of excellent flavor. The fruit is in perfection from November to February.

COLUMBIA, *Columbian Virgalieu.* A large native Pear of oblong or pyramid form, and fine yellow color, tinged with red; flesh rich, firm, juicy, and excellent; from November to January. Tree productive and of very handsome form.

EASTER BEURRÉ, *Bergamotte de la Pentecôte, Beurré d'Hiver de Bruxelles, Doyenne d'Hiver, de Bruxelles, Bezi Chaumontelle Très Gros.* Of all the late-keeping Pears this is considered the best (for England). Fruit large, roundish, oblong; color green, but yellow at maturity, with specks of russet brown; flesh yellowish-white, perfectly buttery and melting, also extremely high-flavored; it is eatable in November, and will keep till May; it is a most profuse bearer, on a quince stock.

ECHASSERY, *Bezy de Chassery, Bezy de Landry, Poire d'Œuf, Ambrette, Walnut, Tilton of New Jersey.* Fruit middle size, of a roundish turbinate figure, something like a Citron, or the Ambrette; skin smooth, greenish-yellow, with grey specks;

flesh melting, juicy, and delicious; from December to March.

GLOUT MORCEAU, *Gloux Morceaux, Beurré d'Aremberg, Roi de Wurtemburg, Gloria, Colmar d'Hiver of Prince, and Beurré de Hardenpont of Downing.* A very large Belgic variety, of great excellence; fruit of ovalish form, pale green color inclining to yellow, with russety specks and blotches; flesh whitish, firm, very juicy, and excellent; in perfection from November to March.

LEWIS. This variety originated on the farm of Mr. I. Lewis, of Roxbury, Mass. The size is medium; form somewhat globular; skin, when ripe, a greenish yellow; the flesh is white. Very melting, juicy, and excellent; from November to March, The tree grows quick, and bears abundance of fruit.

LOUISE BONNE DE JERSEY, *Louise Bonne d'Avranches.* A large Pear; oblong; a good substitute for the old *St. Germain;* skin yellowish green, sometimes tinged with red; flesh extremely tender, and full of an excellent saccharine, well flavored juice. A first-rate fruit, from October till after Christmas.

NEWTOWN VERGALIEU. A large Pear, of a yellow color, with a very short stalk; the tree grows very crooked and of an irregular form, bending by the weight of its fruit, which is excellent to preserve, or for baking; from November to January. Its productiveness renders it desirable in an orchard.

PASSE COLMAR, *Fondante de Panisel, Passe Colmar Gris dit Precet, Poire Precel, Passe Colmar, Epineux, Beurré Colmar Gris dit Precel, Beurré d'Argenson, Present de Malines, Colmar Souverain, Chapman's.* A most valuable Pear, of medium size, conical, flattened next the eye; skin at maturity yellowish, sprinkled with russet, a tinge of red next the sun; flesh yellow ish, melting, rich, and excellent. The tree is a good bearer, and the fruit is in perfection from November to February.

POUND PEAR, *Black Pear of Worcester, Parkinson's Warden, Grande Monarque, Livre, Groote Mogul, Gros Rateau Gris, Love Pear. Winter Bell of Downing.* Fruit very large, of a roundish turbinate figure; skin rough, covered with dull russet;

flesh hard and coarse, but excellent when baked or stewed in winter. Grafted on a Pear-stock, the tree bears so abundantly as to bend like a weeping willow. A specimen of this variety was exhibited at the sixteenth annual fair of the American Institute, October, 1843, weighing 33 oz.

PRINCE'S ST. GERMAIN. Fruit about medium size; form obovate; skin russety yellow, with dull red cheek; flesh melting and good. Mr. Manning says that its abundant bearing, and its ripening gradually in the house during winter, render it a very valuable market fruit; good till after Christmas.

SURPASSE MARIE LOUISE, *Pitt's Prolific Marie, Pitt's Marie Louise.* A large Pear; oblong or calabash-formed; green, covered with brown-yellow russet; flesh melting and rich-flavored; ripe in October and November. It is a very prolific bearer.

SURPASSE ST. GERMAIN. Fruit of medium size; round at the crown, tapering to the stem; it is of very irregular form; the skin is rough; color yellow, mixed with dull brown; flesh coarse-grained, sugary, and high flavored; good from November till January.

SURPASSE VERGALIEU. Fruit large, oblong, some specimens nearly round; the skin smooth, its color yellow, with a light red cheek; flesh rich, juicy, and delicious eating; in October and November. Mr. Manning says the tree bears young, yields large crops, and is worthy of extensive cultivation.

UNEDALES ST. GERMAIN, *Belle de Jersey.* A large fine pyriform Bell Pear, of a brownish-green color, with russety spots; flesh firm and high-flavored. It is considered a first-rate baking Pear, and will keep till March. Mr. Reid, of the Murray Hill Nursery, exhibited some fine specimens of this fruit at the sixteenth annual fair of the American Institute, October, 1843.

VICAR OF WINKFIELD, *Bourgmestre of Boston, Monsieur le Curé, Dumas, Clion of Boston, according to the catalogue of Winter & Co., Flushing.* Fruit oblong, or pyramidal; skin russety-yellow, with ruddy color on one side; flesh firm, sweet, and rich; good as a table fruit, from December to February. This variety is deserving extensive cultivation for its beauty, large size, keeping qualities, and productiveness.

WINTER NELIS, *Nelis d'Hiver*, *La Bonne Malinoise*, *Spreeuw*. All accounts agree that this is a most excellent Winter Pear; ts size is above medium, somewhat oval; its skin green and russety, full of grey dots; flesh yellowish white, melting, high-flavored, with a musky perfume; at perfection in December and January.

PERRY PEARS.

BARLAND. This variety took its name from the original tree, growing in a field called Bare Lands, in Herefordshire, England. The fruit is smallish, of ovate form; skin dull green, russeted with grey. It is deemed excellent for perry.

HOLMORE. Fruit small globular; skin of a dingy yellowish green, tinged with red. Excellent perry is made of this variety in Herefordshire, England.

HUFFCAP. There are several varieties of Pears bearing this name, but the best perry is made of the true Herefordshire Huffcap. The fruit is middle-sized, of pale green color, marked with grey russet.

MONARCH. A new Pear, considered by Mr. Knight as without a rival. The tree is of rapid growth, and an abundant bearer; fruit large, of an extraordinary musky flavor, and deemed excellent for perry; good also for the table; from October to December and January.

OLDFIELD. Fruit below the medium size, of pale green color, with russety spots. An excellent perry fruit. Specific gravity of its juice 1067. From this variety is made the celebrated Ledbury Perry.

LONGLAND. Fruit very handsome, much like the Swan's Egg in shape; skin bright gold color, tinged and mottled with a russety lively orange; specific gravity of its juice 1063. The tree is handsome and upright, and much cultivated in Herefordshire for perry.

TEINTON SQUASH. Fruit middle-sized, of angular shape, skin a muddy russety green, marbled with dull orange, interspersed with ash-colored specks. The perry made from this fruit is of the very highest quality, something approaching in color and briskness to champagne, for which fine samples of it have sometimes been sold.

SELECT DESCRIPTIVE LIST OF PEARS.

THE ONTARIO PEAR. This variety promises well. Those persons who have raised it state that the trees grow vigorously,

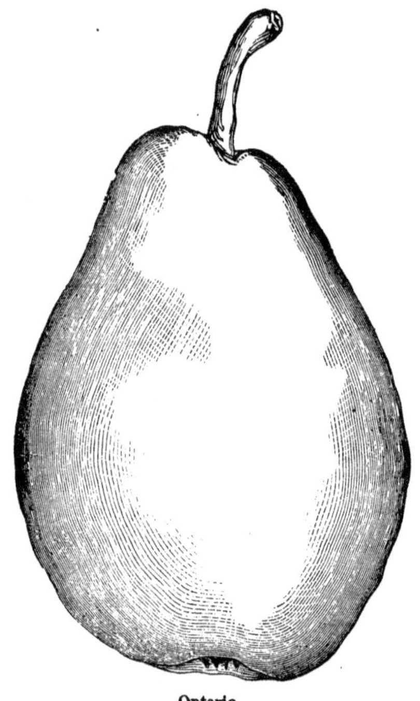

Ontario.

and will doubtless make an excellent pear for market. It is a seedling of the Canandaigua variety.

BEURRÉ D'ANJOU. A first-rate autumn Pear, imported from

France by Col. Wilder, of Boston; fruit rather above medium size; obovate; skin greenish-yellow, a little clouded with russet; flesh very fine-grained, buttery, and melting, with a rich, sprightly vinous flavor.

Bezi de la Motte, *Bein Armudi, Beurré Blanc de Jersey* Fruit of medium size, bergamot-shaped, skin pale yellowish green, sprinkled with russet dots; flesh white, very fine-grained, buttery and juicy, with a sweet perfumed flavor; an old autumn variety, ripe in October.

Bishop's Thumb. An old English autumn Pear, usually considered first-rate; fruit rather large, oblong, and narrow; skin yellowish-green, dotted with russet, and tinged with red; flesh juicy, melting, and of a rich vinous flavor.

Bon Chretien Fondante. A new Flemish Pear, abounding with juice, and having a refreshing and agreeable flavor; skin pale green, mottled, and dotted with russet; ripe in October.

Buffum. A native orchard Pear, from Rhode Island, of the Doyenne family; fruit of medium size, oblong ovate; skin deep yellow, finely suffused with bright red and russet dots; flesh sweet and excellent; ripe in September.

Compte de Lamy, *Beurré Curte, Dingler, Marie Louise the Second.* A rich Flemish autumn Pear, of medium size, roundish obovate; skin yellow, with a brownish-red cheek, and russety; flesh melting and high-flavored.

Duchesse de Mars, Duchess of Mars. A French autumn Pear of medium size, obovate; skin dull yellow, partially covered with brown russet, with a dull red cheek; flesh very melting, and of a rich perfumed flavor.

Dunmore. A truly admirable and hardy Pear from the garden of the London Horticultural Society. Fruit large, oblong obovate; skin greenish, speckled with russet; flesh buttery, melting, and rich; ripe in September.

Eyewood. A hardy and prolific seedling of Mr. Knight's. Fruit of medium size, oblate or flattened; skin much covered with russet; flesh buttery, rich, and melting; in October and November.

Fondante Van Mons. An excellent melting Pear, introduced by Mr. Manning. Fruit of medium size, roundish; skin pale yellow; flesh white, juicy, sweet, and palatable; towards the end of October.

Jalousie de Fontenay Vendée. A fine autumn French Pear, of medium size; turbinate or obtuse pyriform; skin dull yellow and green, with red cheek, marked with russet; flesh melting, with a rich-flavored juice.

Lawrence. A seedling winter pear, from the nursery of Messrs. Wilcomb & King, Flushing. Fruit rather large. obovate; skin yellowish-green, with patches of brown; flesh melting and rich; from November to January.

Paradise d'Automne. A newly imported early autumn Pear, of large size; pyriform, tapering into the stalk; skin dull yellow, russeted; flesh white, fine-grained, melting, and luscious.

Petre. This fine autumn variety originated in the old Bartram Botanic Garden, near Philadelphia, from a seed furnished by Lord Petre of London, in 1735. Fruit of medium size, obovate; skin pale yellow, marked with greenish russet; flesh fine-grained and melting, with a perfumed high flavor.

Queen of the Low Countries, *Reine des Pays-Bas.* Fruit large, broad pyriform; skin dull yellow, mottled with russet, and overspread with fine dark red; flesh melting, with a rich sub-acid vinous flavor; early in October.

Rostiezer. A German Pear of medium size; oblong pyriform; skin yellowish-green, with reddish-brown cheek, and light-colored dots; flesh juicy, melting, sweet, and palatable; in September and October.

St. Ghislain. An excellent Belgium autumn Pear, introduced by S. G. Perkins, Esq., of Boston. Fruit of medium size, pyriform; skin pale yellow, with a few grey specks; flesh white, buttery, juicy, and of a rich sprightly flavor.

Thompson. This fine autumn Pear was named in honor of Mr. Robert Thompson, Superintendent of the London Horticultural Society's garden. Fruit of medium size, obovate;

skin pale lemon-yellow, dotted and streaked with russet; flesh white, buttery, and melting, with an agreeable aromatic flavor; tree hardy and prolific, producing its fruit in October and November.

VAN MONS LEON LE CLERC. A splendid autumn Pear, imported by Col. Wilder of Boston. Fruit large, oblong-ovate; skin yellowish, mingled with brown; flesh yellowish-white, rich, and melting; in October and November.

VAN BUREN. A seedling raised by Gov. Edwards of New Haven. Fruit large, obovate; skin clear yellow, with a rich orange-red blush, and russet spots; flesh sweet and perfumed; excellent for baking and preserving.

SELECTING PEARS ADAPTED TO LOCALITIES.

The reader should bear in mind that many of the foregoing kinds of pears will succeed well in certain localities, and in other places be nearly worthless. Locality is everything with pears. The first question of importance is, when a person is about to plant pear-trees—Will that kind succeed in my locality?

The list of pears might be increased to several times the present length, but those desiring other varieties may find them minutely described in fruit catalogues of nursery-men in various parts of the country. New varieties are originated every year, some of which are much inferior to those that have been grown for a long period. Previous to selecting trees, extensive inquiry should be made, to ascertain, if possible, if there are any trees in that locality, and whether they bear abundantly, or yield but a small crop. Every beginner should heed this caution, and not select a variety that he knows nothing of, because some person has recommended it as worthy of cultivation.

FIRE-BLIGHT AND MILDEW.

The Pear, and also the Quince, aud sometimes other trees, are subject to the fire-blight. This malady may be completely checked on its first appearance, by cutting off and immediately burning the injured branches. Generally speaking, careful pruning, cleaning the bark all over with a brush, applying soap or tobacco-water to the leaves, and occasionally putting good earth and good manure to the roots, will remedy most diseases in fruit-trees. Removing them from a bad to a better soil will, of course, effect this, where it proceeds from a poorness of land; for the old adage, "Remove the cause, and the effect will cease," will be here exemplified. To cure the oozing of the gum, nothing more is necessary than to cut away the diseased parts of the bark; and by thus assisting nature in casting out the excrementitious or noxious juices, a complete cure may be effected.

When a tree is affected by mildew, let it be immediately sprinkled with soapsuds, and then be dusted over with sulphur and tobacco-dust, or snuff; at the same time dig around the tree, and examine the soil and subsoil; if it be wet and cankery, it should be taken away, and replaced with good healthy soil, and the ground drained. On the contrary, if the ground be dry, give it a plentiful watering. The same remedy may serve as a preventive of the extension of blight, if applied in time. When any canker is observed, the part affected must, at the time of pruning, be cut clean out, and the part thus dressed be pared, so that no water can lodge in the wound. When this is done, let a quantity of soot be mixed with water, and a little train-oil well worked among it, but so that the mixture finally remains stiff. This may be plastered over all the wounds that have been pruned. The application of this mixture keeps out the wet from the wounds, where it would be likely to lodge, and both the soot and oil promote vegetation. When trees are cankery from having a bad subsoil, it is in vain to apply any remedy till the ground is properly drained, some fresh soil mixed with the natural soil, and the tree replanted. When trees are known to be so situated as to be particularly liable to the attacks of insects or disease, they should be attended to at the time of winter or early spring pruning, in order to destroy the insects in their larv- state.

MANAGEMENT OF DWARF PEAR-TREES.

The two illustrations of dwarf pear trees-shown under this head will furnish a fair idea of the manner of training dwarf-trees. The short lines will show where the branches must be shortened, or cut off, during the successive years. The knife must be employed freely in order to produce a beautiful dwarf-tree of any kind of fruit.

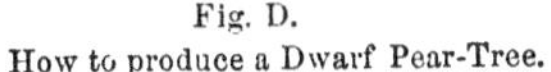

Fig. D.
How to produce a Dwarf Pear-Tree.

Fig. E.
Dwarf Pear-Tree.

Figure D represents a four-year pyramidal tree, pruned three times, each section being shown by the figures 1, 2, 3; and the lines across the branches represent the point where the knife is to be applied at the next pruning. Figure E represents a tree loaded with fruit, after the top has been pruned in the pyramidal form. Such trees are kept in form from year to year, by cutting and punching off the ends of the growing branches.

PLUM. PRUNIER. *Prunus.*

The Plum-tree grows fifteen feet or more in height, branching into a moderately spreading head; the leaves are ovate, serrated, and on short petioles; petals white. The natural color of the fruit is generally considered to be black; but the varieties in cultivation are of yellow, red, blue, and green colors, and of different forms and flavors. There are several good sorts that grow wild in the hedges of Britain, and also in America, but its original country is supposed to be Asia. According to Pliny, it was taken from Syria into Greece, and from thence into Italy. There are many varieties cultivated in France; and in the London Horticultural Garden there are about three hundred sorts kept under name. The Green Gage is considered the best dessert Plum, and the Egg Plum for sweetmeats; but the Damson is the best baking Plum.

The Plum is said to succeed best in a lofty exposure, and may yield well in the mountainous parts of the United States. Plum-trees yield well near Albany, but the fruit is by no means plentiful in the vicinity of the city of New York. Like the Nectarine, it is subject to the attacks of the Curculio and other insects.

It has been observed that Plum-trees growing in frequented lanes or barn-yards, are more generally fruitful than those cultivated in private gardens or secluded situations. This circumstance is by some attributed to the jarring of the trees, by cattle and swine rubbing against them; thus causing the defective fruit to fall on the ground. Geese kept in orchards or fruit-gardens often prove beneficial; as they, by devouring the defective fruit and other corruptible matter, prevent the possibility of insects getting into the ground, so as to perpetuate their existence or multiply their species.

Cobbett attributes the scarcity of Plums in New York to neglect. In his American Gardener he asks: "How is it that we see so few Plums in America, when the markets are supplied with cart-loads in such a chilly, shady, and blighty country as England?"

I would answer this query by informing the reader that the inhabitants of our parent country, with a view to derive the full benefit of the sun's rays for the cultivation of Plums, Peaches, Nectarines, and such other fruit as require extra heat, train their trees against walls, fences, or trellis-work; and from their having these means of support, gardeners have no inducement to plant them deeper than is necessary; whereas, from the circumstance of the American climate being sufficiently warm to ripen those fruits on standard trees, they are generally so cultivated. Many persons, to save the trouble of staking or otherwise supporting their trees, plant them too deep, and thus defeat the operations of nature. That this is a prevalent error has been shown in the articles Nectarine and Peach, to which the reader is referred for a more concise view of the subject.

New varieties of the Plum are produced from seed; and the old kinds are generally propagated by budding on stocks of free-growing Plums, in preference to grafting, because Plum trees are very apt to gum wherever large wounds are made in them. All the sorts produce their fruit on small natural spurs rising at the ends and along the sides of the bearing shoots of one, two, or three years' growth. In most sorts, new fruit branches are two years old before the spurs bear. The same branches and spurs continue fruitful, in proportion to the time which they take to come into bearing.

After the formation of the head is begun, it takes from two to six years before the different sorts come into bearing. Standards must be allowed to expand in free growth, occasionally pruning long ramblers and irregular cross branches. In annual pruning, thin crowded parts, cut away worn-out bearers, and all decayed and cankery wood. The Plum may be cultivated in small gardens, trained as an espalier, or to a close fence, like the Apricot. The tree is of further use than for its fruit as a dessert. The bark dyes yellow; the wood is used by turners;

and the dried fruit, or prune, is formed into electuaries and gentle purgatives. Prunes were originally brought from Damascus, whence the name *damson.*

MANAGEMENT OF PLUM-TREES.

Plum-trees require a soil free from superabundant moisture and well cultivated. The trees may be planted out in the spring, or in autumn, in ground that is kept clear from weeds and grass for at least four or five years. The soil for plums should have a good proportion of clay in it; and if clay predominates, mingle some sand with the clay. Wood-ashes, iron filings, iron turnings, and oxide of iron, which may be collected at the blacksmith's shop, are excellent for plum-trees. Coal-dust, soot, and all such materials, will promote the health of plum-trees and render them eminently productive.

SELECT DESCRIPTIVE LIST OF PLUMS.

American Yellow Gage, *American Wheat.* A beautiful medium-sized oval Plum, of a bright yellow color, when fully ripe; its flavor is rich, equal to the Green Gage. The fruit is not apt to crack nor to be attacked by insects. It is a very suitable variety to cultivate for the market; it ripens in August and September.

Apricot Plum, *Prune Abricote, Abricotée de Tours.* A large freestone Plum; its form is globular, depressed, divided by a deep suture; whitish yellow, but faint red next the sun, and covered with bloom; its flesh is firm, juicy, sweet, musky, and excellent; it ripens in August and September.

Bingham, *Bingham's Yellow Cling.* A delicious clingstone Plum, of large size and oval form; skin bright yellow, spotted and blotched with red; flesh yellow, rich, and delicious; ripening in August and September.

BLEECKER'S GAGE. This fine freestone Plum is stated to have been raised by the Rev. Mr. Bleecker, of Albany, from the stone of a German Prune; it is a large globular fruit, of excellent quality; skin dark yellow, with red spots and blotches; the flesh is rich, saccharine, and juicy; in September.

COE'S GOLDEN DROP, *Coe's Imperial, Bury Seedling, Golden Gage, Fair's Golden Drop.* Raised by Mr. Coe, Bury St. Edmunds, Suffolk, England. The tree is vigorous; fruit oval, of large size; skin greenish yellow, spotted with violet and crimson; the flesh, which separates from the stone, is of gold color, rich, and excellent; the fruit ripens at the end of September, and will keep several weeks. A first-rate fruit, and worthy of general cultivation.

COE'S LATE RED, *Saint Martin, Saint Martin Rouge.* An excellent freestone Plum of medium size, in form almost round; its color is violet purple, with a partial degree of bloom; flesh rich, saccharine, and high flavored. It is one of the best of late Plums; ripening in October and November.

COLUMBIA, *Columbian Gage.* A beautiful native clingstone Plum, of light purple color; the flesh is firm, of a greenish hue, with an abundance of rich-flavored juice. The tree is a great bearer, and ripens its fruit in August.

COOPER'S LARGE RED, *Cooper's Large American, La Delicicuse.* This Plum is of extraordinary size, measuring within an eighth of two inches in each direction; the skin is of a fine dark purple color; the flesh is yellowish green, rich, juicy, and of pleasant flavor; the fruit makes excellent preserves, if gathered in August; its great defect is an inclination to rot, if left long on the tree.

DENNISTON'S SUPERB is an excellent variety. The color is a pale yellowish-green, somewhat similar to the Green Gage plum. It was originated by Isaac Denniston, Albany, N. Y.

DIAMOND PLUM. Some consider this as the largest Plum known; its color is a dark purple; in form it resembles the Magnum Bonum, but its flavor is considered rather superior; it ripens in September, and the flesh separates clear from the stone. The tree, which grows vigorously, originated with Mr. Hooker, Kent, England

Denniston's Superb.

DOWNING'S EMERALD DROP. A beautiful clingstone Plum of medium size, oblong form, and green color; flesh firm and of delicious flavor; this variety originated at the Nursery of A. J. Downing & Co., Newburgh, State of New York.

DOWNTON IMPERATRICE. A superior late Plum, of medium size, shaped similar to the Blue Imperatrice; skin dark yellow, and very thin; the flesh yellow, soft, juicy, with a high-flavored acidity; at perfection in October and November.

DRAP D'OR, *Cloth of Gold, Mirabelle Double. Yellow Perdrigon of Winter & Co.* A small freestone Plum, of a roundish form and bright yellow color, marbled with red; flesh yellow, tender; juice sugary and excellent; ripe in July and August.

DUANE'S FRENCH PURPLE, *Dame Aubert Violet. Purple Magnum Bonum and Purple Egg of some collections.* A very superior clingstone Plum, of large size, and oblong form; the skin dark purple; flesh sweet, juicy, rich, and excellent; ripe in September. This variety, from being imported by Mr. Duane of New York, was named after him, as he had lost the original name.

EARLY ORLEANS, *New Orleans, Early Monsieur, Monsieur Hatif.* A fine freestone plum, above medium size; form round; its suture deep; color dark purple, covered with a fine bloom; flesh greenish yellow, of excellent flavor; sweet, combined with a pleasant acid; it ripens in August.

EARLY TOURS, *Precoce de Tours, Early Violet.* The tree is vigorous and fertile; fruit small, oval, dark purple covered with fine bloom; flesh greenish yellow, tender, juicy, and of very agreeable flavor; one of the best early varieties, and very productive; ripe at the end of July.

ELFRY. *French Cooper of Prince.* A native clingstone Plum, highly esteemed in Pennsylvania and New Jersey for its productiveness and other good qualities; the fruit is below medium size, of oblong shape and dark blue color; flesh firm, very rich and delicious; in September.

GERMAN PRUNE, *Prune d'Allemagne, Damas Gros, Quetsche, Quetzen.* The fruit of the Quetsche Plum is grown for the purpose of drying, and is considered the best for use as prunes; fruit below the middle size; of an oval figure; skin red and purple; flesh yellow; juice sweet, with a slight acid; ripe early in September.

GOLIATH, *Goliah, St. Cloud, Caledonian. Wilmot's Late Orleans.* This fruit is very large, sometimes weighing four ounces; the skin is a deep reddish purple; the flesh pale yellow, firm, and well flavored, but not rich, slightly adhering to the stone; the tree is a great bearer, and the fruit is much used for cooking; ripe in September.

GREEN GAGE, *Great Queen Claude, Dauphine, Grosse Reine Claude Abricot Vert, Verte Bonne, Gros Damas Vert.* A middle-sized round fruit, of a yellowish-green color, and purplish russety red next the sun; the flesh is of a greenish hue, melting, with an abundance of very sweet and highly perfumed juice, of an exquisite taste; it arrives at maturity towards the end of August.

HORSE PLUM, *Large Sweet Damson.* Fruit of medium size, oval, with a deep suture in the middle; skin dark red, inclining to purple when ripe; flesh greenish yellow; juice acid but agreeable. Quantities of these Plums are sold in the New York markets in August and September, for sweetmeats. The trees are generally raised from suckers; and Peaches, Apricots, and Nectarines will bud and thrive well on such stocks.

HULING'S SUPERB, *Keyser's Plum.* This Plum is of monstrous size, and has been known to weigh nearly four ounces; it is of roundish form, and of a greenish-yellow color; the flesh sweet and excellent. It was raised from seed by Mr. Keyser, is of Pennsylvania, and brought into notice by Dr. Wm. Hulings, of that State.

IMPERATRICE, *Imperatrice Violette, Blue Imperatrice. Simiana of som collections.* One of the best of late clingstone Plums; fruit medium size, oval; skin rich deep purple, covered with bloom; flesh yellowish green, a little firm, very sweet, rich, and juicy; the fruit hangs long on the tree, and is at maturity in October and November.

IMPERIAL DIADEM, *Red Imperial, Red Diaper.* A fine fruit, admirably adapted for culinary purposes; shape oval; color pale red, but dark when mature; flesh yellow, and separates from the stone; juice plentiful when perfectly ripe, which is early in September; it is of good flavor, and highly perfumed.

ITALIAN DAMASK, *Damas d'Italie.* This fruit is of medium size, nearly round, a little flattened at the base; its color blue or violet, and covered with a purple bloom; its flesh is yellow, rich, and juicy, and the tree, which matures its fruit in August, is very productive.

KIRKE'S PLUM. This variety is said to be as hardy and prolific as the Orleans, as handsome as the Damask, and as good as the Green Gage; fruit large, roundish; skin covered with a close, firm, azure bloom, through which appear a few golden specks; flesh greenish-yellow, firm, juicy, and rich; in perfection the early part of September.

LA ROYALE, *Royale.* A large and excellent freestone Plum, of a homely dull red color, but concealed by a thick violet or azure bloom; flesh fine, yellowish-green, firm, juicy, high-flavored, and delicious; a superior Plum; at maturity early in September.

LATE PURPLE DAMSON, *Purple Winter Damson, Blue Damascene, Blue Damson.* This variety is in great esteem for preserves, and generally commands a high price. It is of a dark purple color, covered with bloom; the flesh has rather too much acidity for a table fruit, but this tartness gives it an agreeable flavor when cooked; and if the fruit remains on the tree until November, it becomes sweet.

LAWRENCE GAGE, *Lawrence's Favorite.* A large round freestone Plum, of a yellowish-green color, tinged with red; flesh firm, and of delicious flavor, similar to the Green Gage. The tree is very fertile, and yields an abundance of fruit in August and September.

LUCOMBE'S NONESUCH. This Plum is large, compressed at the summit and base; its breadth is two inches; its color at maturity, as well as its form, resembles the Green Gage, but more streaked with yellow; flesh firm, rich, and juicy; at maturity in August; tree a good bearer.

MIMMS, *Mimms Plum, Diaprée Rouge.* The fruit is very large, a little oblong; color bright purple, covered with thick bloom; its flesh, which separates from the stone, is yellowish-green, tender, juicy, and very agreeably flavored; ripe in September.

MOROCCO, *Early Black Damask, Black Damascus, Black Morocco, Early Damask, Early Morocco.* This is considered one of the best of early Plums. The tree is very hardy and productive; fruit middle-sized, roundish; skin deep blackish purple, covered with a light blue bloom; flesh greenish-yellow, juicy, rich, and high-flavored; ripe early in August.

NECTARINE PLUM, *Caledonian, Howell's Large, Prune Pêche, Jenkin's Imperial.* One of the most beautiful Plums known; large, nearly round; the skin at maturity varies from red to crimson, covered with azure bloom; flesh yellowish, coarse-grained, astringent; juice abundant, and of a mild, pleasant flavor; at maturity in July and early in August.

NEW YORK PURPLE, *Brevoort's Purple Bolmar, Brevoort's Purple Washington.* An excellent fruit, raised from a seed of Bolmar's Washington Plum, that had been impregnated with the pollen of the Blue Gage. The fruit is very large; skin brown red, covered with purple bloom: flesh yellow, of a rich and brisk flavor, and adheres to the stone; ripe towards the end of August.

OCTOBER GAGE, *Frost Gage.* A beautiful native fruit, a drawing of which has been taken from nature, and may be found in "Hoffy's Orchardist's Companion." Fruit of medium size; form oblong; color dark brownish-purple, covered with a black bloom; flesh firm and juicy; flavor sprightly and agreeable; ripe early in October.

ORLEANS PLUM, *Red Damask, Damas Rouge, Monsieur.* A well known and productive Plum; of medium size, and somewhat oval form; the skin is dark red, approaching to purple, with a thin blue bloom; flesh yellow, firm, and good, separating freely from the stone; ripe in August.

POND'S PURPLE, *Pond's Seedling.* A large round purple clingstone Plum, a native of Massachusetts; it is of peculiar rich flavor, not apt to crack, and is well adapted for the markets. The tree bears wonderful crops, which ripen in August.

PRINCE'S IMPERIAL GAGE, *Flushing Gage, Superior Green Gage, White Gage.* This tree was originated at the Flushing nursery, from a seed of the Green Gage. The fruit is one of the finest of its class; the skin at maturity is yellow, with a whitish bloom; the flesh is rich, luscious, and of excellent flavor. It makes fine preserves, if gathered towards the end of August; at maturity in September.

Prince's Orange Egg. A large, splendid, orange-colored clingstone Plum, of oval form, aud of peculiarly rich flavor; ripe in August. The tree yields abundant crops of truly beautiful fruit, which is never attacked by insects, as many kinds are.

Prune Suisse, *Semiana, Prune d'Altesse, Monsieur Tardif, Swiss Prune.* Fruit very handsome, round, flattened; color varying from bright amber to deep red, and covered with azure bloom; flesh yellow, delicious, melting, and closely adheres to the stone; juice very abundant. An excellent fruit; ripening in September.

Purple Gage,*Blue Gage, Reine Claude Violette, Die Violette Königinn Claudian.* This fruit is of medium size, almost round, and may be considered as one of the finest varieties; its skin is of a violet purple color, with pale yellow dots, and covered with a light blue bloom; flesh greenish-amber, rich, saccharine, and high-flavored: at maturity in August, and good until October.

Queen Victoria, *Sharp's Emperor, Dennyer's Victoria.* An excellent freestone Plum, as large as the *Red Magnum Bonum;* of a roundish oval form, and red color, covered with a fine bloom; the flesh is firm, rich, juicy, and delicious. The tree grows very strong, and yields abundant crops in September.

Red Diaper, *Diaprée Rouge, Roche Carbon.* One of the most beautiful Plums known; form oval, above medium size; color bright red; flesh greenish-yellow, soft and sweet, separating from the stone; the fruit makes excellent prunes, if gathered early in September; and like the Imperatrice, will hang some time on the tree.

Red Magnum Bonum, *Red Imperial, Imperial Violette of the French, Purple Egg of Prince and others.* A large, oval Plum, of deep red color, covered with blue bloom; the flesh, which parts from the stone, is harsh and acid; consequently good for cooking, preserves, etc.: in September and October.

Red Perdrigon, *Perdrigon Rouge.* An excellent Plum, of the first class; of medium size, oval shape, and fine red color, with gold-colored dots, and a fine bloom; flesh bright yellow, transparent, and separates from the stone; juice sweet and delicious; ripe early in September. It makes excellent prunes, not inferior to the White Perdrigon.

Red Queen Mother. The Plum is of medium size, its color bright red and yellow, somewhat spotted, and covered with pale bloom; its flesh is yellow, sweet, and excellent, ripening early in September. A very productive variety, and highly deserving of cultivation.

Royal de Tours. The tree is of extraordinarily vigorous growth; its principal stem rises vertically; the fruit is globular, of medium size; red violet color, and covered with azure bloom; flesh yellow, fine, good; juice abundant and sweet: ripens early in August.

Saint Catharine. A medium-sized, oblong fruit; skin bright gold color, spotted with red at maturity, and covered with bloom; flesh yellow, tender, sweet, and fine flavor; ripens early in September, and will hang some time on the tree. A good market Plum, for which purpose it is much cultivated.

Smith's Orleans. This variety is held in great esteem as a market fruit; the trees are free from gum and insects, and yields abundant crops of large freestone Plums, of an oval form and purple color. The fruit ripens gradually in September.

Surpasse Monsieur. A large fruit, of oval form, and of a dark red purplish color, raised by a Mr. Noisette; it is said to be more beautiful and perfumed than the Monsieur, and the tree yields suckers, which produce fruit in all its beauty and excellence: in September.

Virginale, *White Virginal.* This fruit ranks among the best of Plums; its shape is round; color yellowish, touched with violet or rose, and covered with dense bloom; flesh melting, juice abundant, and very agreeable; it adheres to the stone: ripe in September.

Washington, *New Washington, Bolmar's Washington,*

Franklin. A very large, globular Plum, inclining to oval; color greenish-yellow, with crimson specks, covered with a rich bloom. This Plum has sometimes weighed over four ounces; its flesh is yellow, firm, sweet, and delicious: in August. This variety originated in New York, from suckers of an old root, the tree of which had been some time previously destroyed by lightning.

White Magnum Bonum, *Yellow Magnum Bonum, Grosse Luisante, Imperiale Blanche, Egg Plum, White Mogul, White Holland.* This fruit is of extraordinary size; oval, yellow, covered with pale bloom; the flesh yellow, firm, closely adhering to the stone; excellent for cooking and preserves: in September.

White Perdrigon, *Perdrigon blanc.* A middle-sized, oblong fruit, of a pale yellow, with red spots, and covered with white bloom; flesh yellow, saccharine, and juicy, separating from the stone: it ripens in August.

Autumn Gage, *Roe's Autumn Gage.* A new late Plum, raised by William Roe, Esq., of Newburgh. Fruit of medium size, oval; skin pale yellow, with whitish bloom; flesh juicy, and of delicate pleasant flavor: in September.

Buel's Favorite. An excellent clingstone Plum, raised by Isaac Denniston, of Albany. Fruit pretty large, ovate; skin pale green, sprinkled with lighter dots, and a little red; flesh juicy and high-flavored: end of August.

Cruger's Scarlet, *Cruger's Seedling.* A seedling raised by Henry Cruger, Esq., of New York. Fruit rather larger than the Green Gage, roundish, oval; skin a lively red, covered with thin blue bloom; flesh of a sprightly flavor.

Damson, *Common Damson, Purple Damson, Black Damson.* A favorite fruit with old housekeepers for preserves, of which there are many varieties, which from being frequently raised from seed vary somewhat in character. They ripen in succession from September to November.

Denniston's Superb. Fruit round, a little flattened; skin yellowish-green, with purple blotches, overspread with a thin bloom; flesh very thick, juicy, with a rich vinous flavor; a freestone, ripening towards the end of August.

Ickworth Imperatrice, *Knight's No.* 6. A choice seedling from Mr. Knight, of Downton Castle. Fruit above medium size, obovate; skin purple, embroidered with streaks of golden fawn-color; flesh juicy and rich: it ripens early in October, and may be kept till Christmas if laid away in paper.

Isabella. An attractive-looking English clingstone Plum of medium size; skin dark red in the sun, paler in the shade, and dotted; flesh yellow, rich, juicy, and of delicious flavor: towards the end of August.

Jefferson. A Plum of high merit, raised by the late Judge Buel. Fruit large, oval; skin golden yellow, with a purplish red cheek, covered with a thin bloom; flesh rich, juicy, and high-flavored: towards the end of August.

Lombard, *Bleecker's Scarlet, Beeckman's Scarlet.* This variety was brought into notice by Mr. Lombard, of Springfield, Massachusetts. Fruit of medium size, roundish oval; skin delicate violet, dotted with red; flesh yellow, juicy, and pleasant: in August.

Orange Plum, *Orange Gage.* A plum of extraordinary size from the garden of Mr. Teller, of Rhinebeck, New York. Skin bronze-yellow, clouded with purple; flesh deep yellow, a little coarse-grained, but of a pleasant acid flavor: ripens the last of August.

Purple Favorite. This variety was first introduced by A. J. Downing, Esq., of the Newburgh Nursery. Fruit above medium size, roundish ovate; skin light brown in the shade, purple in the sun, dotted with golden specks and thin light, bloom; flesh pale green, very juicy, tender, luscious, and melting: ripens towards the last of August.

QUINCE. COIGNASSIER. *Cydonia.*

The Quince is of low growth, much branched, and generally crooked and distorted. The leaves are roundish or ovate, entire, above dusky green, underneath whitish, on short petioles. The flowers are large, white, or pale red, and appear in May and June. The fruit, a pome, varying in shape in the different varieties, globular, oblong, or ovate. It has a peculiar and rather disagreeable smell, and austere taste. The fruit takes its name from being a native of the ancient town of Cydon, in the Island of Crete. Some suppose it to be a corruption of *Malus colonea*, by which the Latins designated the fruit. It is used as a marmalade for flavoring apple-pies, and makes an excellent sweetmeat; and it has the advantage over many other fruits for keeping, if properly managed.

Of the several sorts, the following are in greatest esteem: 1. The oblong, or Pear Quince, with ovate leaves, and an oblong fruit lengthened at the base. 2. The Apple Quince, with ovate leaves, and a rounder fruit. 3. The Portugal Quince, the fruit of which is more juicy and less harsh than the preceding, and therefore the most valuable. It is rather a shy bearer, but is highly esteemed, as the pulp has the property of assuming a fine purple tint in the course of being prepared as a marmalade. 4. The mild or eatable Quince, being less austere and astringent than the others. 5. The Orange Quince, a very handsome fruit of peculiar rich flavor. 6. The Musk or Pineapple Quince, very large and beautiful.

The Quince produces the finest fruit when planted in a soft, moist soil, and rather shady, or at least sheltered situation. It is generally propagated by layers, and also by cuttings, and approved sorts may be perpetuated by grafting. In propagating for stocks, nothing more is necessary than to remove the lower shoots from the layer, so as to preserve a clear stem as high as the graft; but for fruit-bearing trees, it is necessary to train the stem to a rod, till it has attained four or five feet in height, and can support itself upright.

When planted in an orchard, the trees may be placed ten or twelve feet apart. The time of planting, the mode of bearing, and all the other particulars of culture, are the same as for the Apple and Pear. The chief pruning they require, is to keep them free from suckers, and cut out decayed wood. The ground should be kept free from grass and weeds; and if the soil be poor, swine manure, chip dirt, or any other kinds of rich manure should be forked into the ground around the trees. If the soil be heavy, containing a large proportion of clay, let a load of sand or fine gravel be spread around each tree, or mingled with the earth before the trees are transplanted.

Raspberry. Framboisier. *Rubus.*

There are several species of the *Rubus* found wild in various parts of Asia, Europe, and America, some of which have upright stems, others prostrate. The American Stone Bramble, and also the common Blackberry, Dewberry, and Cloudberry, are of this family. The *Rubus idæus*, or common Raspberry, grows spontaneously in the province of New Brunswick, and in various parts of the United States, but most of the cultivated varieties are supposed to have originated in England. Loudon describes the true Raspberry as having "stems which are suffruticose, upright, rising to the height of several feet, and are biennial in duration; but the root is perennial, producing suckers which ripen and drop their leaves one year, and resume their foliage, produce blossom shoots, flower, and fruit, and die the next. The leaves are quinate-pinnate; the flowers come in panicles from the extremity of the present year's shoots; they are white, appear in May and June, and the fruit forms about a fortnight afterwards."

The fruit is grateful to most palates, as nature presents it, but sugar improves the flavor; accordingly it is much esteemed when made into sweetmeats, and for jams, tarts, and sauces.

It is fragrant, sub-acid, and cooling; allays heat and thirst. It is much used in distilling. "Raspberry syrup is next to the Strawberry in dissolving the tartar of the teeth; and as, like that fruit, it does not undergo the acetous fermentation in the stomach, it is recommended to gouty and rheumatic patients."

Nichol enumerates twenty-three species and varieties of the cultivated Raspberry, and twenty-one of the *Rubus ronce*, or Bramble; in the latter are included the American Red and Black Raspberry, the Long Island and Virginian Raspberry; also the Ohio Ever-Bearing, and the Pennsylvania Raspberry. The English varieties are, Early Small White; Large White; Large Red; most Large Red Antwerp; Large Yellow Antwerp; Cane, or smooth-stalked; Twice-bearing White; Twice-bearing Red; Smooth Cane, twice-bearing; Woodward's Raspberry; Monthly, or Four Season; Dwarf Red Cane; Victoria Raspberry; Large Red Franconia; Mason's Red Cluster; McKeon's Scarlet Prolific; Chili Red; Cornish Red; Cox's Honey; Brentford Red; Brentford White; Flesh-colored; Barnet Red; Bromley Hill; Cretan Red; Prolific Red; Canada Purple; Rose-flowering, etc.

HOW RASPBERRIES ARE PROPAGATED.

The varieties can be perpetuated by young sucker-shoots, rising plenteously from the root in spring and summer. When these have completed one season's growth, they are proper to detach with roots for planting, either in the autumn of the same year, or the next spring, in March or early in April. These new plants will bear some fruit the first year, and furnish a succession of strong bottom-shoots for full bearing the second season. New varieties are raised from seed, and they come into bearing the second year. Some of the American species are cultivated by layers, which produce fruit the same year.

Raspberry beds are in their prime about the third and fourth year; and, if well managed, continue in perfection five or six years, after which they are apt to decline in growth, and the fruit to become small, so that a successive plantation should be provided in time. Select new plants from vigorous stools in full perfection as to bearing. Be careful to favor the twice-bearers with a good mellow soil, in a sheltered situation, in order that the second crop may come to perfection.

When Raspberries are cultivated on a large scale, it is best to plant them in beds by themselves, in rows from five to seven feet apart, according to the kinds. In small gardens they may be planted in detached stools, or in single rows in different parts of the garden, from the most sunny to the most shady aspect, for early and late fruit of improved growth and flavor. It is requisite to cut out the dead stems early in the spring, and to thin and regulate the successional young shoots. At the same time, the shoots retained should be pruned at the top, below the weak bending part, and some rotten dung worked in around the roots of the plants. Keep them clear of weeds during the summer, by hoeing between the rows, and eradicate all superfluous suckers; but be careful to retain enough for stock in succeeding years.

The Antwerp and other tender varieties of the Raspberry are liable to be more or less injured by the severity of our winters; to prevent which, they should be protected by bending them down to the ground late in autumn, and covering them with earth five or six inches, sloping it off so as to prevent injury from rain or snow.

In order to obtain a good supply of Raspberries in the autumn, cut down some of the twice-bearing varieties close to the ground, which will occasion strong suckers to shoot up, that will yield an abundant crop of fruit at a season when other varieties are not attainable.

SELECT DESCRIPTIVE LIST OF RASPBERRIES.

American Black, *Black Cap*. This fruit is of smallish size, and ripens in June and July. It is a favorite with some

AMERICAN RED, *English Red, Common Red.* This variety is much cultivated for the market. The fruit ripens in June and July successively.

ANTWERP RED, *Large Red Antwerp, Howland's Red Antwerp, Burley.* This species is rather tender, on which account

The Red Antwerp Raspberry.

the branches must be bent down in autumn, and covered with soil. The fruit is large and beautiful, of delicious flavor, and quite fragrant; in June and July.

ANTWERP WHITE, *Yellow Antwerp.* This is also tender or half hardy, but very prolific; the fruit is large, of a pale yellow color, and much esteemed. It ripens in June and July.

BARNET, *Cornwallis Prolific, Lord Exmouth, Large Red.*

This is considered a first-rate fruit, and yields abundantly; in June and July.

BEEHIVE. A new variety, introduced by Messrs. Winter & Co., of the Linnæan Botanic Garden, Flushing. The fruit is large, of round shape and red color; ripe in July.

CORNISH, *Large Cornish.* A hardy and highly productive variety, yielding an abundance of red berries in June and July.

DOUBLE-BEARING RED, *Twice-Bearing.* This species is very prolific, producing its first crop in July, and another in October.

FLESH-COLORED, *Framboisier Couleur de Chair.* A new variety, imported by W. R. Prince & Co. from France. It is described as a highly flavored and much-esteemed fruit.

FRANCONIA, *Red Franconia.* This variety is in great repute for its productiveness and the fineness of its fruit, which ripens gradually in July.

MONTHLY OR FOUR SEASONS, *Perpetual Bearing.* This species, if planted in a shady situation, will produce successional crops throughout the summer.

RED TALL CANE. There are several species of the Cane Raspberry, some of which are worthless. The Tall Red Cane produces fine fruit in July and August, and very frequently in autumn.

VICTORIA. This Queen of Raspberries has been imported by W. R. Prince, and plants are offered for sale at his nursery at Flushing, for twenty-five cents each.

BLACKBERRIES.

This kind of fruit requires about the same kind of management that is essential to raise good raspberries. Clean cultivation and rich ground, with all the old canes removed annually, will seldom fail to secure a bountiful crop. The illustrations of different varieties are not overdrawn as to size. Indeed, in many instances, the fruit grows larger than it is here represented. It must be borne in mind that in order to raise large berries, the soil must be worked deep and enriched with the best kind

The High-bush Blackberry.

of fertilizing material, and the surface mulched in hot weather. Blackberry bushes should be kept as clean of grass and weeds as growing corn or cabbage.

The Kittatinny Blackberry was originated by E. Williams, Montclair, New Jersey, and sustains the reputation of being one of the best, and with some fruit culturists the very best, blackberry in the country. It is a great bearer, endures our cold winters well, and sells quickly in market. We consider it superior to the celebrated New Rochelle Blackberry either for the table or for market.

STRAWBERRY. FRAISIER. *Fragaria.*

The *Cherry*, the *Currant*, and *Strawberry* red,
To the rich and the poor their refreshments have shed;
Pomona has scatter'd her blessings abroad,
The full-bearing branches bend down with their load.

This is a genus of fruit-bearing herbaceous plants, of which there are few in the vegetable kingdom that can equal the Straw-

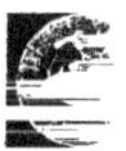

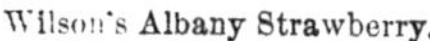

Wilson's Albany Strawberry.

berry in wholesomeness and excellence. The fruit is supposed to receive its name from the ancient practice of laying straw between the rows, which keeps the ground moist and the fruit clean. They are natives of temperate, or cold climates, as of Europe and America. The fruit, though termed a berry, is in botanical language a fleshy receptacle, studded with seeds. It is universally grateful, alone or with sugar, cream, or wine, and has the property, so valuable for acid stomachs, of not undergoing the acetous fermentation. Physicians concur in placing Strawberries in their small catalogue of pleasant remedies; as having properties which render them in most conditions of the animal frame positively salutary. They dissolve the tartareous incrustations of the teeth, and promote perspiration. Persons afflicted with the gout have found relief from using them very largely; so have patients in case of the stone; and Hoffman states that he has known consumptive people cured by them. The bark of the root is astringent.

CULTIVATION AND MANAGEMENT.

In cultivating the Strawberry an open situation and rich loamy soil, rather strong, are required for most varieties; and from their large mass of foliage and flowers, they must, till the fruit is set, have copious supplies of water. The row culture is best calculated to produce fruit; and frequent renewal insures vigorous plants as well as large fruit. Some plant them in single rows, from eighteen inches to two feet apart, according to the sorts. Others form a bed with four rows. If several beds be intended, a space of two or three feet may be left between each bed as a path; and in the second or third season the paths may be manured and dug, to admit the runners taking root. By this means a renewal may be made so often; and the old stools being taken away, leave spaces between the beds as before. Or new plantations may be made every season; because, after the roots are fairly established, they multiply spontaneously, as well by suckers from the parent stem as by numerous runners; all of which, rooting and forming a plant at every joint, require only removal to a spot where there is room for them to flourish. If the runners be taken off, and planted smal! A native of Britain. Some of the varieties are in in August and September, they will produce fine fruit the following season, and will bear in full perfection the second summer. Some, however, prefer spring planting, which answers very well if done in damp weather.

A plantation of the Alpine yields fruit the same year that it is made. The Wood and the Alpine are often cultivated from seed, which generally produces fine fruit. The other species are uniformly propagated by offsets, except the intention be to try for new varieties. The Alpine and Wood species may be planted in situations rather cool and shady, in order that they may produce their fruit late in the season, which is desirable. The Strawberry, with a little trouble of choosing a succession of sorts, may be forced so as to be had at the dessert every month in the year; though during the winter months it has not much flavor.

Some gardeners lay straw an inch or two thick over their beds in March, and set fire to it, in order to promote a stocky growth of plants and early fruit; others recommend mowing off the tops of such as are not required to fruit early, while they are in blossom, with a view to obtain a crop of Strawberries late in the season.

The London Horticultural Catalogue contains the names of about one hundred and fifty varieties of all the species, which are classed according to their nature, color, etc. Class 1. Scarlet Strawberries; 2. Black Strawberries; 3. Pine Strawberries; 4. Chili Strawberries; 5. Hautbois Strawberries; 6. Green Strawberries. 7. Alpine and Wood Strawberries. To select all the most esteemed from this, or any other extensive catalogue, is a difficult task. The following description of species and varieties may serve to direct the choice.

SELECT DESCRIPTIVE LIST OF STRAWBERRIES.

THE WOOD STRAWBERRY, *Fragaria vesca*, with oval serrated leaves; the fruit red, white, and green, which is round and

great repute, as they are very productive and continue long in bearing.

Triomphe de Gande.

THE SCARLET. *Fragaria Virginiana*, with leaves like the preceding; the fruit roundish and scarlet-colored. A native of Virginia. Varieties—Methven Scarlet, Knight's Scarlet, Austrian Scarlet, Early Scarlet, Wilmot's Late, Common Late, Wilmot's Early Scarlet, etc.

THE ROSEBERRY, *Fragaria, Virg. Var.* An Aberdeen seedling, introduced in 1810. The plants have few roundish leaves, larger fruit than the scarlet, and are very prolific; continues bearing till August.

THE BLACK Var. *Downton.* Dark Scarlet Strawberry, originated by Mr. Knight. The fruit is large, irregular, and cock's-comb-like; plant hardy and prolific.

THE CAROLINA *Fragaria Carolinensis.* Color dark red; a native of America. There are several choice varieties of this fruit, as—Elton's Seedling, Keen's Seedling, Mulberry, Wilmot's Black Imperial, Blood Pine, North's Seedling, Knevet's Seedling, etc.

THE MUSKY, OR HAUTBOIS, *Fragaria elatio*, with oval, rough, javelin-edged leaves. A native of Britain. Varieties—Black Hautbois, White Hautbois, Globe Hautbois, Conical Hautbois,

Double or Twice Bearing, producing delicious fruit in spring and autumn.

The Chili, *Fragaria Chiliensis*, with large, oval, thick, hairy leaves, and large flowers; the fruit large and very firm; a native of South America. Wilmot's Superb, or Large Cock's comb Scarlet, Knight's Seedling and Greenwell's New Giant are highly esteemed varieties.

Keen's Imperial or New Chili, *Fragaria Chili var.*, raised by Mr. Keen, of Isleworth; a most excellent bearer, ripening early. The fruit is very large, the flesh firm and solid, without any separate core; color scarlet.

The Alpine or Prolific, *Fragaria Collina*, commonly lasts from June till November, and in mild seasons till near Christmas; the varieties of this fruit are red and white. Natives of the Alps of Europe.

The One-Leaved, *Fragaria monophylla*. The pulp of the fruit pink-colored. A native of South America.

The following varieties have been lately propagated from some of the above species:—

Bishop's Orange, *Bishop's Globe, Bishop's New.* Fruit large, of roundish or conical form; orange-scarlet color, and very delicious flavor; ripe early in July.

Garnstone Scarlet. A fine, highly esteemed scarlet variety, of large size, roundish form, and peculiarly rich flavor, which ripens early in June.

Elton, *Elton Pine Strawberry.* Fruit very large; form heart-shaped, or obtusely conical; color bright dark-scarlet; rosy red; flavor very rich, spicy, aromatic, and agreeable. A beautiful drawing of this fruit is given in "Hoffy's Orchardist's Companion," from which the above description was taken.

Grove End Scarlet, *Atkinson's Scarlet.* A Seedling raised by Wm. Atkinson, at Grove End, Marylebone, in 1820; fruit large, oblate, of a bright vermilion color, and rich flavor; ripe by the middle of June.

Hovey's Seedling. This favorite variety was raised by Messrs. Hovey & Co. of Boston, in 1834. Fruit very large;

form round or slightly ovate, conical; color deep shining red, paler in the shade; flesh scarlet and firm, abounding in an agreeable acid and high-flavored juice; not surpassed by any other variety; ripe early in July.

Scott's Seedling.

HUDSON'S BAY, *American Scarlet, Velvet Scarlet, Large Hudson.* Fruit large, of ovate form; represented by Mr Downing as the best for market; early in July.

MONTHLY RED ALPINE. Fruit of medium size, and conical. Continues bearing fruit moderately from June till winter.

MYATT'S BRITISH QUEEN. The fruit of this celebrated variety is said to be of monstrous size; in form roundish, and in quality first-rate; about the middle of July.

MYATT'S PINE. A medium-sized fruit of ovate form, and very rich-flavored; ripening in July.

PRINCE ALBERT. A new variety raised in London, represented as a large fruit of ovate form, very splendid in appearance and delicious in flavor; ripe in July.

PRINCE'S NEW PINE. An excellent seedling variety of large size and ovate form. Raised by Wm. R. Prince, of Flushing; ripe early in July.

ROSEBERRY MONTEVIDEO, *Montevideo Early Scarlet.* An

improved American Seedling, from the common Roseberry: of large size, conical form, and fine flavor; ripe early in July.

SWAINSTONE'S SEEDLING. This variety is described as large, ovate, and of the very first quality, ripening one crop early in June, and a second crop in autumn.

Trolloppe's Victoria.

VICTORIA, *Higgin's Seedling.* The fruit of this variety is greatly esteemed; it is extra large, of roundish form, and exquisite flavor; early in July.

WARREN'S SEEDLING, *Warren's Methven.* This is represented as a peculiar fruit, being of large size, and in form nearly flat; it is moreover of a rich pineapple flavor, and yields abundantly throughout the month of July.

WHITE BUSH ALPINE, *New White Alpine* A medium-sized berry, of ovate form and agreeable flavor; the plant has no runners, and ripens its fruit in June and July.

WALNUT. NOYER. *Juglans.*

From the circumstance of our having an abundance of the fruit, and from the many species of this genus of trees growing spontaneously around us, it is presumed that the culture of the

Juglans regia, commonly called English Walnut, or Madeira Nut, has been neglected by many of our citizens. It is a native of Persia, and is cultivated in France, England, and in other parts of Europe, both as a fruit and timber tree. The fruit, in England, is much used in a green state for pickling, and also as an adulteration of soy sauce. In France, an oil, which supplies the place of that of Almonds, is made from the kernel. In Spain, they strew the gratings of old and hard nuts, first peeled, into their tarts and other meats. The leaves strewed on the ground, and left there, annoy moles; or macerated in warm water, afford a liquor which will destroy them. The unripe fruit is used in medicine for the purpose of destroying worms in the human body. Pliny says: "The more Walnuts one eats, with the more ease will he drive worms out of the stomach."

The timber is considered lighter, in proportion to its strength and elasticity, than any other, and therefore commonly used in England for gun-stocks. It is used in cabinet work in most parts of Europe. The young timber is allowed to make the finest colored work, but the old to be finest variegated for ornament. When propagated for timber, the nut is sown; but when fruit is the object, inarching from the branches of fruit-bearing trees is preferable. Budding is also practised by some. The buds succeed best when taken from the base of the annual shoots. Ordinary-sized buds from the upper part of such shoots generally fail.

Walnut-trees that have not been grafted or budded may be induced to produce blossoms by ringing the bark, that is, cutting out a streak of the bark around the body or main branches of the tree. Walnut-trees seldom yield much fruit until fifteen or twenty years old. The nuts are produced on the extremities of the preceding year's shoots. The trees should sta d forty or fifty feet apart, and be permitted to branch out in their natural order. They need but little pruning, merely to regulate any casual disorderly growth, to reduce over-extended branches, and to prune up the low stragglers.

Lest any of our native Walnuts should be neglected or abandoned by any, I annex a description of the different kinds:

Juglans catharticus is known under the name of Butternut, Oilnut, and White Walnut; these nuts are used by the Indians as a medicine.

Juglans nigra, the Black Walnut, is a tree of large size; its fruit is known to be excellent.

Juglans olivæformis, Pecan, or Illinois nut, is delicious. The nuts of *Juglans sulcata*, which is called Thick Shell-bark Hickory, and Springfield, and Gloucester nut, are large and well tasted. The Shell-bark Hickory, shag-bark, or scaly-bark Hickory, *Juglans alba*, is so called on account of its bark, which is torn lengthwise in long loose strips, as in *Juglans sulcata*. The *Juglans tomentosa*, the Mucker nut, White-heart Hickory, or common Hickory, and most of the other kinds enumerated, are worth cultivating where there is none, for timber for mechanical purposes; and that of the *Juglans glabra*, or Hog nut, is useful for making the old-fashioned splint-brooms.

HOW TO PROPAGATE.

Any or all of the foregoing nuts may be made to vegetate by planting them late in autumn in a well prepared soil free from superabundant moisture, and covered with about one inch in depth of firm mould. When the young trees are three or four years old they may be transplanted where they are to produce fruit. In some localities White Walnuts will succeed well, and the trees will yield fruit in ten to fifteen years; while in other parts of the country, or in an uncongenial soil, all efforts to make any of the species of the Juglans productive will prove ineffectual.

Mr. Bridgeman alludes to grafting the Juglans. I have heard others speak of grafting Walnut-trees, and I have seen it performed, but have never known a scion to grow, nor have I ever met with a person who had seen a living graft on a Butternut, or Black or White Walnut-tree. I have raised

Black Walnut-trees twenty feet high in eight years, all of which were loaded with large nuts when they were seven years old. Large and excellent nuts of all kinds may be raised by improved cultivation, as well as different kinds of fruit.

Reviser.

INDEX.

A.

B.

C.

F.

G.

H.

I.

L.

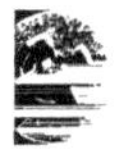

M.

N.

O.

P.

Q.

R.

S.

T.

V.

W.

Y.

PART III.

FLOWER-GARDENING.

CHAPTER I.

INTRODUCTION.

"Awake! the morning shines, and the fresh field
Calls you: ye lose the prime, to mark how spring
The tended plants, how blows the Citron grove;
What drops the Myrrh, and what the balmy Reed;
How Nature paints her colors; how the bee
Sits on the bloom, extracting liquid sweets."

How delightful is this fragrance! It is distributed in exquisite proportion; neither so strong as to oppress the organs, nor so faint as to elude them. We are soon cloyed at a sumptuous banquet; but this pleasure never loses its poignancy, nor palls the appetite. This balmy entertainment not only regales the sense, but cheers the very soul; and, instead of clogging, elates its powers.

"The soft green grass is growing
O'er meadow and o'er dale;
The silv'ry founts are flowing
Upon the verdant vale;
The pale Snow-drop is springing
To greet the glowing sun;
The Primrose sweet is flinging
Perfume the fields along;
The trees are in their blossom,
The birds are in their song;
As Spring upon the bosom
Of Nature's borne along.

"So the dawn of human life
Doth green and verdant spring;
It doth little ween the strife—
Like the Snow-drop it is fair,
And like the Primrose sweet,
But its innocence can't scare
The blight from its retreat."

The pious Hervey, in his Meditations on the Flower-Garden, has furnished us many sublime ideas respecting the order, variety, and beauty of the flower tribe. It is in vain to attempt a catalogue of those amiable gifts. There is an endless multiplicity of their characters, yet an invariable order in their approaches. Every month, almost every week, has its peculiar ornaments; not servilely copying the works of its predecessors, but forming, still forming, and still executing, some new design; so lavish is the fancy, yet so exact is the process of Nature. Were all the flower tribe to exhibit themselves at one particular season, there would be at once a promiscuous throng, and at once a total privation.

We should scarcely have an opportunity of adverting to the dainty qualities of half, and must soon lose the agreeable company of them all. But now, since every species has a separate post to occupy, and a distinct interval for appearing, we can take a leisurely and minute survey of each succeeding set. We can view and review their forms, enter into a more intimate acquaintance with their charming accomplishments, and receive all those pleasing sensations which they are calculated to yield.

Before the trees have ventured to unfold their leaves, and while the icicles are pendent on our houses, the Snow-drop breaks her way through the frozen soil, fearless of danger. Next peeps out the Crocus, but cautiously and with an air of timidity. She shuns the howling blasts, and cleaves closely to her humble situation. Nor is the Violet last in the shining embassy which, with all the embellishments that would grace a royal garden, condescends to line our borders, and bloom at the feet of briers. Freely she distributes the bounty of her emis sive sweets, while herself retires from sight, seeking rather to administer pleasure than to win admiration;—emblem, expressive emblem, of those modest virtues which delight to bloom in obscurity. There are several kinds of Violets, but the fragrant, both blue and white, are the earliest. Shakspeare compares an exquisitely sweet strain of music to the delicious scent of this flower:

> "Oh! it came o'er my ear like the sweet South,
> That breathes upon a bank of Violet,
> Stealing and giving odor."

The devout Hervey, in his admonitions to those who indulge in sloth, has thrown out the following sublime ideas: What sweets are those which so agreeably salute my nostrils? They are the breath of the flowers, the incense of the gardens. How liberally does the Jasmine dispense her odoriferous riches! How deliciously has the Woodbine embalmed this morning walk! The air is all perfume. And is not this another most engaging argument to forsake the bed of sloth? Who would be involved in senseless slumbers, while so many breathing sweets invite him to a feast of fragrancy, especially considering that the advancing day will exhale the volatile dainties? A fugitive treat they are, prepared only for the wakeful and industrious. Whereas, when the sluggard lifts his heavy eyes, the flowers will droop, their fine sweets be dissipated, and, instead of this refreshing humidity, the air will become a kind of liquid fire.

With this very motive, heightened by a representation of the most charming pieces of morning scenery, the parent of mankind awakes his lovely consort. There is such a delicacy in the choice, and so much life in the description of these rural images, that I cannot excuse myself without repeating the whole passage. Whisper it, some friendly genius, in the ear of every one who is now sunk in sleep, and lost to all these refined gratifications!

Our subject is so enchanting that we had inadvertently wandered from the path we first entered. We now retrace our steps, and take a glance at surrounding objects. The fields look green with the springing grass. See the Daffodil how it spreads itself to the wind! The leaves of Honeysuckles begin to expand; the Lilacs, or Syringas, of various hues, unfold their buds. The Almond exhibits its rosy clusters, and the Corchorus its golden balls. Many of the lowlier plants exhibit their yellow and purple colors, and the buds of Lilies, and other perennial plants, prepare to show themselves. If we turn our attention to the orchard, we behold the Apricots, Nectarines, and Peaches lead the way in blossoming, which are followed by the Cherry and the Plum. These form a most agreeable spectacle, as well on account of their beauty as of the promise they give of future benefits. It is, however, an anxious time for the possessor, as the fairest prospect of a plentiful increase is often blighted.

Now we return to the garden. Before we have time to explore Nature's treasures, many flowers disappear; among which are the humble Daisy, which shrinks from the intense heat, and the several varieties of Primulas, or early spring flowers. The various grades of Polyanthus deserve a close inspection. These for awhile exhibit their sparkling beauties; but, alas! soon disappear. Scarcely have we sustained this loss, but in comes the Auracula, and more than retrieves it. She comes arrayed in a splendid variety of amiable forms, with an eye of crystal, and garments of the most glossy satin. A very distinguished procession this! the favorite care of the florist, which soon disappear.

> "Fair-handed Spring
> Throws out the Snow-drop and the Crocus first,
> The Daisy, Primrose, Violet darkly blue,
> And Polyanthus with unnumbered dyes.
> Then comes the Auracula, enriched with shining meal,
> O'er all their velvet leaves."

While we reluctantly dispense with the sweet perfumes of the Hyacinth and Narcissus, we behold the Tulips begin to raise themselves on their fine wands or stately stalks. They flush the parterre with one of the gayest dresses that blooming Nature wears. Here one may behold the innocent wantonness of beauty. Here she indulges a thousand freaks, and sports herself in the most charming diversity of colors. In a grove of Tulips or a bed of Pinks, one perceives a difference in almost every individual. Scarcely any two are turned and tinted exactly alike. What colors, what colors are here! these so nobly bold, and those so delicately languid!

What a glow is enkindled in some! what a gloss shines upon others! With what a masterly skill is every one of the varying tints disposed! Here they seem to be thrown on with an easy dash of security and freedom; there they are adjusted by the nicest touches of art and accuracy. Those colors which form the ground are always so judiciously chosen as to heighten the lustre of the superadded figures; while the verdure of the impalement, or shadings of the foliage, impart new liveliness to the whole. Fine, inimitably fine, is the texture of the web on which these shining treasures are displayed. What are the labors of the Persian looms; what all the gay attire which the shuttle or the needle can furnish, compared with Nature's works? One cannot forbear reflection in this place on the too-prevailing humor of being fond and ostentatious of dress. What an abject and mistaken ambition is this! How unworthy the dignity of man, and the wisdom of rational beings! Especially since these little productions of the earth have indisputably the preëminence in such outward embellishments.

"Bright TULIPS, we do know,
  Ye had your coming hither,
And fading time doth show,
  That ye must quickly wither.

"Your sisterhood may stay,
  And smile here for an hour,
But ye must quickly die away,
  E'en as the meanest flower.

"Come, virgins, then, and see
Your frailties, and bemoan ye;
For lost like these—'twill be
As time had never known ye."

But let us not forget the fragrant, the very fragrant Wall and Gillyflowers; some of these regale us with their perfumes through various vicissitudes and alternations of the season, while others make a transient visit only.

In favored climates the Anemone appears encircled at the bottom with a spreading robe, and rounded at the top into a beautiful dome. In its loosely flowing mantle, you may observe a noble negligence; in its gently bending tufts, the most exquisite symmetry. This may be termed the fine gentleman of the garden, because it seems to possess the means of uniting simplicity and refinement, of reconciling art and ease. The same month has the merit of producing the Ranunculus. All bold and graceful, it expands the riches of its foliage, and acquires by degrees the loveliest enamel in the world. As persons of intrinsic worth disdain the superficial arts of recommendation practised by fops, so this lordly flower scorns to borrow any of its excellences from powders and essences. It needs no such attractions to render it the darling of the curious, being sufficiently engaging from the elegance of its figure, the radiant variety of its tinges, and a certain superior dignity of aspect.

We had intended to confine our meditations to the beauties of April and May, but Nature seems to improve in her operations. Her latest strokes are the most masterly. To crown the collection, she introduces the Carnation, which captivates our eyes with a noble spread of graces, and charms another sense with a profusion of exquisite odors. This single flower has centred in itself the perfection of all the preceding. The moment it appears, it so commands our attention that we scarcely regret the absence of the rest.

"Maternal Flora, with benignant hand,
Her flowers profusely scatters o'er the land;
These deck the valleys with unnumbered hues,
And far around their pregnant sweets diffuse,
The broad CARNATIONS, gay and spotted Pinks,
Are showered profuse along the rivers' brinks."

The field we have entered is so extensive and so enchanting that we cannot extricate ourselves without taking a cursory glance at the airs and habits, the attitude and lineaments, of each distinct class. See the Pæonia of China, splendid and beautifully grand! View the charming Rose, delicate and languishingly fair! and while you inhale its balmy sweetness, you will be constrained to admire it, notwithstanding its thorny appendages.

"Rose! thou art the sweetest flower
That ever drank the amber shower;
Rose! thou art the fondest child
Of dimpled Spring! the wood-nymph wild!
Resplendent Rose! the flower of flowers,
Whose breath perfumes Olympus' bowers;
Whose virgin blush, of chasten'd dye,
Enchants so much our mental eye."

Behold all the pomp and glory of the parterre, where Nature's paint and perfumes do wonders. Some rear their heads as with a majestic mien, and overlook, like sovereigns or nobles, the whole parterre. Others seem more modest in their aims, and advance only to the middle stations; a genius turned for heraldry might term them the gentry of the border; while others, free from all aspiring airs, creep unambitiously on the ground, and appear like the commonalty of their species. Some are intersected with elegant stripes or studded with radiant spots. Some affect to be genteelly powdered, or neatly fringed; while others are plain in their aspect, unaffected in their dress, and content to please with a naked simplicity. A few assume the monarch's purple, or are arrayed in the becoming robe of virgin whiteness, while doleful black is never seen in the wardrobe of spring. The weeds of mourning would be a manifest indecorum when Nature holds a universal festival. She would now inspire none but delightful ideas; and therefore always makes her appearance in some amiable attire. Here stands a warrior clad with crimson. There sits a magistrate robed in scarlet. Yonder a pretty flower seems to have dipped its petals in the rainbow, and glitters in all the gay colors of that resplendent arch. Some rise into a curious cut, or fall into a set of beautiful bells. Others spread themselves in a swelling tuft, or crowd into a delicious cluster. In some the predominant stain softens by the gentlest diminutions, till it has even stolen away from itself. The eye is amused at the agreeable delusion, and we wonder to find ourselves insensibly decoyed into quite a different lustre. In others one would think the fine tinges were emulous of preëminence. Disdaining to mingle, they confront one another with the resolution of rivals, determined to dispute the prize of beauty; while each is improved, by the opposition, into the highest vivacity of complexion.

"Mrs. Pæony came in quite late in a heat,
With the Ice-plant, dew-spangled from forehead to feet;
Lobelia, attired like a queen in her pride,
And Dahlias, with trimmings new furbish'd and dyed,
And the Bluebells and Harebells in simple array,
With all their Scotch cousins from highland and brae,
Ragged Ladies and Marigolds clustered together,
And gossip'd of scandal, the news, and the weather;
What dresses were worn at the wedding so fine
Of sharp Mrs. Thistle and sweet Columbine."

OBSERVATIONS ON THE FLOWER-GARDEN.

"If you would have a vivid, vigorous breed
Of every kind, examine well the seed;
Learn to what ELEMENTS your plants belong,
What is their constitution, weak or strong;
Be their physician, careful of their lives,
And see that every species daily thrives;
These love much AIR; those on much HEAT rely;
These, without genial MOISTURE, droop and die."

Previous to forming a flower-garden, the ground should be made mellow and rich, by being well pulverized, manured, and prepared in every respect as if intended for a kitchen-garden. A flower-garden should be protected from cold and chilling winds by tight fences, or plantations of shrubs, forming a close and compact hedge, which should be neatly trimmed every year. Generally speaking, a flower-garden should not be on a large scale; and the beds or borders should not be broader in any part than the cultivator can reach without treading on them. The shape and number of the beds must be determined by the quantity of the ground and the taste of the person laying out the garden.

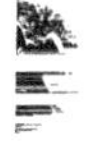

Much of the beauty of a pleasure-garden depends on the manner in which it is laid out. A great variety of figures may be indulged in for the flower-beds. Some choose oval or circular forms; others squares, triangles, hearts, diamonds, intersected with winding grass-paths and gravel-walks. In the design of an ornamental garden, nature, however, should be imitated as closely as practicable, not only in the formation and regulation of the flower-beds, but in the adaptation of each species to its peculiar element, soil, and situation; taking into consideration that the inmates of a garden, constituting as they do a mingled group, collected from all the different climates and soils of the vegetable creation, require each its most essential aliment to promote a luxuriant growth.

A flower-garden should be so situated as to form an ornamental appendage to the house; and, where circumstances will admit, it should be located before the windows exposed to a southern or south-eastern aspect. The principle on which it is laid out ought to be that of exhibiting a variety of color and form, so blended as to produce one beautiful whole. In a small flower-garden, viewed from the windows of a house, this effect is best produced by beds, or borders, formed side by side, and parallel to the windows whence they are seen, as in that position the colors show to the best advantage. In a retired part of the garden, a rustic seat may be formed, over and around which grape-vines, or honeysuckles, and other sweet and ornamental creepers and climbers, may be trained on trellises, which will afford a pleasant rural retreat.

CONSTRUCTING A ROCKERY.

In extensive pleasure-grounds a rockery, formed of rough stones, and rich light soil, may be erected in imitation of a mountain, on which may be cultivated various plants natives of mountainous districts, and such indigenous plants as are calculated for the situation; also herbaceous plants, procumbent and trailing, such as Mesembryanthemums, Climbing Cordydalis, the various species of Silene or Catch-fly, Gypsophila, Lotus, Ricota or Syrian Honesty, Godetia, etc. These, being interspersed with dwarf plants of different species, as Mountain Lychnis, Violets, Daisies, etc., and so arranged as to cover a great proportion of the rocky surface, must necessarily produce a very pleasing effect.

Although the greatest display is produced by a general flower-garden—that is, by cultivating such a variety in one bed or border as will insure an almost constant blooming—yet bulbous-rooted plants, though essential to the perfection of the flower-garden, lose something of their peculiar beauty when not cultivated by themselves. The extensive variety of bulbous roots furnishes means for the formation of a garden, the beauty of which, arising from an intermixture of every variety of form and color, would well repay the trouble of cultivation, particularly as, by a judicious selection and management, a succession of bloom may be kept up for some length of time. As, however, bulbous flowers lose their richest tints about the time that annuals begin to display their beauty, there can be no well founded objection to the latter being transplanted into the bulbous beds, so that the opening blossoms of the annuals may fill the place of those just withered, and continue to supply the flower-beds with all the gaiety and splendor of the floral kingdom.

DELIGHTFUL EMPLOYMENT FOR LADIES.

The cultivation of annual flowers is a delightful employment, and well adapted to the amusement of a lady, who, with the assistance of a laborer to prepare the ground, may turn a barren waste into a beauteous flower-garden with her own hands. Sowing the seed, transplanting, watering, and training the plants, tying them to sticks as props, leading them over trellis-work, and gathering their seed, are all suitable feminine occupations; and from their affording motives for exercise in the open air, they contribute greatly to health and tranquillity of mind.

But the taste of the florist will be exercised to little purpose, in the selection of flowers, if strict attention is not paid to the general state of the garden. If there are lawns or grass-walks, they should be frequently trimmed, and more frequently mowed and rolled, to prevent the grass from interfering with the flower-beds, and to give the whole a neat, regular, carpet-like appearance. If there are gravel-walks, they should be frequently cleaned, replenished with fresh gravel, and rolled. Box, and other edgings, should be kept clear of weeds, and neatly trimmed every spring. Decayed plants should be removed, and replaced by vigorous ones from the nursery-bed. Tall flowering plants must be supported by neat poles or rods; and all dead stalks and leaves from decayed flowers must be frequently removed. Treatment should be one of the pro-dominating characteristics in the management of a flower-garden.

In the summer season, all kinds of insects must be timely destroyed, and in the evenings of warm days the flowers will require frequent watering.

SELECTING SOIL ADAPTED TO FLOWERS.

Some seeds germinate in two or three days after having been deposited in the earth; others will exhibit no signs of vegetation in as many weeks. These and other distinguishing features arise, in a great measure, from their having originated in various soils and climates. Natives of cool or temperate climates and moist soils are generally tardy in germinating when cultivated in a warm climate and dry soil, for want of a due share of their most essential aliment, MOISTURE; and natives of warm climates and light soils require artificial culture in cool seasons and unpropitious climates, in order to their being accommodated with their natural and most important aliment, HEAT. AIR also is a more necessary aliment to some species than to others, but these three elements collectively constitute the food of plants in general. It may also be observed that the adaptation of plants to a soil congenial to them is of the utmost importance; as plants will not thrive well when their roots are surrounded by improper food.

Under favorable circumstances, annuals, in general, will produce their flower-buds within two months from the period of sowing the seed. Some species, soon after exhibiting their brilliant blossoms and ripening their seed, disappear, while others embellish the borders with a succession of flowers for two or three months. An assortment of seed judiciously selected, and sown in due season, will afford amusement to the cultivator the greater part of a summer, and yield seed for the propagation of the species in succeeding years, if gathered when ripe, and carefully preserved.

Annual plants will grow from one to four feet in height, in

a soil of uniform character and situation; but as these are diversified in almost every garden, no correct conclusion can be drawn in this particular. An attempt, however, has been made, in the annexed Catalogue, to describe the various species as nearly as possible, which may serve as a guide to the gardener in planting; the most dwarfish being adapted to the front or outer edge of the borders, and others in regular gradation.

Those species marked thus § are tender. Those marked thus * should be sown in the spot where they are intended to blossom, as they are apt to droop and die by being transplanted. Those marked thus †, though cultivated as annuals, from their facilities in blossoming and ripening their seed the first season, are in reality perennial, as are also some other varieties from warm climates, usually denominated annuals; but as such could not be cult vated at all by those who have no means of protecting their plants during our severe winters, they may with great propriety be treated as tender annuals, by sowing the seed every spring.

With a view to render this work more generally useful and interesting, a classification and definition of the various species and varieties embraced in the annexed Catalogue are given. Precision, however, in the performance of this task is impracticable, as it must be evident that the vegetable family, having been collected from every variety of climate and soil, will differ as to height, color, time of blossoming, and in many other essential points, when cultivated out of their natural Element.

A CATALOGUE OF ANNUAL FLOWER SEEDS.

Graines de fleurs annuelles.

§ Denotes tender. † Perennial. * Difficult to transplant.

		Feet High.
† Ageratum, Mexican, blue,	*Ageratum Mexicana,*	1 to 2
Alkekengi, or Kite Flower, lilac,	*Atropa physaloides,*	3 to 4

		Feet High
† Alyssum, Sweet, white,	*Alyssum maritima,*	1
§ Amaranthus, three-colored,	*Amaranthus tricolor,*	2 to 3
* Argemone, or Prickly Poppy, yellow, cream-colored, and white,	*Argemone, Mexicana, grandiflora, ochroleuca, etc.,*	2 to 4
Aster, Chinese and German, white, red, striped, purple, etc.,	*Aster, Chinensis, var., alba, rubra, striata, purpurea, etc.,*	1 to 2
§ Balsams; three species and numerous varieties, scarlet, striped, purple, crimson, white, etc.,	*Balsamina hortensis, Mastersiana, cornuta, coccinea, striata, purpurea, alba, etc.,*	1 to 2
§ Bartonia, the Golden,	*Bartonia aurea,*	2 to 3
Bladder Ketmia, buff, dark centre,	*Hibiscus trionum,*	1 to 2
Blue Bottle, Great,	*Centaurea cyanus, major,*	3 to 4
Blue Bottle, Small,	*Centaurea cyanus, minor,*	1 to 2
Blumenbachia, white,	*Blumenbachia insignis,*	*under* 1
§ Browallia, or Amethyst, blue, white,	*Browallia elata, alba, etc.,*	1 to 2
§ Cacalia, scarlet,	*Cacalia coccinea,*	1 to 2
Calliopsis; Drummond's Coreopsis,	*Calliopsis Drummondii,*	2 to 3
Calandrina, Annual, crimson,	*Calandrina speciosa, etc.,*	1 to 2
† Calandrina, rose and purple tinged,	*Calandrina discolor, etc.,*	2 to 3
* Candytuft, white and purple,	*Iberis alba, purpurea, etc.,*	1
* Catch-fly, purple and red,	*Silene purpurea, muscipula, etc.,*	2 to 3
* Catch-fly, dwarf pink, spotted, etc.,	*Silene Armeria, picta, etc.,*	1 to 2
* Caterpillars, Hedgehogs, and Snails, curious,	*Medicago circinnata, intertexta, scutellata, etc.,*	1 to 2
Centaurea, or pink Sultan,	*Centaurea Americana,*	2 to 3
China Pink, of every shade,	*Dianthus Chinensis, annuus,*	1 to 2
§ Cleome, rose-colored, white, etc.,	*Cleome rosea, spinoca, etc.,*	2 to 3
Chrysanthemum, white, yellow, and three-colored,	*Chrysanthemum coronarium, alba, lutea, tricolor, etc.,*	2 to 3
Clarkia, rose, purple, white, etc.,	*Clarkia elegans, pulchella, etc.,*	1 to 2
§ Clintonia, elegant blue,	*Clintonia elegans,*	1 to 2
§ Cockscomb, crimson and yellow,	*Celocia cristata, lutea,*	2 to 3
§ Collinsia, lilac, white, two-colored,	*Collinsia heterophylla, bicolor,*	2 to 3
† Commelina, blue-flowering,	*Commelina cœlestis,*	1
* Convolvulus, dwarf variegated, etc.,	*Convolvulus minor, bicolor, etc.,*	1 to 2
Coreopsis, Golden, dark centre,	*Calliopsis tinctoria,*	2 to 3

		Feet High
§ Cotton Plant, cream,	*Gossypium herbaceum,*	3 to 4
Crotalaria, purple, yellow, and white,	*Crotalaria verrucosa, etc.,*	1 to 2
Cuphea, Mexican, scarlet, variegated,	*Cuphea lanceolata, silenoides,*	1 to 2
† Dahlia, Mexican, various,	*Dahlia superflua,*	3 to 6
Devil in the Bush, or Love in a Mist, blue, yellow, purple, white, etc.,	*Nigella damascena, Hispanica, orientalis, sativa, etc.,*	1 to 2
Dwarf Love in a Mist, various,	*Nigella nana,*	1
† Dew Plant, crimson,	*Mesembryanthemum glabrum,*	1 to 2
† Didiscus, azure blue,	*Didiscus cœruleus,*	2 to 3
§ Egg-plant, white, for ornament,	*Solanum melongena,*	1 to 2
Erissimum, orange,	*Erissimum perofskianum,*	1 to 2
† Eschscholtzia, or Chryseis, yellow, red, and orange,	*Eschscholtzia, crocea, cristata, Californica, etc.,*	1
Eternal Flower, yellow, purple, and white,	*Xeranthemum lucidum, var., lutea, bracteatum, alba,*	2 to 3
Euphorbia, variegated,	*Euphorbia variegata,*	2 to 3
* Evening Primrose, dwarf annual, white, yellow, red, etc.,	*Œnothera linearis, Drummondii, tetraptera, micrantha, etc.,*	1 to 2
* Evening Primrose, large yellow,	*Œnothera grandiflora,*	2 to 3
* Evening Primrose, willow-leaved,	*Œnothera salicifolia,*	3 to 4
Feather Grass,	*Stipa pinnata, avenacea.*	1 to 2
* Flos Adonis, or Pheasant Eye, red,	*Adonis minata,*	1 to 2
† Francoa, pink and purple,	*Francoa appendiculata,*	1 to 2
§ Galardia, orange and crimson,	*Galardia picta,*	1 to 2
Garidella, Nigella like,	*Garidella nigellastrum,*	1 to 2
Gilia, blue, pink, variegated, etc.,	*Gilia capitata, tricolor, etc.,*	1 to 2
§ Globe Amaranthus, crimson, white,	*Gomphrena globosa,*	1 to 2
Grove Love, blue,	*Nemophila insignis,*	1
† Godetia the Twiggy, purple,	*Godetia viminea,*	3 to 4
Godetia the Ruddy, annual,	*Godetia rubricunda,*	2 to 3
Godetia, dwarf, purple, and spotted,	*Godetia lepida, Lyndleyana, etc.,*	1 to 2
* Gypsophila, pink and white,	*Gypsophila elegans, viscosa,*	1 to 2
Hawkweed, yellow and red,	*Crepis barbata rubra,*	1 to 2
§ Hibiscus, yellow, reddish centre,	*Hibiscus Africanus,*	2 to 3
* Horned Poppy, yellow and scarlet,	*Glauceum luteum, phœniceum,*	2 to 3
† Hunnemania, brilliant yellow,	*Hunnemania famerix, folia,*	3 to 4
Hypecoum, three species, yellow,	*Hypecoum procumbens, etc.,*	1 to 2

		Feet High
§ Ice Plant, white,	*Mesembryanthemum, var.,*	1
† Jacobea, purple, spotted, etc.,	*Senecio purpurea, elegans, etc.,*	1 to 2
Job's Tears, grey,	*Coix lachryma Jobi,*	2 to 3
Larkspur, dwarf Rocket, white, blue, purple, pink, and other colors,	*Delphinium ajacis, alba, cœrulea, purpurea, etc.,*	1 to 2
Larkspur, branching, various colors,	*Delphinium consolida, etc.,*	2 to 3
Lavatera, red, purple, and white,	*Lavatera, trimestris, alba, etc.,*	4 to 6
Love-lies-bleeding, crimson,	*Amaranthus melancholicus,*	1 to 2
Lunaria, purple,	*Lunaria purpurea,*	1 to 2
* Lupins, dwarf annual, yellow, purple, rose, two-colored, etc.,	*Lupinus nanus, densiflorus, bicolor, etc.,*	1 to 2
Malesherbia, blue,	*Malesherbia coronata,*	2 to 3
* Malope, tall scarlet, etc.,	*Malope grandiflora, etc.,*	3 to 4
* Malope, dwarf crimson, rose,	*Malope trifida, malacoides,*	1 to 2
Marigold, African, yellow, orange,	*Tagetes erecta,*	3 to 4
Marigold, French, variegated,	*Tagetes patula,*	2 to 3
Marigold, sweet, yellow striped,	*Calendula officinalis,*	1 to 2
§ Marigold, Fig, yellow,	*Mesembryanthemum annuus,*	1
Martynia, or Cuckold's Horn,	*Martynia proboscidea,*	2 to 3
† Marvel of Peru, or Four O'Clocks, white, yellow, red, striped, scented,	*Mirabilis jalapa, lutea, rubra, striata, longiflora, etc.,*	2 to 3
† Mignonette, sweet scented,	*Reseda odorata,*	*under* 1
† Monkey Flower, yellow, scarlet, rose, etc., variegated,	*Mimulus moschatus, cardinalis, rivularius, roseus, etc.,*	1 to 1
§ Nierembergia, several varieties of various colors,	*Nierembergia intermedia, violacea, phœnicea, etc.,*	2 to 3
Nolana, in varieties, blue,	*Nolana paradoxia, prostrata, etc.*	1 to 2
* Oats, animated, green,	*Avena sensitiva,*	2 to 3
† Pansy, or Heart's-Ease, purple, blue, yellow, and numerous shades, variegated,	*Viola tricolor, grandiflora, atropurpurea, cœrulea, lutea, etc., under*	1
Pentaptes, scarlet,	*Pentaptes phœnicea,*	1 to 2
Phlox, annual, rosy red, etc.,	*Phlox Drummondii, etc.,*	1 to 2
Pimpernel, blue and scarlet,	*Anagallis indica, arvensis,*	1
* Poppy, large, white and scarlet,	*Papaver somniferum, coccinea,*	3 to 4
* Poppy, dwarf, scarlet, white, yellow, striped, Persian red, etc.,	*Papaver rhœas, nudicale, Persicum, rubra, striata, etc.,*	1 to 2
Portulaca, two var., purple, scarlet,	*Portulaca splendens, coccinea,*	1
Prince's Feather, crimson,	*Amaranthus hypochondriacus,*	2 to 3

		Feet High
Rocket Candytuft, white, etc.,	*Iberis coronaria, etc.,*	1 to 2
Rose Campion, annual, dwarf red, purple, white, striped, etc.,	*Agrostemma cœli, rosea, githago, lacla, etc.,*	1
Salpiglossis, variegated, purple, etc.,	*Salpiglossis, atro-purpurea,*	2 to 3
Saphonaria, or Silene, rose,	*Saphonaria vaccaria,*	2 to 3
† Schizanthus, in variety, orange, wing-leaved, etc.,	*Schizanthus retusus, pinnatus, obtusifolia, etc.,*	1 to 2
§ Sensitive Plant, red,	*Mimosa sensitiva,*	*under* 1
Shortia, yellow,	*Shortia Californica,*	1 to 2
§ Stevia, Vanilla-scented, white,	*Stevia serrata,*	1 to 2
Stock Gilly, Virginian, lilac,	*Malcomia maritima,*	1
Strawberry Spinach, red fruit,	*Blitum capitatum,*	1 to 2
Strephtanthus, rose-colored,	*Strephtanthus obtusifolius,*	2 to 3
Sunflower, yellow,	*Helianthus annuus,*	6 to 8
Sunflower, dwarf, yellow,	*Helianthus minor, nanus,*	2 to 3
Sun Rose, spotted,	*Helianthemum guttatum,*	1 to 2
* Sweet Balm, blue,	*Melissa odoratum,*	1 to 2
* Sweet Basil, blush, lilac,	*Ocymum basiliacum,*	1 to 2
Sweet Sultan, white, yellow, purple,	*Centaurea moschata, etc.,*	1 to 2
* Ten Week Stock, scarlet, purple, white, etc.,	*Mathiola annua, var., græca, tenella, etc.,*	1 to 2
§ Tobacco in varieties, scarlet, yellow, [etc.,	*Nicotiana tabacum, rustica,*	3 to 4
Touch-me-not, yellow,	*Noli me tangere,*	1
Trefoil, crimson and scented,	*Trifolium incarnatum, etc.,*	3 to 4
* Venus's Looking-glass, lilac,	*Campanula speculum,*	1 to 2
Vesicaria, in varieties, yellow,	*Vesicaria grandiflora, etc.,*	2 to 3
† Verbena, in varieties, scarlet, rose, blue, lilac, pink, etc.,	*Verbena aubletia, bonariensis, Drummondii, pulchella, etc.,*	1 to 3
Zinnia, scarlet, yellow, violet-colored, red, etc.,	*Zinnia coccinea, latea, grandiflora, rubra, etc.,*	2 to 3

The following are climbing and trailing plants, which should be planted in situations where they can be supported by poles, twine, or trellises. The tallest growing vines and creepers are best adapted to the covering of arbors, to create shade, or conceal any unsightly object; the procumbent trailing and low climbing plants, such as the Nasturtium, Loasa, Petunia, Sweet Pea, &c., may be trained on trellis-work of an ornamental form, as that of a fan, balloon, or pyramid, which should be on a scale corresponding to the situation and extent of the garden.

		Feet High
Balloon Vine, or Love in a Puff,	*Cardiospermum halicacabum,*	*over* 10
§ Balsam Apple and Pear,	*Momordica balsamina,*	*over* 10
Bean Hyacinth, white and purple,	*Dolichos alba, purpurea,*	*over* 10
§ Bean, scarlet flowering,	*Phaseolus multiflorus,*	*over* 10
Bean, Castor Oil, or Palma Christi,	*Ricinus communis,*	5 to 6
§ Cypress Vine, scarlet and white,	*Ipomœa coccinea, alba,*	*over* 10
Gourd, Mock Orange, in varieties,	*Cucurbita bicolor, aurantia,*	*over* 10
Gourd, the Bottle, in varieties,	*Cucurbita lagenaria, elevata,*	10
§ Loasa or Chilian Nettle, orange,	*Loasa lateritia, aurantiaca, etc.,*	3 to 6
Maurandia, blue,	*Maurandia Barclayana,*	*over* 10
§ Morning Glory, scarlet striped, etc.,	*Ipomœa coccinea, striata, etc.,*	*over* 10
Morning Glory, of the Convolvulus tribe, purple, striped, yellow, pink, white, etc.,	*Convolvulus major, purpurea, cœrulea, striata, lutea, incarnata, alba, etc.,*	*over* 10
Nasturtium, orange, and crimson, variegated,	*Tropœolum atrosanguineum, nana, etc.,*	4 to 6
§ Thunbergia, wing-leaved, purple,	*Thunbergia alata, etc.,*	4 to 6
† Petunia, purple, white, rose, etc.,	*Petunia nyctaginiflora, etc.,*	2 to 3
Sweet Peas, various complexions, white, purple, red, rose, striped, etc.,	*Lathyrus odoratus, var., alba, purpurea, rosea, striata, etc.,*	3 to 4

As many city gardens are so limited as not to admit of an extensive assortment of flowers, a select list may be made from the above Catalogue, to suit the taste of such as may be so situated; and amateurs, who cultivate on a larger scale, can obtain such additional sorts as may be desired at the different seed-stores, under their various names.

Previous to providing annual flower seeds, the cultivator should lay out a plan of his garden; and in making allotments of ground for any particular purpose, provision should be made for a select assortment of such bulbous, tuberous, and perennial plants as may be deemed most worthy of attention, not forgetting to leave room for some of the choicest varieties of the Dahlia, the qualities of which will be described hereafter.

Another consideration is to have at hand suitable implements, so that the work may be performed in a skilful manner and at the proper season. A spade, rake, hoe, trowel, drilling machine, and pruning-knife, may be deemed essential; and in order to have the beds laid out with the edges straight and even, a garden-line should be in readiness. If labels should be required, they may be made of shingles, which, being split into strips about an inch wide, and sharpened at one end, will serve for marking distinct kinds, either in pots, or on the borders. In order to have the names or numbers written in legible characters, the labels should be painted on the smooth side with white lead, and then marked with a black-lead pencil before the paint gets dry. Inscriptions made in this way will be as durable as the label itself.

The next, and perhaps the most important, consideration is to have the ground in good condition to receive the seed. In order to attain this desirable object, let some good rich compost or very old manure be provided and well mixed with the soil. Mingle it with the soil a full spit deep, pulverizing every particle. It would be an advantage if the ground could be dug to a great depth at the commencement of winter, and then again at the period of sowing seed in the Spring.

PREPARATION OF THE SOIL.

A mellow loam, which is a medium earth between the extremes of clay and sand, enriched with pulverized manure or compost, is adapted to the generality of flowering plants; but ground of a boggy nature, composed of black earth, decayed leaves, etc., and in a low situation, is essential to the luxuriant growth of amphibious plants, as Water Lilies, Iris, Lobelia, and the like. As the cultivator has not always a choice, he may select such plants only as are most congenial to his peculiar soil and situation.

Previous to preparing flower-beds or borders, care must be taken to arrange them in such a manner that the ground may be a little elevated in the middle. This is essential to the draining off of a redundancy of water, as well as to the exhibition of plants to the greatest possible advantage.

All kinds of annual flower seeds may be sown early in the

spring, on borders or beds of pulverized earth. The beds should be levelled, and the seed sown either in small patches, each kind by itself, or in drills, from an eighth to half an inch deep, according to the size or nature of the seed. Lupins, Peas, &c., should be planted about half an inch deep. Those who would have their plants flower early should sow the hardy kinds early in the season. Those varieties marked thus †, and thus §, may be sown in boxes or pots of light earth, at the same time. These, if exposed to the sun every day, and sheltered in cold nights, will be forwarded in growth, and be fit to transplant early in June. Those marked * may also be sown in small pots; and as these plants will not bear transplanting, they should be turned out of the pots with the balls of earth entire, and placed in the ground where they are intended to flower; or, if the seed be sown in a bed with other kinds, the plants should be carefully transplanted with a trowel, without disturbing their roots.

HOW TO GROW EARLY FLOWERS

The most eligible way to obtain early flowers is to prepare a slight hotbed for the tender kinds, and either plunge the pots therein up to their brims, or sow the seed in the earth in shallow drills, not more than a quarter of an inch deep. It may be necessary to state that, although, in favorable seasons, flower seed in general will come up in from one to three weeks after it is sown, the seed of the Cypress vine will not grow until settled warm weather, unless in a hotbed. It should be soaked for about half an hour in moderately warm water previous to being sown. If some of the hardy annuals be sown in September, they will grow large enough to survive the winter, if slightly covered with straw or litter; and if plants thus raised be transplanted early in the spring, they will produce very early flowers.

To prevent disappointment, I would recommend that great care be taken to keep the seed-beds as clear from weeds as possible. It cannot be denied that young plants are apt to get smothered, and sometimes pulled up with weeds. To obviate this, I would suggest that the seed be sown in shallow drills, each kind by itself; and that an account be kept of the contents of each drill in a book; also of all seeds that are sown at different times; and by being particular in the dates, you may always know when to expect your plants to come up. Those persons totally unacquainted with plants will, by this means, be enabled to identify each particular kind, and thus become familiarly acquainted with them.

These pots may be either marked with letters or figures on the outside, to answer with the book, or notches may be cut in wood, or other labels affixed to the pots, and entered accordingly.

If these numbers be continued to one hundred, or even one thousand, there can be no mistake, provided the rows are all marked according to the entry in the book; or if No. 1 be noted, plain sticks will answer afterwards, if one be stuck at each end of every row. In this case it would be well to leave a space every ten or twenty rows, and note the number of rows. By this means they can be more easily traced.

Some species of Dwarf Annuals, such as Sweet Alyssum, Candytuft, Clarkia Pulchella, Mignonette, Pimpernell, and such others as grow not over a foot in height, may be cultivated in small beds, either separate or two or three kinds mixed together. Clarkia Pulchella suits very well with Mignonette, as it will thrive in moderately poor soil, which is the best adapted for that plant when fragrance is an object.

MANAGEMENT OF VARIOUS KINDS OF FLOWERS.

The best way to manage the mixed species is to level a narrow border of rather poor soil, and sow it all over with Mignonette, then with Clarkia Pulchella. When the plants are up, both kinds should be thinned out equally, so as to leave the plants from one to two inches apart all over the bed. These, when they come into blossom, will form a rich mass, and have a very pretty effect, the bushiness of the Mignonette hiding the naked stalks of the Clarkia. The White Alyssum and Purple Candytuft form a pleasing contrast when mixed in equal proportions, and also the Dwarf Gilia and Blue Pimpernell.

The new species of Dwarf Annual Phlox (*Phlox Drummondii*) is described in a London magazine as a splendid sight when cultivated in a bed. "Every flower, though of the deepest carmine, has its petals of a pale blush color on the under side, and every petal, though of the palest pink, has a dark carmine spot at its base. Thus the variety of colors displayed in a bed of these flowers almost exceeds description; and when they are seen under a bright sun, and agitated by a gentle breeze, the effect is extraordinarily brilliant."

When seeds are intended to be sown in patches, which is often done for want of an unoccupied border, the best way to perform this business is, after having pulverized the soil, to form circular drills in the surface with the rim of a flower-pot, which may be large or small according to fancy. By sowing seed in such circular drills, the plants can be more easily traced than when scattered promiscuously over the ground; and the weeds can be destroyed with less risk and trouble. Such kinds as are marked in the Catalogue thus * may remain as sown; or, if parted, they should be removed with a scoop trowel in a careful manner, in small tufts; and this business, as well as transplanting in general, should always be done immediately preceding or after rain, and in cloudy weather.

The risk and trouble of transplanting may be avoided by adopting the following method of sowing the seed: Take a dollar package of twenty varieties, and number the bags from one to twenty; then sow a circle from each bag in the order in which they are numbered, and insert a short stick in the centre of each circle as a mark. By this method the twenty varieties are distributed along the border in succession, and as each bag will be sufficient for three circles, sixty circles, or three assortments of twenty varieties, may be sown in three different aspects of the garden, which will not only give the various flowers the best possible chance with regard to exposure, but show the varieties to the greatest possible advantage. By preserving the bags, the mere novice, by referring to the name and number on each, will become acquainted with the different varieties from the order in which they stand in his garden. This system may be practised to advantage either on a large or small scale.

Herbaceous plants in general will not flower well if grown in clusters. They should, therefore, be thinned or transplanted into the regular beds, at all favorable opportunities, after they have grown about an inch in height; and as there is always a risk of some plants not taking root, it is safest to plant a few of each sort every time, taking care to diversify the colors, and also to leave a few plants in the seed-beds, for the purpose of substituting in the room of such plants whose period of flowering may be over; as is the case generally with early perennial plants and bulbs at about the season that the last of the annuals are fit to remove. The transplanting may be done with a small trowel, or a neat dibble made for the purpose.

BIENNIAL AND PERENNIAL FLOWER SEED.

The remarks preceding our Catalogue of Annuals will, with few exceptions, apply to that of Biennials and Perennials; and the circulation of the sap in the roots and stalks of plants is influenced by like causes and subject to the same vicissitudes as the germination of seed. This principle is exemplified by some plants of various species putting forth their leaves and flowers at a later period than others in the same location, as if waiting for nature to replenish the earth with food adapted to their respective requirements, which by the gradual changes from cool to temperate, and from that to warm weather, is affected to that degree as to enable all the various species of plants, collected from every climate and soil under the sun, to reward the industrious cultivator by a gradual exhibition of their fascinating blossoms, and a distribution of their odoriferous sweets, throughout the three propitious seasons of the year.

In distinguishing between biennials and perennials, I have only marked such as are apt to die after once blossoming, and which can only be renewed from seed. Some of those species, frequently classed with biennials, as *Aquilegia* or Columbines, *Dianthus*, etc., are in reality perennial, and may be easily perpetuated from year to year, by suckers, layers, or any of the ordinary methods of propagation. Frequent renewal of the roots of perennials is absolutely necessary to their prosperity or very existence. Many species are by nature best adapted for propagation at the footstalks, from their yielding little or no seed at the top of the plant. This is particularly the case with choice double-flowering plants, the roots of which in many cases constitute the seed, which must be perpetuated by root offsets, cuttings, etc.

The annexed Catalogue embraces a great proportion of the most desirable of what are termed fibrous-rooted herbaceous plants, the seed or roots of which may be obtained at seed-stores and nurseries. The estimated height applies to plants of a year's growth. Some will arrive to more than three times that height when cultivated in a green-house; and even in open-ground culture the same plants will vary considerably, according to the soil or situation in which they are grown. The specified height, however, although unavoidably imperfect, may serve as a guide to the gardener in arranging his flower-beds. Those marked thus †, being tender and half-hardy, will need protection in the winter. Those marked thus ‖ are biennials. Those marked thus * yield little or no seed. There are also many other species of which the seed is unattainable, from its being suffered to be scattered by the wind, and in some cases, from the climate being unfavorable to its ripening. These, as will be shown hereafter, may be perpetuated by other methods.

A CATALOGUE OF BIENNIAL AND PERENNIAL FLOWER SEEDS.

Graines de fleurs bisannuelles et vivaces.

† Denotes tender. ‖ Biennial. * Seed unattainable.

		Feet High.
Adonis, Spring-flowering, yellow,	*Adonis vernalis,*	2 to 3
Alpine Columbine, purple,	*Aquilegia Alpina,*	1 to 2
Alyssum, yellow,	*Alyssum saxatile,*	1
Asclepias, orange, purple, etc.,	*Asclepias incarnata, etc.,*	2 to 3
Asiatic Globe Flower, yellow,	*Trollius Asiaticus,*	3 to 4
† Auricula, variegated,	*Primula auricula,*	*under* 1
† Balm of Gilead, fragrant,	*Dracocephalum canariense,*	1
Bee Larkspur, blue and brown,	*Delphinium elatum,*	4 to 6
Bergamot, crimson, blue,	*Monarda Kalmiana, didyma,*	2 to 3
*† Canary Aster, purple,	*Cineraria amelloides,*	1
† Calceolaria, various colors,	*Calceolaria variabilis,*	2 to 3
Campanula, Peren., blue, white, etc.,	*Campanula persicafolia, etc.,*	2 to 3
‖ Canterbury Bells, blue, white,	*Campanula medium,*	2 to 3
† Caper Tree, green,	*Cuphorbia lathyrus,*	2 to 3
Cardinal Flower, in varieties, scarlet.	*Lobelia cardinalis, etc.,*	3 to 4
Cassia, Maryland, yellow,	*Cassia Marylandica,*	3 to 4
† Carnation Pink, various colors,	*Dianthus caryophyllus,*	1 to 2
*† Celsia, red and yellow, variegated,	*Celsia orientalis,*	1 to 2
Chinese Imperial Pink, variegated,	*Dianthus Chinensis,*	1 to 2
† Chinese Primrose, lilac, white,	*Primula Chinensis,*	*under* 1
† Cistus, yellow,	*Cistus guttatus,*	1 to 2
† Clandanthus, white,	*Clandanthus arabicus,*	2 to 3
† Clerodendron, scarlet,	*Clerodendron speciosum,*	4 to 5
Clove Imperial Pink, crimson,	*Dianthus hortensis,*	1 to 2
† Colutea, scarlet,	*Sutherlandia frutescens,*	2 to 3
* Coreopsis, Perennial, in varieties, yellow,	*Calliopsis grandiflora, lanceolatum, auriculata, etc.,*	2 to 3
*† Coronilla, yellow,	*Coronilla glauca,*	2 to 3
* Coronet, or double Lychuis, scarlet.	*Lychnis coronata,*	2 to 3

		Feet High
‖ Clary, purple-topped,	*Salvia sclara,*	1 to 2
Columbine, various colors,	*Aquilegia vulgaris,*	1 to 2
*† Daisy, Garden, various colors,	*Bellis perennis, hortensis,* *under*	1
Dragon's Head, bluish pink,	*Dracocephalum Virginianum,*	3 to 4
Dragon's Head, purple and striped,	*Dracocephalum argumense,etc.,*	1 to 2
European Globe Flower, yellow,	*Trollius Europæus,*	2 to 3
‖ Evening Primrose, yellow,	*Œnothera biennis,*	3 to 4
Eupatorium, blue, white,	*Eupatorium cœrulea, etc.,*	2 to 3
‖ Foxglove, purple, white,	*Digitalis purpurea, alba,*	3 to 4
Fraxinella, red, white,	*Dictamnus rubra, alba,*	1 to 2
Gentian, purple, yellow, white,	*Gentiana purpurea, lutea, etc.,*	1
Gentian, porcelain-flowered,	*Gentiana adscendens,*	2 to 3
† Geranium, various colors,	*Pelargonium zonale,*	2 to 3
Globe Thistle, purple,	*Echinops sphærocephalus,*	2 to 3
† Hepatica, blue, pink,	*Anemone hepatica,* *under*	1
Hibiscus, pink, white, purple,	*Hibiscus palustris, speciosus,etc.*	3 to 4
Hollyhock, Antwerp, China, and English, of various colors,	*Althea rosea Chinensis, Anglica, etc.,*	4 to 5
‖ Honesty, or Satin Flower, blush,	*Lunaria biennis,*	2 to 3
† Indian Shot, yellow, scarlet,	*Canna Indica, lutea, coccinea,*	1 to 2
†‖ Ipomopsis, scarlet,	*Ipomopsis elegans,*	3 to 4
Ivy-leaved Toad Flax, pink,	*Lunaria, cymbalaria,*	1 to 2
Jacob's Ladder, blue,	*Polemonium cœruleum,*	1 to 2
† Jerusalem Cherry, red fruit,	*Solanum pseudo, capsicum,*	2 to 3
Larkspur, Perennial, purple, pink, white, etc.,	*Delphinium grandiflorum, perennis,*	2 to 3
* Liatris, long spiked, purple,	*Liatris spicata, elegans, etc.,*	3 to 4
* Lily of the Valley, white,	*Convallaria majalis,*	1
† Lotus, brown,	*Lotus jacobeus,*	2 to 3
† Lisianthus, scarlet,	*Lisianthus Russellianus,*	2 to 3
† Lupin, Perennial, blue, white, changeable, etc.,	*Lupinus perennis, mutabilis, variabilis, etc.,*	2 to 3
* Lychnidea, or American Phlox, lilac, purple, red, white, etc.,	*Phlox puniculata, acuminata, pyramidalis, odorata, etc.,*	3 to 4
* Lychnidea, early, pink, etc.,	*Phlox subulata, stolonifera,etc.,*	1 to 2
* Lychnis, Mountain, variegated,	*Lychnis Alpina,*	1 to 2
Lychnis, scarlet,	*Lychnis Chalcedonica,*	3 to 4
London Pride, variegated,	*Dianthus deltoides,*	1
† Mesembryanthemum, variegated, yellow, white, purple, etc.,	*Mesembryanthemum acinaciforme, spectabile,tricolor,etc.,*	1 to 2
*† Mexican Sage, scarlet,	*Salvia splendens,*	2 to 3

		Feet High.
Monk's Hood, white, blue, etc.,	*Aconitum album, versicolor, etc.,*	4 to 6
MonkeyFlower, yellow, purple spots,	*Mimulus ringens, luteus, etc.,*	1 to 2
† Oleander, pink, white,	*Nerium Oleander,*	2 to 3
* Pardanthus, Chinese, orange,	*Pardanthus Chinensis,*	1 to 2
Pentstemon, purple,	*Pentstemon campanulata*	2 to 3
Perennial Flax, purple,	*Linum perennis,*	2 to 3
† Periwinkle, Madagascar, rose, white,	*Vinca rosea, alba,*	1 to 2
Pink, Pheasant-eyed, variegated,	*Dianthus plumarius,*	*under* 1
† Polyanthus, variable and splendid,	*Primula polyanthus,*	*under* 1
Poppy, Perennial, red, yellow,	*Papaver orientale, bracteata,*	2 to 3
Potentilla, rose, puce, yellow,	*Potentilla formosa, splendens,*	1 to 2
†‖ Pyramidal Bell Flower, blue,	*Campanula pyramidalis,*	3 to 4
* Queen of the Meadows, white, rose,	*Spiræa ulmaria, lobata, etc.,*	3 to 4
* Ragged Robin, or Red Lychnis,	*Agrostemma flos cuculi,*	1 to 2
Rocket, Garden, purple,	*Hesperis matronalis,*	2 to 3
‖ Rose Campion, or Mullen Pink, rose, white, etc.,	*Agrostemma coronaria rosea, alba, etc.,*	2 to 3
Rudbeckia, yellow, purple,	*Rudbeckia, lutea, purpurea,*	3 to 4
Saphonaria, rose blush,	*Saphonaria officinalis, etc.,*	1 to 2
* Saxifrage, rose white, purple,	*Saxifraga umbrosa, crassifolia,*	1
‖ Snapdragon, white, red, variegated, in several splendid varieties.	*Antirrhinum bicolor, versicolor, coccinea, spartium, etc.,*	1 to 2
Sophora, white, blue, etc..	*Sophora alba, australis,*	2 to 3
†‖ Stock Gilliflower, numerous varieties, scarlet, white, purple, striped,	*Matthiola incana, coccinea, alba, purpurea, striata, etc.,*	1 to 2
* Sunflower, yellow,	*Helianthus perennis, altissimus,*	3 to 4
‖ Sweet Scabious, purple, brown,	*Scabiosa atra, purpurea, etc.,*	2 to 3
Sweet William, various colors,	*Dianthus barbatus,*	1 to 2
* Thrift, pink and red,	*Statice vulgaris, speciosa, under*	1
Valerian, Garden, red, white,	*Valeriana rubra, alba,*	2 to 3
Valerian, Sweet-scented, blue,	*Polemonium cærulea,*	3 to 4
Veronica, variegated, blue,	*Veronica variegata, cærulea,*	2 to 3
* Violet, Fragrant, white, blue, etc.,	*Viola odorata, alba, cærulea, under*	1
†‖ Wallflower, bloody, yellow,	*Cheiranthus Cheiri,*	1 to 2
*† Wallflower, double perennial,	*Cheiranthus perennis,*	1 to 2
†‖ Wall-leaved Stock Gilliflower,	*Cheiranthus glaber,*	1 to 2
* Windflower, various colors,	*Anemone coronaria,*	1 to 2
Yucca, or Adam's Needle, white,	*Yucca filamentosa, gloriosa, etc.,*	3 to 4

CLIMBING PLANTS.

The reader is here reminded that our Catalogue of Annua Flower Seeds contains a few varieties of perennials, which were there introduced because of their aptness to blossom the first season of the seed being sown; these, with those marked † in the last Catalogue, may be sown and treated in the manner recommended for tender annuals. Those intended to be cultivated as green-house plants should be taken up before the approach of cold weather, transplanted into flower-pots, and sheltered either in a garden-frame, green-house, or light room. Those plants with tuberous roots, such as Dahlias, Marvel of Peru, and also some others of the Bean and Pea tribe, may be cut down late in the autumn, and the roots taken up and preserved in the same manner as those of other tuberous and bulbous-rooted plants, of which I shall treat hereafter.

Hardy biennial and perennial flower seeds may be sown in the month of April, in shallow drills. If this business be performed in the manner recommended for annuals, they can be easily distinguished from each other; and as these plants do not flower the first year, they may be thinned out, or removed from the seed-beds as soon as they are well rooted, and planted either in different parts of the flower-beds or in a nursery-bed. If the latter plan be adopted, they should be planted in rows a foot or more apart, and kept free from weeds by means of a small hoe, which will greatly promote their growth, and prepare them for transplanting into the regular and permanent blossoming-beds, either in the autumn or early in the ensuing spring.

It may be here observed that biennials seldom survive the second winter to flower in perfection, unless they are renewed by cuttings of top shoots, young flower stalks, or casual offsets, layers, etc. It will be unnecessary to take this trouble, unless with some extraordinary double-flowering plants. Some of the perennials may be increased by root offsets detached from the old plants, and planted in spring or autumn; others by bottom suckers and slips of top shoots, layers, pipings of young shoots, etc. Pinks, Sweet-Williams, Pansies, and double Violets, also Periwinkle, or running Myrtle, and many other similar plants, may be increased by simply laying their branches an inch or two under the surface, in July and August. After roots have formed, which may be expected in six or eight weeks, each tuft or plant may be transplanted into the borders.

Many sorts of biennial and perennial flower seeds may be sown in September, or as soon as ripe; and if the plants get strong before winter sets in, some of them will flower the ensuing summer.

It may be necessary here to remind the reader of those species of beautiful double-flowering perennial herbaceous plants which do not produce seed; some of these are included in our Catalogue; they may be obtained at the nurseries, and should be introduced into the regular flower-beds either in autumn or early in the spring; the best mode of increasing these, and all double-flowering perennials raised from seed, is by layers, cuttings, offsets, etc., detached from the old plants.

It may here be observed that the most certain method of obtaining double flowers is by propagation from perennial plants. Many seed customers feel disappointed if they do not in every case procure double flowers from seed, which is unreasonable, because, although seed will, under ordinary circumstances, reproduce its species, it will by no means uniformly produce the particular variety by which it was borne. The experience of numerous amateurs will corroborate this fact, who frequently, after saving seed from their most perfect flowers, have the mortification of witnessing such degeneracy the following season as would lead them to doubt its identity, had the seed been obtained from any other source. Seed gathered from double Balsams, or Lady Slippers, for instance, will frequently produce semi-double and single flowers the next season.

RENEWING FLOWER-BEDS.

As the earth in the flower-beds will require to be fresh dug and replenished with good compost or manure once in two or three years, it may be necessary to take up all the perennial plants at such times. Such roots as are overgrown should be deprived of their surplus offsets, and either planted in a nursery-bed, or returned with the parent plants into the regular flower-beds; they should be inserted a little deeper than before, and the fine fresh earth distributed well about the fibres.

In removing plants into the beds where they are intended to blossom, great pains should be taken to preserve some of the earth to their roots. The ground should be previously brought into good condition, so that they may strike freely, and produce their flowers in perfection. The plants should be so arranged that they may all be seen, the most dwarfish being placed in front, and the taller kinds in regular gradations behind; or the tallest may be planted along the middle of the beds, and the others on each side, according to their varied heights and colors.

GROUPING FLOWERS ARTISTICALLY.

There is no part of gardening which requires so much the exercise of taste and fancy, as in setting off a border or bed of intermixed flowers to advantage. In association with other flowers, the different kinds of hardy bulbs may be planted in small clumps of six, seven, or eight inches in diameter, three, four, five, or more roots in each, according to their size and growth, and these at suitable distances from each other. Likewise observe to diversify the kinds and colors, so as to display, when in bloom, the greatest possible variety of shades and contrasts.

If green-house plants be plunged into the flower borders in the month of May, they will not only tend to ornament the garden by their diversity of foliage and blossom, but the roots will receive a more uniform supply of moisture than if the pots were exposed to the sun and wind; care should, however, be taken to give the different species a situation suitable for them. Hydrangeas, Primulas, Daisies, Oleanders, Camellias, China Roses, and half-hardy plants in general, thrive best in a moderately shaded situation. Geraniums, Jasmines, Heliotropes, etc., may be plunged in a sunny situation, provided they be regularly supplied with water. Many species planted for ornament in the flower borders may at the same time be propagated by layers. The *Fuchsia* or Ear-drop, Passion Flower, Heliotrope, Carnation, Petunia, running Verbena, etc., will, if laid in June or July, exhibit their blossoms in perfection, and yield young plants, which, being preserved through winter, may be used to replenish flower-beds the ensuing spring.

CHANGEABLE FLOWER-GARDENS.

"First flowers of the spring-time,
  Bright gems of the year,
All lovely and blooming,
  How fresh ye appear;
Springing up in the garden,
  The hedge-row, and vale,
Enriched by the showers,
  And fann'd by the gale."

In some countries the wealthy have *changeable flower-gardens*, which are so arranged that their productions can be changed at pleasure, so that whenever any plant, or group of plants, begins to decay, it can be removed, and its place supplied by others coming into bloom. To effect this, a large reserve-nursery is requisite, in which the plants must be kept in pots, and removed and plunged in the borders as wanted. Sir W. Chambers informs us that the Chinese excel in this mode of gardening; and that he has known a mandarin (or noble) to have the whole furniture and style of his parterre changed in a single night, so as to present next morning not only a different description of flowers, shrubs, and dwarf trees, but a different arrangement of the beds and compartments. Something of the same kind is practised in the gardens of the Tuileries in Paris, in some of the imperial gardens at St. Petersburg, and in the viceroyal gardens at Monza. Gardens of this description admit of a very perfect arrangement of the flowers, whether in the mingled manner, in select groups, or according to the natural method. It is only with such resources that a flower-gardener can "paint his way," as Sir W. Chambers says the Chinese artists do, "not scattering their flowers indiscriminately about their borders, but disposing of them with great circumspection along the skirts of the plantations, or other places where flowers are to be introduced. They reject all that are of a straggling growth, and of harsh colors and poor foliage, choosing only such as are of some duration, grow either large or in clusters, are of beautiful forms, well leaved, and of tints that harmonize with the greens that surround them. They avoid all sudden transitions, both with regard to dimension and color, rising gradually from the smallest flowers to those of the boldest growth; and varying their tints, by easy gradations, from white, straw-color, purple, and incarnate, to the deepest blues, and most brilliant crimsons and scarlets. They frequently blend several roots together, whose leaves and flowers unite, and compose one rich, harmonious mass; such as the white and purple Candytuft, Larkspurs, and Mallows of various colors, double Poppies, Lupins, Primroses, Pinks, and Carnations; with many more of which the forms and colors accord with each other; and the same method they use with flowering shrubs, blending white, red, and variegated roses together, purple and white lilacs, yellow and white jasmines, altheas of various sorts, and as many others as they can with any propriety unite. By these mixtures they increase considerably the variety and beauty of their compartments. In their large plantations, the flowers generally grow in the natural ground; but in flower-gardens, and all other parts that are highly kept, they are in pots buried in the ground, which, as fast as the bloom goes off, are removed, and others are brought to supply their places; so that there is a constant succession for almost every month in the year; and the flowers are never seen but in the height of their beauty."

It may be observed, further, that established plants will always produce their blossoms earlier and stronger in the spring than those recently transplanted; it should, therefore, be an object with gardeners to do the business of forming permanent flower-beds, and of transplanting hardy perennial and biennial plants, in September or October.

The hardy bulbous roots must also be planted in October or November, which, on being properly preserved through the winter, will embellish the parterre in spring by their early and First Flowers.

WALKS AND EDGINGS.

In my preliminary observations, I directed the attention of my readers to some important points respecting walks, edgings, etc. Although box is superior to anything else for edgings, yet, in extensive gardens, dwarf plants of various kinds may be used for such purpose. Thrift is the neatest small evergreen next to box; but Violets, Pinks, Periwinkle, Pansy, Iris, Stone Crop, or even Parsley, Thyme, Strawberry plants, etc., may be used for the sake of diversity. These will require frequent watering and trimming, and the Thrift, etc., should be sometimes taken up, divided at the roots, and replanted.

Box edgings will also require frequent pruning and trimming;

and once in from seven to ten years the whole may be taken up, divided, and replanted, and the surplus slips may be planted in a nursery-bed, in rows about a foot apart; these will be suitable for making edgings the year following.

Flower-beds should be kept free from weeds, and watered occasionally in the summer. In the autumn they should be covered with leaves, straw, or light litter; this should be taken off in the spring, and the ground hoed and dressed in such a manner as to enliven the earth around the roots of the plants, and to give the whole a neat appearance.

FLOWERING AND ORNAMENTAL SHRUBS.

Arbrisseaux d' Ornement.

Shrubs are so closely connected with flowering plants, and, indeed, so many of them are embellished with flowers, that they may be considered as essential to the completion of an ornamental garden. They are all perennial, and are divided into two classes, deciduous and evergreen; the former lose their leaves in the winter, the latter only shed them when others are ready to supply their places.

Shrubs are not only necessary to the embellishment of a flower-garden, but many kinds are eligible for hedges to it, and may be planted at a trifling expense. These hedges should be frequently trimmed and trained, the sides cut even, and the tops sparingly clipped, so as to make them ornamental as well as useful, and also to increase the vigor of their growth. When hedges become open or naked at the bottom, they should be plashed down; this is done by cutting the branches half through near the ground; they will then bend easily, and may be interwoven with the adjoining branches.

When shrubs, creepers, or climbers are planted against walls or trellises, either on account of their rarity, delicacy, or to conceal a rough fence, or other unsightly object, they require different modes of training; some attach themselves naturally, as the Ivy, and merely require to be occasionally guided, so as to cause a regular distribution of their shoots; others must be treated like fruit-trees, trained thinly, if blossoms are the object, and rather thick, if the intention be to show the foliage to the greatest possible advantage.

Ornamental shrubs grow from one foot to twelve or more feet in height; and where such are planted for ornament, the height of each plant, when full grown, should be considered, and also the mode of growth, that every one may be so planted as to show to advantage, observing that the tall-growing kinds should be planted in the back part of the borders, and those of low growth in front; but if they are required to be planted in clumps, they should be so arranged as to rise gradually from the sides to the middle, and be afterwards neatly trimmed.

Shrubs require an annual pruning, at which time cut out all irregular and superfluous branches, and head down such as require it, forming them into handsome bushes. Apply stakes to such as need support, and see that the low-growing ones do not injure each other, or interfere with other dwarfish plants near them.

Many kinds of shrubs may be raised from seed sown early in the spring, but are more commonly propagated by suckers, layers, or cuttings. Like other plants, they require a good soil, which should be manured every two or three years, and some of the tender kinds should have some protection in winter.

The following list contains the most of those usually planted in gardens and on lawns. These will afford a succession of flowers from spring until autumn, and may be obtained at the nurseries at moderate prices.

CATALOGUE, Etc.

Amorpha fruticosa, Indigo shrub, produces handsome bunches of purple flowers in June and July.

Amygdalus nana, Dwarf double-flowering Almond; a very beautiful shrub, about three feet high; blossoms early in April.

Aralia spinosa, or Angelica tree, about ten feet high; flowers in very large bunches, and continues a long while in bloom.

Cytisus Laburnum, or Golden Chain; a most elegant shrub, producing long racemes or bunches of yellow flowers in June and July; there are two kinds, the English and the Scotch Laburnum. The Scotch is the largest, forming a pretty large shrub; the English kind is greener, more compact, and by some thought to be the handsomest; they ought to be in every garden.

Calycanthus Floridus, Allspice, or sweet-scented shrub, a native of the Southern States; the flowers are of a very dark chocolate color, and the fragrance very much resembles ripe strawberries; easily kept when once introduced. This shrub generally grows about five feet high in gardens, and blossoms from May to August.

Ceanothus Americanus, Red Root, or Jersey Tea tree; a plant or two in the collection, as it flowers in profusion, is worth having.

Cercis siliquastrum, or Judas tree. The flowers appear very early in the spring, before the leaves come out, and make a fine appearance; as it grows rather tall, it is calculated for the back row of the shrubbery.

Colutea arborescens, or Bladder Senna, having bunches of yellow flowers in June and July, which are succeeded by seed in a kind of bladder; calculated for the back or centre row of shrubberies.

Cratægus oxyacantha, the Hawthorn. It makes a pretty appearance planted out singly in the back or centre row; the flowers are very fragrant; it is sometimes called the Pride of

May; the double white, double scarlet, and single scarlet Hawthorn, are very beautiful, and ought to be in every plantation. Hawthorn hedges are much used in England, where they look very handsome when clipped; but they do not answer so well in this country, the heat of our summers causing the leaves to fall off early, often in July; on that account they are not much used. We have several things which are better calculated for that purpose.

Cydonia Japonica, or Pyrus Japonica, a very beautiful scarlet flowering shrub, from Japan. It is found to be very hardy, resisting our most severe frosts; it flowers very early, and continues a long time in bloom. A second flowering takes place in the latter part of the summer. It is every way a desirable shrub.

Daphne mezerion, one of our most early flowering shrubs, which blooms freely in April and May, and is very sweet-scented. It is rather tender in some situations, but will stand our ordinary winters very well in a sheltered situation.

Dirca palustris, or Leather Wood; a pretty little shrub, growing very regular in shape, and has the appearance of a large tree in miniature: it is a native of our Northern States; the flowers, which appear very early in the spring, are yellow, and come out before the leaves.

Gymnocladus Canadensis, or Kentucky Coffee tree. The berries bear a resemblance to coffee, and are said to be a good substitute for it; however, it is a beautiful tree, with handsome feathered leaves, and makes a fine contrast with others. It should be planted in the back or the centre of the plantation; it is very hardy.

Halesia diptera, and *Halesia tetraptera*, two-winged and four-winged Silver Bell, or Snow-drop tree. They are both natives of the Southern States, but are perfectly hardy here; our most severe winters do not injure them. The former kind flowers in April, and the latter withholds its blossoms until May. They are elegant shrubs.

Hibiscus Syriacus, fl. pleno, the double flowering Althea

frutex, of which there are several varieties; the double white, double red, double red and white, and striped, are the most showy; they begin to flower late in July, and continue until autumn. The single kind, of which there are many varieties, are scarcely worth cultivating, the double ones being raised quite as easily, and are equally hardy. These are indispensable in every plantation.

Hypericum frutescens, Shrubby Hypericum. There are several species of this small but beautiful shrub, all natives of the Southern States, but perfectly hardy here. They all flower profusely in the summer, and continue for a long time. They should be planted in the front row.

Kerria Japonica, or *Corchorus Japonica*, yellow Japan Globe Flower; although a native of Japan, like many other Japanese flowers, it is perfectly hardy here. It flowers in the greatest profusion at all times, except in the very dead of winter, and will grow in almost any soil or situation.

Kœlreuteria paniculata, Japan Bladder tree, or *Kœlroterius.* This is another hardy shrub from Japan. It has long racemes of flowers succeeded by a bladder-like fruit, and is worthy of cultivation in every good collection.

Ligustrum vulgare, virens, large European Privet, a very handsome evergreen shrub, flowering profusely in June, and producing bunches of black round berries. It bears slipping well, and is therefore very suitable for hedges, or to inclose ornamental plantations. It grows quick, and is well adapted to our climate. When planted in a hedge-row, and kept clipped, the American Privet makes a beautiful hedge, and ought to be in more general use.

Philadelphus coronarius, or common Syringa, is very ornamental, producing its sweet-scented flowers early in the spring, and in abundance.

Philadelphus inodorous, and *P. Grandiflorus*, Garland Syringa, are both natives of the Southern States, but quite hardy here. Their flowers are large, and continue for several months, in wreaths or garlands. They are well calculated for the centre row, and also to hide unsightly objects, and have a beautiful effect when mixed with monthly honeysuckles, etc.

Persica, or *Amygdalus Persica*, *fl. rosea pleno*, or double flowering Peach, is very beautiful in shrubberies. It blossoms early, and sometimes bears fruit, but it is cultivated entirely for its beautiful blossoms. A few trees of the Chinese double flowering Apple (*Pyrus spectabilis*) have also a beautiful effect.

Rhus cotinus, Venetian Sumach, Aaron's Beard, sometimes called fringe-tree, is a fine shrub, calculated for the centre of the clump or shrubbery. Its large branches of fringe remain all the summer, and give it a curious and striking effect.

Ribes Missouriensis, or Missouri Currant; there are two species of this very ornamental shrub from Missouri, introduced by Lewis and Clarke; they are quite hardy, and flower profusely from April to June.

Robinia glutinosa and *Robinia hispida;* the former a pretty large shrub, producing fine branches of flowers in great abundance throughout the summer; the latter is a smaller shrub; both of them are, however, worthy of a place in large collections.

Robinia pseudo-acacia, or Yellow Locust tree. This tree is introduced here rather on account of its usefulness than beauty, though the latter is very considerable. The timber is superior to any other kind of wood for ship-trunnels, mill-cogs, and fence-posts, as well as for various other purposes. Its culture is very easy, and may be propagated in great abundance, by sowing the seed in March, April, or May, in a bed of good sandy loam, which is its favorite soil, and covering them half an inch deep. Previous to sowing, put the seed in a basin, pour on scalding water, and let it stand all night; pick out such seed as are swollen and plant them immediately; next evening repeat the same process with such as did not swell the first night, mix the whole and sow them; they will come up in the course of the following month numerously; for no seed grow more freely, notwithstanding what some say to the contrary. When the plants are a year old, transplant them out of the seed-bed into nursery rows, four feet distant, and plant from plant one foot

Having had two or three years' growth on these rows, they may be planted successfully in any warm and tolerably rich sandy soil. They may also be propagated by suckers, which they throw up abundantly, especially if some of the wide-extending roots be cut through with an axe. An acre of these trees, planted at two feet distant each way, will contain 10,890; and four feet distant, 2,722; and it is said that no appropriation of land is more lucrative than that devoted to this purpose. The Three-thorned Acacia seed (*Gleditschia*) should be prepared in the same manner.

Rosa, or Roses, a very numerous variety of these; some reckon five or six hundred kinds. They are accounted the most beautiful of Flora's productions. Perhaps a handsome collection might be made out of about fifty of the best sorts, which by taking such quantity I suppose might be obtained at about fifty cents each, under name; and generally, a fine collection unnamed at half that amount. No good garden or shrubbery should be without them.

Sorbus aucuparia, Mountain Ash, or Roan tree. This is a very beautiful shrub of the larger size; the leaves are ornamental; the flowers and fruit, which are produced in large bunches, are beautiful; the fruit remains till late in the autumn. It is a native of Europe.

Sorbus Canadensis. This is a native of our Northern frontiers and mountains, but it does not grow so large as the former; the berries are smaller and red, the former larger and of an orange color; but otherwise much resembles it.

Spartium junceum, Gentista, etc. Two or three species of Broom, producing numerous bunches of yellow flowers in May and June; the *Genista*, or Spanish Broom, which has white flowers, is also very pretty, but not quite so hardy as the former.

Symphoria racemosa, or Snow-berry, sometimes called St. Peter's Wort, a pretty little shrub; the bunches of wax-like white berries which it produces during the whole summer give it a beautiful appearance.

Syringa vulgaris, or common Lilac, blossoming in May, is well known to all, and needs no comment. The white variety is not quite so common. They are only used for outside plantings, as they sucker very freely, and soon make themselves common.

Syringa Persica, or Persian Lilac, is a delicate low shrub, the flowers very abundant, and the leaves small and delicate. There are two varieties of the Persian Lilac: the white flowering, and the blue or purple flowering.

The *Chinese* cut-leaved Lilac is very curious; the leaves are cut like Parsley, the flowers growing in longer racemes than the former.

Siberian, or large Persian Lilac. The bunches of flowers are very large, and continue in bloom a long time after the common Lilac.

Tamarix Gallica, or French Tamarix, and the *Tamarix Germanica*, German Tamarix, are two pretty shrubs; the leaves and branches are small and slender, producing quantities of beautiful flowers, which form a very striking contrast to the other parts of the shrubbery.

Viburnum opulus, or Guelder Rose, otherwise called Snowball, is a very showy shrub, producing large balls of snow-white flowers in May, and is indispensably necessary to every shrubbery.

Vitex agnus castus, or Chaste tree, a pretty and singular shrub, flowering the most part of the summer.

CLIMBING PLANTS.

Ampelopsis hederacea. This plant, on account of the largeness of its leaves and rapidity of its growth, is well adapted for covering walls. There are several species, all resembling the vine in habit and flower.

Aristolochia sipho, Birthwort, or Dutchman's Pipe. A very curious blooming plant, with extraordinarily large foliage, well calculated for an arbor; affording a dense and cooling shade.

Atragene alpina. A free-growing deciduous shrub, with small pinnated foliage, and large blush-colored flowers, which continue from May to July.

Bignonia crucigera is a desirable evergreen, being of a luxuriant growth. It will cover in a few years an area of fifty feet, and bloom from May to August; color, orange.

Bignonia radicans, or Trumpet Creeper, produces large bunches of red trumpet-shaped flowers in July and August.

Bignonia grandiflora is much like the former in habit and appearance, but the flowers are much larger. It is said to be a native of China, and the former a native of this country. They are both perfectly hardy, and will climb up brick-work or wooden fences, without any assistance.

Clematis, or Virgin's Bower. There are several species, some of them tender, or not sufficiently hardy for our severe winters, without protection. The *Clematis azurea, bicolor*, and *flama*, are splendid varieties. The *Clematis Virginica, Viorna, Viticelli*, and *Vitalba*, are perfectly hardy, and blossom throughout the summer.

Glycine Sinensis, or *Wistaria Sinensis*, is a handsome Chinese Creeper of recent introduction from China, and is not yet common in our nurseries. It is a beautiful vine, running to a great height, and loaded with long racemes of purple flowers throughout the summer.

Glycine frutescens, or *Wistaria frutescens.* This beautiful brother of the Chinese kind is a native of our Southern States, grows much in the same way as the others, and is, perhaps, not inferior. Although this fine creeper has been long known in England, we have not heard much about it by English writers; the conclusion seems to be that it does not flower well in England. In fact none of our Southern plants do well in that country, while those from China do very well; here, however, it is quite the reverse. I have the Chinese *Wistaria Sinensis* from fifteen to twenty feet high, and the American *Wistaria* about the same height. The Chinese does not look so vigorous and green as his American brother. The American *Wistaria* should be planted in every garden with othet creepers, or to run up the trees in shrubberies, according to its natural habit.

Hedera Helix, Irish Ivy, is a desirable evergreen for covering naked walls, or any other unsightly object. The leaves are of a lively green, and from three to five angled. There are several varieties of it, all calculated for growing in confined, shady situations, where plants in general will not thrive.

Jasminum officinale, Garden Jasmine. This delicious climbing shrub has from time immemorial been common in Europe for covering arbors. Its delicate white fragrant flowers render it very desirable; but it is rather tender for our Northern winters, unless well protected. In the Southern States, this plant, and also the yellow Jasmine (*revolutum*), grow luxuriantly and bloom profusely, and even *Jasminum grandiflora* will endure the winters of South Carolina and Georgia.

Lonicera, comprehending all the fine sweet-scented honeysuckles. Of the Italian kinds, the monthly honeysuckle is decidedly superior, continuing to flower all through the summer, until late in autumn, and is very fragrant. Some of the other European kinds may be occasionally introduced into large shrubberies. There is a white honeysuckle, lately introduced from France, denominated *Hedysarum coronarium*, which is in great repute. Two or three American kinds deserve particular notice.

Lonicera sempervirens, or Coral Trumpet, monthly honeysuckle, is extremely beautiful, flowering the whole of the summer, with its thousands of scarlet bunches; it is, however, destitute of scent.

Lonicera Fraseri, also an American; the flowers are like the other kind in almost every particular except color, this being a bright yellow.

Lonicera pubescens, or *Caprifolium pubescens*, a large and beautiful honeysuckle from the North-west coast; the flowers are large, and of a bright copper color, inclining to orange. They are all perfectly hardy.

Lonicera flexuosa, Chinese Honeysuckle, of late introduction; it is perfectly hardy, withstanding our most severe frosts without the least injury; it is a very sweet-scented honeysuckle, grows rapidly, and to an immense height. It flowers in pairs and threes all up the branches, covering the whole plant completely with flowers. It blossoms in spring and autumn, and is a very valuable acquisition to our gardens and shrubberies.

Lonicera Japonica, or Japan Honeysuckle. This bears flowers in great profusion, which are white, afterwards becoming of a light yellow. It is not so hardy as the Chinese, and requires a little protection in the winter.

Passiflora, or Passion Vine. There are several hardy species, but the best is the *Passiflora incarnata;* this, although it dies to the ground every winter, will, during the summer, grow from twenty to thirty feet, and yield abundance of beautiful purple flowers.

Periplaca græca, or Silk Vine. A prolific climber; wood slender, twining, and elastic; leaves smooth, ovate, lanceolate. Established plants will grow thirty or forty feet in one season, and yield flowers in clusters, of a brownish-yellow color, from May to July.

I shall only add to the above the running kind of Roses; although there are many other things which might be mentioned.

Rosa multiflora, from China, is pretty well known, producing thousands of small double red roses in bunches. It requires a sheltered situation from some of our keen north-westers. *Rosa multiflora alba*, from the same country, is of late importation, but as it increases readily may be obtained at about the same price as the former; the bunches of flowers are white. *Rosa Grevillia*, a running rose, also from China, the flowers of various colors. *Rosa rubifolia*, Raspberry-leaved Rose, from our Northern frontiers, and extending over the Western country; although a single flowering rose, it produces large bunches of flowers, which are differently colored on the same bunch, exactly like the former China kind, and is another instance of the similarity of the native Chinese plants to those of our country.

Rosa canina, fl. pleno, English double Dog Rose, is a very pretty little double rose, and will run to a great height. *Rosa Banksii*, Lady Banks's double white China running Rose; it runs up and spreads much: it may be easily known from others of the running roses, by its being entirely destitute of prickles. *Rosa Noisette*, and Champney's, are said to have been raised from China seed in Carolina; they are not strictly running roses, but as they grow tall are fine ornaments for the shrubbery, flowering during the whole of the summer and autumn, in large clusters. The Madeira Rose, or double white cluster, musk, flowers throughout the summer and autumn months, and is therefore well adapted for the shrubbery. *Rosa Cherokensis*, called the Nondescript, or Georgia Rose; the flowers are very large, being white, with yellow centre. This is a running rose, growing very high around trees, etc.

Rosa rubiginosa, or Sweetbrier, is too well known to need description.

PROPAGATION OF FLOWERING SHRUBS.

Flowering shrubs are variously propagated by slips, cuttings, layers, suckers, buds, or scions; and these may be thus defined:

1. Slips are simply small branches, slipped down from the side of a large branch, or from the main stem. These should

be taken from the parent plants carefully, so as to leave an eye or heel at the lower or butt end.

2. Cuttings should be made from shoots or stalks of a prior year's growth; and such should be selected as are well ripened, having their joints not far apart: they may be cut so as to have three or four joints in each cutting. In some species of succulent plants, the joints being near together, cuttings need not be more than from four to six inches long; but shrubby plants in general will admit of their being from ten to twelve inches.

3. Layers differ from cuttings in nothing, except that they strike root into the soil, while yet adhering to the parent plant.

4. Suckers are in reality young plants, connected to the parent at the root, which should be carefully separated in spring or autumn, and transplanted in the same manner as plants raised by any other method; either in a nursery-bed, shrubbery, or flower-border.

5. Scions are of two sorts: scions properly so called, and buds. A scion is a cutting, or portion of a plant, which is caused to grow upon another plant, from which it extracts fluid for the nourishment of its leaf-buds; these thus fed gradually grow upwards into branches, and send woody matter downwards, so as to become connected with the stock grafted on. The business of planting slips, cuttings, etc., of the tender kinds into nursery pots, and the hardy kinds into borders, is generally performed in spring and autumn.

MANAGEMENT OF HARDY FLOWERING SHRUBS.

For the purpose of raising hardy flowering shrubs by slips or cuttings, let a border be prepared in a shaded and sheltered situation, by manuring and deep digging. Provide cuttings about a foot long, and insert them into the ground full one-third of their length; the rows may be about two feet apart, and the cuttings nine inches from each other in the rows. Press the ground around the stems, and rake it smooth. The after-management of nursery-beds, made in spring, is to keep them watered in dry weather, hoe them occasionally, and by autumn the cuttings will be rooted.

In cold climates, plantations made in autumn should be protected by a covering of leaves, straw, or litter, merely sufficient to screen the plants from wind and the sun's rays in time of freezing, the heat of the sun being more destructive to vegetation in winter than the cold weather.

To increase flowering shrubs, rose bushes, or any other plants, by layers, dig the ground about the plants to be operated on to a good depth; then with a sharp knife cut between two joints half through the stalk or branch on the under part, turn the edge of the knife upwards and make a slit, carrying it past the first joint half way to the next above; make a hollow in the ground, and insert the cut part from one to three inches deep, according to the nature of the plant operated on, keeping the branch perpendicular, and the slit open. Each layer should be pegged down with a hooked stick, made from small branches of trees, to keep it in its proper position, as well as to prevent the cut part from uniting where the roots form for the young plants.

BUDDING, GRAFTING, AND INARCHING.

Budding, grafting, and inarching are often practised on shrubs, with a view to perpetuate improved varieties. Budding may be performed on roses of different descriptions, as the White Moss, Unique, Tuscany, and other fine varieties, upon such wild kinds as are of a strong habit. The best time for performing the operation is towards the end of July or early in August, as the buds are then generally matured so that the bark parts freely from the wood, which is essential to the successful accomplishment of the business.

Grafting is generally performed in the spring. There are many methods practised on trees, as cleft grafting, whip grafting, saddle grafting, side grafting, root grafting, inarching, or grafting by approach, etc., which methods are all fully explained under the head of "Budding and Grafting," in the fruit department. I shall, however, here present a short view of the mode best adapted for shrubs.

Scallop budding is performed by cutting from a small stock a thin narrow scallop of wood, about an inch in length, and taking from the chosen twig a thin scallop of wood of the same dimensions; this is instantly applied, and fitted perfectly at top and bottom, and as nearly as possible on its sides, and firmly bound with bass matting. This may be performed in spring, and if it fails, it may be repeated in the month of July. The French practise this mode on Roses.

The most simple method of grafting is to cut off the stock in a wedge-like manner; then prepare a graft having three or four eyes; proceed to cut a slit in it upwards, and thrust it on the stock, taking care to join the bark of each together; tie them firmly together with bass, and immediately cover the grafted part with clay and horse-dung mixed; which, being well prepared, should be closed securely round the graft in an oval form.

Inarching, or grafting by approach, may be performed as follows: The shrubs to be grafted must be growing very near to those which are to furnish the grafts; a branch of each must then be prepared by making a long sloping cut nearly to its centre; the two must be brought together, and secured by a bandage of matting, so that the bark may meet as nearly as possible. The graft may then be covered with clay composition; and when a complete union has taken place, the plants may be separated with a sharp knife, by cutting off below the junction.

As the above directions are applicable to the propagation

and management of green-house, tender, and half-hardy plants as well as to hardy shrubs and vines, it may be necessary here to remind the reader that delicate roses and half-hardy woody plants left out during the winter should be protected either by bending down the branches and covering them with soil, or by tying them up to stakes, and binding straw snugly around them. At the same time throw some dung on the ground about the roots; the longest of which may be raked off on the approach of spring, and the shortest forked in, so as to manure the plants, and thus give vigor to their rising shoots.

TRANSPLANTING DECIDUOUS PLANTS.

Deciduous shrubs may be transplanted at any time after they lose their leaves, and before the buds begin to expand in spring, provided the ground can be brought into good condition to receive them; the holes should be dug capacious enough to hold the roots without cramping them, and some earth, well pulverized, must be thrown equally among the fibres of the roots, which should be well shaken, and the earth trodden down around the plants, until brought to the level required. Evergreens should be removed carefully with a ball of earth connected with their roots, and some good mould should be provided to fill in with.

The spring pruning of shrubs and vines should be attended to before the buds begin to rise; say March in the Northern, and January in the Southern States. In performing this business, use a sharp knife, in order that all amputations and wounds be cut and pared smooth, and in a slanting manner. Divest the plants of all dead wood, superfluous branches, and those which cross each other. Regulate the plantation in such manner that the natural form and habit of each plant may be retained as much as possible, and train the branches so that the sun can have free access to every part; bearing in mind the hints thrown out in the Introduction to our Catalogue. Some shrubs and vines will need a summer pruning, merely to thin out young shoots, superfluous wood, etc., and to train straggling branches.

THE CULTIVATION OF BULBOUS AND TUBEROUS-ROOTED PLANTS.

These plants exhibit a striking variety of the beauties of Nature. It would seem as if every change she is capable of forming was included in the radiant colors of the Tulip. Never was a cup either painted or enamelled with such a profusion of tints. Its stripes are so glowing, its contrasts so strong, and the arrangement of them both so elegant and artful, that it may, with propriety, be denominated the reigning beauty of the garden in its season. The Hyacinth is also an estimable flower for its blooming complexion, as well as for its most agreeable perfume and variety.

The Double Dahlia, in its numerous varieties, is inconceivably splendid. It was only at the latter part of the eighteenth century that the first of these, which were single, were introduced into Europe from Mexico.

Double Dahlias of three colors were first known in the year 1802, and since that time the varieties have increased so rapidly, that those which a few years ago were considered beautiful are now thrown away to give place to the more beautiful sorts. I have good authority for stating that upwards of twenty thousand seedlings are raised yearly in England, only a few of which are introduced into the collections of amateurs, to take the place of such old sorts as may from time to time be rejected. This is done, in order that none but the very choicest may be retained in such collections.

In some gardens in Holland, they cultivate, by distinct names, about eleven hundred varieties of Tulips, thirteen hundred of

Hyacinths, and six hundred of Ranunculuses and Anemones, some of which are sold as high as sixty dollars the single root. It is stated in the travels of Mr. Dutens, of his having known ten thousand florins, equal to $4,000, refused for a single Hyacinth; and Dodsley says, in his Annual Register for 1765, that the Dutch of all ranks, from the highest to the lowest, during the years from 1634 to 1637 inclusive, neglected their business to engage in the Tulip trade. Accordingly in those days the *Viceroy* was sold for £250, the *Admiral Liefkeens* for £440, and the *Semper Augustus* at from £500 to £1,000 each; and a collection of Tulips was sold by the executors of one Wouter Brockholsmentser for £9,000. It is stated that in one city in Holland, in the space of three years, they had traded for a million sterling in Tulips.

DIFFERENCE BETWEEN BULBOUS ROOTS AND HYACINTHS.

"The Hyacinth, purple, white, and blue,
Which flung from its bells a sweet peal anew,
Of music so delicate, soft, intense,
It was felt like an odor within the sense."

It may here be necessary to define the difference between bulbous and tuberous roots. Those designated bulbous have skins similar to Onions, or the *Allium* tribe; and tuberous roots imply all such as produce tubers something similar to Potatoes.

The soil for bulbous and tuberous roots in general should be light, and yet capable of retaining moisture; not such as is liable to become bound up by heat, or that, in consequence of too large a portion of sand, is likely to become excessively hot in summer; but a medium earth between the two extremes. As many city gardens do not contain a natural soil of any depth, a suitable compost should be provided in such cases, which may consist of equal parts of sand, loam, rotten manure, mould, etc.

When ready, the beds may be laid out, from three to four feet wide, and they should be raised two or three inches above the level of the walks, which will give an opportunity for all superfluous moisture to run off. Let the beds thus formed be pulverized to the depth of fifteen or eighteen inches; and at the time of planting, let a small quantity of beach sand be strewed in the apertures or trenches prepared for the roots to grow in, both before and after placing them therein, which will prove beneficial.

A southern exposure, dry and airy, and sheltered from the north-west winds, is preferable for most bulbs. But Anemones and Ranunculuses should be in some measure sheltered from the intense heat of noon. Buds of hardy bulbous and tuberous roots should be covered on the approach of winter with litter, leaves, straw, or such earth as is formed by the decay of leaves, to the depth of two or three inches, as it prevents any ill effects which a severe season may have on the roots; but it should be carefully raked off in the spring.

MANAGEMENT OF BULBOUS ROOTS.

Bulbous roots in general should be taken up in about a month or six weeks after the bloom is exhausted, or when the foliage is about half decayed. If fine warm weather, the bulbs may be dried on the beds they grow on, by placing them in separate rows, being careful not to mix the several varieties. To prevent such an accident, labels may be affixed to, or placed in, the ground opposite each bulb. They will keep much better when dried gradually. To this end, a little dry earth may be shaken over them, to screen them from the heat of the sun. If it should rain before they get dry, take them in, or cover them with boards. When dry, clear them of the fibres and stems, and then put them away in dry sand; or if wrapped in paper, they may be kept in boxes or drawers until the season of planting returns.

The tender tuberous roots, such as Dahlias, will have to be taken up before the cold becomes severe. As the Dahlia exhibits its flowers in all their splendor, until nipped by the frost, the roots ought, in the event of a very sudden attack, to be secured from its blighting effects. They are not apt to keep well if taken up before they are ripened. The tops should therefore be cut down as soon as they have done flowering; and the ground covered around the roots with dung or litter. This will enable them to ripen without being injured by frost; and in about a week after being cut down, or on the appearance of severe weather, they should be dug up and packed in dry sand, and then stowed away in a dry place out of the reach of frost. The temperature suited to keep green-house plants will preserve them in good order.

WINTER MANAGEMENT OF BULBS.

Some people complain of the difficulty of keeping Dahlia roots through the winter. I am of opinion that they are often killed from being taken up before they are ripe, and then put in a confined, damp place; or are by some, perhaps, subjected to the other extreme, and dried to a husk. I keep mine on shelves in the green-house, and seldom lose one in a hundred. If it be an object with the cultivator to have the names perpetuated from year to year, each plant should have a small label affixed to the old stalk, by means of small brass or copper wire, as twine is very apt to get rotten.

Cape bulbs, and such tuberous roots as are cultivated in pots, on account of their tenderness, should be kept dry after the foliage is decayed, until within about a month of their period of regerminating, at which time they should, after having been deprived of their surplus offsets, be repotted in good fresh earth.

There are some descriptions of bulbous and tuberous roots that need not be taken up oftener than once in two or three years, and then only to deprive them of their young offsets, and to manure the ground. These will be described hereafter, under their different heads.

In the articles which follow, I have named the preferable

season for planting the various kinds of bulbous and tuberous roots; but as some bulbs will keep in good condition several months, there can be no objection to retaining such out of the ground, to suit any particular purpose or convenience.

AMARYLLIS—HOW TO CULTIVATE.

Of this genus of flowering bulbs there are about eighty species, and upwards of one hundred varieties; they are natives of South America, and in Europe are generally kept in the hot-house; some of the varieties are hybrids, produced by cultivation; these succeed very well in the green-house, and in this country we frequently have very perfect flowers in the borders. A few of the choicest varieties are as follows:

Amaryllis Aulica, or Crowned Amaryllis, is one of the most beautiful; it produces four flowers, about seven inches in diameter, on an erect stem, about two feet and a half high, with six petals of green, crimson, and fine transparent red colors.

A. Ballota produces three or four rich scarlet flowers on the stem, each about five inches in diameter; there are two or three varieties of this species, all beautiful.

A. Johnsoniensis. The stem of this variety rises about two feet, and exhibits four beautiful scarlet flowers, with a white streak in the centre of each petal, each flower about six inches in diameter. It sometimes produces two stems.

A. Longifolia, or *Crinum Capense*, is perfectly hardy; it flowers in large umbels of a pink color, inclining to white, and is a good garden variety.

Amaryllis formosissima, or Jacobean Lily, produces a flower of great beauty; although a low-priced plant, it throws out gracefully its glittering crimson-colored petals, which have a brilliancy almost too intense for the eye to rest upon.

The *A. Lutea* produces its bright yellow flowers in October, in the open air; but the bulb requires a little protection in winter, or it may perish.

The most suitable soil for the Amaryllis is a clean new earth, taken from under fresh grass sods, mixed with sand and leaf mould; the latter ingredient should form about a third of the whole, and the sand about a sixth. Some of the varieties may be planted in pots during the month of April, and others will do very well in the open ground, if planted early in May, in a sunny situation. The bulb should not be set more than half its depth in the ground; as, if planted too deep, it will not bloom; the plant deriving its nourishment only from the fibres. When the bulbs have done flowering, such as are in pots should be watered very sparingly, so that they may be perfectly ripened, which will cause them to shoot stronger in the ensuing season, and those in the ground should be taken up, and preserved in sand or paper.

ANEMONE AND RANUNCULUS.

These are medium, or half-hardy roots, producing beautiful little flowers of various hues, and are highly deserving of cultivation. The bulbs should be planted in a fresh, well pulverized, loamy soil, enriched with cow-dung. If planted in the garden, the beds ought not to be raised above one inch higher than the alleys, and the surface should be level, as it is necessary for the prosperity of these plants rather to retain than to throw off moisture. The plants will generally survive our winters; but it is always safest to plant them in such a manner that a temporary frame of boards can be placed over them when the weather sets in severe; and if they are to be shaded while in flower, the posts intended for the awning may be fixed in the ground at the same time; these will serve to nail the boards to, and thus answer two purposes.

Anemones and *Ranunculuses* may be planted during October or November, in drills two inches deep and six inches apart; the roots should be placed with claws downwards, about four inches distant from each other, and covered up, leaving the bed quite level. The awning need not be erected over the beds until they come into bud, which will be early in May The extreme heat of the American climate is, however, unfavorable to the perfect development of their beautiful blossoms in ordinary seasons, even when shaded.

CROCUS.

These are hardy little bulbs, said to be natives of Switzerland. There are in all about fifty varieties of this humble, yet beautiful plant, embracing a great variety of hues and complexions, and their hardiness, and earliness of flower, offer a strong motive for their cultivation. The bulbs may be planted in October or November, in rows about six inches from the edgings; if in beds, they may be placed in ranks of distinct colors, about four inches apart, and from one to two deep, which will afford to their admirers considerable amusement and gratification, and that at a very early season. They are generally in full perfection early in April.

CROWN IMPERIAL.

This is a species of the genus *Fritillaria*, of which there are about twenty species and varieties, chiefly natives of Persia. These squamose bulbs produce tall, luxuriant stems, embellished with green glossy foliage, and flowers of various hues; but there are only a few of the most curious cultivated, perhaps on account of their odor, which to some persons is disagreeable. They are, however, very hardy, and produce singular and showy flowers in April and May, suited to make variety in the flower borders, in which they may be planted in August and September, from three to four inches deep. They need not be taken up every year as other bulbs; and when they are, which may be about every third year, they ought not to be retained too long out of the ground before they are replanted.

COLCHICUM.

This curious little bulb, being planted in the month of June, about two inches deep, produces its flowers in October. It then dies, without leaving any external appearance of seed; the vital energies, however, lie buried in the bulb all the winter, and in the spring produce a stalk with seeds, which get ripe by the first of June, just in time to plant for flowering in the ensuing autumn. How wonderful are the provisions of Nature!

CYCLAMEN.

There are several species of the Persian Cyclamen which are worthy of cultivation in pots. The varieties Coum and Persicum will bloom in a green-house, or warm room, from January to April, if planted in good, light compost early in September. The foliage of these plants is of a dark green velvet color; and the flowers of the variety Coum are of a dark crimson color. Those of the variety Persicum are of a delicate French white, tipped with pink; and their fragrance is similar to that of the wild rose.

DOUBLE DAHLIA.

This may, with propriety, be denominated one of the most important perennial tuberous-rooted plants that can be introduced into a garden; and from the circumstance of its having become so fashionable, of late years, I have felt anxious to furnish, in this work, a catalogue of all the choicest varieties attainable. I therefore applied for this purpose to Mr. G. C. Thorburn, 51 John street, New York city, who, from a regular correspondence with connoisseurs, both in England and America, becomes acquainted with all the most beautiful and rare varieties; and he has kindly furnished a list and description of about one hundred, including the choicest seedlings of the last two years. To these I have added about one hundred and twenty varieties, most of which I have had under cultivation in my own garden, and which may be justly denominated preëminently beautiful.

In making this selection, several superb varieties are omitted, not because they are undervalued, but for the sake of brevity, which in a work of this kind must be consulted. Those marked thus † are native American varieties. Those marked thus * obtained the greatest number of premiums at the various Floricultural and Horticultural Exhibitions in Great Britain, as well as in our own country. There are, perhaps, fifty more in this Catalogue, not far beneath them; but none are marked except those which, from having been tested in this climate, can with confidence be recommended, as being free and perfect Bloomers. The choicest seedlings of last year, which have been purchased in England, at from fifteen shillings to five pounds sterling each, are marked thus §. It may be necessary to observe, that many of our choice old varieties, as well as several of the new ones, hereinafter described, have not been offered in competition at public exhibitions. These are, therefore, not to be undervalued for want of the star or asterisk; and it is presumed that the brief description given of the different shades will be sufficient to govern amateurs in thei• choice.

CATALOGUE OF DOUBLE DAHLIAS.

† Denotes American Seedlings. * Free Bloomers. § New Varieties.

* Admiral Stopford, *Trentfield's*, very dark, cupped petals; fine formed flower.
Alba Purpurea, *Young's*, white, edged with purple.
Alexander, *Miller's*, bright orange buff.
Alphonse, *Bavais's*, primrose, edged with violet.
Alkœnig, light scarlet; extra large flower.
§ Andromeda, *Collison's*, primrose, tipped with carmine.
Andrew Hoffer, *Holmes's*, bright maroon, cupped petals.
Antler, *Keynes's*, vivid scarlet; fine formed flower.
* Antagonist, *Bragg's*, pure white; excellent formed flower.
† Apollo, *Schmitz's*, clear golden yellow, cupped petals.
* Arethusa, *Brown's*, bright violet purple; very fine.
* Asmodeus, very dark puce; novel and pretty variety.
Athlete, *Chereau's*, beautiful lilac; extra fine shape.
Beauty of Chelmsford, *Wick's*, white, edged with lavender.
Beauty of the Plain, *Sparry's*, white, deeply margined with rosy purple.
Beauty of Wakefield, *Barrett's*, white, edged with light purple.
* Beauty of Sussex, *Mitchell's*, delicate pink, edged with cherry color; a free bloomer.
§ Berryer, *Turner's*, black; extra fine dark show flower.
* Beeswing, *Drummond's*, rich crimson, splendidly cupped.

† Black Prince, *Kent's*, extra dark maroon.
§ Bohemian Girl, *Proctor's*, white, edged with purple; fine form.
Bridemaid, *Brown's*, white, edged with purple; free bloomer.
† Brooklyn Rival, *Kent's*, beautiful light orange; fine shape.
Burnham Hero, *Church's*, superb deep crimson.
† Caleb Cope, *Schmitz's*, mottled rosy lilac; free bloomer.
§ Captain Warner, *Girling's*, light purple, elegantly shaped.
Charles XII., *Miller's*, plum color, tipped with white.
Charles XII., *Pamplin's*, fine rosy crimson.
* Cheltenham Queen, *Hodge's*, white, round petals, finely cupped.
Cinderella, *Dubras's*, beautiful cherry color, tipped with white.
* Cleopatra, *Atwell's*, beautiful light yellow; a fine show flower.
§ Cloth of Gold, *Edwards's*, extra bright golden yellow; superb show flower.
* Colonel Baker, dark claret; fine form and free bloomer.
* Constantia, *Cox's*, white, beautifully shaded with bright pink.
Countess of Liverpool, beautiful shaped scarlet.
§ Dawn of Day, *Mitchell's*, light lilac; elegantly formed flower.
† Desdemona, *Schmitz's*, primrose, tipped with rosy lilac.
Donna Antonia, *Dickens's*, purple, tipped with white.
* Dowager Lady Cowper, rosy pink; extra fine formed flower.
Duchess of Richmond, *Fowler's*, fine orange and pink.
Duke of Bedford, *Dennis's*, large crimson maroon.
Duke of Wellington, *Smith's*, rich scarlet crimson, finely cupped.
* Duke of York, *Keynes's*, light scarlet, beautifully cupped.
Dupetit Thouars, *Mielliez's*, deep yellow, laced with red.
Eclipse, *Catleugh's*, vermilion rose; superb flower.
Eleame de Beaucour, *Girling's*, white, edged and striped with bright purple.
Engenia, chrome yellow, elegantly tipped with violet.
Enterprise, *Dodd's*, beautiful clear buff color; fine form.
* Essex Champion, *Turvell's*, bright orange; of superior form
Evecque de Bayeux, *Oudin's*, spendid velvety maroon.
* Eximea, *Girling's*, bright rose, finely cupped.
§ Fantasii, *Mielliez's*, bright yellow, edged with scarlet.

Favorite, *Dodd's*, white, tipped with rosy crimson.
Francis, *Jones's*, white, margined with purple.
§ Fulwood Glory, *Teebay's*, light crimson; extra fine form.
† General Houston, *Briell's*, light purple; fine free bloomer.
§ Golden Fleece, *Union's*, bright orange; splendid flower.
Golden Rule, beautiful yellow; finely formed.
§ Goldfinch, crimson and yellow; extra fine fancy variety.
Grace Darling, *Dodd's*, bright salmon; fine formed flower.
Grandis, extra large ruby purple.
* Great Mogul, *Atwell's*, extra fine shaded crimson.
Great Western, *Bragg's*, light purple, mottled with crimson.
* Harlequin, *Dodd's*, white, deeply margined with scarlet.
† Henry Clay, *Schmitz's*, dark claret, beautifully cupped.
† Hero of the States, *Kent's*, light scarlet, dark centre.
† Hero of the West, *Schmitz's*, rosy carmine; finely formed.
* Hero of Stonehenge, *Whales's*, dark crimson; conical form; very fine show flower.
§ Hon. Mr. Herbert, *Brown's*, bright salmon color; exquisite form; a free bloomer.
Hope, *Neville's*, extra fine rose color; free bloomer.
* Illuminator, *Keynes's*, white, edged with scarlet; similar to "Painted Lady."
* Indispensable White, *Tassart's*, French white; flowers of immense size.
§ Isis, *Salter's*, nankeen, edged with white, interspersed with brown; a fancy variety.
Ithuriel, *Harrison's*, bronze, delicately shaded with pink.
King of Lilacs, *Girling's*, beautiful lilac; free bloomer.
* Lady Ann Murray, *Catleugh's*, white, mottled with purple.
* Lady Antrobus, *Sparry's*, white, tinted with scarlet lake; fine form, and free bloomer.
† Lady Ashburton, *Russell's*, pure white, elegantly tipped with carmine lake.
§ Lady Cornwallis, *Whales's*, blush white; extra fine form.
Lady Catharine Jermyn, white, mottled with crimson.
§ Lady Featherstone, *Sparry's*, white, margined with purple.

* Lady Sale, *Smith's*, yellow, edged with brilliant scarlet.

§ Lady Stopford, *Trentfield's*, lake crimson; fine form, and free bloomer.

* Lady St. Maur, white, delicately tipped with lavender.

† Lady Stewart, *Kent's*, white, lightly tinged; fine formed flower.

* Lady Von Brendenstein, *Degen's*, white, tipped with violet.

§ Lady of the Lake, *Keynes's*, white, beautifully margined with rosy pink.

* La Lione, *Salter's*, creamy white, elegantly edged with scarlet.

* La Tour du Auvergne, orange scarlet; large cupped flower.

Le Grand Bourdain, *Low's*, rosy lilac, centre tinged with bright yellow.

† Lutea Grandiflora, *Kent's*, light yellow; free bloomer.

† Lutea Perfecta, *Kent's*, sulphur yellow; finely formed.

† Lutea Speciosa, *Schmitz's*, extra fine shaped; yellow.

* Madame Chauviere, *Girling's*, light crimson, tipped with white.

Madame Rignou, buff, tipped with pure white.

Madame Villabois, white, beautifully tipped with vermilion.

Madame Wallner, *Girling's*, dark maroon, tipped with white.

* Marchioness of Exeter, *Widnall's*, peach blossom; fine form, cupped petals.

* Marchioness of Ormonde, *Bourne's*, white, tipped with violet purple; fine show flower.

Marshal Soult, *Elphinstone's*, delicate lilac, tinted with red.

§ Marquis of Aylesbury, *Sparry's*, purple; very fine show flower.

§ Magician, *Turner's*, orange, edged with bright yellow.

Maid of Bath, *Davis's*, white, edged with purple.

§ Master George Clayton, a fine fancy show flower.

Maria, *Wheeler's*, deep rose; superb form, free bloomer.

§ Marguerite, *Bailey's*, beautiful crimson, tipped with white.

§ Miss Prettyman, *Turner's*, white, margined with bright purple.

§ Mrs. Caudle, *Turner's*, light orange; profuse bloomer.

† Mrs. Clay, *Kent's*, white; elegantly formed, and slightly shaded with lilac.

† Mrs. Rushton, *Buist's*, white, tipped with rose; a free bloomer.

* Mrs. Shelley, *Mitchell's*, rosy lilac; fine form and free bloomer.

† Negro, *Schmitz's*, fine dark puce; a good show flower.

Nihil, *Bailey's*, fancy bright red, tipped with white.

Novelty, shaded ruby; fine form and free bloomer.

Nonpareil, *Proctor's*, ruby scarlet; first-rate form, and showy

Ophir, *Edwards's*, fine yellow, sometimes tipped with crimson.

* Orb, very fine scarlet crimson; a perfect and free bloomer.

§ Orlando, *Brown's*, pale rosy lilac, of fine form and habit.

§ Pantaloon, *Dodd's*, a first-rate show flower, and free bloomer.

Pickwick, *Cormack's*, purple; fine form; a good show flower.

† Pontiac, *Schmitz's*, orange, edged with bright red; very showy.

§ Princess Radsville, *Gaines's*, white, edged with crimson; fine formed flower.

Princess Royal, *Harwood's*, fine primrose; good form.

Prince of Wales, *Dodd's*, fine yellow, cupped petals.

President of the West, dark crimson; fine form.

Punch, *Dodd's*, bright purple, striped with white; fancy variety.

† Purpurea Perfecta, *Kent's*, light purple; very compact; a free bloomer.

§ Queen of the Fairies, *Cook's*, delicate pink, deeply margined with white; very fine.

* Queen of Perpetuals, *Girling's*, delicate peach blossom; a perfect formed flower.

Queen of Roses, *Widnall's*, pale rosy lilac; very fine.

§ Queen of Sheba, *Wilkinson's*, pure white; elegantly formed

* Queen, *Widnall's*, peach blossom, finely cupped; superb show flower, and free bloomer.

Queen of Trumps, white, edged with rosy lilac.

Raphael, maroon and crimson; a good show flower.
Reliance, *Widnall's*, bright orange, finely cupped.
Rival Prince of Orange, *Widnall's*, bright orange; very fine.
† Rival, *Schmitz's*, maroon, shaded with red.
Rienzi, *Widnall's*, crimson and puce mottled.
§ Rose d'Amour, *Brown's*, extra fine dark lilac; free bloomer.
Rose Superior, *Girling's*, delicate rose color; well formed.
Scarlet Defiance, *Cowdery's*, superb dark scarlet; great bloomer.
§ Scarlet Gem, *Turner's*, vivid scarlet; an extra fine show flower.
Sir E. Antrobus, *Keynes's*, fiery crimson; a fine show flower.
Standard of Perfection, dark crimson; good-formed flower.
Striata Formosissima, *Bates's*, blush white, striped and spotted with crimson.
Suffolk Hero, *Girling's*, fine dark maroon; a good bold flower.
Sulphurea Elegans, *Jones's*, sulphur yellow; large bloomer.
Surprise, *Oakley's*, bright scarlet, tipped with white.
† T. C. Percival, *Schmitz's*, large dark crimson, round petals; fine formed flower.
Trafalgar, *King's*, peach-blossom pink; good form and showy.
Triumph, *Mielliez's*, white, tinted with bright purple.
* Ultimatum, *Bavais's*, bright red; elegantly formed.
* Unique, *Ansell's*, light yellow, beautifully tipped with red.
* Victory of Sussex, *Stanford's*, dark maroon; fine show flower.
Victor, *Widnall's*, bright primrose, edged with crimson.
* Violet Perfection, *Keynes's*, purple, with bright violet shade.
* Viscount Ressigneur, *Dubras's*, purple, tipped with white.
§ Yellow Standard, *Keynes's*, the most perfect flower of its color.
† Yellow Victory, *Schmitz's*, brimstone yellow; free bloomer.

PROPAGATING DOUBLE DAHLIAS FROM SEED.

As some amateurs are apt to fancy that the most economical method of obtaining a supply of Dahlias in their gardens is to raise them from seed, it may be necessary to remind such, that the trouble and expense of raising any quantity of seedlings is equal to that attending the cultivation of the same number of the choicest varieties; and when it is considered that the greatest proportion of a plantation may be single and semi-double, and that but few double-flowering plants can be expected, equal to those above described, it must appear evident that it is the interest of such persons as desire to have their gardens unencumbered with plants, that are not calculated to ornament the same, to procure plants, or roots, of such varieties as have been tested, and highly recommended, as is the case with all those described in the preceding Catalogue, and also those which are generally sold by the regular florists. But as I am writing for young gardeners, it may be necessary to state, that although new varieties are usually raised from seed of the finest double flowers, some successful propagators prefer that procured from semi-double varieties. Sow seed towards the last of March, in pots, and plunge them in a moderate hot-bed; or seed may be deposited in the earth of the beds, in shallow drills.

Nothing is more simple than the cultivation of Dahlia roots. In March or April, they will, if properly kept through the winter, begin to sprout around the old stems and tubers. To forward these sprouts in growth, the roots should either be buried in light earth, on the top of a moderate hot-bed, or else potted, and then set in a warm room, or green-house, and watered. As soon as the shoots have grown to the length of two or three inches, the roots may be divided in such a manner as to have a strong shoot attached to a piece of the tuber, or old stem. Each of these will, if properly managed, make a plant. Those who may commence cultivating at an early season, should put the plants thus separated into small pots and keep them in a growing state until about the middle of May, at which time they may be turned out of the pots, with the balls of earth entire, and planted in the open borders, from three to four feet from each other.

In order to obtain an extra number of plants from any choice varieties, cuttings are frequently taken from the shoots when about three inches in length, which are planted in nursery-pots, and cultivated in hot-beds; they require to be shaded from the sun, by mats, for the first fortnight; after which they may be gradually inured to the air, and treated as plants raised in the ordinary way.

PREPARATION OF THE SOIL FOR DAHLIAS.

Let the ground be well pulverized, and enriched with good old manure, before the plants are set out. If the top soil be shallow, and the subsoil inferior, it would be beneficial to the plants to dig holes to the depth of a foot to eighteen inches, and then replenish the earth with good rich compost, consisting of two-thirds of fresh loam, and one-third of well-rotted manure.

Many cultivators have found late planting to suit better than early; and I myself have had more perfect flowers from plants set out about the middle of June than from those planted in May. This is easily accounted for. In July and August, the weather is generally hot, which brings the most forward plants into bud at an early season; and in the event of a continuation of hot, dry weather, such buds fail to produce perfect flowers; whereas, those plants which are set out late, keep growing through the hot weather, and produce their buds just in time to receive all the benefit of the autumnal rains. From a consideration of these circumstances, I think early in June the safest time to set out Dahlia plants; and if those persons who have no convenience to force their roots set them out in May, in ground prepared as before directed, they will generally succeed very well, provided they take care to cover them in case of a cold change of weather. The roots may be thus cultivated entire, as is frequently done; but if it be desired to have them parted, this business can be easily accomplished without disturbing the roots; and the offsets may be planted in the ground separately or potted.

Previous to setting out the plants, it will be necessary to provide for their preservation, through the varied changes of the season, as a sudden gust of wind may destroy the expectations of a year. The branches of the Dahlia are extremely brittle; and, therefore, a stout pole, or neat stake, should be driven down near each root, of a suitable height, so that the branches, as they progress in growth, may be tied thereto at every joint, which may be done with shreds of matting or twine. If the poles be in readiness, they are much more easily fixed at the time of planting the Dahlias than afterwards; but it may be done at any time after the ground has been softened by rain, provided it be not delayed too long, so as to subject the plants to risk. Sometimes a few forward buds of the Dahlias will exhibit their premature beauties to the beams of a July and August sun; but their lustre is quickly dimmed. The latter part of September, sometimes all October, and part of November, witness the Dahlia in all its glory; and dwarf plants, cultivated in pots, will sometimes blossom at Christmas; but they require more than ordinary care, at a late period of their growth.

GLADIOLUS, CORN-FLAG, OR SWORD LILY.

Of this genus of bulbs there are about fifty species, natives of the Cape of Good Hope. They produce flowers of various colors, in August and September, and are well worthy the attention of those who cultivate tender exotic plants. They may be planted in September or October, about an inch deep, in pots, which must be kept in a green-house or light room, and watered sparingly until they begin to grow. The following are known to be superb species and varieties:

G. alatus, or Wing-Flowered, producing bright orange-colored flowers.

G. blandus produces flowers of a beautiful blush rose color.

G. Byzantinus, or Turkish Flag, has large delicate purple flowers.

G. cardinalis. This variety produces very large flowers of superb scarlet, spotted with white.

G. floribundus, or Cluster Flower, produces large flowers of white and pink color.

The *Gladiolus Natalensis*, or *Psittacina*, is perhaps the most desirable to cultivate of all others. It blossoms freely, and the colors are exquisitely beautiful. In its progress of blooming, it exhibits variable colors, as vermilion, red, yellow, green, white, crimson, etc., which brighten, as the flower arrives at perfection, to the brilliancy of a rainbow. Another good quality displays itself in the bulb, which, if properly managed, will yield an abundance of offsets. These being cultivated will flower the third year in perfection, and thus continue to multiply perpetually.

I have named September and October as the time for planting, because it is considered the preferable season for most bulbs. Yet if these be preserved in good condition through the winter, until early in April, and then planted in a soil consisting of about one-half fresh loam, equal parts of leaf mould and sand, well mixed, they may be forwarded in a warm room, green-house, or moderate hot-bed, until settled warm weather, and then turned out of the pots into a border, where they can be shaded from the sun at noon-day. This will induce each of them to throw up three or four stems, from three to four feet high, each stem producing five or six gorgeous blossoms, in great perfection. Those planted in the autumn or winter may also be turned out of the pots in June; and from the fibres having taken substantial root in the soil, before transplanting, such plants may be taken up again in August, or early in September; and on being planted in large pots, they may be removed, so as to perfect their bloom, within view of the parlor or sitting-room, which will afford considerable amusement and gratification.

HYACINTH.

"Hail to thee! hail, thou lovely flower!
Still shed around thy sweet perfume!
Still smile amid the Wintry hour,
And boast e'en then a spring-tide bloom!
Thus hope, 'mid life's severest days,
Still smiles, still triumphs o'er despair;
Alike she lives in pleasure's rays,
And cold affliction's Winter air."

There are, as has been already stated, about thirteen hundred varieties of this family of plants, comprising all the various hues, as white, pink, red, yellow, blue, purple, crimson, etc.; and some of those with various colored eyes. They begin to produce their flowers in the open borders, early in April, on short, erect stems covered with florets or small bells; and each floret is well filled with petals rising towards the centre; and is suspended from the stem by short, strong footstalks, the longest at the bottom; and the uppermost florets stand so erect as to form a pyramid. A plantation, or bed of these, has a very beautiful appearance, provided they are well attended to. In planting them, which should be in the months of October or November, care should be taken to have the colors so diversified as to suit the fancy. They may be placed in short rows across the bed, about eight inches apart, and from three to four inches deep, measuring from the top of the bulb, and covered up at the setting in of winter, as before recommended for bulbs in general.

Those who may have a fine collection should have an awning erected in the spring, to screen them from the chilling blast, and also from drenching rains, and the noonday sun; and they should be looked over as soon as they make their appearance above ground, to see if they are all perfect and regular; if faulty or inferior bulbs should appear to have been planted in a conspicuous part of the bed, by accident or mistake, they can be taken out with a trowel, and by shortening the rows, others may be substituted. When all are regulated, look over them frequently, and as the stems shoot up, tie them to wires, or small rods, with shreds of bass matting or thread, being careful not to injure the florets. In about six weeks after they have done flowering, the bulbs may be taken up, and managed as recommended for bulbs in general, in a former page.

IRIS, OR FLOWER DE LUCE.

There are two distinct species of plants cultivated under the name of *Flower de Luce*, each consisting of several varieties. The bulbous species and varieties are designated as English, Spanish, Chalcedonian, and American. These, if introduced into the flower-borders, and intermixed with perennial plants of variable colors, have a very pretty appearance when planted in clumps or patches. This may be done in the month of October, by taking out a spadeful of earth from each place allotted for a plant, and then inserting three or four bulbs, about two inches deep. If the ground be poor, some rich compost may be dug in before the bulbs are planted; and if several sorts be planted in the same border, let them be of various colors. The tuberous-rooted are blue, yellow, brown, spotted, and some other colors; they are easily cultivated; and flower freely in a loose soil inclining to moisture, if planted in March or April.

IXIAS.

These are tender, but very free flowering bulbs, producing on their stems, which vary in height from six inches to two feet, very delicate flowers of various colors, as orange, blush, white, purple, green, crimson, scarlet, and some have two or three colors blended in the same plant. There are, in all, upwards of twenty species, which may be cultivated in the green-house, by planting the bulbs in pots in September or October, and placing them near the light, and watering them sparingly until they begin to shoot. There are some pure white, and others yellow, growing in various parts of the country. Among the foreign genera are several species. Of the *Martagon*, or Turk's Cap Lilies, there are some beautiful varieties; as the *Caligula*, which produces scarlet flowers; and there is one called the Crown of Tunis, of purple color; besides these, are the Double Violet Flamed, the White, the Orange, and the Spotted. These are all hardy, and may be planted in various parts of the garden, by taking out a square foot of earth, and then, after manuring and pulverizing it, the bulbs may be planted therein before the setting in of winter, at different depths, from two to four inches, according to the size of the bulbs. Some of the Chinese varieties are very beautiful, as the Tiger, or Leopard Lily, and the dwarf red, *Lilium concolor*. There are others with elegant silver stripes, which are very showy, and there is one called *Lilium superbum*, that has been known to have twenty-five flowers on a single stalk.

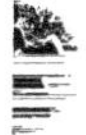

Besides those just enumerated, there are some others which are generally cultivated in green-houses, as the *Calla*, or Ethiopian Lily; and the following, which have been known to endure our winters, by protecting them with mulch or leaves. *Lilium longiflorum*, in two varieties, produce on their stalks, which grow from twelve to eighteen inches high, beautiful rose-colored flowers, streaked with white, which are very sweet-scented. These roots are sometimes kept out of the ground until spring, and then planted in the flower-borders, but they should be preserved carefully in sand or dry mould. *Lilium Japonicum*, of which there are two varieties, produce several stalks at once, yielding very showy flowers. One of the varieties is blue-flowered, and the other produces flowers of the purest white.

NARCISSUS.

The species and varieties of this plant are numerous. The *Incomparable* is perfectly hardy, and produces its flowers in April, which are called by some *pasche*, or *paus* flowers, by others, butter and eggs; perhaps because their bright yellow petals are surrounded with large white ones. Some persons dislike the smell of these, and it is said that the odor has a pernicious effect upon the nerves; but the white fragrant double, as well as the Roman, and Polyanthus Narcissus, are free from this objection, being of a very grateful and agreeable smell. Some of these are justly held in great esteem for their earliness, as well as for their varied colors. The *Grand Monarque de France*, the *Belle Legoise*, and some others, have white flowers with yellow cups. The *Glorieux* has a yellow ground, with orange-colored cups; besides these are some white and citron colored, as the *Luna*, and others entirely white, as the *Reine Blanche* and *Morgenster*. All these varieties are very suitable either for the parlor or green-house, and may be planted in pots, from October to December, from two to three inches deep. The double Roman Narcissus are very sweet-scented; if these be planted in pots, or put into bulb-glasses in the month of October, they will flower in January and February.

Polyanthus Narcissus are more delicate than Hyacinths or

Tulips. When they are planted in the open border, they should be covered about four inches with earth; and before the setting in of winter, it is advisable to cover the beds with straw, leaves, or litter, to the depth of six or seven inches, and to uncover them about the middle of March.

ORNITHOGALUM, OR STAR OF BETHLEHEM.

There are about fifty varieties of these bulbs, natives of the Cape of Good Hope, some of which are from three to five inches in diameter, and shaped similar to a pear; others are much like Hyacinth bulbs. Among those cultivated in America are the *O. lacteum* and the *O. aureum.* The former produces fine white flowers, and the spike is about a foot in length; and the latter produces flowers of a golden color, in contracted racemose corymbs. The *O. maritimum,* or Sea Squill, is curious; from the centre of the root rise several shining glaucous leaves, a foot long, two inches broad at the base, and narrowing to a point. If kept in a green-house, these are green during the winter, and decay in the spring. Then the flower-stalk comes up, rising two feet, naked half way, and terminated by a pyramidal thyrse of white flowers.

These bulbs are generally cultivated in the green-house, and require a compost consisting of about one-half fresh loam, one-third leaf mould, and the remainder sand, in which they may be planted in September. When cultivated in the garden, they should be planted four or five inches deep, and protected with barn-yard or stable manure. They produce their flowers early in June.

OXALIS.

The Oxalis is a native of the Cape of Good Hope; the species are numerous, and their roots are very small bulbs, articulated, jointed, or granulated, in a manner peculiar to this genus. They produce curious flowers of various hues, yellow, purple, rose, red, white, striped, vermilion color, etc. The bulbs should be planted in very small pots, in August and September, in a compost consisting of about two-thirds loam, and one-third leaf or light mould, and treated in the same manner as other Cape Bulbs. They increase in a peculiar manner, by the parent bulb striking a fibre down from its base, at the extremity of which is produced a new bulb for the next year's plant, the old one perishing. These plants will flower freely in a green-house.

PÆONY.

" Pæonia round each fiery ring unfurls,
Bares to the noon's bright blaze her sanguine curls."

Of this genus of splendid plants there are known to be about twenty species, and as many varieties. It is said that the *Pœonia officinalis rubra*, or common double red Pæony, was introduced into Antwerp upwards of two centuries ago, at which time it was sold at an enormous price. It has since been highly esteemed in Europe and America, and is to be found in all well established gardens, exhibiting its vivid crimson petals early in June. Many superb species have of late years been brought from China, a few of which may be noticed, with some others which are in very great repute.

Pœonia alba Chinensis is one of the finest of the herbaceous sorts. The flowers are white, tinged with pink at the bottom of the petals.

P. edulis whitlèji has also white flowers, which are very large and splendid.

P. edulis fragrans is a fine large double scarlet variety, and produces flowers perfumed like the rose.

P. humei has beautiful large double dark blush-colored flowers.

P. paradoxa fimbriata produces fringed double red flowers, which are very beautiful.

These are all hardy, and may be planted about four inches deep in the garden, in October or November. The flowers exhibit themselves to the best advantage when planted on a bed that is elevated, and of a circular form. The following are half-hardy and half-shrubby; and have been known to survive the winter by being well protected, but are kept much better in a green-house; and they also exhibit their flowers to greater advantage than when exposed to the full sun.

P. moutan Banksii, or Tree Pæony, produces very large double blush flowers in abundance, with feathered edges to every petal. This variety is highly deserving of cultivation.

P. moutan rosea is a fine rose-colored double variety, and produces very splendid flowers.

P. moutan papaveracea produces very large white flowers, with pink centres. This splendid variety frequently bears flowers from nine to eleven inches in diameter. Besides the above, are several others of various colors, some of which are semi-double.

TULIP.

"For brilliant tints to charm the eye,
What plant can with the TULIP vie?
Yet no delicious scent it yields
To cheer the garden or the fields;
Vainly in gaudy colors dressed,
'Tis rather gazed on than caressed."

The Tulip is a native of the Levant, and has been in cultiva tion nearly three centuries. It may be justly entitled the King of Flowers, for the brilliancy and endless combination of all colors and shades. The varieties of the Tulip are very numerous, and are divided into different classes. Those cultivated in regular beds by amateurs are rose-colored, *bybloemen*, and *bizarres*. There are a great many beautiful varieties, denominated *Parrot* Tulips, which have notched petals, striped or diversified with green; and also some very dwarfish kinds, both single and double, which are generally cultivated in parlors and green-houses.

Mr. T. Hogg has published "A Treatise on the Cultivation of Florists' Flowers," which comprises the Tulip, Carnation, Auricula, Ranunculus, Polyanthus, Dahlia, German and China Asters, Seedling Heart's Ease, and New Annuals. In that work, which is dedicated to Queen Adelaide, the author remarks that the cultivation of the Tulip is one of the most fascinating and pleasing pursuits imaginable, and that when "the Tulip mania has fairly got hold of any one, it sticks to him like the skin on his back, and remains with him the rest of his life." He instances a Mr. Davey, of Chelsea, as being in his seventy-fifth year, and in whose breast the fancy for Tulips was so predominant, that, in the autumn of 1832, he was induced to part with a hundred sovereigns for one single Tulip, named "Miss Fanny Kemble." Perhaps a better definition of what constitutes the properties of a good Tulip could not be given, than a description of this "precious gem, or loveliest of all Tulips." But, lest my readers should conclude that the old man was in his dotage, I would inform them that this favorite bulb was purchased of the executors of the late Mr. Clarke, with whom it originated, and that it had not only been the pet of its owner, but had excited the envy and admiration of all the amateurs who went to view it.

"This precious gem, a *bybloemen* Tulip, was raised from one of Mr. Clarke's seedling breeders, and broke into color three years ago. It has produced two offsets since, and is adapted to the second or third row in the bed; the stem is firm and elastic; the foliage full and broad, of a lively green; the cup large, and of the finest form; the white pure and wholly free from stain; the pencilling on the petals is beautifully marked with black or dark purple, and the feathering uniform and elegant; it preserves its shape to the last, the outer leaves not sinking from the inner; in a word, it is considered the first flower of its cast, and the best that has ever been produced in England up to this date."

BRIEF DESCRIPTION OF TULIPS.

The following description may serve to govern the choice of amateurs. Tulips exhibited at the show are, in general, classed and distinguished as follows: *Flamed Bizarres*, *Feathered Bizarres*, *Flamed Bybloemens*, *Feathered Bybloemens*, *Flamed Roses*, *Feathered Roses*, and *Selfs* or plain-colored.

A *Bizarre* Tulip has a yellow ground, marked with purple or scarlet of different shades. It is called *flamed* when a broad or irregular stripe runs up the middle of the petals, with short abrupt projecting points branching out on each side. Fine narrow lines, called arched and ribbed, often extend also from this broad stripe to the extremity of the leaves, the color generally appearing strongest in the inside petals. A Tulip, with this broad colored stripe, which is sometimes called beamed or splashed, is also, at the same time, frequently feathered.

The flower is called *feathered* when it is without this broad stripe; but yet it may have some narrow lines, joined or detached, running up the centre of the leaf, sometimes branching out and curved towards the top, and sometimes without any spot or line at all. The petals are feathered more or less around the edges or margin inside and out, the pencilling or feathering being heavy or broad in some, and light or narrow in others, sometimes with breaks or gaps, and sometimes close and continued all around.

A *Bybloemen* Tulip has a white ground, lined, marked, striped, or variegated with violet or purple, only of various shades; and whether feathered or flamed, is distinguished by the same characters and marks which are pointed out and applied to the Bizarres Tulips.

A *Rose* Tulip is marked or variegated with rose, scarlet, crimson, or cherry color, on a white ground; and the Feathered Rose is to be distinguished from the Flamed by the same rules as described before; the Rose is very often both feathered and flamed.

A *Self*, or plain-colored Tulip, properly so called, is either white or yellow, and admits of no further change; other plain-colored Tulips, whether red or purple, are called breeders, and are hardly worthy of being exhibited.

MANAGEMENT OF TULIPS

To describe minutely the mode of planting a regular bed of Tulips would exceed our limits. Suffice it to state that the name of every bulb should be written in a book, and that they should be so classed as to have the varied colors show advantageously. To this end, the tallest should be allotted for the middle of the bed, and others in regular gradation, so as to have the most dwarfish on the sides. The bulbs must be covered with good mould to the depth of three inches from the top of the bulb on the sides of the bed, and about four inches in the middle. Let a spoonful of clean drift sand be used around each bulb, and see that the bed be left sufficiently round from the middle to the edges. The beginner must understand that no unsightly tallies, nor number sticks, are to distinguish the Tulips, but that he must adopt a sort of ground plan, dividing the whole bed into rows of seven bulbs across. For example, write down the names and places of the Tulips in the first row, and continue the same form all through to the other end of the bed.

Row First.

No. 1.	Fenelon, ...	this is a	Bybloemen.
2.	Duchess of Clarence, ...	"	Rose-colored.
3.	Charlemagne, ...	"	Bybloemen.
4.	Louis the Sixteenth, ...	"	Bybloemen.
5.	Memnon, ...	"	Bizarre.
6.	Volney, ...	"	Bybloemen.
7.	Lady Crewe, ...	"	Rose-colored

Good fresh loam, taken from under healthy grass sods, is the most suitable soil for Tulips. Under this soil should be buried well rotted cow or horse droppings, to the depth of a foot, about two inches in thickness. The reason for placing the dung so low is that the fibres may get down to it (which they will do), and that the bulbs may not be injured by it, as is apt to be the case if too much dung is used around them. The best time for planting the bulbs is early in November, and the beds should be made a fortnight previous, in order that the earth may become sufficiently settled. If severe frosts set in after the Tulips show themselves above ground in the spring, some protection should be given. Single mats placed over hoop bends answer very well; and at the time of blooming, an awning should be erected over them to screen them from the intense heat of the sun, which awning should be sufficiently spacious to admit of persons walking under it, to view the beautiful flowers to the greatest possible advantage.

TUBEROSE.

This fragrant and delightful yet very tender flower has been cultivated in English flower-gardens for upwards of two centuries. There the bulbs are generally cultivated in pots early in the spring, and transferred to the flower-borders as soon as the weather becomes settled and warm. They generally succeed very well here, if planted at once in the open border, towards the last of April, and produce flowers, which are pure white, and highly odoriferous, on a stem three to four feet high.

The bulbs produce a number of offsets, which should be preserved with the parent plants through the winter, and then parted off and planted by themselves, in April or early in May, to produce flowering roots for the ensuing year. These roots thrive best in a light rich soil, well pulverized, in which they should be planted about two inches deep, not forgetting to take them up again before the approach of winter.

TIGER FLOWER.

Perhaps there is no flower treated of in this work, that is more beautiful than some of the species of the genus *Tigridia.* Like all Mexican bulbs, these are tender, and should either be cultivated in the green-house, or carefully preserved until settled warm weather, and then planted in rich light soil, in a sheltered situation. A bed of these beautiful flowers would afford as much gratification to some amateurs as a bed of Tulips.

The *Tigridia conchiflora* is of a rich yellow color, tinged and spotted with white and crimson; the colors are vivid and finely contrasted. The *Tigridia pavonia* is of the brightest scarlet, tinged and spotted with brilliant yellow. The corolla, which is about four inches in diameter, is composed of six petals; the outer petals are thrown backwards, and exhibit the blossom in all its splendor, which exists only a single day; but as if to compensate for its transient visit, each plant will produce a number of flowers; and where a bed of them can be collected, they will amuse their admirers for several weeks from July to September. In such case the bulbs may be planted about two inches deep, say nine by fifteen inches apart, towards the end of April, or early in May, and taken up again in October, to preserve for planting the ensuing year.

CULTURE OF BULBOUS ROOTS, IN POTS OR GLASSES, IN THE WINTER SEASON.

The culture of bulbous roots in a green-house, or light room, during the winter, is comparatively easy, provided two points be attended to: the first is to keep them near the light, and turn the pots or glasses around frequently, to prevent their growing crowded; and the second is, when the plants have done growing, to give them little or no water. For want of attention to these points, bulbs have been known to produce foliage year after year, without showing any sign of blossoms. All bulbs, at a certain period of the year, are in a dormant condition. This, in a state of nature, occurs invariably after the seed has ripened; yet as, in a green-house, many of this family do not ripen seed, the cultivator should watch the period when the leaves show indications of decay, at which time the supplies of water should be lessened, and shortly afterwards the earth should be suffered to get dry, and remain so until the season returns when the bulbs regerminate.

Many sorts of bulbs will keep best in pots, under the soil, in a dry, shady place, and in the same temperature as that in which they are in the habit of growing; but others, such as the Hyacinth, Tulip, and Narcissus, may be taken out of the soil, and preserved, as before directed, until the return of the proper season for replanting.

Dutch bulbous roots intended for blooming in pots, during the winter season, should be planted during the months of October and November, and be left in the open air until it begins to freeze; and then be placed in the green-house, or in a room, exposed to the sun. They will need occasional, moderate waterings, until they begin to grow. Then they should have abundance of air in mild weather, and plenty of water from the saucers, underneath the pots, while in a growing state; and should be exposed, as much as possible, to the sun, air, and light, to prevent the foliage from growing too long, or becoming yellow. For this purpose, single Hyacinths, and such as are designated earliest among the double, are to be preferred. Single Hyacinths are by some held in less esteem than double ones. Their colors, however, are more vivid, and their bells, though smaller, are more numerous. Some of the finer sorts are exquisitely beautiful. They are preferable for flowering in winter, to most of the double ones, as they bloom two or three weeks earlier, and are very sweet-scented. Roman Narcissus, double Jonquils, Polyanthus Narcissus, double Narcissus, and Crocuses also make a fine appearance in the parlor during winter.

It is a remarkable circumstance of the Crocus, that it keeps its petals expanded during tolerably bright candle or lamp light, in the same manner as it does during the light of the sun. If the candle be removed, the Crocus closes its petals, as it does in a garden when a cloud obscures the sun; and when the artificial light is restored, they open again, as they do with the return of the direct solar rays.

Hyacinths and other bulbs intended for glasses should be placed in them about the middle of November, the glasses being previously filled with pure water, so that the bottom of the bulb may just touch the water. Then place them for the first ten days in a dark room, to promote the shooting of the roots; after which, expose them to the light and sun as much as possible. They will blossom without the aid of the sun; but the colors of the flowers will be inferior. The water should be changed as often as it becomes impure. Draw the roots entirely out of the glasses, rinse the fibres in clean water, and also the glasses inside. Care should be taken not to suffer the water to freeze, as it will burst the glasses, and often causes the fibres to decay. Soft or rain water is generally preferred.

Forced bulbs are seldom good for anything afterwards. However, those who wish to preserve them, may immerse them wholly in water for a few days; and then, having taken them out, and dried them in the shade for a short time, they may be planted in a good soil, in the garden, where they will sometimes flower the next year. It does not clearly appear in what way the water operates, when the bulb is wholly immersed; but it is certain that bulbs so treated increase in size and solidity, and have an incomparably better chance of flowering the second year, than those which have not been so treated. Most probably their total immersion enables them to obtain a greater proportion of oxygen from the water.

Nosegays should have the water in which their ends are inserted changed, on the same principle as bulbous roots; and a much faded nosegay, if not dried up, may often be recovered for a time, by covering it with a glass bell, or cup, or by substituting salt water for fresh. Very fine Hyacinths have been grown in a drawing-room, in the following novel manner: A quantity of moss, classically called *hypnum*, and vulgarly fog, was placed in a water-tight box, about eight or nine inches deep, into which the bulbs were placed, at the end of September, without mould, and duly watered; and the result of this experiment was highly satisfactory.

GENERAL MANAGEMENT OF GREEN-HOUSE PLANTS.

Having already exceeded my limits, I am compelled to be brief in my observations on such ornamental plants as are generally cultivated in hot and green-houses. This description of plants embraces those which are collected from various climates, and thrive best in a temperature and soil similar to that in which nature first produced them. Hence, those who propagate exotic plants, must provide suitable composts, and also separate departments, where the different degrees of heat may be kept up, according to their nature and description. Some of these are raised from seed sown in the spring, others by layers, suckers, and offsets detached from the old plants, and many by slips or cuttings, planted at different seasons of the year, according to their various natures and state of the plants. Many kinds require the aid of glass coverings and bottom heat, created by fresh horse-dung, tan, etc.

Were I to attempt to give directions for the propagation of all the varieties of useful and ornamental exotic plants cultivated in various parts of our country, it would require several volumes. The catalogue of green-house plants alone, kept by the enterprising proprietor of the Linnæan Botanic Garden, at Flushing, occupies fifty pages of close matter. It would therefore be impossible to do justice to the subject, without dividing upwards of two thousand species of plants into classes, and treating of them under distinct heads. I shall, therefore, not attempt, in this edition, to write largely on the subject.

In order to render this work useful to those who may wish to avail themselves of the pleasure of nursing some of those beauties of nature in dwelling or green-houses during the most chilling days of our severe winters, and to afford amusement to the ladies at a season when our gardens are deprived of their loveliest charms, I shall notice some essential points connected with the management of green-house plants in as explicit a manner as possible, and subjoin a brief catalogue of such species as are most generally cultivated, of which there are innumerable varieties; descriptions of which, with all the varied features of the floral kingdom, may be found in the voluminous works of Loudon, Sweet, Chandler, and other English writers.

Those generally denominated green-house plants, and which are kept in rooms, should be placed where they can have the light of the sun, without being exposed to frost. Air, heat, and moisture are essential to the growth of plants; but these should be given in due proportions, according to circumstances. In frosty weather they should be kept from the external air, and watered very sparingly. When water is necessary, it should be applied in the morning of a mild sunny day. The plants should be kept free from decayed leaves, and the earth at the top of the pots should be sometimes loosened to a moderate depth, and replenished with a portion of rich compost. Plants kept in private houses are often killed with kindness. The temperature of a room in winter need not be more than ten degrees above freezing. If plants are healthy, they may be kept so, by attention to the preceding hints. Unhealthiness generally arises from their being subjected to the extremes of heat, cold, or moisture, or from total neglect.

An amateur florist has suggested the following hints in regard to the management of plants in rooms. He says that he keeps his plants in a room, the windows of which, having a southern exposure, will admit the sun all day. The plants are placed on a table with rollers attached to the legs, which in moderate weather is kept as near to the glass as possible. In cold weather, he removes the table into the middle of the room, and places a pail of water near the plants to attract the frost. He considers it a great mistake to suppose that plants kept in warm rooms require much fire-heat; on the contrary, he contends, that a moderate degree of cold will agree with plants much better than a very high temperature. He, however, considers it needless to attempt to keep plants in a cold room, the windows of which face the north. A south-eastern or even eastern exposure may answer without any fire, except in very cold weather. It may be observed, further, that excessive moisture injures plants more than drought, and that plants, in general, do not require water while the surface of the earth in the pots is moist.

ATTRACTING FROST WITH WATER.

Most persons misapprehend the true philosophy of this subject. We frequently hear of placing a pailful of water beneath a tree, when there is danger of the frost destroying the blossoms, and tying a wet rope to the top of the tree, with the lower end in the pail of water. The water is said to attract the frost. All this is a ludicrous absurdity. There is no efficacy in a vessel of water, except so far as it radiates heat. A pail or tub containing water will tend to keep plants warm by radiating heat, just as a fire in a stove tends to keep up the temperature around it. If a pail of water attracts frost, so does a heated stove. A large vessel of hot water, placed near pots containing plants, will keep them from being injured by cold, for several hours. The same is true if the earth in the pots be warmed, through and through, either by warm water or in some other manner. Such warm bodies of any kind radiate heat, for several hours, modifying the temperature near the growing plants. A large vessel of water in the open air, therefore, can afford but little heat to a plant or tree.—S. E. T.

PLANTS REQUIRE LIGHT.

In order that the ideas above advanced may be duly considered, it may be useful to indulge in a more minute description of the nature of plants, and to show in what manner the elements operate upon them. It is an acknowledged fact, that the roots of plants require moisture, and therefore penetrate the earth in search of it, and that the plants themselves are greatly nourished by air, and spread their branches and leaves to catch as much as possible its enlivening influence. Light also is so far essential, that there can be no color without it. Witness the blanching of celery and endive, where the parts deprived of light become white. Place a plant in almost any situation, it will invariably show a tendency to turn to the light. The sunflower is a striking example of this singular fact. As the leaves supply the plant with air, and the fibres of the roots with nourishment, if we strip off the leaves, or destroy the fibres, we deprive it of part of its means of support.

HEAT ESSENTIAL TO THE GROWTH OF PLANTS.

Having shown that air and water are essential to vegetation, and light to its color, experience shows us that heat, in a greater or less degree, is not less necessary to the growth of plants; it is therefore requisite, that in taking plants into our rooms, we should attend to these particulars. The internal structure of plants consists of minute and imperceptible pores, which serve the same important purpose in the vegetable, as veins in the animal, system, which are the medium of the circulation of the sap in the former, as the veins are of the blood in the latter. But it is by no means settled, as yet, by physiologists, how the food of plants is taken up, and converted into their constituent parts.

From the foregoing considerations and facts, it is evident, that, as air, heat, and moisture are each essential to vegetation, water should only be given in proportion as heat and air are attainable. In the summer season, green-house plants may be exposed to the open air, from the early part of May until the end of September, by being placed on the ledges of windows, or on a stand erected for the purpose, or, in the absence of a nursery-bed of flowering plants, they may be introduced into the regular flower-beds, to supply the place of such plants as may wither and die in the course of the summer, by being turned out of the pots and planted, or plunged in the earth with the pots.

WATERING PLANTS.

In the heat of the summer season plants generally require water every evening, and in the absence of dews, the earth about their roots may sometimes need a little in the morning but experience shows, that the roots of plants more frequently get injured from being soddened with water, than from being kept moderately dry.

Having before intimated that exotic plants will generally thrive best in a temperature and soil similar to that in which nature first produced them, it may be necessary to remind the reader, that we have the means of obtaining suitable composts from our own soils, and from sand, decayed leaves, rotten dung, and various kinds of peat, bog, and rock mould. These ingredients being judiciously mixed and prepared, may be suited to all the various kinds of plants, and should be used as occasion requires.

As the roots of plants make considerable growth in the course of a summer, it will be necessary to examine them by turning them out of the pots. This may be done in the latter part of August, or early in September, at which time all matted and decayed roots should be pared off, and the plants shifted into larger pots, which being filled with suitable compost, and watered, will be ready for removal into the house on the approach of cold nights, which is generally early in October.

Green-house plants require an annual pruning, and should be occasionally headed down, in order that their size and appearance may be improved; the best time for doing this is soon after they have done flowering, and while they are in a growing state.

Having endeavored to furnish my readers with the artificial means of preserving tender plants in a climate foreign to that in which nature first produced them, I shall call their attention to another class of plants well calculated for the windows of a house. I allude to the many beautiful varieties of the Chinese Chrysanthemum, which are frequently cultivated in pots, and may be taken from the ground and put into pots, even when in full bloom, without injury; and when the bloom is over, returned to the garden. In the spring following they will throw up an abundance of suckers.

LIST OF CHRYSANTHEMUMS.

The following list contains some of the best varieties of the Chrysanthemums, which are entitled to a place in every flower-garden. In October and November, when the waning year has left our gardens comparatively cheerless, these, with their various colors, deck them out in gaiety, and prolong the semblance of summer. They are perfectly hardy, and will brave our severest winters.

The gold-bordered red; *the petals are red, striped with golden yellow.*
White quilled.
Pale buff, or orange.
Changeable, *red and orange on same plant.*
Lilac quilled.
Rose-colored, or pink.
Lilac and white, *changeable; the flowers vary to lilac, to white with a purple centre, and to pure white.*
Dark crimson, or Spanish brown.
Straw-colored quilled.
Golden yellow.
Tasselled white.
Semi-double quilled ditto.
Paper white.
Quilled light purple.
Expanded do. do.
Quilled yellow.
Double Indian yellow.
Double Indian white.
Dark purple.
Early blush.
Golden Lotus.
Quilled purple.
Starry purple.
Park's small yellow, *fine.*
Quilled salmon.
Semi-double quilled.
Pale orange.
Two-colored red.
Curled buff or salmon.
Large lilac.
Late pale purple.
Quilled fine yellow.
Sulphur do.
Superb clustered do.
Small do.
Single flame yellow.
Quilled pink.
Quilled orange.
Early crimson.
Curled lilac.
Two-colored incurved.
Blush ranunculus.
Late quilled purple.
Tasselled lilac.
Tasselled yellow.
Yellow waratah.
Pale lilac.
Large buff, *superb.*
Barclay's.
Alton's.
Sabine's.

PROPAGATING CHRYSANTHEMUMS.

Chrysanthemums may be propagated from hardy cuttings and each plant will produce several suckers, which may be separated every spring. As the flowers are liable to be injured by the rain in autumn, it is advisable to take up a few plants, and place them in a light room or green-house, which will preserve them for some time.

Many people keep their late blooming plants in the house through the winter. This is a bad practice, as the heat and want of air will exhaust or destroy the plants altogether. If the flowers fade before hard frost prevails, it is best either to plunge the pots into the ground with the plants, or to turn them out of the pots and plant them, with the balls of earth entire, into the borders of the flower-garden.

Early in May, such as may be intended for potting the ensuing season should be divided at the roots, if not potted, and planted, each kind by itself. One single stem is sufficient for a moderate-sized pot, if the object be to have bushy plants; but if showy plants are desired, one of each of the varied colors may be selected for each pot, which should be sufficiently capacious to hold them without crowding them, as this will cause the plants to grow weak and slender. If this occurs early in the summer, a stocky growth may be produced by clipping the tops, and they will bloom in great perfection in their usual season.

INTRODUCTION TO THE CATALOGUE OF GREEN-HOUSE PLANTS.

To promote brevity and avoid tautology, I here submit the following statement:

That the directions accompanying our Catalogue of Annual, Biennial, and Perennial Flower Seed, will apply to such plants in the green-house department as are ordinarily raised from seed.

The directions annexed to the Catalogue of Flowering and Ornamental Shrubs, including propagation by cuttings, layers, etc., are applicable to a great portion of the plants hereinafter described; and also to such Bulbous roots as are generally embraced in green-house catalogues, from their being adapted to artificial culture, having been already treated of, under each head, in numerous articles; to which the reader is referred.

With the exception of hot-house plants, which require a uniformly warm climate to perpetuate their existence, all such other tender and half-hardy plants as need protection in winter, may come under the denomination of green-house plants; some species, however, may be preserved in frames, pits, cellars, or warm rooms. Many of those species designated thus § and thus † in our first two catalogues, are of such description; and as they have been treated of in the chapters thereto annexed, the following catalogue and explication will be necessarily brief, when compared with one general catalogue of exotic plants.

DESCRIPTIVE CATALOGUE.

Acacia. Of this and the *Mimosa,* which are by some considered as one genus, there are upwards of a hundred species and varieties, suited for artificial culture. The blossoms, which are generally straw-color and yellow, except the most tender, some of which are crimson, succeed each other from February to June.

Agapanthus. A beautiful species of Lily, producing large blue flowers from April to June; some varieties have striped leaves and delicate white blossoms.

Aloe. Of this genus there are numerous species and varieties some of which are very curious, being possessed of all the varied forms and figures peculiar to succulent plants. Some species flower annually from March to September; and all, except the Century Aloe, blossom frequently. The colors are generally yellow, pink, and red. The singular figure and habits of these plants render them desirable for green-house culture.

Alstrœmeria. Of this genus of plants there are several species, which have tuberous roots. The flowers of the varieties are of different shades, as rose-colored, scarlet, yellow, red, etc.; and some are variegated, as the *Alstrœmeria psittacina*, which is red, yellow, and green, and the *A. tricolor*, which is black, white, and yellow. They are beautiful plants when kept in good order.

Arbutus, European Strawberry Tree. A half-hardy evergreen shrub, of which there are several species and varieties, producing crimson and pink blossoms, and fruit, which remain on the plant a considerable time.

Ardesia, Chinese Ardesia. This is generally cultivated as a hot-house plant; and if kept in the green-house, should be placed in a warm situation. There are several species, producing oblong shining leaves, pink flowers, and red berries, which are very ornamental.

Aster argophyllus, Musk Plant. A plant of no great beauty, but esteemed by some for its musky fragrance; leaves ovate, lanceolate, and silky beneath.

Aucuba Japonica. A half-hardy shrub, with pale green leaves spotted with yellow. It produces small purple blossoms, but is desirable for its foliage only: to preserve which in good condition, shade in the summer is absolutely necessary.

Azalea. The Chinese species of Azalea are numerous and beautiful, producing blossoms of various hues, as white, purple, scarlet, yellow, etc., and some are striped and spotted, which succeed each other from February to May, under good cultivation.

A skilful florist, Mr. William Russell, has some hybrids which he raised by crosses between the different species of Azaleas and Rhododendrons, both of the hardy and choicest green house varieties. He has already flowered several plants, which partake of the Rhododendron in the umbels, and embrace all the good qualities of the Azalea.

Banksia. A genus of plants named in honor of Sir Joseph Banks, of which there are over twenty species, all curious in flower, and variable in foliage; colors, yellow and green. They generally blossom from May to August.

Beaufortia. There are two species of this beautiful shrub, yielding scarlet and pink flowers from the sides of their stalks, from May to July.

Bellis perennis. Daisy. This half-hardy dwarf species, of which there are several varieties, as recorded in our Perennial Catalogue, are worthy of further notice, from their yielding thousands of button-formed flowers from January to July, or until checked by the summer heat, from which they should be screened, by being planted in a shaded border in the spring. The colors are white, red, and variegated, and some, called Hen and Chicken Daisies, grow in clusters.

Bletia Tankervilli. A delicate plant, producing spikes of purple flowers, similar to the Hyacinth, from April to July.

Bouvardia. Mexican Bouvardia. A beautiful plant, producing brilliant scarlet flowers from May to September, when carefully cultivated.

Bar[illegible]ia. There are several species of this plant, natives of New Holland; the flowers of some are star-like, rose-colored, and sweet-scented; in perfection in April and May.

Brunia. This species of plants have foliage similar to the *Erica*, but the leaves are three-cornered; the plants when young are very handsome. *Brunia nodiflora* produces chaste white globular flowers in abundance. There are several other varieties highly esteemed by amateurs.

Brunsvigia Josephinæ. This cape bulb produces splendid rose-colored flowers in large umbels, on a stem about two feet high. There are several other species, some of which produce scarlet, others purple, and variegated blossoms, in perfection when cultivated in a warm green-house.

Buddlea madagascariensis. This plant, when properly cultivated, will blossom freely during winter, producing spikes of orange-colored flowers, of an agreeable fragrance.

Buonapartea juncea. This is a curious low-growing plant, with long narrow leaves, and spikes of small blue flowers, which, when cultivated in a warm situation, will continue some time in bloom.

Burchellia. A dwarf evergreen shrub, producing orange-colored flowers in large terminal clusters, from March to June.

Cactus. Of this family of plants there are numerous species, supposed to be of different genera, from the variation of their character and habits. Some are denominated *Cereus*, others *Epiphyllums*, *Mamillarias*, etc. The night-blooming *Cereus* is much celebrated. They all belong to the hot-house, but succeed well in a warm room or good green-house. Some are formed into erect pyramids, others are of a trailing habit; and all produce from the sides of their succulent stalks and leaves, beautiful crimson, scarlet, white, or pink flowers, from March to August.

Calceolaria. Of this species of delicate dwarf plants, there are several splendid varieties annually raised from seed, producing red, yellow, and orange-colored flowers from April to August, when shaded from the noon-day sun. They will otherwise suffer from heat.

Calothamnus. A beautiful evergreen shrub, similar to a dwarf pine, producing scarlet blossoms from the old wood, from April to November.

Callicoma serratifolia. A beautiful plant, producing tufted yellow heads of flowers from May to July.

Camellia. Of this admired winter-blooming genus of plants, there are several distinct species, the varieties from many of which multiply annually. Its durable glossy foliage, and splendid flowers, which excel those of any other plant, will insure it a preëminence in every green-house; as in good collections, flowers of various hues may be gathered from October to May. Those who grow Camellias must supply them moderately with tepid water when in flower, and for those out of flower, the warmest position must be given to induce them to make an early growth. Sponge the leaves weekly, to keep them clean, and to prevent the accumulation of dust upon them.

Cheiranthus. Under this title have been generally embraced all those fragrant and beautiful half-hardy species of Biennial Plants known as Wall and Gilly Flowers; the latter species is now, however, denominated Matthiola in our catalogues. The beautiful blossoms and delicious fragrance of these families, from February to June, entitle them to more than a passing notice. Their perfumes are exquisite.

Cineraria cruenta. Canary Aster. A dwarf half-shrubby plant, producing purple flowers in April and May.

Cineraria maritima. Silvery-leaved Ragwort, or Powdered Beau. A white plant, producing bright yellow globular flowers from April to June or July.

Cistus. Rock Rose. A half-hardy dwarf shrub, of which there are upwards of twenty species, natives of Europe; the flowers, which are white and purple, multiply abundantly in May and June.

Citrus. Orange, Lemon, etc. This genus embraces the Orange, Lemon, Lime, Shaddock, etc., of each of which there are several varieties. They are indispensable in a good greenhouse, for their handsome evergreen foliage, and odoriferous blossoms, and beautiful golden fruit, which by careful cultivation may be kept constantly on the plants. Those varieties with variegated, yellow, and green foliage, are very generally admired.

Clethra arborea variegata. A fine sweet-scented shrub, producing spikes of white downy blossoms; the leaves are oblong and serrated, having a gold-colored edge.

Correa. A genus of dwarf shrubby plants, consisting of several species, producing their orange, white, red, and green blossoms frequently in the winter, and sometimes in May or June.

Coronilla glauca. A desirable green-house dwarf shrub, yielding numerous sweet-scented yellow flowers in clusters, from January to April. There are other varieties which blossom in summer.

Cotyledon orbiculata. Cape Navelwort. A succulent plant, producing finger-like suckers and successional joints, which blossom annually; the curiosity of the foliage, however, is its chief recommendation.

Crassula. A species of dwarf succulent plants, producing scarlet and variegated wax-like flowers from April to June or July.

Crinum amabile. A large beautiful flowering bulb, of which there are several species, chiefly calculated for hot-house culture, where some varieties frequently yield three stems of beautiful crimson, purple, or white flowers in a year.

Cypripedium insignis. This species is known by the name of Lady's Slipper Plant; the flowers, which are green and purple, have a waxy appearance, and are similar in shape to an Indian shoe. It should be cultivated in a warm, moist situation.

Daphne odora. A beautiful dwarf evergreen shrub, yielding white fragrant blossoms in many-flowered terminal heads, from December to March. There are other species and varieties, one of which has its leaves edged with yellow.

Dianthus. Under this name are embraced the admirable species of Carnations, Picotees, Pinks, Sweet Williams, etc., recorded in our Catalogue of Perennials; and which are in universal esteem for the fragrance and beauty of their flowers, which succeed each other from May to August. They are all hardy, except the Carnation and Picotee tribes, which are well deserving green-house or frame culture.

Diosma. A dwarf genus of heath-leaved shrubs, producing numerous small flowers of a white color from March to May. Some of the varieties are sweet-scented.

Dryandrus. To this genus belong several species, similar to the *Banksias;* they are delicate plants, producing orange and straw-colored thistle-like flowers in abundance.

Echeveria. This genus of succulent plants are natives of Mexico and California. Some of the species produce green and red blossoms; the flowers of the variety *pulverulenta* are red, and the foliage is covered with powder, which gives it a beautiful appearance.

Epacris. This is a native of New South Wales, of which there are several species, mostly erect-growing plants, varying from two to four feet; the leaves are small, and the blossoms, which, in different varieties, are crimson, pink, purple, and white, are, under good cultivation, abundant from January to June.

Eranthemum. This species belong to the hot-house, and will not flower in perfection without plenty of heat. The *Eranthemum pulchellum* produces flowers of a fine blue color from December to April; and the *Eranthemum bicolor* will yield purple and white flowers from April to August, under good cultivation.

Erica, Heath. Upwards of five hundred species and varieties of this plant are cultivated in Great Britain, where a continued succession of bloom is kept up from January to December. The most prominent colors are white, scarlet, purple, yellow, and red. They are desirable plants to cultivate in any country, as they furnish material for the bouquet in winter; but they must be screened from the noon-day sun in summer, and only moderately watered, as extremes of drought or moisture are destructive to this family of plants.

Erythrina, Coral Plant. There are several species of this plant, chiefly adapted to the hot-house, producing long spikes of crimson or scarlet flowers. Some keep them in good condition in a green-house; they must, however, be well attended to, and frequently repotted, which will sometimes induce them to bloom two or three times in a year.

Escallonia. There are several species of this plant, some of which will survive the winters of our Southern States. When cultivated in a green-house as half-hardy shrubs, they yield their red, white, and pink flowers throughout a long season.

Euonymus. This plant is called by some the variegated Camellia; the flowers are not very showy, but the silvery and golden-edged foliage of the different varieties renders them very attractive. They are natives of China.

Euphorbia. There are several species of this plant adapted to the green-house, some of which are beautiful, especially the *E. splendens*, and Poinsett's scarlet, or *Euphorbia Poinsetti.* They flower freely from December to May, if kept in a warm part of the house.

Eupatorium elegans. A dwarf plant, producing white sweet-scented flowers early in the spring; to promote bushiness, the plant, after blossoming, should be closely pruned.

Eutaxia myrtifolia. A beautiful little evergreen shrub; foliage small, but very neat, furnishing numerous red and yellow-colored blossoms from March to May, under good culture.

Ficus elastica, India-rubber Tree, and *Ficus australis*, are both evergreen plants, and grow luxuriantly in a green-house; the foliage, which is large and glossy, is pink on the under side.

Ficus, Fig Tree. A plant easily cultivated, of which there are many species and varieties, which, kept in pots or tubs, in a temperature adapted to the Orange tree, will fruit freely, and ripen two crops a year.

Fuchsia, Lady's Ear-drop. Of this beautiful shrub there are several varieties, producing clusters of small scarlet flowers, the stamens of which are encircled with a petal of purple; in bloom from April to September.

Gardenia, Cape Jasmine. A very popular evergreen plant, producing white fragrant rose-like flowers from May to August. There are several species and varieties, some of which are more dwarfish than others, but all are desirable.

Gelsemium nitidum, Carolina Jasmine. A beautiful climbing

evergreen, producing in the month of May large yellow tiumpet-like blossoms, of delicious fragrance.

Gloxinia. A desirable herbaceous plant, of which there are several varieties, yielding beautiful showy flowers; colors, blue, lilac, and white.

Gnaphalium, Everlasting Flower. Of this plant there are several species or varieties, some of which yield clusters of yellow flowers, and others red, from March to June.

Gnidia, Flax-leaved Gnidia. A dwarf shrub, of which there are several varieties, furnishing pretty tubular and corymbose straw-colored flowers in the winter and spring.

Grevillea. There are several species of this evergreen dwarf shrub, which are very handsome in flower and foliage. The flowers of some grow in racemose spikes, and of others on flowering branches; the colors are white, rose, green, and straw or light yellow. They yield seed, and are easily cultivated.

Heliotropium, Peruvian Heliotrope. A species of soft shrubby dwarf plants, which, when cultivated in a warm situation, will yield abundance of delicate blue or purple flowers from January to September.

Helychrysum, Eternal Flower. There are several species and varieties of this plant, producing soft downy foliage and durable flowers, which, if cut before they are too far advanced, will retain their splendor several years.

Hibbertia. A species of climbing evergreen shrubs, which yield fine yellow flowers in succession from May to September, under good culture.

Hibiscus Chinensis. This half-hardy herbaceous plant is worthy of a place in the green-house, as some species will yield flowers six inches in diameter, if well attended to and frequently watered; the colors are crimson and blush.

Hovea. This is a pea-flowering evergreen shrub, of which there are several species, natives of New South Wales. The *Hovea celsii* is a beautiful runner, yielding numerous blue flowers.

Hoya, Wax Plant. A fine climbing species, adapted to the

hot-house; the leaves being succulent, green, and fleshy, they require considerable heat and but little water. Some produce pink flowers, and others white, in April and May.

Hydrangea hortensis. The Hydrangea is a well known deci duous, half-hardy, soft-wooded shrub, producing large pink balls of blossom, when cultivated in a shaded border, from May to October; and by mixing iron dust from a blacksmith's shop with the soil, or by growing the plants in swamp earth, or mould from decayed leaves, the flowers will become blue.

Illicum, Aniseed Tree. A dwarf species of shrub, the leaves of which, when rubbed, smell like anise; some produce red, and others yellow flowers in March and April.

Indigofera, Indigo Tree. A free flowering shrub, of which there are several species; the flowers, which grow in long pinnacles, are red, yellow, and pink.

Jacarandus. A genus of evergreen shrubs, of easy culture, containing five species, most of which produce blue or purple flowers, on loose branching panicles, in abundance.

Jambosa vulgaris. This species of evergreen shrub is generally called Rose Apple, from its producing rose-scented fruit, which is about an inch in diameter, and eatable. There are several varieties, yielding either white, rose, green, or straw-colored flowers in erect spreading stamens. They are of easy culture.

Jasminum, Jasmine. Of this favorite genus there are several species, of various complexions. The Catalonian Jasmine, or *J. grandiflorum*, produces white fragrant blossoms in winter; the Indian Jasmine, or *J. odoratissimum*, and also the *J. revolutum*, yield very sweet-scented yellow flowers from April to June, and the *J. officinale*, a climbing plant, blossoms through the summer.

Justicia. The plants of this genus are generally cultivated in the hot-house; some produce scarlet flowers in large terminal spikes, from December to March, and others purple.

Kennedia. A beautiful evergreen climber, of which there

are several species, producing blossoms of various hues, as scarlet, blue, crimson, and purple, from February to June.

Lagerstrœmia. A half-hardy deciduous plant, the roots of which, if planted in the garden in March, will produce large spikes of red flowers, from May to August.

Lantana. A genus of dwarf shrubs, which being cultivated in the hot-house, or warm green-house, will yield their blossoms in April and May; the species are of various colors; yellow, orange, pink, white, purple, and variable.

Laurus nobilis, Laurel. This evergreen shrub is by some esteemed for its fragrant leaves; there are several species distinguished as sweet bay, royal bay, etc., and some species are without scent.

Lavandula, Lavender. A species of soft-wooded, half-hardy plants, with narrow, scented leaves, yielding spikes of fragrant blue flowers in May and June.

Lechenaultia formosa. A dwarf plant with heath-like foliage and bright scarlet blossoms; in bloom a long season under good culture.

Leptospermum. This genus is somewhat celebrated from the leaves of the species *L. scoparium* being used by the crew of Captain Cook's ship as a substitute for Tea, the leaves having an agreeable bitter flavor; the blossoms, which are small, are white.

Leucodendron, Silver Tree. A neat evergreen shrub, with silver-like foliage, of which there are several species, all admirable for their beauty.

Linum, Flax. Two species of this plant are worthy of cultivation in a green-house, where they will bloom in February and March. The *Linum trigynum* produces large yellow flowers in clusters, and *Linum ascyrifolium* yields spikes of blue and white flowers, which are similar to those of the Convolvulus.

Lobelia. There are several species of this plant, which are generally herbaceous; they produce an abundance of little flowers of brilliant colors. The *Lobelia crinus* is a pretty trailing plant, yielding numerous blue flowers all the summer.

Lychnis coronata, Coronet-flowered Lychnis. This half-hardy plant, embraced in our Catalogue of Perennials, is worthy of protection, from its furnishing trusses of beautiful orange scarlet flowers, from June to August. As it yields no seed, the roots should be taken from the ground in autumn, and returned the ensuing spring.

Magnolia. Most of the species of this justly admired genus are hardy, and blossom in the summer; there are, however, some of the Chinese varieties, which, cultivated in a greenhouse, will produce their beautiful purple, yellow, and white blossoms, from January to April.

Melaleucas. A beautiful genus of plants, natives of New Holland; the diversity of their foliage and singularity of flowers, some of which are scarlet, and shoot from the wood like fringes, render them worthy of good cultivation.

Menettia. This is a desirable climber, of which there are several species; some produce variegated flowers, others bright scarlet, and the variety *cordiflora* is curious as well as beautiful.

Mesembryanthemum. A genus of succulent plants, consisting of hundreds of species and varieties, chiefly natives of the Cape of Good Hope. They vary greatly in their forms, attitudes, and habits of growth; some are upright, others procumbent; some are thick, others cimeter or slender-leaved. They are all singular, and many of them beautiful. The colors of the flowers, which are of every shade, are great ornaments from May to August; some species and varieties are cultivated as annuals in the flower-garden, where they prove a great acquisition.

Metrosideros. A genus of Australasian shrubs, some species of which are willow and others spear-leaved, producing their cones of scarlet or white flowers from March to May.

Myrtus, Myrtle. A genus of dwarf evergreen shrubs, of which there are several species and varieties; the foliage is chiefly glossy and fragrant, yielding numerous small flowers.

There are some species known as Cape Myrtles, or *Marsines*, which also yield abundance of white and purple flowers from March to May.

Nandina domestica, Japan Nandina. A half-hardy evergreen shrub; leaves supra-decompound, with entire lanceolate leaflets; a kind of foliage that is very rare.

Nerium, Oleander. A well known and admired shrub, yielding clusters of rose-like flowers from May to September. The *Nerium splendens* is the most esteemed of the red varieties; the true double white and striped are very rare; but some of those cultivated for sale, producing semi-double flowers, are by no means desirable.

Olea fragrans, Dwarf Olive. This variety of the Olive recommends itself to notice, for its dwarf habit of growth, and from the foliage and white blossoms being highly odoriferous; from March to May.

Passiflora, Passion Flower. Of this celebrated genus of climbing plants, there are several species and varieties, which produce splendid flowers of various colors, red, blue, white, purple, scarlet, etc., beautifully contrasted, and some species yield fruit. They generally blossom from May to September, and some will flower in the hot-house in winter.

Pelargonium, Geranium. The species and varieties of this beautiful genus are supposed to exceed a thousand, which are of every character, color, and lineament, and some so beautifully blended as to astonish the beholder; the agreeable fragrance also, of which many of them are possessed, will always render them favorites to amateur florists. The best blooming season is from April to June or July.

Pittosporum. A Chinese evergreen shrub, with handsome glossy foliage, yielding numerous white clusters of flowers in April and May, which are of delicious fragrance. There are several species, one of which is variegated.

Plumbago capensis, Cape Plumbago. A beautiful dwarf plant, with oblong leaves, yielding numerous spikes of showy blue flowers nearly all the summer.

Polygata cordata, Heart-shaped Polygata. A beautiful little plant, producing abundance of rich purple flowers nearly all the winter.

Protea. A beautiful race of plants, the foliage of which is very diversified, and the flowers also; being red, white, straw, brown, green, and purple, and most of these colors are frequently to be seen on the same plant; in flower from March to June.

Primula. In this genus are embraced all the varieties of the Primrose, Polyanthus, Auricula, Cowslip, Oxlip, etc., already inserted in our Biennial and Perennial catalogues. The flowers, which appear early in spring, are mostly sweet-scented, and of various colors, red, white, yellow, lilac, purple, crimson, etc., which in some are beautifully variegated. The above are natives of England; besides which are two varieties, white and pink, natives of China, producing umbels of flowers from January to May.

Pyrus Japonica alba, or Cydonia Japonica. One of the earliest flowering dwarf shrubs of the garden, producing beautiful blush flowers; there is another variety, which produces scarlet blossoms, already described in our catalogue of shrubs.

Reseda, Mignonette. This fragrant little plant has been already treated of as an annual; it may, however, be kept under cultivation from January to December, by sowing seed at different seasons in a green-house or warm room.

Rhododendron, Rose Bay. A beautiful genus of plants, chiefly natives of India, furnishing clusters of flowers of various shades, as purple, scarlet, or crimson, and these variegated in spots and flakes; in flower from March to May.

Rosea, Rose. This Queen of Flowers, so universally admired, nature seems to have distributed over the whole civilized world; and varieties have been so multiplied of late years, as to render it difficult to make a judicious choice; many of the new varieties, however, being shy bloomers, are not so desirable for green-house culture as the common China Rose, a select assortment of which, carefully cultivated, will produce blossoms from January to December.

Rosmarinus, Rosemary. A fragrant, half-hardy, slender-leaved plant, which has been held in great esteem for ages. In some parts of Europe it is customary to distribute sprigs among the guests at weddings and funerals.

Ruella. A desirable plant, of which there are several species; they produce purple or scarlet tunnel-shaped flowers from December to March.

Salvia, Mexican Sage. A free-blooming plant, producing, in the different species, scarlet and blue flowers in spiked whorls; cuttings of which, if taken from stock plants in the green-house early in spring, and planted in good garden soil, will embellish the borders three or four months of the summer.

Sempervivum arboreum, Tree House Leek. A succulent plant, similar to the common house leek, on a dwarfish stem; by some admired as an evergreen.

Stapelia. A genus of dwarf succulent plants, producing beautiful purple, striped, freckled, and star-like flowers, within six inches of the surface; in its varieties from May to November.

Stevia serrata, Vanilla-scented Stevia. This plant, although usually cultivated as an annual, is worthy of green-house culture, from its affording fragrant and ornamental materials for bouquets the whole winter.

Strelitzia regina, Queen's Strelitz. A beautiful dwarf plant, producing from a stalk, from one to two feet long, several flowers of a bright yellow, contrasted with blue, from May to September.

Tecoma capensis. A perennial plant, producing orange-colored trumpet-flowers in clusters, very similar to the Bigonia tribe, towards the end of summer.

Thea, Tea. Of this celebrated Chinese plant, which supplies a great portion of the human family with their domestic beverage, there are two varieties, *Thea viridis* and *Thea bohea*

The plants, when cultivated in a green-house, are by no means of rapid growth, nor are the flowers, which are white, of any great beauty.

Tussilago fragrans. A half-hardy herbaceous perennial plant, by some much esteemed for its heliotrope-scented blossoms, which spring up in clusters from December to March.

Verbena triphylla, named in some catalogues *Aloysia citriodora.* A deciduous shrub, generally admired for the fragrance of its leaves, which is its chief recommendation, the blossoms, which are white, being small.

Verbena, Splendid Verbena. A tribe of plants increasing in variety annually, and which already embrace every shade of color, scarlet, blue, rose, lilac, white, pink, etc. Planted in the flower-borders, they impart beauty and variety through the summer, and cultivated in the green-house, they embellish it a great part of the winter.

Viburnum tinus, Laurustinus. A much-admired half-hardy evergreen shrub, producing clusters of white blossoms from January to May. There are other species very similar in habit, and one with striped leaves.

Viola, Violet. Of these beauties of the garden, some of which are denominated " Florists' Flowers," there are upwards of a hundred species and varieties. The early Violets are highly fragrant, and the variety and beauty of the Pansy tribe almost exceed description or conception. As these splendid dwarf plants decorate the green-house and flower-borders from January to December, they are worthy of careful cultivation.

Yucca aloe-folia, and its beautiful variety, *variegata*, are desirable plants to cultivate, from their singular appearance, contrasted with other plants. Their blossoms, which are white, grow in spikes, but the plants do not flower much until several years old.

MANAGEMENT OF GREEN-HOUSE PLANTS IN COLD WEATHER.

> "Descending snow, the yellow leaf and sear,
> Are indications of old Time's career;
> The careful florist tends his sheltered plants,
> Studies their nature, and supplies their wants."

Green-house plants will need constant care and attention. When water is necessary, let it be given in mild weather (99). In case of accidents happening from frost, I would remark, that the sudden transition from cold to heat is often more destructive to plants than frost itself. If plants get frozen, and cannot be screened from the rays of the sun, they should be watered as the air becomes warm, and before they begin to thaw. If sufficient attention be paid, so as to have the temperature of the house rise gradually as the water is sprinkled over the leaves, it may be a means of preserving plants that would otherwise be destroyed.

See that the green-house, or room, in which plants are kept, is so secure as to prevent the intrusion of cold air, or the escape of warm air in the night season. All kinds of tender plants in pots should be set into frames or pits, and plunged in old tan or light mould; and in the event of severe frosts, coverings of mats, straw, etc., must be laid over them.

In the early part of October, preparation must be made for the housing of green-house plants. Previous to this being done, let the room or green-house be whitewashed with lime, which will prove pernicious to insects, and prevent their generating among the plants. Begin the first week in this month to place all the shrubby plants, such as Orange and Lemon trees, on the back shelves; others should be so placed that they can be cultivated to advantage; and they should all be arranged in regular gradation, so as to have the low-growing or dwarf plants on the front shelves.

Such green-house plants as may have been repotted and pruned in the course of the last month, should be looked over, and if they have taken root, they should be exposed gradually to the sun, and watered moderately in dry weather. If any of the green-house plants were plunged in the flower-beds, they should be taken up and pruned early in October, and then put into suitable-sized pots. Half-hardy perennials, such as Carnations, Daisies, Primulas, Lilies, Hydrangeas, etc., should be taken up, divided carefully at the roots, and then put into moderate-sized pots, and attended to as before directed for green-house plants. Many hardy kinds of flower seed may be sown this month. This is a good season to propagate all kinds of hardy perennial plants, by parting the roots; and those that were raised from seed in the spring, may be transplanted into regular flower-beds, in cloudy or wet weather. Such Chrysanthemums as are intended to be protected while in blossom, should now be taken up and planted in moderate-sized pots. Before the winter sets in severely, let such Chrysanthemums as may have been cultivated in pots be planted in the garden, or as soon as they have done blossoming.

Mignonette, and other tender seedling plants under protection, will require attention at all seasons. They should not be over-watered, or the plants will perish with mildew.

Camellias should be frequently syringed while in bud, or watered over the foliage with a rose attached to the watering-pot, as should all other shrubby plants.

WATERING GREEN-HOUSE PLANTS.

Temperance in the use of water is of the utmost importance in the winter season, for several reasons which may be given. In the first place, water will attract frost, and, therefore, should be used very sparingly in frosty weather; another consideration is, that in the absence of heat and air, plants cannot absorb much moisture, and, consequently, must become injured from excessive watering; and it may be observed further, that it is not prudent to keep plants in an extremely vigorous state, until the season arrives when the external air is soft and salubrious; they can then have a due proportion of heat, air, and moisture at the same time.

A Fahrenheit thermometer is indispensable in a green-house, or room where plants are kept, and the temperature should be always kept up as nearly as possible to forty degrees, in the absence of the sun. If the gardener retire to rest in this variable climate, leaving the mercury much below forty, he may expect to find his plants frozen in the morning.

A good brick flue is better calculated for heating a small green-house than any other contrivance; because, after a sufficient fire has been made to heat the bricks thoroughly, they will retain the heat through a winter night, whereas an iron stove with its metal pipes will cool as the fire gets low, and expose the plants to cold towards morning, which is the time they most need protection. The heat from iron is, moreover, too dry and parching, while an evaporation or salubrious steam may be raised from bricks, by sprinkling the flue occasionally, which would operate on plants similar to healthful dew-drops.

In cold weather sitting-rooms or parlors are generally heated in the daytime to full twenty degrees higher than what is necessary for the preservation of plants; consequently, as the heat decreases in the night season, plants often get injured, unless a fire is kept up. Air must be admitted to plants kept in this way, at all opportunities; and more water will be necessary for such plants, than those kept in a green-house would require.

Green-house plants will need daily care in hot and dry weather. They should be watered every evening. Such Geraniums as may have grown large and unwieldy, should be pruned, in order that their size and appearance may be improved.

Garden Roses, having done flowering for the season, should also be pruned. Cut out all old exhausted wood, and where it is too thick and crowded, shorten such shoots as have flowered, to a fresh strong eye, or bud, accompanied with a healthy leaf

All wood that grows after this pruning will ripen perfectly, and produce large flowers the ensuing year.

If the weather be warm and dry, it may be necessary to water such flowering shrubs and Roses as were planted in the spring; and if Dahlia plants could be watered two or three times a week, it would be beneficial to their growth. Give regular sprinklings from the rose of a watering-pot, or syringe, to shrubby plants in general, but particularly Camellias, Orange and Lemon trees, etc., in order to keep them in a healthy state.

Bulbous roots in pots, whose foliage has withered, should be kept dry until the period of regermination. Others may be taken up as soon as ripe; after which the offsets may be parted off, and both these and the parent bulbs dried for planting in autumn.

The flower-garden should be kept weeded and watered, and the seeds gathered as they ripen. Apply neat rods to tall-growing and running kinds of plants. Nip off curled and dead leaves, and destroy insects. Hydrangeas, Daisies, Polyanthus, Primulas, etc., should be kept shaded from the noon-day sun, or they will droop, and some may die. Carnations and Pinks will need frequent waterings at the roots, and the branches should be tied neatly to rods.

Such flowering shrubs as may have been planted late in the spring season, should be regularly watered in dry weather. Give frequent waterings to the flower-beds, in general; cut down dead flower-stalks; remove decayed plants, and carefully replace them with vigorous ones from the nursery-bed.

CAMELLIAS, OR JAPAN ROSES.

Camellias, or *Japan Roses.* There are numerous varieties of this valuable class of plants, exhibiting every shade of color, from deep crimson to the purest white; in some imperceptibly blended, in others strikingly contrasted. They are unrivalled objects of beauty from October to May, being set in a fine glossy foliage.

Double Camellias are generally propagated on stocks of the single, which are procured by planting cuttings of the young shoots in light mould under bell-glasses; on these, when grown to a sufficient size, are inarched the finer kinds of double. Sometimes these latter are also struck by cuttings; but as their progress by such method is generally slow and uncertain, it is seldom resorted to. These valuable plants are too often injured by amateurs, from misapplied care bestowed upon them, so that their whole compensation and enjoyment are reduced to the mere possession of a handsome green shrub. Destined, from the extreme beauty and unrivalled delicacy of their flowers, to become the chief pride and ornament of the green-house and drawing-room in the winter season, Camellias should have a fair chance given them to exhibit their fine bloom in perfection.

It should be observed, that Camellias are by no means tender shrubs, but require to be kept in a medium, even temperature, and they generally succeed best in a green-house, where the atmosphere is damp. As the buds begin to swell, they will require more water than at any other time, which may be applied from the rose of a watering-pot, or syringe, while in bud, but when in blossom it should be applied to the earth.

If Camellias be kept where there is dry air occasioned from fire-heat, they must have plenty of the natural air at all opportunities, or the buds will become brown and fall off; and if they are exposed to extreme cold at night, which is too often the case when kept in rooms of an uneven temperature, premature decay of the buds will inevitably be the consequence.

To preserve Camellias in a healthy condition, they should be kept in a fresh, moderately light soil, consisting of sandy loam taken from under grass-sods, and leaf-mould well mixed; nothing being more injurious to them than overpotting, they should not be shifted into larger pots, until the projection of their roots shows evidently that they are in need of it. Few plants bear privation of sunshine in summer better than these; they should, however, be kept in an open situation, where they can have a full share of light and air.

Such bulbous roots as may be in progress of blooming, will require attention in due time; turn them frequently to the light, as recommended on page 95, and increase the supplies of water as they advance towards perfection.

Attend to *Campanula Pyramidalis*, *Hepaticas*, *Mimulus*, *Senecios*, and herbaceous plants in general; those not in bud should be watered very sparingly. Shrubby plants, especially those which bud and blossom in winter, and the early part of spring, as the several varieties of the Acacias, Azaleas, Calceolarias, Correas, Coronillas, Daphnes, Diosmas, Eupatoriums, Eutaxias, Fuchsias, Gnidias, Heaths, Laurustinuses, Lemon trees, Rhododendrons, Orange trees, etc., will require water once or twice a week, according to circumstances, and air should be given at all opportunities, or the plants will not blossom in perfection.

For the benefit of such as may wish to raise early plants from seed, or to force Dahlia or other roots, I subjoin the following brief directions for making a small hot-bed: In a border exposed to the morning sun, let a pit be dug about thirty inches deep, five feet wide, and six long; this will admit of two sashes, each three feet by five. A frame of suitable dimensions may be made of plank; the back plank may be two feet wide, and the end ones sloped so as to make fifteen-inch plank do for the front. The frame being made, set it over the pit, and then get a load of horse-dung, fresh from the livery stables, (not such as has lain long, or may have been soddened with water,) spread it evenly in the pit until full, then put into the frame rich light mould, or compost, to the depth of ten or twelve inches, and the seed may be sown as soon as it gets warm. It may be necessary to observe, that in making hot-beds, the quantity of top mould should be regulated according to the substance of the manure in the pit, and this may vary according to the use the beds are intended for, or to other circumstances. After the seeds are sown, the beds will require constant attention; cover up warm in cold nights, and give air at all opportunities, to prevent the plants from growing weak.

MANAGEMENT OF GREEN-HOUSE PLANTS IN WARM WEATHER.

"The '*Yellow Crocus*,' in her simple dress,
And the '*pale Primrose*,' chaste in loveliness,
Though the fierce Storm King rides upon the gale,
Foretell of Spring, 'midst snow and cutting hail."

As the spring progresses, the external air will be soft and salubrious; at which time it should be freely admitted to plants kept in rooms and green-houses. In proportion as the plants get air, they should have water applied from the rose of a watering-pot.

Monthly Roses will require attention this month. It should be recollected, that it is from the young wood of these plants that buds are to be expected; their growth should, therefore, be encouraged, by admitting sun and air at all opportunities, and water when necessary.

Primulas. There are several species of plants under this name, which exhibit their blossoms in March and April; some of which are very beautiful, as the Polyanthus, English Spring Flowers, Auricula, etc.; but I would now direct the reader's attention to the Chinese varieties, some of which are pure white, and others of a lilac color. They are first raised from seed sown in the spring, and will keep two or three years.

Plants that are full grown, will commence blooming in December, and continue to produce umbels of flowers for five or six months, if well attended to; they are generally in their prime this month, at which time a little water should be applied to the earth about twice a week.

Many species and varieties of seed may be sown in hot-beds prepared as previously directed.

Auricula, Polyanthus, and all other species of *Primula* seed, should now be sown. Mignonette, Ten Week Stock, and Dahlia seed, from choice varieties, may also be sown in pots, and care should be taken, when the plants are up, that they be not injured by excess of moisture.

There are some splendid varieties of the Schizanthus which deserve attention at an early season. They are rather difficult of cultivation in pots, being apt to suffer by excess of heat or moisture; and often, when in full bloom, die off suddenly by decays at the bottom of the stem. No plants will, however, more amply repay all the care and trouble that may be bestowed on them, than those of the elegant genus Schizanthus. The best soil for them is loam and leaf-mould, with a small portion of sand. They should be repotted as often as the pots are filled with roots, till they come into full flower.

All the different varieties of tender annual, biennial, and perennial flower seed, designated thus § and thus † in our Catalogues, pages 99 and 118, may be sown early in hot-beds, or in pots kept in the green-house.

Hyacinths, Narcissus, and other bulbs in glasses, must have the water shifted every week, and the glasses should be thoroughly washed every two or three weeks.

Towards the end of the month, roots of *Amaryllis formosissima*, *Gladiolus psittacinna*, Tiger Flower, Tuberose, and such other bulbs as may have been preserved dry through the winter, may now be planted in pots and kept in a green-house or light room, or else plunged in a hot-bed. Those who have no such conveniences may, however, delay the planting of sound bulbs, until the weather will admit of their being planted in warm borders in the spring of the year.

Dahlia roots should be plunged in a hot-bed, to forward

them, with a view to their being separated as soon as the eyes are discernible.

As the warm weather progresses, the gardener should be on the alert, in order to conquer the various kinds of insects. Burn tobacco leaves in the green-house, so as to fumigate the plants well, before they are removed into the open garden; and such plants as may show any indications of being infested with the eggs of insects, should be sponged with soap-suds, and afterwards well syringed and watered. Frequent sprinkling from the rose of a watering-pot will prevent insects from accumulating; especially if the water be impregnated with tobacco, by a bag of the leaves being steeped therein a few hours previous to using it.

Choice Geraniums will need timely attention in order that they may exhibit their flowers to advantage. When in full bloom, care should be taken not to wet the foliage or flowers; but this may be done freely before the buds are expanded.

TIME TO TRANSPLANT GREEN-HOUSE FLOWERS.

Green-house plants may be set out early in the growing season, and it should be done in cloudy weather, in order that they may be prepared gradually for the shining of the sun upon them. A situation exposed to the sun for only one-half the day is preferable for most plants, especially if they can be shaded at noon.

Many plants, such as Coronillas, Heaths, Aucubas, Myrtles, Oleanders, and several other sorts, are subject to be infested with white and brown scaly insects; if these cannot be effectually taken from the plants by washing and sponging, let the plants be headed down early in the month of May, and if they are well attended to, new branches will shoot out on the old stem.

Such Orange trees as were budded last July or August should be headed down early in the spring. Auriculas, Polyanthus, and Daisies, should be separated into single tufts, and planted in a shady border for increase, as soon as they have done blossoming. Such Carnations as may have been wintered in frames should now be exposed to the open air, in the flower-borders. Tulips, which will be in full perfection in the fore part of the season, will require constant attention. Such green-house plants as may have done blossoming may be pruned carefully, and if the cuttings be planted at this time they will strike freely. Cuttings of *Salvia splendens* and *fulgens* will produce strong plants for blossoming in August, if planted early in the season. Chrysanthemum cuttings should now be put down, and the suckers divided, and planted singly in borders, or in pots, for flowering in the autumn.

Those who may have a number of plants in various sized pots, should provide a few new pots a size larger than the largest in use; the largest plants being shifted into the new pots, leaves the next sized pots for the second sized plants, and by pursuing this plan of shifting until the whole are done, the smallest pots will be left for such plants as have been propagated in the course of the summer.

The shifting of plants requires considerable attention and judgment, as some plants, if kept in too large pots, will sustain considerable injury; therefore, in such cases, where the fibrous roots have not spread around the pot, nothing more is necessary than to rub off a little of the outside mould, and then to substitute fresh compost for the roots to run in.

Such plants as may have become pot-bound, and whose roots are matted around the pot, will, in many cases, bear reducing. If the matted roots are carefully pared off, and the plants shifted into good fresh compost, they will soon take root, and grow freely; but it will be necessary to prune off all surplus branches of the plants previous to repotting them.

and to shade them for a week or ten days. Pieces of tile, or broken pots, should be laid over the aperture at the bottom of the pots, to enable the surplus moisture to drain off, or the roots will sustain injury.

CHAPTER II.

AN OUTLINE OF THE PRINCIPLES OF HORTICULTURE.

By JOHN LINDLEY, F.R.S.,
Professor of Botany in the University of London, and Associate Secretary of the Horticultural Society.

I. General Nature of Plants.

1. Horticulture is the application of the arts of cultivation, multiplication, and domestication to the vegetable kingdom. Horticulture and Arboriculture are branches of Agriculture.

2. The vegetable kingdom is composed of living beings, destitute of sensation, with no power of moving spontaneously from place to place, and called plants.

3. Plants are organized bodies, consisting of masses of tissue, which is permeable by fluids or gaseous matter.

4. Vegetable tissue consists either of minute bladders, or tubes adhering by their contiguous surfaces, and leaving intermediate passages where they do not touch.

5. Tissue is called *Cellular* when it is composed of minute bladders, which either approach the figure of a sphere, or are obviously some modification of it, supposed to be caused by extension or lateral compression.

6. When newly formed it is in a very lax state, and possesses great powers of absorption, probably on account of the excessive permeability of its membrane, and the imperfect cohesion of its cells.

7. Cellular tissue, otherwise called Parenchyma, constitutes

the soft and brittle parts of plants, such as pith, pulp, the spaces between the veins of leaves, and the principal part of the petals.

8. Succulent plants are such as have an excessive development of cellular tissue.

9. It may be considered the most essential kind of tissue, because, while no plants exist without it, many are composed of nothing else.

10. Tissue is called *Woody Fibre* when it is composed of slender tubes, which are conical and closed at each end, and placed side by side.

11. Woody fibre is what causes stiffness and tenacity in certain parts of plants; hence it is found in the veins of leaves, and in bark, and it constitutes the principal part of the wood.

12. *Vascular Tissue* is that in which either an elastic tough thread is generated spirally within a tube that is closed and conical at each end; or rows of cylindrical cellules, placed end to end, finally become continuous tubes by the loss of their ends.

13. The most remarkable form of vascular tissue is the *Spiral Vessel*, which has the power of rolling with elasticity when stretched.

14. Other kinds of vascular tissue are incapable of unrolling, but break when stretched.

15. Spiral vessels are not found in the wood or bark, and rarely in the roots of plants.

16. Vascular tissue of other kinds is confined to the root, stem, veins of leaves, petals, and other parts composed of leaves. It is not found in bark.

17. The common office of the tissue is to convey fluid or air, and to act as the receptacle of secretions.

18. Cellular tissue conveys fluids in all directions, absorbs with great rapidity, is the first cause of the adhesions that take place between contiguous parts, and is the principal receptacle of secreted matter.

19. Adhesion will take place at all times during the growing

season, when the cellular tissues of two different parts, or of two different plants, are kept for some time in contact; but as none but tissues of nearly the same nature will adhere, grafting and budding, which are caused by the adhesion of contiguous parts, can only take place either between different varieties of the same species, or between nearly related species; and even then only when the corresponding parts of the scion or bud and the stock are placed in contact.

20. Woody fibre conveys fluid in the direction of its length, gives stiffness and flexibility to the general system, and acts as a protection to spiral and other delicate vessels.

21. Spiral vessels convey oxygenated air.

22. Other vessels probably conduct fluid when young, and air when old.

23. As the bodies of which all tissue is composed are perfectly simple, unbranched, and regular in figure, having, when elongated, their two extremities exactly alike, they are more or less capable of conveying gaseous matter or fluids in any direction, and, consequently, a current may be reversed in them without inconvenience; hence inverted cuttings or stems will grow.

[If cuttings will grow when the top ends are stuck in the ground, I have never had the satisfaction of seeing them. I have often heard that sprouts of trees and bushes will grow with the top end down, but I have never met with a person who has seen such a thing.—S. Edwards Todd.]

24. All parts of plants are composed of tissue, whether they be soft, as pulp, or hard, as the bony lining of a peach.

25. With regard to Horticultural operations, the parts of plants should be considered under the heads of *Root* (II.); *Stem* (III.); *Leaf Buds* (IV.); *Leaves* (V.); *Flowers* (VI.), *Sexes* (VII.); *Fruit* (VIII.); and *Seed* (IX.).

II. Root.

26. The Root is the part that strikes into the earth when a seed begins to germinate, and which afterwards continues to lengthen beneath the soil.

27. It is also the part which is sometimes emitted by the stem, for the purpose of absorbing nutriment from the atmosphere; as in Ivy, Air-plants, Vines, etc.

28. It is distinguished from the stem by the absence of leaves in any state; of regular leaf-buds (IV.); of evaporating pores or stomata (131); and of pith in Exogenous plants.

29. Therefore, such underground bodies as those called Tuber (61) in the Potato, Bulb (96) in the Onion, and solid Bulb or Cormus (61) in the Crocus, are not roots.

30. The office of the root is to absorb food in a fluid or gaseous state; and also to fix the plant in the soil, or to some firm support.

31. The latter office is essential to the certain and regular performance of the former.

32. It is not by the whole of their surface that roots absorb food; but only by their young and newly formed extremities, called *Spongioles.*

33. Hence the preservation of the spongioles in an uninjured state is essential to the removal of a plant from one place to another.

34. A spongiole consists of very young vascular tissue (12) surrounded by very young cellular substance (5).

[Some modern botanists discard entirely the idea that there are *spongioles* on the ends of roots. Dr. Webster says that spongioles are *supposed* expansions of minute parts, at the termination of radicles, resembling a sponge, for absorbing the nutriment of plants.—S. Edwards Todd.]

35. Spongioles secrete excrementitious matter, which is unsuitable to the same species afterwards as food; for poisonous

6*

substances are as fatal to the species that secrete them as to any other species.

36. Hence whatever is known to produce any specific deleterious action upon leaves or stems, such as certain gases (298) and mineral or vegetable poisons, will produce a much more fatal effect upon the spongioles.

37. These organs have no power of selecting their food, but will absorb whatever the earth or air may contain, which is sufficiently fluid to pass through the sides of their tissue.

38. So that if the spongioles are developed in a medium which is of an unsuitable nature, as they will still continue to absorb, they cannot fail to introduce matter which will prove either injurious or fatal to life, according to its intensity.

39. This may often explain why trees suddenly become unhealthy, without any external apparent cause.

40. Plants have the power of replacing spongioles by the formation of new ones; so that an individual is not destroyed by their loss.

41. But this power depends upon the cooperation of the atmosphere, and upon the special vital powers of the species.

42. If the atmosphere is so humid as to hinder evaporation, spongioles will have time to form anew; but if the atmosphere is dry, the loss by evaporation will be so much greater than can be supplied by the injured roots, that the whole system will be emptied of fluid before the new spongioles can form.

43. This is the key to Transplantation.

44. As roots are destitute of leaf-buds, and as leaf-buds are essential to the multiplication of an individual (108), it should follow that roots can never be employed for the purpose of multiplication.

45. Nevertheless, roots when woody have, occasionally, the power of generating adventitious leaf-buds (IV.); and when this is the case, they may be employed for the purpose of multiplication; as those of Cydonia Japonica, etc.

46. The cause of this power existing in some species, and not in others, is unknown.

47. It is therefore a power that can never be calculated upon, and whose existence is only to be discovered by accident.

48. Although roots are generated under ground, and sometimes at considerable depths, yet access to a certain quantity of atmospheric air appears indispensable to the healthy execution of their functions. This is constantly exemplified in plants growing in the earth at the back of an ill-ventilated forcing-house, where the roots have no means of finding their way into the earth on the outside of the house.

49. It is supposed by some that the introduction of oxygen into their system is as indispensable to them as to animals.

50. It seems more probable that the oxygen of the atmosphere, seizing upon a certain quantity of carbon, forms carbonic acid, which they absorb and feed upon.

51. It is at least certain that the exclusion of air from the roots will always induce an unhealthy condition, or even death itself. This may be one of the reasons why stiff tenacious soils are seldom suited to the purposes of the cultivator, until their adhesiveness has been destroyed by the addition of other matter.

52. It is therefore one of the most delicate parts of plants, and the most easily injured.

53. But to the other species the excrementitious matter is either not unsuitable or not deleterious.

54. Hence soil may be rendered impure (or, as we inaccurately say, worn out) for one species, which will not be impure for others.

55. This is the true key of the theory of rotation of crops.

56. This also may serve to explain in part why light soil is indispensable to many plants, and heavy or tenacious soil suitable to so few; for in the former case the spongioles will meet with little resistance to their elongation, and will consequently be continually leaving the place where their excrementitious matter is deposited; while in the latter case, the reverse will occur.

III. Stem.

57. The Stem is that part of a plant which is developed above ground, and which took an upward direction at the period of germination.

58. In consists of a woody axis, covered by bark having stomata (131) on its surface, bearing leaves with leaf-buds in their axillæ, and producing flowers and fruit.

59. The points where leaves are borne are called *Nodi;* the spaces between the leaves are *Internodia.*

60. The more erect a stem grows, the more vigorous it is; and the more it deviates from this direction to a horizontal or pendulous position, the less is it vigorous.

61. Some stems are developed under ground, such as the Tubers of the Potato and the Cormus of the Crocus; but they are known from roots by the presence of leaves, and regular leaf-buds, upon their surface.

62. Stems increase in diameter in two ways.

63. Either by the addition of new matter to the outside of the wood and the inside of the bark; when they are *Exogenous;* ex. Oak.

64. Or by the addition of new matter to their inside; when they are *Endogenous;* ex. Cane.

65. In Exogenous stems, the central portion, which is harder and darker than that at the circumference, is called *Heart Wood;* while the exterior, which is softer and lighter, is called *Alburnum*, or *Sap Wood.*

66. The inside of the bark of such stems has also the technical name of *Liber.*

67. The heart wood was, when young, Alburnum, and afterwards changed its nature by becoming the receptacle of certain secretions peculiar to the species.

68. Hence the greater durability of heart wood than of sap wood. While the latter is newly formed empty tissue, almost as perishable as bark itself, the former is protected against

destruction by the introduction of secretions that become solid matter, which is often insoluble in water, and never permeable to air.

69. The secretions by which heart wood is solidified are prepared in the leaves, whence they are sent downwards through the bark, and from the bark communicated to the central part of the stem.

70. The channels through which this communication takes place are called *Medullary Rays*, or *Silver Grain.*

71. Medullary rays are plates of cellular tissue, in a very compressed state, passing from the pith into the bark.

72. The wood itself is composed of tubes consisting of woody fibre and vascular tissue, imbedded longitudinally in cellular substance.

73. This cellular substance only develops horizontally; and it is to it that the peculiar character of different kinds of wood is chiefly due.

74. For this reason the wood of the stock of a grafted plant will never become like that of its scion, although, as will be hereafter seen (IV.), the woody matter of the stock must all originate in the scion.

75. The stem of an exogenous plant may therefore be compared to a piece of linen, of which the weft is composed of cellular tissue, and the warp of fibrous and vascular tissue.

76. In the spring and autumn a viscid substance is secreted between the wood and the liber, called the *Cambium.*

77. This cambium appears to be the matter out of which the cellular horizontal substance of the stem is organized.

78. In Endogenous stems the portion at the circumference is harder than that in the centre; and there is no separable bark.

79. Their stems consist of bundles of woody matter, imbedded in cellular tissue, and composed of vascular tissue surrounded by woody fibre.

80. The stem is not only the depository of the peculiar secretions of species (67), but is also the medium through

which the sap flows in its passage from the roots into the leaves.

81. In exogenous stems (63) it certainly rises through the alburnum, and descends through the bark.

82. In endogenous stems (64) it probably rises through the bundles of wood, and descends through the cellular substance; but this is uncertain.

83. Stems have the power of propagating an individual only by means of their Leaf-buds. If destitute of leaf-buds, they have no power of multiplication, except fortuitously.

IV. Leaf-buds.

84. Leaf-buds are rudiments of branches, inclosed within scales, which are imperfectly formed leaves.

85. All the leaf-buds upon the same branch are constitutionally and anatomically the same.

86. They are of two kinds; namely, *regular* or *normal*, and *adventitious* or *latent* (119).

87. Regular leaf-buds are formed at the axillæ of leaves.

88. They are organs capable of propagating the individual from which they originate.

89. They are at first nourished by the fluid lying in the pith, but finally establish for themselves a communication with the soil by the woody matter which they send downward.

90. Their force of development will be in proportion to their nourishment; and, consequently, when it is wished to procure a young shoot of unusual vigor, all other shoots in the vicinity are prevented growing, so as to accumulate for one shoot only all the food that would otherwise have been consumed by several.

91. Cutting back to a few eyes is an operation in pruning to produce the same effect, by directing the sap, as it ascends, into two or three buds only, instead of allowing it to expend itself upon all the others which are cut away.

92. When leaf-buds grow, they develop in three directions;

the one horizontal, the other upwards, and the third down wards.

93. The horizontal development is confined to the cellular system of the bark, pith, and medullary rays.

94. The upward and downward developments are confined to the woody fibre and vascular tissue.

95. In this respect they resemble seed; from which they differ physiologically in propagating the individual, while seed can only propagate the species.

96. When they disarticulate from the stem that bears them, they are called *Buds.*

97. In some plants, a bud, when separated from its stem, will grow and form a new plant if placed in circumstances favorable to the preservation of its vital powers.

98. But this property seems confined to plants having a firm, woody, perennial stem.

99. Such buds, when detached from their parent stem, send roots downwards and a stem upwards.

100. But if the buds are not separated from the plant to which they belong, the matter they send downwards becomes wood and liber (66), and the stems they send upwards become branches. Hence it is said that wood and liber are formed by the roots of leaf-buds.

101. If no leaf-buds are called into action, there will be no addition of wood; and, consequently, the destruction or absence of leaf-buds is accompanied by the absence of wood; as is proved by a shoot, the upper buds of which are destroyed and the lower allowed to develop. The lower part of the shoot will increase in diameter; the upper will remain of its original dimensions.

102. The quantity of wood, therefore, depends upon the quantity of leaf-buds that develop.

103. It is of the greatest importance to bear this in mind in pruning timber trees; for excessive pruning must necessarily be injurious to the quantity of produce.

104. If a cutting with a leaf-bud on it be placed in circum-

stances fitted to the development of the latter, it will grow and become a new plant.

105. If this happens when the cutting is inserted in the earth, the new plant is said by gardeners to be *upon its own bottom.*

106. But if it happens when the cutting is applied to the dissevered end of another individual, called a *stock,* the roots are insinuated into the tissue of the stock, and a plant is said to be *grafted,* the cutting being called a *scion.*

107. There is, therefore, little difference between cuttings and scions, except that the former root into the earth, the latter into another plant.

108. But if a cutting of the same plant without a leaf-bud upon it be placed in the same circumstances, it will not grow, but will die.

109. Unless its vital powers are sufficient to enable it to develop an adventitious leaf-bud (119).

110. A leaf-bud separated from the stem will also become a new individual, if its vital energy is sufficiently powerful.

111. And this whether it is planted in earth, into which it roots like a cutting, or in a new individual, to which it adheres and grows like a scion. In the former case it is called an *eye,* in the latter a *bud.*

112. Every leaf-bud has, therefore, its own distinct system of life and of growth.

113. And as all the leaf-buds of an individual are exactly alike, it follows that a plant is a collection of a great number of distinct identical systems of life, and, consequently, a compound individual.

114. Regular leaf-buds being generated in the axillæ of the leaves, it is there that they are always to be sought.

115. And if they cannot be discovered by ocular inspection, it may nevertheless be always inferred with confidence that they exist in such situations, and may possibly be called from their dormant state into life.

116. Hence, wherever the scar of a leaf, or the remains of a

leaf, can be discovered, there it is to be understood that the rudiments exist of a system of life which may be, by favorable circumstances, called into action.

117. Hence, all parts upon which leaves have ever grown may be made use of for purposes of propagation.

118. From these considerations it appears that the most direct analogy between the Animal and Vegetable kingdoms is with the Polypi of the former.

119. Adventitious leaf-buds are in all respects like regular leaf-buds, except that they are not formed at the axillæ of leaves, but develop occasionally from all and any part of a plant.

120. They are occasionally produced by roots, by solid wood, or even by leaves and flowers.

121. Hence roots, solid wood, or even leaves and flowers, may be used as means of propagation.

122. But as the development of adventitious buds is extremely uncertain, such means of propagation can never be calculated on, and form no part of the *science* of cultivation.

123. The cause of the formation of adventitious leaf-buds is unknown.

124. From certain experiments it appears that they may be generated by sap in a state of great accumulation and activity.

125. Consequently, whatever tends to the accumulation of sap in an active state may be expected to be conducive to the formation of adventitious leaf-buds.

V. Leaves.

126. Leaves are expansions of bark, traversed by veins.

127. The veins consist of spiral vessels inclosed in woody fibre; they originate in the medullary sheath and liber; and they are connected by loose parenchyma (7), which is full of cavities containing air.

128. This parenchyma consists of two layers, of which the upper is composed of cellules perpendicular to the cuticle, and the lower of cellules parallel with the cuticle.

129. These cellules are arranged so as to leave numerous open passages among them for the circulation of air in the inside of a leaf. Parenchyma of this nature is called *cavernous.*

130. Cuticle is formed of one or more layers of depressed cellular tissue, which is generally hardened, and always dry and filled with air.

131. Between many of the cells of the cuticle are placed apertures, called *stomata,* which have the power of opening and closing as circumstances may require.

132. It is by means of this apparatus that leaves elaborate the sap which they absorb from the alburnum, converting it into the secretions peculiar to the species.

133. Their cavernous structure (129) enables them to expose the greatest possible surface of their parenchyma to the action of the atmosphere.

134. Their cuticle is a non-conducting skin, which protects them from great variations in temperature, and through which gaseous matter will pass readily.

135. Their stomata are pores that are chiefly intended to facilitate evaporation; for which they are well adapted by a power they possess of opening or closing as circumstances may require.

136. They are also intended for facilitating the rapid emission of air, when it is necessary that such a function should be performed.

137. The functions of stomata being of such vital importance, it is always advisable to examine them microscopically in cases where doubts are entertained of the state of the atmosphere which a particular species may require.

138. Leaves growing in air are covered with a cuticle.

139. Leaves growing under water have no cuticle.

140. All the secretions of plants being formed in the leaves, or at least the greater part, it follows that secretions cannot take place if leaves are destroyed.

141. And as this secreting property depends upon specific vital powers connected with the decomposition of carbonic

acid, and called into action only when the leaves are freely exposed to light and air (279), it also follows that the quantity of secretion will be in direct proportion to the quantity of leaves, and to their free exposure to light and air.

142. The usual position of leaves is spiral, at regularly increasing or diminishing distances; they are then said to be alternate.

143. But if the space, or the axis, that separates two leaves is reduced to nothing at alternate intervals, they become opposite.

144. And if the spaces that separate several leaves be reduced to nothing, they become verticillate.

145. Opposite and verticillate leaves, therefore, differ from alternate leaves only in the spaces that separate them being reduced to nothing.

VI. Flowers.

146. Flowers consist of two principal parts, namely, *Floral Envelopes* (149), and *Sexes* (VII.).

147. Of these, the former constitute what is popularly considered the flower; although the latter are the only parts that are absolutely essential to it.

148. However different they may be in appearance from leaves, they are all formed of those organs in a more or less modified state, and altered in greater or less degree by mutual adhesion.

149. The floral envelopes consist of two or more whorls of transformed leaves; of which part is calyx, its leaves being called sepals, and part corolla, its leaves being called petals.

150. The sexes are also transformed leaves (187).

151. The calyx is always the outermost, the corolla is always the innermost whorls; and if there is but one floral envelope, that one is calyx.

152. Usually the calyx is green, and the corolla colored and

more highly developed; but the reverse is frequently the case, as in Fuchsia, Ribes sanguineum, etc.

153. A flower being, then, an axis surrounded by leaves, it is in reality a stunted branch; that is, one the growth of which is checked, and its power of elongation destroyed.

154. That flowers are stunted branches is proved, first, by all their parts, especially the most external, occasionally reverting to the state of ordinary leaves; secondly, by their parts being often transformed into each other; and, thirdly, by the whorls of flower-buds being dislocated and actually converted into branches whenever anything occurs to stimulate them excessively.

155. Their most essential distinctive character consists in the buds at the axillæ of their leaves being usually dormant, while those in the axillæ of ordinary leaves are usually active.

156. For this reason, while leaf-buds can be used for the purpose of propagation, flower-buds cannot usually be so employed.

157. Being stunted branches, their position on the stem is the same as that of developed branches.

158. And as there is in all plants a very great difference in the development of leaf-buds, some growing readily into branches, others only unfolding their leaves without elongating, and many remaining altogether dormant, it follows that flower-buds may form upon plants of whatever age and in whatever state.

159. But to produce a general formation of flower-buds it is necessary that there should be some general predisposing constitutional cause, independent of accidental circumstances.

160. This predisposing cause is the accumulation of sap and of secreted matter.

161. Therefore, whatever tends to retard the free flow of sap, and causes it to accumulate, will cause the production of flower-buds, or fertility.

162. And, on the other hand, whatever tends to produce excessive vigor, causes the dispersion of sap, or prevents its elaboration, and causes sterility.

163. Transplantation with a partial destruction of roots, age,

or high temperature accompanied by a dry atmosphere, training obliquely or in an inverted direction, a constant destruction of the extremities of young growing branches, will all cause an accumulation of sap, and secretions; and, consequently, all such circumstances are favorable to the production of flower-buds.

164. But a richly manured soil, high temperature, with great atmospheric humidity, or an uninterrupted flow of sap, are all causes of excessive vigor, and are consequently unfavorable to the producing of flower-buds.

165. There is a tendency in many flowers to enlarge, to alter their colors, or to change their appearance by transformation and multiplication of their parts, whenever they have been raised from seed for several generations, or domesticated.

166. The causes of this tendency are probably various, but, being entirely unknown, no certain rules for the production of varieties in flowers can be laid down, except by the aid of hybridizing (201).

167. It often happens that a single branch produces flowers different from those produced on other branches. This is technically called a *sport*.

168. As every bud on that branch has the same specific vital principle (113), a bud taken from such a branch will produce an individual, the whole of whose branches will retain the character of the sport.

169. Consequently by buds an accidental variety may be made permanent, if the plant that sports be of a firm woody nature (98).

170. As flowers feed upon the prepared sap in their vicinity, the greater the abundance of this prepared food, the more perfect will be their development.

171. Or, the fewer the flowers on a given branch, the more food they will severally have to nourish them, and the more perfect will they be.

172. The beauty of flowers will therefore be increased either by an abundant supply of food, or by a diminution of their num-

bers (thinning), or by both. The business of the pruner is to cause these by his operation.

173. The beauty of flowers depends upon their free exposure to light and air, because it consists in the richness of their colors, and their colors are only formed by the action of these two agents (281).

174. Hence flowers produced in dark or shaded confined situations are either imperfect or destitute of their habitual size and beauty.

175. Double flowers are those in which the stamens are transformed into petals; or in which the latter, or the sepals, are multiplied. They should not be confounded with *Proliferous* (183) and *Discoid Compound Flowers* (184).

176. Although no certain rules for the production of double flowers can be laid down, yet it is probable that those flowers have the greatest tendency to become double in which the sexes are habitually multiplied.

177. In Icosandrous and Polyandrous plants either the stamens or the pistilla are always very numerous when the flowers are in a natural state; and it is chiefly in such plants that double flowers occur when they become transformed.

178. It is therefore in such plants that double flowers are to be principally expected.

179. In proportion as the sexes of flowers habitually become few in number, do the instances of double flowers become rare.

180. Double flowers are therefore least to be expected in plants with fewest stamens.

181. Whenever the component parts of a flower adhere by their edges, as in monophyllous calyxes, monopetalous corollas, and monadelphous, or di-, or poly-adelphous stamens, the tendency to an unnatural multiplication of parts seems checked.

182. Therefore, in such cases, double flowers are little to be expected; they are, in fact, very rare.

183. Proliferous flowers are those in which parts that usually have all their axillary buds dormant accidentally develop such buds; as in the Hen and Chickens Daisy, in which the

bracteæ of the involucrum form other Daisy-heads in their axillæ; or, as in certain Roses, in which the capillary leaves develop leaf-buds in their axillæ, so that the flower becomes a branch the lower leaves of which are colored and transformed, and the upper green, and in their ordinary state.

184. Discoid compound flowers are those in which the cen tral florets of a flower-head acquire corollas, like those of the circumference, as in the Dahlia; the cultivated variety of which should be called discoid, and not double.

185. These two last are so essentially different from double flowers, that whatever laws may be supposed to govern the production or amelioration of double flowers, can have no relation to proliferous or discoid compound flowers.

VII. Sexes.

186. The sexes consist of two or more whorls of transformed leaves, of which the outer are called *Stamens* (188), and the inner *Pistillum* (191).

187. They are known to be modifications of leaves, because they very frequently are transformed into petals, which are demonstrably such (149), and because they occasionally revert to the state of leaves.

188. The stamens bear at their apex an organ, called the *anther*, which contains a powder called *pollen.*

189. When the anther is full grown it opens and emits the pollen, either dispersing it in the air in consequence of the elasticity with which it opens; or depositing it upon the stigmata (191); or exposing it to the action of wind, or such other disturbing causes as may liberate it from its case.

190. The pollen consists of exceedingly minute hollow balls, or cases, containing myriads of moving particles, which are the fertilizing principle of the stamens.

191. The pistillum has at its base one or more cavities or *cells*, in which bodies called *ovula* are placed; and at its apex one or more secreting surfaces, called *stigmata.*

192. The ovula are the rudiments of seed.

193. If the fertilizing powder of the pollen comes in contact with the stigmata, the ovula in the cells of the pistillum are vivified, and become seed.

194. But if this contact does not take place, the ovula cannot possibly be vivified, but shrivel up and perish.

195. The phenomenon of vivification takes place in consequence of the descent of a portion of the moving particles (190) of the pollen into the ovula, where such particles form the commencement of future plants.

196. In wild plants, stigmata is usually acted upon only by the pollen of the stamens which belong to it.

197. In this case, the seed thus vivified will, when sown, produce new individuals, differing very little from that by which they were themselves produced.

198. And, therefore, wild plants are for the most part multiplied from generation to generation without change.

199. But it is possible to cause deviations from this law by artificial means.

200. If the pollen of one species be placed upon the stigmata of another species, the ovula will be vivified; and what is called a *hybrid* plant will be produced by those ovula when they shall have grown to be seed.

201. Hybrid plants are different from both their parents, and are generally intermediate in character between them.

202. They have little power of perpetuating themselves by seed; but they may, if woody, be perpetuated by cuttings (312), buds (354), scions (335), etc.

203. Therefore, no hybrids but such as are of a woody perennial character can be perpetuated.

204. It usually happens that the hybrid has the constitution and general aspect of the polliniferous parent; but is influenced in secondary characters by the peculiarity of the female parent

205. This should always be borne in mind in procuring new hybrid plants.

206. Really hybrid plants must not be confounded with

such as are spurious, in consequence of their origin being between two varieties of the same species, and not two species of the same genus.

207. Hybrid plants, although incapable of perpetuation by seed, are often more abundant flowerers than either parent.

208. This is, probably, connected with constitutional debility (162).

VIII. Fruit.

209. Fruit, strictly speaking, is the pistillum arrived at maturity.

210. When the calyx adheres to the pistillum, and grows with it to maturity, the fruit is called *inferior;* as the Apple.

211. But when the pistillum alone ripens, there being no adhesion to it on the part of the calyx, the fruit is called *superior;* as the Peach.

212. The fruit is, therefore, in common language, the flower, or some part of it, arrived at its most complete state of existence; and, consequently, is itself a portion of a stunted branch (153).

213. The nature of its connexion with the stem is therefore the same as that of the branches with each other, or of leaves with their stem.

214. A superior fruit consisting only of one, or of a small number of metamorphosed leaves, it has little or no power of forming a communication with the earth, and of feeding itself, as real branches have (89).

215. It has also very little adhesion to its branch; so that but slight causes are sufficient to detach it from the plant, especially at an early age, when all its parts are tender.

216. Hence the difficulty of causing Peaches and the like to *stone*, or to pass over that age in which the vascular bundles that join them to the branch become woody, and secure them to their place.

217. For the same reason they are fed almost entirely by

other parts, upon secreted matter which they attract to themselves, elaborate, and store up in the cavities of their tissue.

218. The office of feeding such fruit is performed by young branches, which transmit nutriment to it through the bark (69).

219. But as young branches can only transmit nutriment downwards, it follows that, unless a fruit is formed on a part of a branch below a leaf-bud, it must perish.

220. Unless there is some active vegetation in the stem above the branch on which it grows; when it may possibly live and feed upon secretions attracted by it from the main stem.

221. But inferior fruit, consisting at least of the calyx in addition to the pistillum, has a much more powerful communication with the branch; each division of its calyx having *at least* one bundle of vascular and fibrous tissue, passing from it into the branch, and acting as a stay upon the centre to prevent its breaking off.

222. Such fruit may be supposed much more capable of establishing a means of attracting secretions from a distance; and, consequently, is less liable to perish from want of a supply of food.

223. It is therefore not so important that an inferior fruit should be furnished with growing branches above it.

224. Fruit is exclusively fed by the secretions prepared for it by other parts; it is therefore affected by nearly the same circumstances as flowers.

225. It will be large in proportion to the quantity of food the stem can supply to it; and small in proportion to the inability of the stem to nourish it.

226. For this reason, when trees are weak, they should be allowed to bear very little, if any, fruit; because a crop of fruit can only tend to increase their debility.

227. And in all cases each fruit should be so far separated from all others as not to be robbed of its food by those in its vicinity.

228. We find that nature has herself in some measure pro-

vided against injury to plants by excessive fecundity, in giving them a power of throwing off flowers, the fruit of which cannot be supported.

229. The flavor of fruit depends upon the existence of certain secretions, especially of acid and sugar; flavor will, consequently, be regulated by the circumstances under which fruit is ripened.

230. The ripening of fruit is the conversion of acid and other substances into sugar.

231. As the latter substance cannot be obtained at all in the dark, is less abundant in fruit ripened in diffused light, and most abundant in fruit exposed to the direct rays of the sun, the conversion of matter into sugar occurs under the same circumstances as the decomposition of carbonic acid (141 and 279).

232 Therefore, if fruit be produced in situations much exposed to the sun, its sweetness will be augmented.

233. And in proportion as it is deprived of the sun's direct rays, that quality will diminish.

234. So that a fruit which, when exposed to the sun, is sweet, when grown where no direct light will reach it will be acid, as Pears, Cherries, etc.

235. Hence acidity may be corrected by exposure to light, and excessive sweetness or insipidity by removal from light.

236. It is the property of succulent fruits which are acid when wild, to acquire sweetness when cultivated, losing part of their acid.

237. This probably arises from the augmentation of the cellular tissue, which possibly has a greater power than woody or vascular tissue of assisting in the formation of sugar.

238. As a certain quantity of acid is essential to render fruit agreeable to the palate, and as it is the property of cultivated fruits to add to their saccharine matter, but not to form more acid than when wild, it follows that, in selecting wild fruits for domestication, those which are acid should be preferred, and those which are sweet or insipid rejected.

239. Unless recourse is had to hybridism, when a wild

insipid fruit may possibly be improved (204), or may be the means of improving something else.

240. It is very much upon such considerations as the foregoing that the rules of training must depend

IX. Seed.

241. The seed is the ovulum arrived at perfection.

242. It consists of an integument inclosing an *embryo*, which is the rudiment of a future plant.

243. The seed is nourished by the same means as the fruit, and, like it, will be more or less perfectly formed, according to the abundance of its nutriment.

244. The plant developed from the embryo in the seed will be in all essential particulars like its parent species.

245. Unless its nature has been changed by hybridizing (204).

246. But although it will certainly, under ordinary circumstances, reproduce its species, it will by no means uniformly reproduce the particular variety by which it was borne.

247. So that seed are not the proper means of propagating varieties.

248. Nevertheless, in annual or biennial plants no means can be employed for propagating a variety except the seed; and yet the variety is preserved.

249. This is accomplished solely by the great care of the cultivator, and happens thus:

250. Although a seed will not absolutely propagate the individual, yet as a seed will partake more of the nature of its actual parent than of anything else, its progeny may be expected, as really happens, to resemble the variety from which it sprang more than any other variety of its species.

251. Provided its purity has not been contaminated by the intermixture of other varieties.

252. By a careful eradication of all the varieties from the neighborhood of that from which seed is to be saved; by

taking care that none but the most genuine forms of a variety are preserved as seed-plants; and by compelling by transplan tation a plant to expend all its accumulated sap in the nourishment of its seed instead of in the superabundant production of foliage, a crop of seed may be procured, the plants produced by which will, in a great measure, have the peculiar properties of the parent variety.

253. By a series of progressive seed-savings upon the same plan, plants will be at length obtained, in which the habits of the individual have become, as it were, fixed, and capable of such exact reproduction by seed as to form an exception to the general rule, as in Turnips, Radishes, etc.

254. But if the least neglect occurs in taking the necessary precautions (252) to insure a uniform crop of seed possessing the new fixed properties, the race becomes deteriorated in proportion to the want of care that has occurred, and loses its characters of individuality.

255. In all varieties those seed may be expected to preserve their individual characters most distinctly which have been the best nourished (243); it is, consequently, those which should be selected in preference for raising new plants from which seed is to be saved.

256. When seed are first opened, their embryo is a mass of cellular substance, containing starch, fixed carbon, or other solid matter, in its cavities; and in this state it will remain until fitting circumstances occur to call it into active life.

257. These fitting circumstances are, a temperature above 32° Fahrenheit, a moist medium, darkness, and exposure to air.

258. It then absorbs the moisture of the medium in which it lies, inhales oxygen (278), and undergoes certain chemical changes; its vital powers cause it to ascend by one extremity for the purpose of finding light, and of decomposing its carbonic acid (279), by parting with its accumulated oxygen, and to descend by the other extremity for the purpose of finding a constant supply of crude nutriment.

259. Unless these conditions are maintained, seed cannot

germinate, and, consequently, an exposure to light is fatal t their embryo, because (278) oxygen will not be absorbed i sufficient quantity to stimulate the vital powers of the embryo into action, for the purpose of parting with it again, by the decomposition of the carbonic acid that has been formed dur ing its accumulation.

X. Sap.

260. The fluid matter which is absorbed either from the earth or from the air is called Sap.

261. When it first enters a plant, it consists of water holding certain principles, especially carbonic acid, in solution.

262. These principles chiefly consist of animal or vegetable matter in a state of decomposition, and are energetic in proportion to their solubility, or tendency to form carbonic acid by combining with the oxygen of the air.

263. Sap soon afterwards acquires the nature of mucilage or sugar, and subsequently becomes still further altered by the admixture of such soluble matter as it receives in passing in its route through the alburnum or newly formed woody issue (65).

264. When it reaches the vicinity of the leaves, it is attracted into them, and there, having been exposed to light and air, is converted into the secretions peculiar to the species.

265. It finally, in its altered state, sinks down the bark, whence it is given off laterally by the medullary rays, and is distributed through the system.

266. No solid matter whatever can be taken up by the roots; for this reason, metals, which in the state of oxides are poisonous, are perfectly harmless in their metallic state, as mercury; and this is, no doubt, the cause why liquid manure, which contains all the soluble parts of manure in a fluid state, acts with so much more energy than stimulating substances in a solid state.

267. The cause of the motion of the sap is the attraction of the leaf-buds and leaves.

268. The leaf-buds, called into growth by the combined action of the increasing temperature and light of spring, decompose their carbonic acid (279), and attract fluid from the tissue immediately below them; the space so caused is filled up by fluid again attracted from below, and thus a motion gradually takes place in the sap from one extremity to the other.

269. Consequently, the motion of the sap takes place first in the branches and last in the roots.

270. For this reason, a branch of a plant subjected to a high temperature in winter will grow while its stem is exposed to a very low temperature.

271. But growth under such circumstances will not be long maintained, unless the roots are secured from the reach of frost; for if frozen they cannot act, and will consequently be unable to replace the sap of which the stem is emptied by the attraction of the buds converted into branches, and by the perspiration of the leaves (XII.).

272. Whatever tends to inspissate the sap, such as a dry and heated atmosphere, or an interruption of its rapid flow, or a great decomposition of carbonic acid by full exposure to light, has the property of causing excessive vigor to be diminished, and flower-buds to be produced.

273. While, on the other hand, whatever tends to dilute the sap, such as a damp atmosphere, a free and uninterrupted circulation, or a great accumulation of oxygen in consequence of the imperfect decomposition of carbonic acid, has the property of causing excessively rapid growth, and an exclusive production of leaf-buds.

274. Inspissated or accumulated sap is, therefore, a great cause of fertility.

275. And thin fluid, not being elaborated, is a great cause of sterility.

276. The conversion of sap into different kinds of secretion

is effected by the combined action of *Air* (XI.), *Light* (XI.), and *Temperature.*

XI. Air and Light.

277. When an embryo plant (242) is formed within its integuments, it is usually colorless, or nearly so; but, as soon as it begins to grow, that part which approaches the light (the stem) becomes colored, while the opposite extremity (the root) remains colorless.

278. The parts exposed to the air absorb oxygen at night, absorb carbonic acid and part with oxygen again in daylight; and thus in the daytime purify the air, and render it fit for the respiration of man.

279. The intensity of this latter phenomenon is in proportion to the intensity of solar light to which leaves are directly exposed.

280. Its cause is the decomposition of carbonic acid, the extrication of oxygen, and the acquisition by the plant of carbon in a solid state; from which, modified by the peculiar vital actions of species, color and secretions are supposed to result.

281. For it is found that the intensity of color, and the quantity of secretions, are in proportion to the exposure to light and air, as is shown by the deeper color of the upper sides of leaves, etc.

282. And by the fact that, if plants be grown in air from which light is excluded, neither color nor secretions are formed, as is exemplified in blanched vegetables; which, if even naturally poisonous, may, from want of exposure to light, become wholesome, as Celery.

283. When any color appears in parts developed in the dark, it is generally caused by the absorption of such coloring matter as preëxisted in the root or other body from which the blanched shoot proceeds, as in some kinds of Rhubarb when forced.

284. Or by the deposition of coloring matter formed by

parts developed in light, as in the subterranean roots of Beet, Carrots, etc.

285. What is true of color is also true of flavor, which equally depends upon light for its existence; because flavor is produced by chemical alterations in the sap caused by exposure to light (229).

286. The same thing occurs in regard to nutritive matter, which in like manner is formed by exposure of leaves to light. Thus the Potato, when forced in dark houses, contains no more amylaceous matter than previously existed in the original tuber, but acquires it in abundance when placed in the light, and deposits it in proportion as it is influenced by light and air. Thus, also, if Peaches are grown in wooden houses, at a distance from the light, they will form so little nutritive matter as to be unable to support a crop of fruit, the greater part of which will fall off. And for a similar reason, it is only the outside shoots of standard fruit-trees that bear fruit. Considerations of this kind form in part the basis of pruning and training.

287. Light is the most powerful stimulus that can be employed to excite the vital actions of plants, and its energy is in proportion to its intensity; so that the direct rays of the sun will produce much more powerful effects than the diffused light of day.

288. Hence, if buds that are very excitable are placed in a diffused light, their excitability will be checked.

289. And if buds that are very torpid are exposed to direct light, they will be stimulated into action.

290. So that what parts of the tree shall first begin to grow in the spring may be determined at the will of the cultivator.

291. This is the key to some important practices in forcing.

292. This should also cause attention to be paid to shading buds from the direct rays of the sun in particular cases; as in that of cuttings, whose buds, if too rapidly excited, might exhaust their only reservoir of sap, the stem, before new roots were formed to repair such loss.

293. As plants derive an essential part of their food from the

air (280) by the action of light, it follows that in glass houses those which admit the greatest portion of light are the best adapted for purposes of cultivation.

294. The proportion of opaque matter in the roof of a glass house constructed of wood varies from one-third to one-seventh; that of an iron house does not exceed one twenty-third.

295. Therefore, iron-roofed houses are in this respect better suited for cultivation than wooden-roofed houses.

296. And it has been found by experiment that light passes more freely through a curvilinear than through a plane roof, and through glass forming an acute angle with the horizon than through perpendicular glass; it follows that a curvilinear roof is best, and a plane roof with glass perpendicular sides the worst, adapted to the purposes of the cultivator.

297. For the same reason common green glass is less fitted for glazing forcing-houses than white crown glass.

298. Poisonous gases in very minute quantities act upon vegetation with great energy. A ten-thousandth part of sulphurous acid gas is quickly fatal to the life of plants; and hence the danger of flues heated by coal fires, and the impossibility of making many species grow in the vicinity of houses heated by coal-fires, or in large towns.

XII. Perspiration.

299. It is not, however, exclusively by the action of light and air that the nature of sap is altered. Evaporation is constantly going on during the growth of a plant, and sometimes is so copious that an individual will perspire its own weight of water in the course of twenty-four hours.

300. The loss thus occasioned by the leaves is supplied by crude fluid, absorbed by the roots, and conveyed up the stem with great rapidity.

301. The consequence of such copious perspiration is the separation and solidification of the carbonized matter that is produced for the peculiar secretions of a species.

302. For the maintenance of a plant in health, it is indispensable that the supply of fluid by the roots should be continual and uninterrupted.

303. If anything causes perspiration to take place faster than it can be counteracted by the absorption of fluid from the earth, plants will be dried up and perish.

304. Such causes are, destruction of spongioles, an insufficient quantity of fluid in the soil, an exposure of the spongioles to occasional dryness, and a dry atmosphere.

305. The most ready means of counteracting the evil consequences of an imperfect action of the roots is by preventing or diminishing evaporation.

306. This is to be effected by rendering the atmosphere extremely humid.

307. Thus, in curvilinear iron hot-houses, in which the atmosphere becomes so dry, in consequence of the heat, that plants perish, it is necessary that the air should be rendered extremely humid, by throwing water upon the pavement, or by introducing steam.

308. And in transplantation in dry weather, evergreens, or plants in leaf, often die, because the spongioles are destroyed, or so far injured in the operation as to be unable to act, while the leaves never cease to perspire.

309. The greater certainty of transplanting plants that have been growing in pots is, from this latter circumstance, intelligible.

310. While the utility of putting cuttings or newly transplanted seedlings into a shady, damp atmosphere is explained by the necessity of hindering evaporation

XIII. Cuttings.

311. When a separate portion of a plant is caused to produce new roots and branches, and to increase an individual, it is a Cutting.

312. Cuttings are of two sorts: cuttings properly so called, and *eyes* (319).

313. A cutting consists of an internodia, or a part of one, with its nodi (59) and leaf-bud.

314. When the internodia is plunged in the earth, it attracts fluid from thes oil, and nourishes the bud until it can feed itself.

315. The bud, feeding at first upon the matter in the internodia, gradually elongates upwards into a branch, and sends organized matter downwards, which becomes roots.

316. As soon as it has established a communication with the soil, it becomes a new individual, exactly like that from which it was taken.

317. As it is the action of the leaf-buds that causes growth in a cutting, it follows that no cutting without a leaf-bud will grow.

318. Unless the cutting has great vitality and power of forming adventitous leaf-buds (119), which sometimes happens.

319. An eye is a leaf-bud without an internodia.

320. It only differs from a cutting in having no reservoir of food on which to exist, and in emitting its roots immediately from the base of the leaf-bud into the soil.

321. As cuttings will very often, if not always, develop leaves before any powerful connexion is formed between them and the soil, they are peculiarly liable to suffer from perspiration.

322. Hence the importance of maintaining their atmosphere in a uniform state of humidity, as is effected by putting bell or other glasses over them.

323. In this case, however, it is necessary that, if air-tight covers are employed, such as bell-glasses, they should be from time to time removed and replaced, for the sake of getting rid of excessive humidity.

324. Layers differ from cuttings in nothing except that they strike root into the soil while yet adhering to the parent plant.

325. Whatever is true of cuttings is true of layers, except

that the latter are not liable to suffer by evaporation, because of their communication with the parent plant.

326. As cuttings strike roots into the earth by the action of leaves or leaf-buds, it might be supposed that they will strike most readily when the leaves or leaf-buds are in their greatest vigor.

327. Nevertheless, this power is controlled so much by the peculiar vital powers of different species, and by secondary considerations, that it is impossible to say that this is an absolute rule.

328. Thus Dahlias and other herbaceous plants will strike root freely when cuttings are very young; and Heaths, Azaleas, and other hard-wooded plants, only when the wood has just begun to harden.

329. The former is, probably, owing to some specific vital excitability, the force of which we cannot appreciate; the latter either to a kind of torpor, which seems to seize such plants when the tissue is once emptied of fluid, or to a natural slowness to send downwards woody matter, whether for wood or not, which is the real cause of their wood being harder.

330. If ripened cuttings are upon the whole the most fitted for multiplication, it is because their tissue is less absorbed than when younger, and that they are less likely to suffer either from repletion or evaporation.

331. For, to gorge tissue with food, before leaves are in action to decompose and assimilate it, is as prejudicial as to empty tissue by the action of leaves, before spongioles are prepared to replenish it.

332. For this reason, pure silex, in which no stimulating substances are contained (silver sand), is the best adapted for promoting the rooting of cuttings that strike with difficulty.

333. And for the same reason, cuttings with what gardeners call a *heel* to them, or a piece of the older wood, strike root more readily than such as are not so protected. The greater age of the tissue of the heel renders it less absorbent than tissue that is altogether newly formed.

334. It is to avoid the bad effect of evaporation that leaves are usually for the most part removed from a cutting, when it is first prepared.

XIV. Scions.

335. A Scion is a cutting (311) which is caused to grow upon another plant, and not in the earth.

336. Scions are of two sorts: scions properly so called, and *buds* (354).

337. Whatever is true of cuttings is true also of scions, all circumstances being equal.

338. When a scion is adapted to another plant, it attracts fluid from it for the nourishment of its leaf-buds until they can feed themselves.

339. Its leaf-buds, thus fed, gradually grow upwards into branches, and send woody matter downwards, which is analogous to roots.

340. At the same time, the cellular substance of the scion and its *stock* adheres (19), so as to form a complete organic union.

341. The woody matter descending from the bud passes through the cellular substance into the stock, where it occupies the same situation as would have been occupied by woody matter supplied by buds belonging to the stock itself.

342. Once united, the scion covers the wood of the stock with new wood, and causes the production of new roots.

343. But the character of the woody matter sent down by the scion over the wood of the stock being determined by the cellular substance, which has exclusively a horizontal development (73), it follows that the wood of the stock will always remain apparently the same, although it is furnished by the scion.

344. Some scions will grow upon a stock without being able to transmit any woody matter into it; as some *Cacti.*

345. When this happens, the adhesion of the two takes

place by the cellular substance only, and the union is so imperfect that a slight degree of violence suffices to dissever them.

346. And in such cases the buds are fed by their woody matter, which absorbs the ascending sap from the stock at the point where the adhesion has occurred; and the latter, never augmenting in diameter, is finally overgrown by the scion.

347. When, in such instances, the communication between the stock and the scion is so much interrupted that the sap can no longer ascend with sufficient rapidity into the branches, the latter die; as in many Peaches.

348. This incomplete union between the scion and its stock is owing to some constitutional or organic difference in the two.

349. Therefore, care should be taken that, when plants are grafted on one another, their constitution should be as nearly as possible identical.

350. As adhesion of only an imperfect nature takes place when the scion and stock are, to a certain degree, dissimilar in constitution, so will no adhesion whatever occur when their constitutional difference is very decided.

351. Hence it is only species very nearly allied in nature that can be grafted on each other.

352. As only similar tissues will unite (19), it is necessary, in applying a scion to the stock, that similar parts should be carefully adapted to each other; as bark to bark, cambium to cambium, alburnum to alburnum.

353. The second is more especially requisite, because it is through the cambium that the woody matter sent downwards by the buds must pass; and also because cambium itself, being organizing matter in an incipient state, will more readily form an adhesion than any other part.

354. The same principles apply to *buds*, which are to scions precisely what eyes (319) are to cuttings.

355. Inarching is the same with reference to grafting, that layering (324) is with reference to striking by cuttings.

356. It serves to maintain the vitality of a scion until it can form an adhesion with its stock; and must be considered the most certain mode of grafting.

357. It is probable that every species of flowering plant, without exception, may be multiplied by grafting.

358. Nevertheless, there are many species and even tribes that never have been grafted.

359. It has been found that in the Vine and the Walnut this difficulty can be overcome by attention to their peculiar constitutions; and it is probable that the same attention will remove supposed difficulties in the case of other species.

XV. Transplantation.

360. Transplantation consists in removing a plant from the soil in which it is growing to some other soil.

361. If in the operation the plant is torpid, and its spongioles uninjured, the removal will not be productive of any interruption to the previous rate of growth.

362. And if it is growing, or evergreen, and the spongioles are uninjured, the removal will produce no further injury than may arise from the temporary suspension of the action of the spongioles, and the non-cessation of perspiration during the operation.

363. So that transplantations may take place at all seasons of the year, and under all circumstances, provided the spongioles are uninjured.

364. This applies to the largest trees as well as to the smallest herbs.

365. But as it is impossible to take plants out of the earth without destroying or injuring the spongioles, the evil consequence of such accidents must be remedied by the hindrance of evaporation.

366. Transplantation should therefore take place only when plants are torpid, and when their respiratory organs (leaves)

are absent; or, if they never lose those organs, as evergreens, only at seasons when the atmosphere is periodically charged with humidity for some considerable time.

367. Old trees, in which the roots are much injured, form new ones so slowly that they are very liable to be exhausted of sap by the absorption of their very numerous young buds before new spongioles can be formed.

368. The amputation of all their upper extremities is the most probable prevention of death; but in most cases injury of their roots is without a remedy.

369. Plants in pots, being so circumstanced that the spongioles are protected from injury, can, however, be transplanted at all seasons without any dangerous consequences.

INDEX.

A.

B.

C.

D.

E.

F.

G.

H.

I.

J.

L.

M.

N.

O.

P.

R.

S.

T.

V.

W.

Charles Dickens' Complete Works.

AUTHOR'S EDITION. With eight Illustrations to each volume. Large 12mo. 14 volumes. . . . . Per vol. $1.00

PICKWICK PAPERS,
OLIVER TWIST; Pictures from Italy; and American Notes,
NICHOLAS NICKLEBY,
OLD CURIOSITY SHOP; and Reprinted Pieces,
BARNABY RUDGE; and Hard Times,
MARTIN CHUZZLEWIT,
DOMBEY AND SON,
DAVID COPPERFIELD,
CHRISTMAS BOOKS; Uncommercial Traveller; and Additional Christmas Stories,
BLEAK HOUSE,
LITTLE DORRIT,
TALE OF TWO CITIES; and Great Expectations,
OUR MUTUAL FRIEND,
EDWIN DROOD; Sketches; Master Humphrey's Clock, Etc., Etc.

☞Any volume in cloth binding sold separately.☜

CHILD'S HISTORY OF ENGLAND. By CHARLES DICKENS. 12mo. Illustrated. Cloth, extra, black and gold, . . $1.00

"Dickens never did any thing in its way better than his 'Child's History of England.' It may be doubted whether it will not last longer than many of his novels; its interest and value are not transient, and do not depend on the caprices of popular taste. It is all as bright and attractive as a fairy-tale." N. Y. EVENING POST.

The International Series of Novels.

Each large 12mo., printed on fine paper, in large clear type, bound in English cloth, with ornamental black stampings. Price, per vol., . . . $1.25

IN THE DAYS OF MY YOUTH. By Amelia B. Edwards.

"Miss Edwards is, in our estimation, the most sparkling and pleasing of the lady writers of light fiction. Her style is animated, fresh and graceful, and her characters are always conceived and drawn with remarkable skill and fineness." BOSTON GAZETTE.

CHARLOTTE ACKERMAN. By Otto Müller.

"The author of this romance has acquired a solid reputation in Germany, and it is evident, from this translation, that it is deserved." SAN FRANCISCO DAILY RECORD.

THE CROSS OF BERNY. By Mme. De Girardin, Mm. Gautier, Sandeau, and Mery.

"The various episodes are skilfully wrought out and blended so as to form a harmonious whole, and make a book not only interesting as a literary curiosity, but entertaining as a love story." PHILA. EVENING BULLETIN.

THE SON OF THE ORGAN GRINDER. By Marie Sophie Schwartz.

"It is full of interesting incidents, is really a study of character. . . . The characters retain a natural impress throughout, and Swedish life, so peculiar and striking, is limned with a touch of Frederika Bremer's power. . . . The translation is so fine as to add a new indebtedness for the provision of the story." AMERICAN AND GAZETTE, PHILA.

The International Series of Novels (Continued.)

NO ALTERNATIVE. By Annie Thomas.

"A charming domestic tale, full of good thoughts and well-wrought incidents that cannot fail to impress the reader's favorable attention and touch his deeper moral nature." ST. LOUIS TIMES.

GERDA. By Marie Sophie Schwartz.

"We seldom have seen a novel that is better calculated to make a favorable impression. The translators have preserved the sense and the spirit, the vigor and the vivacity of the original; and the publishers have given it an elegant dress." BOSTON EVENING TRAVELLER.

THE VICISSITUDES OF BESSIE FAIRFAX. By Holme Lee.

"The book abounds in charming descriptions of country life, and for these Summer days is peculiarly attractive." CHICAGO INTER-OCEAN.

VALENTINE THE COUNTESS. By Carl Detlef.

"'Valentine the Countess,' is a fresh and beautiful series of pictures of German life, containing also, in its working up, many flowers of German thought." ST. LOUIS REPUBLICAN.

CHASTE AS ICE PURE AS SNOW. By Mrs. M. C. Despard.

"We rate it among the good novels—good in its diction, in its scope and power, in its reflective philosophy, in its idealization, and in its artistic execution." CHRISTIAN AT WORK.

GENTIANELLA. By Mrs. Randolph.

"It is a story of marked power, dealing with high life, an intermixture of strong sensational adventures and scenes, and its plot, which has numerous threads, is well woven and direct. . . . As a literary work the novel is worthy of all attention." BOSTON EVENING TRAVELLER.

KATERFELTO. By G. J. White-Melville.

"The novel is full of life and is vigorous. Excellent paintings of scenery and good drawings of character are added to an artistically conceived and well carried out plot." BOSTON EVENING TRAVELLER.

OLDBURY. By Annie Keary.

"When we say the story has for its centrepiece a pretty parsonage, for its leading personages a widowed minister, his son, a country flower named Elsie, with lots of interesting people, old and young, that its romance is mingled with green fields and spreading oaks, that its descriptions can be read with close and careful attention, that its plot and management are thoroughly artistic and beautiful, we say enough to commend the novel to all who love simplicity, purity and nature, in the hands of a fascinating writer." CHICAGO INTER-OCEAN.

AT CAPRI. A story of Italian life. By Carl Detlef.

"The sketches of life at Capri—in the little colony of artists, and among the peasants—are exceedingly well drawn, and the account of the tarantella is a remarkable specimen of graphic description." LITERARY WORLD.

The International Series of Novels (Continued.)

AFRAJA; OR, LIFE AND LOVE IN NORWAY. From the German of Theodore Mügge. By Hon. E. Joy Morris.

"This is a remarkable book, and the admirable representation it gives of life in Norway is really delightful." BOSTON COURIER.

CASTLE DALY. By Annie Keary.

"It is really a great pleasure to come across so unpretending, clear, natural, and if the word may be used, so unmorbid a novel as 'Castle Daly'. It reminds us strongly of some of the best of Miss Edgeworth's novels with the strong bias taken out." NATION, NEW YORK.

A MARRIAGE IN HIGH LIFE. By Octave Feuillet.

"The book is full of wit, satire, sparkling dialogue, piquant situations and worldly wisdom, and has lost, perhaps, less of its brilliancy by translation than is too often the case." LIBRARY TABLE.

ON DANGEROUS GROUND; OR, AGATHA'S FRIENDSHIP. By Mrs. Bloomfield Moore.

"The story is told with the utmost skill, the dialogue being sparkling, the characters unexaggerated, and the whole marked by a well-bred familiarity with the subject; which has been conspicuously absent from the majority of the preceding efforts to depict fashionable society." NEW YORK WORLD.

AN ODD COUPLE. By Mrs. Oliphant.

". . . There is not a dull page in the book." PHILA: INQUIRER

THE PRIME MINISTER. By Anthony Trollope.

"'The Prime Minister' is interesting because of its realistic representation of scenes and people not elevated a great way above those we meet with in ordinary life. It is the lifelikeness which pleases us; it is this which gives Mr. Trollope his enduring success." NEW YORK TELEGRAM.

UNTIL THE DAY BREAK. By Birch Arnold.

"'Until the Day Break' is a well constructed and entertaining story, with an attractive plot and a number of skilfully drawn characters. Its strength lies in its more intense scenes, but it is thoroughly interesting throughout. As an attempt at a story of American life the book is successful beyond the average." BOSTON GAZETTE.

DOLLY: A Love Story. By Frances Hodgson Burnett.

"We have seldom read a better novel than 'Dolly.' It abounds in interest from beginning to end, and when once begun it will be laid down with great difficulty until it is finished." BALTIMORE GAZETTE.

Samuel Lover.

HANDY ANDY. A tale of Irish life. By Samuel Lover. New Library Edition, with two original illustrations by Geo. G. White. 12mo. Cloth, extra, black and gold. . . . . . . $1.50.

"This boy Handy will be the death of us. What are the police about, to allow the uttering of a publication that has already brought us to the brink of apoplexy fifty times?" SPORTING REVIEW.

Charles Lever.

CHARLES O'MALLEY, the Irish Dragoon. New Library Edition, with two original illustrations by F. O. C. Darley. 12mo. Cloth, extra, black and gold, ... $1.50

HARRY LORREQUER. New Library Edition, with original illustrations by G. G. White. 12mo. Cloth, extra, black and gold, . $1.50

"The author is pre-eminent for his mirth-moving powers, for his acute sense of the ridiculous, for the breadth of his humor, and for his power of dramatic writing, which renders his boldest conceptions with the happiest facility." LONDON ATHENAEUM.

Marie Sophie Schwartz.

STANDARD NOVELS. Translated from the Swedish by Selma Borg and Marie A. Brown. Cloth, extra, ... $1.50
Paper covers, ... 1.00

"The works of Mme. Schwartz are standard in Europe, nearly all of them having been rendered into at least three languages." HEARTH AND HOME, N. Y.

BIRTH AND EDUCATION.

"A novel of modern Swedish life, written with the descriptive ability of Miss Bremer, and with far more animation and interest." ROUND TABLE.

GERDA.

(See International Series of Novels.)

GOLD AND NAME.

"This is a powerful book; in plot and style it is equally good." CHRISTIAN STANDARD, CINCINNATI.

GUILT AND INNOCENCE.

"A thrilling and romantic drama is constructed, which keeps the attention riveted to the end, the denouement of which will perhaps surprise the most experienced novel reader." N. Y. CHRISTIAN ADVOCATE.

THE RIGHT ONE.

"Brighter, fresher and better worth reading than nine-tenths of modern novels." WORCESTER GAZETTE.

THE SON OF THE ORGAN GRINDER.

(See International Series of Novels.)

TWO FAMILY MOTHERS.

"The plot is carried forward by characters lifelike and interesting, the whole leading to scenes everywhere fascinating and instructive." ALBANY EVENING POST.

THE WIFE OF A VAIN MAN.

"The book is an admirable one, and raises our opinion of the talents of the Swedish novelist. She is very unlike Frederika Bremer, and has a much more powerful conception of certain phases of life than that good woman ever attained." SPRINGFIELD REPUBLICAN.

Sir Walter Scott.

THE WAVERLEY NOVELS.

HOUSEHOLD EDITION. Large 12mo. Illustrated. 23 vols., at $1.00 each.
GLOBE EDITION. 16mo. Illustrated. 23 vols., at, . . . 1.00 "

WAVERLEY.
GUY MANNERING.
ANTIQUARY.
ROB ROY.
BLACK DWARF; & Old Mortality
HEART OF MIDLOTHIAN,
BRIDE OF LAMMERMOOR; and Legend of Montrose.
IVANHOE.
MONASTERY.
ABBOT.
KENILWORTH.
PIRATE.
FORTUNES OF NIGEL.
PEVERIL OF THE PEAK.
QUENTIN DURWARD.
ST. RONAN'S WELL.
RED GAUNTLET.
BETROTHED; and Talisman.
WOODSTOCK.
FAIR MAID OF PERTH.
ANNE OF GEIERSTEIN.
COUNT ROBERT OF PARIS; and Castle Dangerous.
CHRONICLES OF THE CANONGATE.

(Each volume sold separately.)

Lord Macaulay.

HISTORY OF ENGLAND. From new Electrotype Plates, from the last English edition, with all of Macaulay's corrections, carefully revised.

STANDARD EDITION. With a steel portrait of the author. 5 vols. 12mo.

Cloth, extra, black and gold, per set, ... $5.00
Sheep, marbled edges, " 7.50
Half Calf, gilt, marbled edges, " . . . 15.00

FINE EDITION. 5 vols. Large 12mo. Beveled boards. Superior paper.

Cloth, gilt top, per vol., ... $1.50

8vo EDITION. 5 vols. in one, with portrait. Cloth, extra, black and gold, ... $3.00
Sheep, marbled edges, ... 3.50

This is the best edition of Macaulay, and the only one suitable for general use. In order to supply the demand for a really good edition of this standard work, the publishers have gone to a great expense in making new electrotype plates, and they can confidently recommend this as the best and cheapest edition for general use.

Harriet Martineau.

HISTORY OF ENGLAND. From the beginning of the 19th Century to the Crimean War. Complete in 4 vols., with full index.

Cloth, ... $4.00
Sheep, marbled edges, ... 6.00
Half Calf, gilt back, marbled edges, 12.00

"The work is one which deserves to be in every private library, and it is not too much to say that if a similar history of the United States up to the breaking out of the rebellion could be written, it would be a political event of undeniable importance." NATION, N. Y.

Comte de Paris.

HISTORY OF THE CIVIL WAR IN AMERICA. Translated, with the approval of the author, by LOUIS TASISTRO. Edited by HENRY COPPEE, L.L.D. Vols. 1 and 2, embracing, without abridgment, the first 4 of the French edition. With maps faithfully engraved from the originals and printed in three colors. 8vo. Satin Cloth, per vol., . $3.50
Red Cloth, extra, Roxburgh style, gilt top, uncut edges, . 3.50
Sheep, library style, ... 4.50
Half Turkey Morocco, ... 6.00

(To be completed in 4 volumes.)

"By all odds the best history of the civil war that has yet appeared." EVENING TELEGRAPH, PHILADELPHIA.

"The most impartial, the most thorough, and the most valuable history of the civil war." JOURNAL, BOSTON.

Horace E. Scudder.

RECOLLECTIONS OF SAMUEL BRECK, with passages from his Note Books (1771–1862). 12mo. Cloth, extra. gilt top, uncut edges, . $2.00

"It is one of those contemporary pictures which one is always glad to meet, by whomsoever sketched; but Mr. Breck was not a commonplace man, and had no ordinary opportunities. He was rich and well connected, occupied a high social position, and had some political prominence; lived both in Boston and in Philadelphia, and travelled more than once in Europe; his reminiscences are of personages as far removed in every way as Mirabeau and Marryat, including a large proportion of the most prominent public men of this country during the first half-century of the republic." NATION, N. Y.

Mrs. Anna Harriette Leonowens.

THE ENGLISH GOVERNESS AT THE SIAMESE COURT. Being Recollections of Six Years in the Royal Palace at Bangkok. With eight full-page illustrations, from photographs presented to the Author by the King of Siam. 12mo. Cloth, extra, black and gold, . . $1.25

"No one can read this book without strong interest; whether one regards it merely from the superficial point of view, as an entertaining narrative, or with the deeper significance it bears as an important page in the great book of ethnology." BOSTON COURIER.

THE ROMANCE OF THE HAREM. With eight full-page illustrations. 12mo. Cloth, extra, black and gold, . . . $1.25

"It would hardly be possible to commend too highly 'The Romance of the Harem.' No fiction can equal in interest these thrilling stories of real but far away life. In all the realm of romance it would be hard to find one heroine who bears her ideal woes with a nobility and courage worthy to be compared, for instance, with that of 'Tuptim,' a girl of scarcely sixteen; . . . The stories are not all so sad as this one; but there is a wonderful, fascinating interest about them all." N. Y. TRIBUNE.

Thomas Percy, D. D., (Bishop of Dromore.)

RELIQUES OF ANCIENT ENGLISH POETRY. Consisting of Old Heroic Ballads, Songs and Other Pieces of the earlier Poets, with some of later date not included in any other edition. To which is now added a Supplement of Many Curious Historical and Narrative Ballads, reprinted from rare copies: and a Copious Glossary and Notes. With two engravings on steel. 8vo. Cloth, beveled boards, gilt top, . . $3.75
Sheep, marbled edges, ...
Full Turkey Morocco, Gilt edges, ...

"I do not think that there is an able writer in verse of the present day, who would not be proud to acknowledge his obligations to the 'Reliques.' I know that it is so with my friends; for myself, I am happy to make a public avowal of my own." WORDSWORTH.

William Shakespeare.

COMPLETE WORKS OF WILLIAM SHAKESPEARE, Dramatic and Poetical, with the "Epistle Dedicatorie," and the address prefixed to the first edition of 1623, a Sketch of the Life of the Poet, by ALEXANDER CHAMBERS, A. M., and glossarial and other Notes and References. Edited by GEORGE LONG DUYCKINCK. With 6 steel illustrations, superb portrait on steel and engraved title. 8vo. Sheep, marbled edges, . . $3.50

☞ This is the best one volume edition of Shakespeare published. ☜

FINE EDITION. On extra calendered paper, with a Full and Comprehensive Life, by J. PAYNE COLLIER, A. M. Half calf, gilt, marbled edges. Price, ... $8.00
Full Turkey morocco, gilt edges, ... 8.00

WINDSOR EDITION. 8 vols., 16mo, on laid and tinted paper, with steel illustrations in each vol. Cloth, extra, black and gold, per vol., . $1.25
Half calf, gilt, marbled edges, . . . " . 2.75

FALSTAFF EDITION. 4 vols., crown 8vo, with steel illustrations in each vol. Cloth. extra, black and gold, per vol. $1.75
Half calf, gilt, marbled edges, " 3.75

The American Chess Player's Hand-Book.

Teaching the Rudiments of the Game, and giving an Analysis of all the recognized openings. Exemplified by appropriate Games actually played by Paul Morphy, Harrwitz, Anderssen, Staunton, Paulsen, Montgomery, Meek and others. From the works of Staunton and others. Illustrated. 16mo. Cloth, extra, ... $1.25

"It is the best manual for the beginner with which we are acquainted, and is exceedingly clear and intelligible." NEW ORLEANS PICAYUNE.

The American Gardener's Assistant.

Containing complete Practical Directions for the Cultivation of Vegetables, Flowers, Fruit Trees, and Grape Vines. By THOMAS BRIDGEMAN. New Edition, revised and enlarged, by S. Edwards Todd. With seventy illustrations. 12mo. Cloth, extra, black and gold, . . . $2.00

Famous Horses of America.

Containing 59 Portraits of the Celebrities of the American Turf, Past and Present. 4to. Cloth, extra, ... $1.50

"There is no type of equinal beauty, so far as speed is concerned, that is not represented in this gallery of portraits; and the studying of the varying points in the build of the famous horses must be of great interest to every lover of this noble animal." BOSTON HOME JOURNAL.

J. H. Walsh, F.R.C.S. (Stonehenge.)

THE HORSE IN THE STABLE AND THE FIELD. His Management in Health and Disease. From the last London edition, with an Essay on the American Trotting Horse, and Suggestions on the Breeding and Training of Trotters, by Ellwood Harvey, M. D. Illustrated with over 80 engravings, and full-page engravings from photographs. 12mo. Cloth extra, beveled boards, black and gold, . . . $2.00

"This Americanizing of 'Stonehenge' gives us the best piece of Horse Literature of the season. Old horsemen need not be told who 'Stonehenge' is in the British Books, or that he is the highest authority in turf and veterinary affairs. Add to these the labors of such American writers as Dr. McClure and Dr. Harvey, with new portraits of some of our most popular living horses, and we have a book that no American horseman can afford to be without." OHIO FARMER.

ENCYCLOPEDIA OF RURAL SPORTS. Comprising Shooting, Hunting, Coursing, Fishing, Boating, Racing, Pedestrianism, Cricket, Base Ball, and the various Rural Games and Amusements. With 200 engravings. Crown 8vo. Cloth, extra, black and gold, . . . $4.50

This book is an indispensable companion to every one who enjoys a good horse, a good gun, a good dog, a good boat, a good rod, a game of ball, or in fact even a walk, or any species of manly exercise. The English edition has for many years been the only standard upon the subject, and the American edition is now presented with enlargements, additions and revisions, for American readers, in the assurance that it will supply a want long felt.

Hiram Woodruff.

THE TROTTING HORSE OF AMERICA. How to Train and Drive him, with Reminiscences of the Trotting Turf. By Hiram Woodruff. Edited by Charles J. Foster. Including an Introductory Notice, by George Wilkes, and a Biographical Sketch by the Editor. 19th edition, revised and enlarged, with an Appendix and a copious Index. With a steel portrait of the Author, and six engravings on wood of celebrated trotters. 12mo. Cloth, extra, black and gold, ... $2.50

"We believe it to be the most practical and instructive book that ever was published concerning the trotting horse; those who own or take care of horses of other descriptions may buy and read it with a great deal of profit. Besides all this, it is a work of great interest." WILKES' SPIRIT OF THE TIMES.

George E. Waring, Jr., (of Ogden Farm.)

BOOK OF THE FARM; or, The Handy-Book of Husbandry. Containing Practical Information in Regard to Buying or Leasing a Farm; Fences and Farm Buildings, Farming Implements, Drainage, Plowing, Subsoiling, Manuring, Rotation of Crops, Care and Medical Treatment of the Cattle, Sheep and Poultry; Management of the Dairy; Useful Tables, etc. By the author of "Draining for Profit and for Health," etc. New edition, thoroughly revised by the Author. With 100 illustrations. 12mo. Cloth, extra, black and gold, ... $2.00

"Written by a practical farmer, it is precisely such a book as every farmer should have and should read." N. Y. TRIBUNE.

"It is one of the cheapest and best books on Agriculture with which I am acquainted, and should be in the hands of every farmer." W. S. CLARK, PRESIDENT OF MASSACHUSETTS AGRICULTURAL COLLEGE.

Alexander Wilson.

AMERICAN ORNITHOLOGY; or The Natural History of the Birds of the United States. With a Life of the Author, by GEORGE ORD, F.R.S. With Continuation by CHARLES LUCIEN BONAPARTE, (Prince of Musignano). This edition contains all the plates of the large folio edition, reproduced in a smaller size and embracing nearly four hundred figures of birds, and the entire letterpress of the three volume edition. One volume, imperial 8vo. Cloth, extra, ... $6.00

☞ This is the cheapest work in the market on the subject. ☜

Joseph A. Seiss, D. D.,

A MIRACLE IN STONE; or, The Great Pyramid of Egypt. By the author of "Last Times," "Lectures on the Gospels," "Lectures on the Apocalypse," etc. Cloth, extra, black and gold, . . $1.25

"Dr. Seiss' work is more fascinating than any romance. Yet it records possibly only the beginning of yet more wonderful developments to follow in the future. We have already found 'Sermons in Stones,' such as Shakespeare never dreamed of. What was once only an object of curiosity for travellers, has become the subject of most intense historical, scientific and religious interest." THE CHURCHMAN, N. Y.

M. Laird Simons.

SUNDAY HALF-HOURS WITH THE GREAT PREACHERS. With brief Biographical Notices and a complete Index. With six portraits on steel. Cloth, extra, gilt, ... $3.75
Sheep, Library style, ... 4.50
Cloth, paneled, full gilt, gilt edges, ... 4.75
French morocco, full gilt, gilt edges, ... 6.00

"In all particulars the volume constitutes the finest collection of sermons now in print." DAILY WHIG, BANGOR, ME.

"The volume appears to me to be well adapted to the closet and the family circle; and many of its discourses could be profitably read in whole or in part by lay readers." REV. C. M. BUTLER.

William Smith, (Author of "Biography and Mythology," etc.)

THE DICTIONARY OF THE BIBLE. Comprising its Antiquities, Biography, Geography and Natural History. With an engraving on steel, and 125 engravings of Ancient Cities and Memorable Places of the Holy Land, etc., and Maps. 8vo. Cloth, extra, black and gold, . $3.00
Sheep, marbled edges, ... 3.75

The only edition published in America that is abridged by Dr. Smith himself.

William Bacon Stevens, D. D.

THE SUNDAY AT HOME. A Manual of Home Service, intended for those who are occasionally hindered from attending the House of God. With Sermons and a selection of Hymns. 12mo. Cloth, extra, . $1.50

Hugh Blair.

LECTURES ON RHETORIC AND BELLES-LETTRES. With a memoir of the author's life. To which are added copious questions and an analysis of each Lecture, by ABRAHAM MILLS. 8vo. University Edition. Sheep, sprinkled edges, ... $2.75

It is now used as a Text-Book at Hamilton College, N. Y.; Wittenberg College, Springfield, Ohio; Central College, Fayette, Mo.; St. Ignatius College, Chicago, Ill.; St. Xavier College, Cincinnati, Ohio; St. Louis University, St. Louis, Mo.; Kentucky Wesleyan College.; University of Georgia; Roanoke College; and many other Colleges and Academies.

William Blasius.

STORMS: Their Nature, Classification and Laws. With the means of predicting them, principally from their embodiments, the Clouds, and the connection of these with Aerial Currents, their originators. With numerous maps, plates, and figures. 12mo. Cloth, extra, . . $2.50

"It deserves a place among the choice reference-books of shipmaster, yachtman, and in fact all who have to look to the sky for weather warnings. Chapter X is worth the price of the whole work." NAUTICAL GAZETTE, N. Y.

E. B. Duffey.

LADIES' AND GENTLEMEN'S ETIQUETTE. A Complete Manual of the Manners and Dress of American Society. Containing Forms of Letters, Invitations, Acceptances and Regrets. With a copious Index. 12mo. Cloth, extra, black and gold, ... $1.50

"It is peculiarly an American book, especially adapted to our own people, and its greatest beauty is found in the fact that in every line and precept it inculcates the principles of true politeness, instead of those formal rules that serve only to gild the surface without affecting the substance. It is admirably written, the style being clear, terse and forcible, and as a specimen of book manufacture it is very attractive. The compendium covers the entire ground that it is meant to cover; we have never seen a book of its class which we can more cheerfully recommend to Americans." ST. LOUIS TIMES.

Rufus W. Griswold.

THE PROSE WRITERS OF AMERICA. With a survey of the Intellectual History, Conditions and Prospects of the Country. New and Revised Edition to the present time. With a supplementary Essay on the Present Intellectual Condition of the Country. With twelve portraits on steel. Printed on laid and tinted paper. Imperial 8vo. Cloth, extra, gilt top, beveled boards, ... $5.00
Sheep, marbled edges, Library style, ... 6.00
Half calf, gilt, marbled edges, ... 7.50
Turkey morocco, antique, gilt edges, . . . 10.00

"An important and interesting contribution to our national literature. The range of authors is very wide; the biographical notices full and interesting. I am surprised that the author has been able to collect so many particulars in this way. The selections appear to me to be made with discrimination, and the criticisms show a sound taste and a correct appreciation of the qualities of the writers, as well as I can judge." WM. H. PRESCOTT.

Frederic H. Hedge, D. D.

THE PROSE WRITERS OF GERMANY. With Introduction, Biographical Notices and Translations. With portraits on steel and engraved titel. Printed on laid and tinted paper. Imperial 8vo. Cloth, extra, gilt top, beveled boards, ... $5.00
Sheep, marbled edges, ... 6.00
Half calf, gilt, marbled edges, ... 7.50
Turkey morocco, antique, gilt edges, ... 10.00

"There is no book accessible to the English or American reader which can furnish so comprehensive and symmetrical a view of German literature to the uninitiated; and those already conversant with some of the German classics will find here valuable and edifying extracts from works to which very few in this country can gain access." PROF. A. P. PEABODY, in NORTH AMERICAN REVIEW.

Thomas Hood.

COMPLETE WORKS. With engravings on steel. 5 vols. 12mo. Tinted paper.

SERIOUS POEMS.	**HUMOROUS POEMS.**
UP THE RHINE.	**MISCELLANIES; & Hood's Own**

WHIMSICALITIES, WHIMS AND ODDITIES.

Cloth, extra, black and gold, per vol., ... $1.50
Half calf, gilt, marbled edges, " 3.25

HOOD'S COMICALITIES. A series of 200 Comical Pictures. Fully equal to Leech's and Cruikshank's admirable drawings. Oblong quarto. Half morocco, extra, ... $1.50

Evert A. and George L. Duyckinck.

CYCLOPEDIA OF AMERICAN LITERATURE. Embracing Personal and Critical Notices of Authors, and Selections from their Writings, from the Earliest Period to the Present Day. With portraits, autographs and other illustrations. Edited to date by M. Laird Simons. Illustrated with 1000 engravings. 2 vols. Imperial 8vo. Cloth, extra, . . . $12.00
Sheep, marbled edges, ... 14.00
Half morocco, marbled edges, ... 16.00

Richard Holt Hutton.

ESSAYS IN LITERARY CRITICISM. Contents: Goethe and his Influence—Nathaniel Hawthorne—Arthur Hugh Clough—Wordsworth and his Genius—George Eliot—Matthew Arnold. 12mo. Cloth, extra, gilt. Price, ... $1.50

"The essays are of a very high standard of excellence. They display a depth of insight, subtlety of analysis, and felicity of expression not often met with in these days of hasty work and rapidly-formed impression." CHICAGO INTER-OCEAN.

Charles Knight.

HALF-HOURS WITH THE BEST AUTHORS. With short Biographical and Critical Notices.

HOUSEHOLD EDITION. With six portraits on steel. 3 vols. Thick 12mo. Cloth, extra, ... per set, $6.00
Half calf, gilt, marbled edges, . . . " 12.00

LIBRARY EDITION. Printed on fine laid and tinted paper. With 24 portraits on steel. 6 vols. 12mo. Cloth, extra, . per set, $9.00
Half calf, gilt, marbled edges, . . . " 18.00

The variety of reading is so great that no one will ever tire of these volumes. It is a library in itself.

Mrs. Sarah T. Paul.

COOKERY FROM EXPERIENCE. A Practical Guide for Housekeepers in the Preparation of Every-day Meals, containing more than One Thousand Domestic Recipes, mostly tested by Personal Experience, with Suggestions for Meals, Lists of Meats and Vegetables in Season, etc. 12mo. Cloth, extra, black and gold, ... $1.50

INTERLEAVED EDITION. Cloth, extra, black and gold, . $1.75

"Every recipe given has been carefully tested by either myself or my friends; it has been my aim to give only those that are reliable and practical, and I have made the instructions so explicit that the most inexperienced housekeeper may undertake the preparation of her own dishes or give intelligent instructions to her servants, with the certainty of attaining a happy result." EXTRACT FROM THE AUTHOR'S PREFACE.

ART AT HOME SERIES.

We have the pleasure of announcing that we have begun the publication of the ART AT HOME SERIES, a number of volumes devoted to the subject of home decoration and the cultivation of a more refined taste in all the surroundings of private life. Three volumes of the Series have been published:

1. **A PLEA FOR ART IN THE HOUSE.** By W. J. LOFTIE, B.A., F.S.A., author of "In and Out of London." 12mo. Cloth, flexible. Illustrated. Price, ... $1.00
2. **HOUSE DECORATION in Painting, Woodwork and Furniture.** By RHODA AND AGNES GARRETT. 12mo. Cloth, flexible. Illustrated. Price, ... $1.00
3. **MUSIC IN THE HOUSE.** By JOHN HULLAH, L.L.D. 12 mo. Cloth, flexible. Illustrated. Price, ... 75 cts.

☞ These will be followed by—

DRAWING AND PAINTING. By W. H STACEY MARKS, A.R.A.

DRESS. By MRS. OLIPHANT.

DOMESTIC ARCHITECTURE. By J. J. STEVENSON.

Other volumes on Gardening, Sculpture and Carving, Needle-work and Lace-making, and other subjects connected with Art at Home, will follow.

BEST EDITIONS OF POPULAR 12MOS.

Printed on fine paper, in large clear type. Illustrated. Fine English cloth, extra. Each book nicely covered with Manilla paper.

AT $1.00

ROBINSON CRUSOE.
ARABIAN NIGHTS.
SWISS FAMILY ROBINSON.
SCOTTISH CHIEFS.
THADDEUS OF WARSAW.
GIL BLAS.
CHILDREN OF THE ABBEY.
DON QUIXOTE.
GULLIVER'S TRAVELS.
VICAR OF WAKEFIELD; AND PAUL AND VIRGINIA. In One volume.

AT $1.25

MODERN CLASSICS.
TRAVELER IN AFRICA.
IN THE ARCTIC SEAS.
PILGRIM'S PROGRESS.
BUNYAN'S HOLY WAR.
EMPRESS JOSEPHINE.
CELEBRATED FEMALE SOVEREIGNS.
PIONEER WOMEN OF THE WEST.
BATTLES OF THE REPUBLIC.
CAMP FIRES OF NAPOLEON.
LIFE OF NAPOLEON.
LIFE OF WASHINGTON.
DANIEL BOONE.
DAVID CROCKETT.
KIT CARSON.
GRIMM'S HOUSEHOLD TALES
GRIMM'S POPULAR TALES.
DUCHESS OF ORLEANS.
GUSTAVUS ADOLPHUS.
LADY GREEN SATIN.
ROMAIN KALBRIS.
EVENING AMUSEMENTS.
SOUTH MEADOWS.
REMARKABLE EVENTS IN THE WORLD'S HISTORY.
TRAVELS AND ADVENTURES OF BARON MUNCHAUSEN.
ROMANCE OF THE REVOLUTION.

www.ingramcontent.com/pod-product-compliance
Lightning Source LLC
LaVergne TN
LVHW021307110826
845150LV00003B/512

* 9 7 8 1 4 2 5 5 5 8 7 3 4 *